Democracy after Communism

A *Journal of Democracy* Book

•

BOOKS IN THE SERIES

Edited by Larry Diamond and Marc F. Plattner

Political Parties and Democracy (2001)
(Edited by Larry Diamond and Richard Gunther)

The Global Divergence of Democracies (2001)

Globalization, Power, and Democracy (2000)
(Edited by Marc F. Plattner and Aleksander Smolar)

The Democratic Invention (2000)
(Edited by Marc F. Plattner and João Carlos Espada)

Democratization in Africa (1999)

Democracy in East Asia (1998)

Consolidating the Third Wave Democracies (1997)
(with Yun-han Chu and Hung-mao Tien)

Civil-Military Relations and Democracy (1996)

The Global Resurgence of Democracy, 2nd ed. (1996)

Economic Reform and Democracy (1995)

Nationalism, Ethnic Conflict, and Democracy (1994)

Capitalism, Socialism, and Democracy Revisited (1993)

Published under the auspices of
the International Forum for Democratic Studies

Democracy
after
Communism

Edited by Larry Diamond
and Marc F. Plattner

pg 3-25 9/6 - 9/15

Baltimore and London

9 8 7 6 5 4 3 2 1

Chapters in this volume appeared in the following issues of the *Journal of Democracy:*
Chapters in this volume appeared in the following issues of the *Journal of Democracy:*
chapter 5, October 1994; chapter 2, July 1995; chapter 7, October 1995; chapters 4 and 6,
January 1996; chapter 3, April 1996; chapter 1, October 1996; chapters 8, 9, 10, and 12,
January 1999; chapter 11, July 1999; chapter 13, April 2000; chapter 16, July 2000;
chapter 14, January 2001; chapter 15, July 2001; and chapters 17, 18, 19, 20, 21, 22, 23,
24, 25, and 26, October 2001. For all reproduction rights, please contact the Johns Hopkins
University Press.

The Johns Hopkins University Press
2715 North Charles Street
Baltimore, Maryland 21218-4363
www.press.jhu.edu

Library of Congress Cataloging-in-Publication Data

Democracy after communism / edited by Larry Diamond and Marc F. Plattner.
    p. cm. — (A Journal of Democracy book)
    Includes bibliographical references and index.
    ISBN 0-8018-7076-3 (pbk. : alk. paper)
    1. Democracy. 2. Democratization. 3. Post-communism. I. Diamond, Larry Jay. II.
Plattner, Marc F., 1945- III. Series.

JC421 .D4613 2002
306.2091717--dc21

                                            2002016046

A catalog record for this book is available from the British Library.

CONTENTS

ACKNOWLEDGMENTS

Democracy After Communism is the thirteenth *Journal of Democracy* book to be published by the Johns Hopkins University Press and the third to focus on the progress and problems of democracy in a particular region of the world. Having previously gathered collections of *Journal* articles on East Asia and Africa, respectively, we here bring together a set of essays focusing on Eastern Europe and the former Soviet Union. Once again we are responding to requests from professors who find articles from the *Journal* useful in their teaching and, in this case, have suggested that we assemble a volume which they can use in courses on East European and post-Soviet politics. We hope that this collection will meet their expectations.

Of course, as the title of this volume suggests, the countries that it addresses are not united simply by their geographical proximity. More importantly, they all share the experience of having lived for many decades under communist rule. Attempts to build democracy face certain problems in the postcommunist world that they do not confront in other settings. The question of whether and to what extent this makes postcommunist transitions to democracy fundamentally different from transitions elsewhere is one that is explicitly addressed in our Introduction and in several of the essays in this collection.

The 25 essays gathered here all originally appeared in the *Journal of Democracy* between 1994 and 2001. The essays in the opening section were first published in the mid-1990s, and those in the two subsequent sections between 1999 and 2001. Many of the shorter essays in the two later sections were written in connection with the tenth anniversaries of the downfall of communist rule in Eastern Europe in 1989 and in the USSR in 1991. We regret that limitations of space did not permit us to include some of the other important articles on postcommunist countries that have previously appeared in the *Journal*.

Our colleagues on the staff of the *Journal* once again merit our thanks for their fine work on this volume. Current editors Phil Costopoulos, Zerxes Spencer, Jordan Branch, and Stephanie Lewis did much of the editorial work on the original articles and also helped to prepare this volume for publication. The latter task fell primarily on the shoulders of Stephanie Lewis, and she once more accomplished it with speed, accuracy, and good cheer. Past editors whose editorial contributions are reflected in the pages that follow include Mark Eckert, Annette Theuring, Miriam Kramer, Mahindan Kanakaratnam, and Kristin Helz.

We are pleased to have another opportunity to thank some of the other institutions and individuals who have given crucial support to our work. The Lynde and Harry Bradley Foundation has continued to provide the *Journal* with invaluable financial assistance. The Board of Directors of our parent organization, the National Endowment for Democracy, and its president Carl Gershman have been unstinting in their support. Our colleagues at the journals division of the Johns Hopkins University Press have been most reliable partners. And a special word of thanks is due to Henry Tom, our editor at the books division of the Press, who enthusiastically backed the idea of producing this volume.

INTRODUCTION

Marc F. Plattner

The last quarter of the twentieth century was marked by two dramatic political trends that altered many of the world's regimes: the global resurgence of democracy and the collapse of communism. While the second trend might be considered merely a subset of the first, the relation between the two is not nearly so straightforward as it might at first appear.

What Samuel P. Huntington has termed the "third wave" of democratization began in the mid-1970s with the downfall of dictatorships and the installation of democratic regimes in Portugal, Greece, and Spain. Beginning in the early 1980s this democratic wave washed over most of Latin America, and later in the decade it spread to such Asian nations as the Philippines, South Korea, and Pakistan. Thus, by the time that communist regimes in Eastern Europe collapsed in 1989, the movement toward democracy in these countries could be seen simply as one more step in a worldwide process.

Yet what made possible the emergence of regimes aspiring to democracy in the former Soviet bloc was the internal decay of communism, a process with origins distinct from those which first had given rise to the third wave. Though the debility of communist regimes may be traced much further back, the proximate cause of their death was the reforms launched by Mikhail Gorbachev soon after he came to power as the General Secretary of the Communist Party of the Soviet Union in 1985. Though *glasnost'* and *perestroika* were intended to revitalize communist regimes, they ended up destroying them.

The eclipse of Soviet hard-liners and the relaxation of Communist Party control from Moscow paved the way for nascent opposition movements to come to power in Central Europe, where communist regimes, widely viewed as agents of Russian hegemony, had never enjoyed much popular backing. The wave of communist collapse then quickly moved to the Balkans and soon flooded back not only into the USSR's non-Slavic republics but also into the Soviet heartland. By the end of 1991, the leaders of Russia, Ukraine, and Belarus themselves proclaimed the dissolution of the Soviet Union, which was succeeded by

15 independent states, all expressing some commitment to democratization.

In a formal sense, those formerly communist countries that were able to establish and maintain democratic regimes must surely be counted as part of the third wave (after all, Huntington defines a "wave" of democratization simply in temporal terms as a period during which transitions to democracy outnumber democratic breakdowns). But the larger questions remain: Was the process that brought down communism in some sense fundamentally different from the process that gave birth to new democracies in other regions of the world? Were the democratic transitions away from communism mostly like or mostly not like the transitions away from various forms of authoritarianism that took place elsewhere? And is the challenge of building and consolidating democracy under postcommunist conditions unique, meaning that one cannot hope to understand it properly by applying lessons learned from other new democracies?

The Exit from Communism

Our volume begins with two essays, by Ghia Nodia and Valerie Bunce, respectively, that focus directly on the question of the distinctiveness of postcommunist transitions. Nodia questions whether the postcommunist transitions can meaningfully be said to belong to the third wave at all. Communist regimes, he points out, were largely immune to the "diffusion effect" that spurred the downfall of authoritarian regimes, and opposition movements in the Soviet bloc looked to Western models rather than to examples of democratization in developing countries. At the same time, he insists that postcommunist transitions should be viewed within the broader context of the project of building liberal democracy, "the central political enterprise not just of recent decades, but of modernity as a whole." Comparisons should be made, he argues, not only with third-wave cases, but with the American and French Revolutions, and the postfascist transitions following World War II. Such comparisons are both possible and fruitful because these are all cases of transitions "to something that *is* or *tries to be* or at least *pretends to be* democracy."

What is unique about postcommunist transitions is not their goal but their starting point. Their peculiar challenges stem from the peculiar features of communism. Foremost among these is the absence of a market economy. This means, of course, that postcommunist countries must take on the additional task of building a new economic system, but for Nodia this is only part of the story. For he sees the communist abolition of private property as having stunted the human personality. By severing "the links that connect freedom with responsibility and order" and destroying all public-spiritedness, communism destroyed the qualities that democracy requires of its citizens. The most difficult task of the postcommunist transition is "to cure postcommunist man of the traumatic communist experience."

Valerie Bunce focuses directly on the question of whether the concepts and categories developed by scholars of the democratic transitions in Southern Europe and Latin America should be applied to the post-communist world. Her conclusion is that comparisons between the two regions are useful primarily if we focus on the *differences* that they reveal. In her view, the postcommunist cases are different in a number of crucial respects. First, communist dictatorships were both more deeply entrenched and more "invasive" than the authoritarian regimes of Southern Europe and Latin America. Second, the way in which the old regimes collapsed was different from one region to the other. The distinction between transition through "elite pacts" and through mass mobilization, so important to analysts of the South, is not terribly relevant to the East, where the changes sometimes combined both these modes and sometimes featured neither of them.

Above all, however, Bunce emphasizes the broader reach of the transitions in the East, which extended not only to politics but also to economic and social life and (with 22 of the 27 postcommunist countries representing new states) often to nation-building and state-building as well. She sums up this fundamental distinction as follows: "Simply stated, recent developments in Latin America and Southern Europe can accurately be termed regime transitions. The transformation of Eastern Europe from 1989 to the present, on the other hand, is more than a political transition; it is a revolution—in identity, economics, social structure, and the state." Given this massive difference, Bunce concludes that the most useful comparisons for understanding postcommunist efforts at democratization are to be drawn *within* the universe of the 27 post-communist countries, which share basic characteristics but differ in important political details.

In chapter 3, John Higley, Judith Kullberg, and Jan Pakulski emphasize not the revolutionary aspects of the exit from communism but the strong elements of continuity. Focusing on the role of political, economic, and cultural elites, they note that a surprisingly large proportion of top-level positions in 1993 were occupied by people who also held top-level or mid-level jobs in 1988 under the communist regimes. The authors attribute this continuity of elites not so much to the lingering legacy of communism as to an evolution that had already begun during the latter years of the old regime, when younger, better-educated persons increasingly began to fill higher-level positions. These cadres were well-placed to adapt to and to survive the communist collapse.

Thus, while not minimizing the importance of the coming to power of such opposition leaders as Václav Havel and Lech Wałęsa, the authors conclude that the absence of a "revolutionary" circulation of elites indicates that the changes in Central and Eastern Europe did not constitute real revolutions. The ability of the communist elites to survive in the new order explains why most of them did not "go down fighting" and why most of the transformations were relatively peaceful. The authors go even further, arguing that a moderate degree of elite continuity has actually aided the progress of democracy by contributing to a climate of interelite security and compromise and to acceptance of the norms of electoral competition. They note, however, that in the Balkans and the former Soviet Union, where often there were "really high degrees" of elite continuity and former communist leaders remained in power, the results were unfavorable for the emergence of democracy, typically leading to authoritarian or semi-authoritarian regimes.

In chapter 4, Aleksander Smolar looks at the exit from communism from the very different perspective of "civil society." As Smolar explains, the concept of "civil society" was revivified by democratic opposition groups in Eastern and Central Europe who reacted to previous failures to reform communism from within by formulating a strategy of "society first." The idea was to create "islands of social independence," wholly separate from and in peaceful opposition to the communist party-state. This strategy proved remarkably successful, especially in Poland, where it became the basis of Solidarity, a truly mass movement. Some of the intellectuals who developed the concept of civil society came to view it not just as a potent weapon against communist tyranny but as a new model of political life also superior to Western-style parliamentary democracy.

The euphoria generated by the sudden collapse of communism gave rise to the illusion of "civil society in power." But as Smolar points out, "the myth of civil society as united, antipolitical, and supportive of radical reform was one of the first casualties of the postcommunist era." Broadly based civic fronts like Solidarity in Poland and Civic Forum in Czechoslovakia quickly broke up, competing political parties began to form, and conflicting economic interests began to emerge. Political leaders soon abandoned any thought of seeking a "third way" and set out to build Western-style democratic institutions. Moreover, it turned out that the civil society that had seemed so heroic in ousting communism was not in good shape to fulfill the very different functions required under democracy. Much of the old network of state-run social institutions had collapsed, and economic and cultural circumstances were not propitious for building new ones. As a result, Smolar concludes that in the mid-1990s postcommunist society was "no less—indeed, perhaps even more—atomized than it was in the final years of communism."

The two subsequent essays, written by prominent political leaders of two of the region's most successful transitions, examine the challenges of democratic reform as they confront policy makers. Leszek Balcerowicz, Poland's former deputy prime minister and finance minister and the architect of its economic reforms, highlights the factors that distinguish postcommunist transitions from all earlier cases of both political and economic transformation. The most important and distinctive characteristic of the postcommunist cases is the imperative to proceed with both political and economic reform. Balcerowicz intentionally avoids speaking of a "simultaneous transition," however, precisely because he wants to underline the difficult problems of timing and sequencing that beset such twofold transitions. For the key political change—the organizing of free elections—can be achieved much more rapidly than the creation of a privatized market economy.

This in turn means that many economic reforms, especially those second-stage reforms involving fundamental institutional restructuring, have to take place under democratic political arrangements. Given the difficult initial conditions and the unfavorable external environment that accompanied postcommunist transitions, discontent will inevitably be generated among those groups whose short-term economic interests are harmed by the reforms. The problem is compounded by what Balcerowicz calls the "visibility effect"—the tendency of newly free media to accentuate adverse phenomena like crime and poverty that may have already been prevalent before the transition, but for which it tends to be blamed. There is no easy solution to these difficulties, but Balcerowicz strongly argues for the superiority of radical reform over gradual reform. In his view, political leaders must move quickly to enact key reforms during the period of "extraordinary politics" that immediately follows political change. For once there is a return to the "ordinary politics" of competition for group advantage, reform becomes much harder to achieve.

Mart Laar, prime minister of Estonia from 1992 to 1994 (and again from March 1999 onwards), also favors radical reform, although he presents the desired sequencing in a somewhat different manner. In his brief essay, Laar cites the need to "take care of politics first, and then to proceed with economic reform." Estonia ratified a new constitution in June 1992 and a few months later held its first free and democratic elections since before World War II. Radical reformers came to power, and they sought to take quick advantage of the period of "extraordinary politics," enacting a forceful program of economic "shock therapy." Standards of living, after bottoming out in 1992–93, began to rise. This did not save the reform government from being voted out of office in March 1995, but Laar confidently (and rightly) predicted that its left-of-center successor would not reverse the process of reform or derail Estonia from its track toward democratic consolidation.

With its striking success at political and economic reform and at state-building, Estonia represents one extreme in the postcommunist experience. At the other end of the spectrum are the more anarchic successor states of the Soviet Union and Yugoslavia, along with the breakaway ministates that have sought to achieve their independence.

(The latter category includes such largely unrecognized entities as Chechnya, Bosnia's Republika Srpska, Kosovo, and Nagorno-Karabakh.) As Charles Fairbanks recounts in chapter 7 in an essay focused on postcommunist civil-military relations, the weakness or absence of the state in these places has given rise to a wide range of armed formations that do not really merit being called armies. These bands of irregulars or militiamen range from wholly nongovernmental forces to others with a tenuous or ambiguous connection to the state. Not only do they lack training, discipline, and a clear chain of command, but their members tend to wear civilian clothes and to join or leave their units at will.

Given this situation, it is easy to understand why there has been a great deal of desultory and brutal warfare in the Balkans and the former USSR. Yet as Fairbanks points out, it is a surprising paradox that all this unchecked and irregular military activity has not resulted in the birth of any military regimes in the postcommunist world. He speculates that the commanders of these forces want wealth and power, but have no interest in the potential glory or the responsibility that political rule involves. This may be part of a larger postcommunist trend toward a radical "antipolitics." In reaction to the discipline and regimentation of communism, some parts of the postcommunist world have witnessed "a near-total flight from the public world as such"—a development evident in the growth of crime and corruption as well as the rise of irregular armed forces.

The East European Experience

The essays in the opening section of this volume, all originally written in the mid-1990s, are remarkable attempts to analyze and think through the momentous transformations—then still quite new—that had been launched in 1989–91. By contrast, the authors of the essays in the remaining two sections, all first published between 1999 and 2001, enjoyed the advantage of having seen more "post-transition" history unfold. Many of their essays, in fact, were explicitly written in connection with the tenth anniversaries of the events that brought down communism in Eastern Europe in 1989 and in the former Soviet Union in 1991. These occasions naturally prompted not only reflections on the revolutions of a decade earlier but also consideration of how much had changed since then. After a decade of postcommunism, there was an increasingly obvious divergence among the countries belonging to this category. To a considerable extent, this divergence separates the former republics of the Soviet Union from the East European countries that were not under direct rule from Moscow. In part for this reason, we have divided the remaining portions of this volume into a section on "The East European Experience" and another on "The Post-Soviet Experience."

Our section on Eastern Europe begins with a series of short essays marking the tenth anniversary of the revolutions of 1989. In the first of these, Jacques Rupnik emphasizes the vastly different outcomes of the postcommunist transitions, even going so far as to claim that "the word postcommunism has lost its relevance." He identifies a broad divide separating Central Europe (a category that here includes the Baltic states), which has been a clear "success story," from the Balkans, where the transitions have often been "derailed." While the Central European countries are well on their way to democratic consolidation, the former Yugoslavia fell victim to war and ethnonationalist conflict, and Romania and Bulgaria occupy an intermediate position. Rupnik seeks to account for this "uneven progress" by briefly comparing the differential impact in these subregions of six factors: 1) the legacies of communism; 2) the market and civil society; 3) the rule of law and the "Habsburg factor"; 4) nation-state building and "homogeneity"; 5) culture; and 6) the international environment.

In chapter 9, Richard Rose concentrates on situating the countries of the region within the broader European context. Focusing on the ten leading candidates for membership in the European Union (EU), he draws a largely optimistic picture. All of these countries have already changed their governments at least once at the ballot box, and, even by West European standards, only a small portion of their electorates has given support to extremists. After considerable initial pain, economic prospects are looking brighter, and (outside the former Yugoslavia) ethnic conflict seems less of a threat than in the past. Weaknesses remain with respect to political parties, the rule of law, and corruption, all problems that stem from the legacy of communist rule. Yet there is no reason to think that these countries cannot overcome their pasts and establish normal democracies. After all, a majority of the current 15 members of the EU also had a relatively recent history of dictatorial rule.

In chapter 10, Vladimir Tismaneanu focuses more directly on the revolutions of 1989, asserting that their importance "cannot be overestimated." Countering those who emphasize the "ambiguous legacies" of these events or deny that they achieved fundamental change, he argues that they were genuine *political revolutions* that transformed the existing order decisively and irreversibly." It is true that the anti-communist upheavals in the region had certain illiberal and authoritarian aspects and that these have subsequently given rise to a resurgence of ethnic conflict, populism, and tribalism in some places, but the revolutions of 1989 "have succeeded in their most important task: The old Leninist order, based on suspicion, fear, and mass hopelessness, is gone forever, and the citizens of these countries are now free to shape their own destinies."

The next two essays are by authors who were leading dissidents under communist rule, Poland's Bronisław Geremek and Hungary's G.M. Tamás. Geremek, a key adviser to Lech Wałeşa from the earliest days of Solidarity, was serving as Poland's foreign minister when he wrote his essay, a time at which NATO was engaged in the war in Kosovo. Geremek contends that Poland's Solidarity movement was "not just a rebellion against a constraining system, but a positive force shaping an attractive new alternative in the form of democracy, free markets, and a bond with European and Euro-Atlantic structures." In his view, Poland (along with other Central European states) has succeeded in implementing this vision, not only rapidly attaining the complementary goals of building democracy and free markets, but also "becoming a part of the transatlantic zone of security and prosperity." He sees the expansion of this zone, through the enlargement of NATO and the EU to include other parts of the postcommunist world, as the great challenge ahead.

Tamás, a philosopher who helped found Hungary's Free Democratic Alliance and later served in parliament, has a perspective very different from that of Geremek. For Tamás, the great victory of 1989 threatens to be lost. In his view, resistance to communism was born of "antipathy, not hope" (although he does acknowledge that "Poland is different from the rest"). The peoples of Eastern Europe actively did away with their old regimes, but, lacking a new social idea of their own, they accepted the new capitalist order only passively, and still regard it as an alien imposition. The experience of living under communism produced deep skepticism, an unwillingness to accept any concepts of legitimacy. The resulting moral exhaustion remains, and while "there is no radical alternative . . . on the horizon," widespread sympathy with anticapitalist and antimodern ideas indicates that liberal democracy is not secure.

A key reason for the relative success of democratization in Central Europe since 1989 has been the impact of international factors. In chapter 13, Jacques Rupnik offers a fascinating comparison of the current situation with the failed efforts to maintain the new nations established in the region after World War I. He notes three crucial differences between the two periods. In the post–World War I era, the new states were internally weakened and embroiled with their neighbors by the problem of national minorities; they had to contend with the overwhelming strength of undemocratic Germany; and their nominal independence was in fact compromised by the balance-of-power considerations of Europe's great powers. After 1989, by contrast, the new democracies of Central Europe (though not the Balkan countries) had more homogeneous populations and peaceful relations with one another; Germany had become a "model of democracy"; and the process of European integration had largely replaced the old balance-of-power conflicts.

Rupnik goes on to examine the nature and the effects of European and Euro-Atlantic integration in greater detail. He explains why the expansion of NATO has proceeded faster than that of the EU: The Central Europeans feared a "security void" and saw the United States as the "guarantor of European democracy"; they viewed NATO as a more "value-infused institution"; and NATO membership required less onerous preparations on their part than joining the EU. At the same time, joining the EU was, for political, cultural, and economic reasons, regarded as the "ultimate goal" of the transition begun in 1989. As the case of Slovakia shows, the "democratic conditionality" associated with EU membership has had a powerful effect on countries wishing to join. Rupnik notes, however, that for democratic conditionality to work, aspirant countries must think they have a realistic prospect of membership, and he warns against the danger of creating "hard borders" around the EU that could again divide the continent in two.

In chapter 14, Richard Rose draws upon public opinion data to illuminate the condition of democracy in postcommunist Europe. He notes that most of these countries hold free elections, and that Freedom House rates all ten candidates for initial consideration for EU membership as "Free." In these ten Free countries (all in Eastern and Central Europe and the Baltics), 55 percent of citizens are positive about their new regime, while in six "Partly Free" or "Not Free" countries (all in the former USSR or the former Yugoslavia) only a third are positive. Similarly, in almost all the Free countries, a substantial majority is opposed to any alternative to democratic rule, while in most of the other countries, a majority endorses one or more undemocratic alternatives.

In response to other questions, however, the divergence among the postcommunist countries is less pronounced. By wide margins, postcommunist publics report that they enjoy much greater freedom than they had under communism. Rose points out, however, that they reply quite differently when asked about another critical aspect of democracy—government responsiveness and fairness to its citizens. Respondents feel they are treated no more fairly and that they actually have *less* influence on government than they did under communism. And a very substantial majority believe that their new regimes are more corrupt than their predecessors. Based on these data, Rose concludes, "The weakness of the rule of law is the biggest obstacle to completing democracy in Europe today." Free elections and the widening of individual liberties are not enough to achieve solid democracies capable of meeting the standards for EU membership. There must also be progress in fighting corruption, which not only is a significant threat to post-communist democracy but also has become a major obstacle to European unity.

In the concluding essay of this section, Aleksander Smolar reflects on the contrast between the momentous importance of the revolutions of 1989–91 and the surprisingly low-key celebrations of their tenth anniversary. Those revolutions, spearheaded by intellectuals and courageous democratic activists who invoked the language of morality, human rights, and civil society, had "fascinated the entire world." In addition to transforming the international political landscape, these peaceful revolutions seemed to promise a revitalization of the civic spirit that appeared to be waning in Western democracies. There were widespread hopes that the East would bring to a newly united Europe the moral and spiritual resources it had accumulated in the struggle against totalitarianism. Yet postcommunist reality quickly proved disappointing.

Rather than establishing a new and more moral civic order that would improve upon existing democracies, the emerging postcommunist societies turned out to be rife with xenophobia, ethnic conflict, corruption, and authoritarian tendencies. In building their political institutions, they quickly abandoned the idea of looking for something new, choosing instead to imitate the West. Instead of "the dreamed-of union of equals," the reuniting of Europe took the form of the enlargement of the European Union, with the newcomers rigorously forced to comply with a huge slate of "commandments" from Brussels. Within the postcommunist countries themselves, there is also deep disappointment (though not a desire to return to the past). "The difficulty in embracing the changes of 1989–91," Smolar concludes, "has its source above all in the huge material, social, and psychological costs that resulted from the breakdown of the old system." The romantic vision of a society combining "what were perceived as the good sides of both capitalism and socialism" could not be achieved. Instead, Poland and its Central European neighbors opted for Western-style capitalism and democracy, and whatever the costs of this choice, it has offered them a chance "to join the prosperous and stable countries at the forefront of world civilization."

The Post-Soviet Experience

The collapse of the Soviet Union did not come until two years after the fall of communism in Eastern Europe. The defeat of the August 1991 coup attempt by communist hard-liners was the decisive event, quickly leading to the official dissolution of the USSR at the end of that year. The key figure in the Soviet demise was Boris Yeltsin. Chosen as chairman of the Russian Supreme Soviet in May 1990 and popularly elected as president of the Russian Republic in June 1991, Yeltsin spearheaded the resistance to the coup attempt and the subsequent break-up of the USSR, and then went on to lead Russia for eight more eventful and tumultuous years. During this period Russia displayed the most mixed picture of any postcommunist country, featuring alongside one another elements of genuine democratic transformation, lingering communist influence, and the rise of crime and corruption. In a characteristically surprising move, Yeltsin suddenly resigned from Russia's presidency on 31 December 1999. Stating that Russia should enter a new millennium with a new generation of leaders at the helm, he appointed his young and relatively unknown prime minister Vladimir Putin as acting president until constitutionally mandated elections could take place three months later.

This section of our volume begins with an essay by Michael McFaul assessing Putin's subsequent victory in the March 2000 presidential elections. McFaul cites four reasons why Putin was able to win with a 52.9 percent first-round majority: 1) popular support for his decisive prosecution of the second Chechen war; 2) a national craving for stability after a period of revolutionary volatility; 3) the ineffectiveness of opposition forces, still dominated by old-style communists; and 4) Yeltsin's decision to move the election (originally scheduled for June) forward to March, when the newly appointed Putin was still near the peak of his popularity. The elections demonstrated the weakness both of liberals and of independent nationalist leaders and parties; and although Communist leader Gennady Zyuganov was much more successful, finishing second with 29.2 percent of the vote, his party seemed ready to work with Putin on many key issues. Thus Russia's political future would principally depend on the course chosen by Vladimir Putin.

But evaluating the overall intentions of Putin, who "ran an issue-free campaign," is not easy. His first priority seems to be strengthening the state and the authority of the federal government. At the same time, he appears to favor market-oriented economic reform and foreign-policy cooperation with the West. Most worrisome to McFaul, however, is Putin's apparent indifference to democracy, his willingness to use state power to override individual rights. This is reflected not only in his treatment of independent media, but above all in "the egregious violations of human rights" that have characterized his policy in Chechnya. This does not mean that Putin, a former KGB officer, is an out-and-out "antidemocrat." He is "too modern and too Western-oriented" to want to reestablish a dictatorship, which in any case would be a formidable task in present-day Russia. Thus "neither popular desires for stability and security nor Putin's lack of commitment to democracy need necessarily translate into authoritarianism."

There follows a symposium on "Ten Years After the Soviet Breakup," consisting of ten short essays written during the summer of 2001 in response to questions posed by the *Journal of Democracy*. The charge that we gave to our authors was as follows:

It is now ten years since the failed August 1991 coup attempt by Soviet hard-liners set in motion a series of events that led to the voluntary dissolution of the USSR and the transformation of its 15 constituent republics into independent states. Most of them claimed to be setting out on the road to democracy, and there was great optimism in some quarters, and considerable skepticism in others, about their ability to reach this destination. A decade later, the picture may still be sufficiently mixed to give some support to the optimists as well as the skeptics, but the last couple of years clearly have not been propitious for the fortunes of democracy in "the post-Soviet space." Apart from the Baltic states, democracy today seems to be in retreat throughout the region.

In light of the sobering experience of the past ten years, how would you evaluate post-Soviet efforts at democratization? How would you account for the differences in performance among the 15 successor states of the Soviet Union, and between them and other postcommunist states? What have been the critical obstacles to democratic success? The legacy of communism? Culture? Poor institutional choices? Bad leadership? Economic mistakes? Western policy? Other factors?

We ask that you write a short essay of no more than 3,000 words addressing these questions and drawing out what you consider to be the chief lessons of the post-Soviet experience. Although we would like you to keep in mind the broader picture, you may seek to illuminate it by focusing primarily on one or a few states or on a specific aspect of post-Soviet democratization.

In the first response (chapter 17), Zbigniew Brzezinski emphasizes the primacy of history and culture in accounting for the divergences among the post-Soviet states. These factors explain why, among the former Soviet republics, only the Baltic states have succeeded in following a path toward stable and secure democracy. They also explain why the economic shock therapy that succeeded in Poland and Estonia failed in Russia. Although Western policy was flawed in numerous respects, it is doubtful that even the most enlightened Western policies would have brought a comparable success in Russia. Nonetheless, the situation in Russia (as well as Ukraine and perhaps Georgia) remains ambiguous: "Theirs are unstable authoritarian and yet also semi-anarchic political systems, in which democratic institutions operate at some levels but are absent at others." Hope for the longer run may be found in Russia's geopolitical situation, as the potential threat it faces from the Chinese in the East and the Muslims along its southern border gives it a strong incentive to seek an accommodation with the West.

In chapter 18, Ghia Nodia also emphasizes the cultural factor. He notes that the 15 post-Soviet states, "despite coming out of the same Soviet institutional environment, and despite following (or trying to follow) the same democratic-capitalist path since independence . . . persistently display glaring differences while they have in common little more than what is vaguely referred to as a 'shared postcommunist mentality.'" While Nodia acknowledges that their level of democratic success largely correlates with the fault lines that divide the cultural realms of Western Christendom, Eastern Christendom, and Islam, he denies that there is "a specific set of cultural preconditions" which makes democracy possible. Instead, he sees a process in which "cultural belonging" influences political choices. Since democracy is widely viewed as "Western," those countries where nationalism assumes a pro-

Western character are more likely avidly to pursue democracy, while those countries where nationalism assumes an anti-Western character are more likely to embrace authoritarianism.

Archie Brown opens chapter 19 by asserting that Russia's transition from communism was actually achieved under Gorbachev prior to the breakup of the Soviet Union. In his view, the disintegration of the USSR was not in itself a "democratic gain" (though he acknowledges that the independence of the Baltic states would have been inevitable in a democratized Soviet Union). Unlike the Baltic elites, who were committed to building democratic institutions, Boris Yeltsin and the Russian political elite gave priority to pursuing their own wealth and power. Thus, "ordinary Russian citizens cannot be blamed for taking a dim view of what has been presented to them in the name of democracy." In the near term, the choices of Russia's new and younger political elite will be decisive in determining whether it moves beyond "manipulated democracy" or regresses into full authoritarianism. In the longer run, however, the Russian people are unlikely to remain as manipulable as they have been so far.

In the following essay, Anders Åslund offers a comparative analysis of market-oriented economic reform in the former Soviet Union and its relation to democratization. He concludes that the correlation between the two is very close: "The more far-reaching the democratization, the more radical the market reform has been, and both democracy and market reform have been positively correlated with economic growth." Echoing Brown, he argues that selfish elites, seeking to exploit the state for their own benefit, have posed the greatest threat to democratization, but he sees the strategy of so-called gradual reforms as the vehicle for this exploitation. Radical reform, by contrast, is a path that leads to economic growth and fosters democracy, as is shown by the Baltic states, full-fledged democracies where more than two-thirds of GDP now comes from the private sector. At the other end of the spectrum, countries like Belarus and Turkmenistan, where less than a quarter of GDP originates in the private sector, are also the most undemocratic. The majority of post-Soviet states, however, are "semidemocratic, rent-seeking societies with over half of GDP coming from the private sector."

In chapter 21, Charles Fairbanks analyzes the regimes of the Caucasus and Central Asia, distinguishing three political patterns. One is to be found in the "strong-state autocracies" of Uzbekistan and Turkmenistan, where the old communist system (minus the Communist Party and rule from Moscow) persists. At the other extreme is the "stateless community," exemplified by Chechnya, where the state lacks the power to control its own territory or to raise taxes, but there is a powerful sense of communal solidarity. The most common pattern, however, is that of weak states with some political competition and not wholly fraudulent elections. Most of these states have suffered devastating economic declines and often do not control their own officials, who frequently raise their own revenue by preying on the people. The space emptied by the shrinking state is filled by "clans, ethnic groups, clientelistic networks, and criminal gangs," but also sometimes by prodemocratic NGOs. Fairbanks believes that these patterns cannot endure and that change is coming. Echoing some of the arguments made by Nodia, he suggests that over the long term "civilizational identities" may pull these areas (especially the Caucasus) toward democratization.

In chapter 22, Nadia Diuk looks at Ukraine, the largest and most strategically important of the Soviet successor states apart from Russia. Evaluating Ukraine's performance on the three major tasks of its transition—state-building, economic reform, and democratization—she concludes that Ukraine did surprisingly well in establishing and maintaining its independence but unexpectedly poorly in reforming its economy. As far as democratization is concerned, she notes that Ukraine lies at the midpoint between the genuinely democratic Baltic states and the wholly authoritarian Central Asian states. It has all the trappings of democracy, including relatively free elections, but power continues to be distributed and exercised from the top down. The functions formerly performed by the Soviet Communist Party "simply passed more or less intact into the hands of the newly created presidency and its executive arm, known as the *vertikal*." Accompanying this "super-presidentialist" system is a set of political parties largely controlled by corrupt business interests. Although there have been signs of growing strength in civil society, it is not clear whether this will be enough to overcome the power of entrenched interests opposed to a more open system of government.

The following three essays focus primarily on Russia. In chapter 23, Lilia Shevtsova emphasizes that, outside the Baltic states, post-Soviet transitions have been decisively influenced by "the inability of the political class (including its liberal-democratic wing) to transcend the previous civilizational model," which featured attempts to impose modernization "from above" and reliance on personalized networks rather than on institutions. As a result, Russia has wound up with a "hybrid regime" that uneasily combines "personalistic leadership and democratic legitimation." Although democratic elements are present, the government seeks to manipulate them, and the main pillars of its rule are the bureaucracy and the security services. Shevtsova acknowledges that such a regime (which she labels "bureaucratic quasi-authoritarianism") might survive for quite a while if the country can avoid any social or economic crises, but she contends that the system's structural flaws and incompatible principles will doom its efforts to achieve both economic modernization and political stability.

In chapter 24, M. Steven Fish focuses on the "political transformation" of Russia being attempted by Vladimir Putin since his ascension to the presidency in 2000. The four key elements of this effort are 1) recentralizing state power; 2) fostering the allegiance of citizens to the state; 3) restoring state control of communication; and 4) restructuring the party system. While Putin's pursuit of these policies is often viewed as constituting a restoration of authoritarianism, Fish argues that the consequences "may prove to be both mixed and complex." In some respects, Putin's policies may actually be favorable for democracy, especially since "a feeble central state can impede democratization as surely as an overly strong one." Moreover, Fish argues that the Russian electorate knew very well that Putin was "a stern, cunning statist who placed competent administration and public order above rights but who also did not reflexively detest liberalism and modernity." So despite Russia's profound shortcomings in protecting individual rights and ensuring official accountability, it has at least fulfilled that aspect of democracy which entails "people getting to vote for whom they want and then getting what they voted for."

Grigory Yavlinsky, a member of the Russian State Duma, leader of the Yabloko party, and the leading liberal presidential candidate in 2000, takes a very different view of Putin's Russia in chapter 25. For him, recent developments represent a clear step backwards, as symbolized by official encouragement of popular nostalgia for "the most stagnant Soviet times and traditions." Russia today has only an "artificial, formal, sham democracy." Despite the demise of communism, the system of *nomenklatura* government has been preserved; the whims of officials and personal ties are decisive, while laws count for almost nothing. Now Putin's administration is seeking to stifle whatever independent voices remain by bringing both civil society organizations and the media under state control. The greatest danger today is not a return of communism but "the formation of a new authoritarian or totalitarian system that is completely compatible with a banal market economy." Unless the Russian people themselves recognize that the "development of Russia as a full-fledged European country" is their own responsibility, their country will continue to drift in the direction of dictatorship, while at the same time failing to overcome economic stagnation.

In the final essay of this section, Michael McFaul seeks to draw together some of the themes highlighted by the other contributors to the symposium. Noting the competing explanations offered for the variations among post-Soviet regimes, he argues that both culture and elite choice matter, but neither by itself offers a complete answer. He adds that the balance of power between prodemocratic and antidemocratic forces in any particular country must also figure prominently in any attempt to account for its political development. Like a number of the other authors, McFaul stresses the centrality of Russia in determining the prospects of democracy in the region, and in his view the future of democracy in Russia is a very open question. It has the most "ill-defined" of all postcommunist regimes, and both a democratic and a dictatorial outcome still remain possible. Even if Putin wishes to move the country toward full-blown authoritarianism, it is far from clear that he can attain this objective, as "societal support for democratic norms" remains strong. Russia may be stuck for some time in "a twilight zone between dictatorship and democracy." Yet it is also possible that some kind of crisis will arrive, posing dangers but also opportunities for movement toward democratic change.

From Postcommunism to Democracy

McFaul's essay (chapter 26) concludes not only the symposium and the section on "The Post-Soviet Experience," but also this volume as a whole. It is especially fitting, then, that in its opening pages McFaul takes up the theme with which this volume began: the relationship of the regime changes in the postcommunist world to the global third wave of democratic transitions that was launched in Portugal in 1974. McFaul contends that analysts of post-Soviet developments, by assuming that these were part of the third wave, have been misled by a "distorting interpretive framework." The metaphor of "transition," he suggests, is imperfect because it refers only to political change, which is "only one component of the grand post-Soviet transformation." Moreover, given the importance of securing national independence and reviving crippled economies, "democratization was only one of many aims, and a lesser priority to boot" for the rulers who came to power after the fall of the Soviet Union.

The debate about whether the postcommunist cases are fundamentally different from other third-wave transitions is illuminating in many ways, but it probably does not admit of a definitive answer. There is no question that the postcommunist transformations were broader in scope than the transitions in Southern Europe and Latin America, that they unfolded in different ways, and that they posed greater challenges for would-be democratizers. It is also true that some of the postcommunist cases, like Uzbekistan or Turkmenistan, probably should not be classified even as failed democratic transitions, since democratization was never really attempted. Yet the great majority of postcommunist states were guided to a considerable degree by the goal of democratization, if only because they had no compelling alternative model. And in organizing elections or designing institutions or building a democratic culture, they face problems similar to those encountered by would-be democracies elsewhere.

For many years to come, the postcommunist countries will continue to share many characteristics deriving from the fact that they attempted to build democracy after enduring communism. But those that succeed in their efforts to build democracy will eventually come to be regarded not as "postcommunist" countries, but as democratic ones.

I

The Exit From Communism

1

HOW DIFFERENT ARE POSTCOMMUNIST TRANSITIONS?

Ghia Nodia

Ghia Nodia is chairman of the board of the Caucasian Institute for Peace, Democracy, and Development (CIPDD) and professor of sociology at Tbilisi State University. He wrote this essay, which was originally published in the October 1996 issue of the Journal of Democracy, *while he was a fellow at the International Forum for Democratic Studies in Washington, D.C., from January to June 1996.*

Transitions toward democracy in countries once ruled by communism almost invariably are described as "troubled" or "painful." However appropriate such adjectives might be, and however much legitimate doubt might persist about the degree or quality of democracy in these lands, we should not underestimate the sheer significance of their desire to claim the title of "democracy." Whatever arguments students of democracy may have about its definition, peoples and governments today assume that 1) "democracy" means something universal and general, and 2) the best models of it are to be found in the West. Their understanding of democracy may often be vague and superficial, but some level of understanding is there. Everybody knows, for instance, that under democracy you are supposed to have competitive multiparty elections, that parties must be free to take their messages to the voters, that some independent media and associations should be allowed, and so on. Superficial or not, this vision is indeed derived from the Western democratic experience.

Postcommunist transitions, however "troubled," may still be regarded as transitions to democracy—if only because leading political actors recognize that there is nothing else to make a transition *to*. Even those who come closest to openly rejecting the Western model of democracy, such as President Alyaksander Lukashenka of Belarus or Russia's unrepentant communists, can offer no real alternative vision. They may do a lot of harm, but cannot challenge the centrality of the democratic project. Even if we exclude Belarus or the Central Asian states, where transitions seem hardly to have begun, there remains a vast swath of post-

Soviet countries whose governments do recognize the compelling character of the democratic project, and do comply with at least some of its rules.

Although mainstream, empiricist political science tends to explain political life by reference to material interests, personal ambitions, and the *libido,* none of these things is enough to give us a full understanding of politics. To gain that full understanding, one must take into account the primary role of ideas. Certainly, political actors are driven by their desire for power and their other passions, and they are greatly influenced by economic interests. Their behavior, one may add, is also significantly determined by the cultural traditions of their societies. Granted all that, however, there is also a world of ideas that are not merely subjective, "personal" notions, but are "out there," exerting immense influence over human behavior and creating the basis of political *legitimacy.* What is on the minds of political actors, what ideas are popular or fashionable in a society (on elite or popular levels), is of tremendous importance. Political leaders set their agendas or create their projects on the basis of such ideas. Whether or not they really believe them is secondary in defining the nature of political regimes. If political leaders recognize the compelling power of the idea of democracy and the values and rules that come with it, and see the need to accept— or at least to give the appearance of accepting—those values and rules, then the strength of the idea of democracy is manifest. The resulting regime is eligible to be regarded as democratic—which does not detract from the importance of scrutinizing how "authentically" democratic it really is.

An analogy can be drawn between the crafting of democratic transitions and the art of shoemaking. Shoes may be produced in different fashions, from different materials, with different tools, for different markets, and by different shoemakers, who can vary widely in skill, motivation, work habits, and so on. In the postcommunist situation, the quality of the "shoes" may be so poor that they barely deserve the glorious name of shoes. Someone familiar with the customs of the communist economy might suspect that the shoemaker has been cheating, that he has used the wrong materials and put them together badly, so that the shoes will come apart very soon. Perhaps he has only been making a show of producing shoes, having in mind not consumers, but the prospect of loans from the International Monetary Fund. If the shoemaker is cheating, he needs to be watched carefully (election monitoring). Or he may lack essential skills, so that technical assistance is the solution. In any case, to assess his way of doing business and his product, we need to have some idea of what makes for good shoes, and possibly some knowledge of the history of shoemaking. The latter is likely to be especially useful because the shoemaker tends to be interested in how others made shoes before him, and he may well adjust his business accordingly (whether to produce better shoes or to cheat more effectively).

To Compare or Not to Compare?

These considerations can help us to evaluate the strange debate among political scientists as to whether postcommunist transitions can be usefully compared with other transitions to democracy.[1] The only valid argument against the enterprise of comparison would be not that the differences are too great—after all, comparison implies differences as well as similarities—but that the postcommunist cases aim at some destination other than democracy and hence do not belong to the category of democratic transitions at all. As indicated above, however, most postcommunist transitions are indeed transitions from something that is not democracy to something that *is* or *tries to be* or at least *pretends to be* democracy. It is the universality of the modern democratic project that creates a conceptual space in which it becomes sensible—and indeed necessary—to compare different attempts to implement this project. What is unique about postcommunist transitions is that they are transitions *from communism*. The only interesting question is *how* different this makes them and in what this specific difference consists.

Certain common characteristics of the transitions that began in 1989–91 may not be distinguishing features of postcommunist transitions as such. Take the matter of ethnic conflict. In the course of the transitions, three countries broke up, and in a number of cases bloody ethnoterritorial wars followed. Most Western television coverage of postcommunist transitions has focused on these wars. But can one say that such ethnic strife is intrinsic to postcommunist transitions? To be sure, the legacy of communism affects interethnic relations, and nationalism has played a role in postcommunist transitions.[2] Yet there is no inherent link between communist breakdown on the one hand and ethnic conflict and state breakups on the other. In a number of postcommunist cases, including Poland and Hungary, ethnic factors played no significant role. Moreover, the breakup of the Soviet Union in many ways resembled the breakup of the Russian Empire seven decades earlier in the wake of Russia's unsuccessful attempt to make the transition from Czarist autocracy to liberal democracy. Many other ethnoterritorial conflicts in the postcommunist world also echo conflicts that occurred around the beginning of this century and had nothing to do with communism.

The recent debate among political scientists, with its focus on how far generalizations drawn from "third wave" transitions in Southern Europe and Latin America can be "stretched" to cover the postcommunist cases, has been excessively narrow. In fact, Samuel P. Huntington's idea of a "third wave" that includes all the democratic transitions of the past two decades itself has serious limitations. There was a demonstrable diffu-

sion effect among various "southern" democratizations, so that a democratic transition in one country made it much harder for the authoritarian
regime in another country to hold out. Yet it is doubtful that these events
had any real impact on postcommunist transitions—and if they had none,
why speak of a "wave" at all? The leaders of the postcommunist transitions had in mind the "classic" democratic models presented by Western
Europe and the United States, not the "third wave" democratizations that
began in the mid-1970s. Latin America's experience was typically seen
as negative; indeed, relatively few people in postcommunist countries
knew that democracy had met with much success in Latin America.[3]

By all means let postcommunist transitions be placed in comparative
perspective, but let this perspective not be narrowed to "third wave"
democratizations only. The project of liberal democracy provides the
ground for the comparison, and that project is the central political enterprise not just of recent decades, but of modernity as a whole. It makes
sense to compare attempts to democratize Russia or Hungary not just
with the crafting of democracy in Taiwan or El Salvador, but with the
American and French revolutions of the late eighteenth century, the
postfascist transitions in Germany and Italy after the Second World War,
and so on. Comparisons are legitimate and necessary because what
postcommunist political actors do when changing the previous regime
and consolidating the new one is basically the same thing that anybody
who had the same democratic project in mind has ever done. Of course
the postcommunist leaders do it 1) under very different circumstances;
2) possibly with a different sense of commitment; and 3) with differing
success. But these are exactly the kinds of things that one has to talk
about when making a comparison.

"Ideological" versus "Organic" Transitions

A major distinction to keep in mind when comparing transitions is
that between "organic" and "ideological" modes or elements. By the
"organic" mode of democratization, I mean a gradual societal transformation *followed* by a change of political regime, with the societal transformation serving as a "precondition" of the political shift. Britain and
the United States present classic cases of this mode. The societal changes
are usually discussed under the rubric of "modernization," a process
centering around the rise of personal autonomy as the basic regulative
principle in social relations. Interpersonal relationships are increasingly
ruled by laws rather than sacralized traditions, and status becomes more
a matter of personal achievement than of birth.

The adjective "organic" imperfectly describes this gradual development, for it calls to mind a natural process, whereas the modern transformation definitely involves human effort. At the same time, the notion
of human autonomy was not just a "subjective" idea developed by intel-

lectuals for later implementation by a benevolent tyrant or a vanguard party. Real and profound changes occurred across broad swaths of the social realm, until human autonomy and liberty gradually came to seem normal and "natural." The theory of natural rights developed not only because logical argument led to a conception of human liberties as "natural," but because members of certain societies had enjoyed those liberties long enough to treat them as part of the nature of things. Thus the English and American revolutions were based not on the *idea* of revolution but on the urge to protect existing rights and liberties from infringement by despotic regimes. Principles mattered, but less than the reality of freedom. Indeed, on the formal level of conventional principles, Britain has yet to complete its democratic transition. The British remain subjects rather than citizens, and they live without a written constitution.

The tradition of a predominantly ideological transition began with the French Revolution in 1789. Those who stormed the Bastille were not inspired by the desire to protect anything they already had; rather, they wanted to destroy the old world and build a new one. This new world existed only in the imagination, and was based on general ideas and principles, or the revolutionary project. The latter first had to be elaborated in the minds of intellectuals, and afterwards implemented by the deliberate efforts of an ideologized revolutionary elite. The role of the "people" or the "masses" in this endeavor was ambiguous. Revolutionary leaders declared the "will of the people" sacred; but the actually existing people often lacked a correct grasp of the revolutionary project, while the work of persuading and teaching them promised to be lengthy and uncertain of success. The revolutionary elite solved this problem by mobilizing the masses through appeals to the "will of the people" and by encouraging hatred of the existing regime. Once the redoubt of oppression was leveled, however, the masses had to be demobilized and their enthusiasm tempered, while the revolutionary project had to be forced into reality by means of terror and the modern centralized, bureaucratic state. This became the predominant pattern in modern democratizations. Democratic transition is usually viewed as an elitist enterprise, in which mass enthusiasm must be instrumentalized as carefully as possible.

More recently, however, there has been a very important change in this pattern. Following the Bolshevik Revolution in Russia, which represented the climax of the predominant pattern, the cult of revolutionary exaltation and violence gradually went out of fashion; its brief rebirth in the 1960s proved to be operational mostly in the sexual sphere. Elites had learned the hard way that revolutions have a strong tendency to devour their own children. Revolutions became discredited as too bloody, messy, and unpredictable.

Now, at the end of the twentieth century, it is popular to speak of democratic "transition" rather than democratic "revolution." Of course, broad popular support is still needed to defeat the *ancien régime,* so mass mobilization may remain unavoidable. Yet considerable skill is needed to arouse just enough popular enthusiasm to sweep aside the forces of the past without endangering the initiators themselves. Hence all the talk about how transitions must be carefully "crafted."

"Crafting," of course, further heightens the elitist character of modern democratic transitions. In Latin America or Taiwan, an aspiring "crafter" of democracy would do well to have an Ivy League degree or two in law, political science, or economics. Of course, the virtuoso precision of Taiwan's ruling-party democratizers is hard to match: The moment of *ruptura* itself, the actual change of the regime per se, is still unpredictable and fraught with risk.

The Question of Prerequisites

As recently as the 1960s, the belief was prevalent that any democratic transition had to follow roughly the pattern that I described in discussing "organic" transitions: democratization was held to be possible only in countries that met certain prerequisites regarding culture, the economy, and modernization. The experience of "third wave" democratizations gave birth to an alternative "transitological" theory, represented by the work of Philippe C. Schmitter, Guillermo O'Donnell, Giuseppe Di Palma, and others. This theory holds that the "prerequisites" are no longer so necessary. If, for one reason or another, the idea of democracy becomes powerful enough on the elite level, a democratic transition may proceed with reasonable prospects of success whatever the "objective" conditions of the country. To be sure, there remains an important correlation between the level of economic development and the *sustainability* of democracy: The higher the level of economic development, the greater the chances for democracy to survive without a relapse into autocracy.[4] Yet at the moment of transition itself, no such correlation has been detected.

If so, why do transitions occur? A major reason is imitation (which is what political scientists are talking about when they use terms like "demonstration effect" and "diffusion").[5] The greatest victory of democracy in the modern world is that—for one reason or another—it has become fashionable. To live under autocracy, or even to *be* an autocrat, seems backward, uncivilized, distasteful, not quite *comme il faut*—in a word, "uncool." In a world where democracy is synonymous less with freedom than with civilization itself, nobody can wait to be "ready" for democracy.

Does this diffusion effect follow geographical lines so that the wave spreads from one country to a neighboring one? Yes and no. The geography involved seems to be more cultural than physical. Most Christian countries are currently democratic, while most others are not, with Muslim ones having the least statistical chance. All other things being equal, democratization in a Catholic country is relatively more likely to encourage transition in another Catholic country, but is relatively less likely to exert similar influence on a neighboring Muslim country.

This makes it tempting to rehabilitate the theory of prerequisites, but with the stress less on economic development or modernization than on culture (defined as fairly stable and objective sets of values, traditions, and behaviors). Culture's importance as a possible help or hindrance to democracy has often been underestimated by mainstream political science, yet there are clear limits to the cultural approach, which become apparent if one considers the phenomenon not statically but dynamically. Several decades ago, one could plausibly have argued that democracy is largely for Protestants and unlikely to be achieved by Catholics. Yet time has proved this argument wrong. Now the line has moved eastward, and is said to coincide with the historic boundary between the Western and Eastern branches of Christianity. Or should it be between Christianity and Islam? And what about Confucianism? Yet if a certain culture precluded democratization yesterday, why should it not do so today?

Culture is not merely something objectively "given," but a matter of self-conscious orientation or identity. Nations usually have some broad sense of their place in the panoply of human civilization. They have some idea of their special "function" or "mission," and some sense of where to seek role models. Samuel P. Huntington tried to divide humanity into several civilizational areas (West European, East European, Latin, and so on), and got lots of criticism.[6] If he meant these divisions to be understood rigidly, so that a Muslim country, say, is supposed to be doomed to follow certain ways and have certain loyalties, I would join the critics. But one can consider his discussion of these realms as descriptions of the civilizational areas that nations and their leaders use as reference points when defining their cultural-political orientation. A people looks less to humanity in general for role models than to others within the same civilizational realm. If leading nations within a realm become democratic, others are likely to follow suit: the democratic transitions of the 1970s in Portugal and Spain influenced those in Latin America. The sense of belonging to a civilizational realm affects a people's *will* to democratize, not just its "objective chances" of achieving democracy. Yet there is no determinism at work here, either. Other influences besides membership in a broader grouping can affect a nation's sense of itself. Then, too, the "demonstration effect" can work *across* as well as *within* civilizational boundaries, even if in weaker form. The argument that "democracy is incompatible with our cultural traditions" can be a powerful barrier to the spread of democratic "waves," but its power is far from being absolute.

"Designer Democracies"

The elite-driven and nonrevolutionary character of recent democratic transitions changes the role of values and convictions in such events. In revolutionary transitions, commitment to certain values was absolutely necessary. The convictions of Jefferson, Robespierre, and Trotsky differed greatly, but each had beliefs for which he was ready to fight and sacrifice. In classic revolutionary situations, a critical mass of the revolutionary elite had to be committed to revolutionary ideas, and a critical mass of the general public had to accept them as well.

While a degree of genuine commitment may be desirable for the actors involved in modern democratic "crafting," it is no longer indispensable. Modern transitology has introduced the strange but insightful notion of "democracy without democrats," which is another aspect of "democracy without prerequisites." A "third wave" democratizer no longer needs to feel profound commitment to human rights, respect for minority opinion, the rule of law, and the like. It is enough to believe that making the transition to democracy is necessary and useful for your country, or maybe just for your class or personal interests. Likewise, the general public of a "third wave" country need not have a deep-rooted attachment to democratic values, and neither the level nor the intensity of its political participation should be too high. The general public mainly needs to get used to democracy as a matter of routine, until its procedures and norms come to seem "normal" and "natural."

Of course, this notion of "democracy without democrats" should not be taken too literally. Democratic society certainly needs some committed democrats, and the ideas and values of democracy must gain a certain level of public acceptance as well. The phrase was coined to describe a situation in which democrats are probably present and making an impact, but are too weak to push forward a transition on their own. Stronger political forces must then come into play to convince major actors that it is necessary to resort to democratic practices. Democratic leaders need not be "genuine" democrats, but they should be reasonable and artful politicians.

Here lies one of the roots of that cynicism toward democracy so much complained of around the world today. The upside is that unimpassioned democrats seem to be facing similarly lukewarm antidemocrats. To put it another way, those who would otherwise be cynical autocrats are now cynical democrats. Full-dress restorations of autocracy are rarer, though the subtler erosion of democracy is becoming more common. With intense prodemocratic convictions lacking in civil society, those in power feel a strong temptation to cheat when no one is looking. As Huntington shrewdly observes, "With third-wave democracies, the problem is not overthrow but erosion: the intermittent or gradual weakening of democracy by those elected to lead it."[7]

The coldblooded crafting of democracies along ready-made lines often evokes protests both in the West and in democratizing countries. The enterprise is denounced as part and parcel of Western "cultural imperialism," with advanced capitalist countries using their economic might to impose their commodities—from Coca-Cola and Arnold Schwarzenegger movies to patterns of political and economic order—upon the weaker developing and postcommunist worlds. On the "local" level, this resentment leads to a search for models of democracy that suit local cultures (and eventually tend to become local models of antidemocracy and antimodernity). This line of criticism might seem legitimate, yet home-grown models never really grow out of native life: They are invariably the constructs of intellectuals enchanted by ideological fantasies of organic order. The real native soil might be quite unreceptive to these constructs: Witness the toilings of those Russian intellectuals who have been trying vainly to invent a peculiarly "Russian" model of democracy. Having failed to think of anything viable, they have had to base the idea of Russia's singularity versus Western imperialism on the lingering presence of that earlier Western import—communism. Even the late Ayatollah Khomeini of Iran and his followers, far more successful seekers after a nativist alternative, spent years in Paris—the capital of modern ideological revolution—before they were able to export their model of Islamic revolution and overthrow the modernizing autocracy that ruled their homeland. In this they were reminiscent of the Bolsheviks who labored in the dusty obscurity of Western libraries before they got a chance to "craft" the Russian Revolution.

The diffusion of democratic models, or, to use a more derogatory expression, the dissemination of "designer democracies," is much more "natural" and rooted in human nature than critics think. Democratic (as well as macroeconomic) models are not so much imposed by the West as sought by local elites. In this, they follow the familiar human instinct to seek higher status through imitation. The urge may be so potent that it leads to collective political suicide—Gorbachev and his reform communists being a case in point. The West need not feel guilty about "imposing" its models on "the rest": It is "the rest" who recognize the centrality of the modern Western democratic project and want to participate in it. Intellectuals on both sides may sneer—and concerns about the trivialization of democracy through its superficial dissemination are legitimate—but going against the drive for "status through imitation" is a doomed effort. It may be good news that democracy has become, if not the only game in town, the most popular game in the global village. Yet this implies that the spread of the game depends much more on conformity and envy than on creativity and conviction.

Private Property and Ordered Liberty

If the global spread of the democratic pattern implies a movement from "solid" democracies "rooted" in economic or cultural "prerequisites" to shallower imitations skillfully "crafted" for mass production, and if the passion for freedom has become diluted into a halfhearted recognition of democratic procedures as conventions of postmodern civilization, then there is much less special about postcommunist transitions than one might otherwise suppose. Postcommunist transitions are still unique in many ways, but that is merely another way of saying that thanks to the communist legacy, these transitions are only the most extreme expressions of the general trends described above.

First, if the trend is toward fewer prerequisites, then postcommunist democracy has the fewest. This assertion may be contested: Communism did forcibly modernize various societies in certain ways, which arguably had the side effect of helping to prepare those societies for democracy. Postcommunist Russia is more urbanized, industrialized, and literate than was the agrarian Russia of the czars. Despite this, it remains true that Russia was much more out of step with modernity in 1986 than it was in 1913. The reason is that communist modernization is perverted modernization: It ostensibly builds up the body of modernity, but kills its soul.[8] The communists laid down roads, erected hydroelectric plants, and the like, but they killed (or tried their best to kill) the human capacity for autonomous action.

In general, the lack of market economies and market relations is the most evident—and possibly the most important—peculiarity of postcommunist transitions. Everybody agrees that the correlation between the market economy and democracy is very high (democracy is hardly possible without a market economy, although the reverse does not hold). This may seem too commonplace a point to admit of much elaboration, but not all of its aspects are duly appreciated. The lack of a market economy is usually understood as *adding to the tasks* of transition. Unlike transitions from right-wing autocracies, where crafting a new political regime is the major objective (though some economic reforms may also be required), postcommunist democratizations must create *both* a new economic system and a new political system. Moreover, measures aimed at accomplishing these two tasks tend to clash with each other—the enactment of necessary but painful and unpopular economic reforms can throw off the process of political transition.

This line of analysis is absolutely true, but it is not the whole truth. The market economy is not simply a vehicle for more efficient resource allocation and higher growth, just as the communist economy was not merely an alternative way to provide for the general welfare. A crucial but underappreciated element here is the institution of private property. Communism was primarily about the abolition of private property. But as Hegel says, private property is the necessary correlate of human personality: The notion of personality emerged thanks to the institution of private property; where there is no private property, personality is not possible. The communist project was to change human nature, and the abolition of private property was communism's major—and indeed very powerful—means of doing so, that is, of destroying human personality.[9]

This point is worth stressing because the real root—or, if you wish, the major prerequisite—of democracy is the autonomous individual who treats his or her personal freedom as something "natural" and "inalienable" and at the same time understands (from lived experience) that freedom implies responsibility for one's choices, and that establishing and following rules is a normal way to exercise one's freedom. It is private property, and the whole ensemble of social relations and institutions that goes with it, that provides the ground upon which human autonomy can naturally conjoin with a sense of responsibility and order. The abolition of private property destroys human personality because it severs the links that connect freedom with responsibility and order.

As Jean-Paul Sartre observed, humans are free even in jail, and the drive for freedom cannot be extinguished by any political regime, however totalitarian. Yet communism did terrible damage, for it succeeded all too well in divorcing the natural human love of liberty from the sense of freedom to *do* real things, and reduced it to its most elementary, indeed infantile, form: the freedom of play, dreaming, and defiance. Notions of responsibility, order, and work came to be associated with the realm of oppression and slavery. The niches of freedom that had opened up thanks to Khruschev's liberalization were soon filled by expressions of defiance toward the regime (dissidence) and abstract yearnings for a better world (an idealized West), mostly expressed through art. The dissident movement, whether in the form of heroic public resistance or the much safer and more widespread mode of "kitchen dissidence," greatly contributed to the delegitimization of the communist regime and helped to pave the way for its downfall. Yet by its nature it could contribute little to the positive work of transition. Through the work of figures like Aleksandr Solzhenitsyn, Václav Havel, Joseph Brodsky, Milan Kundera, and Andrei Sakharov, dissident culture produced brilliant descriptions of communist atrocities, penetrating analyses of the corruptions and absurdities of life under totalitarianism, high-quality works of art and literature, and some truly heroic deeds. Yet when the old regime finally fell and the time to build a new one came, most from this milieu either took no major part or met with little success if they did. *Doing* was not their specialty.

To mass infantilization, the communist attack on human personality added large-scale "idiotization." This latter term I derive from the Greek *idiotēs*, which means a purely private person who is unwilling or unable to act in the public sphere. An idiot, in this sense, is the opposite of a citizen. Authors such as Havel, G.M. Tamás, and Charles H. Fairbanks, Jr., have written excellent studies of the delegitimization of the public space under communism, to which I have little to add.[10] By turning the public space into a realm of total falsity, communism made any public activity other than protest and destruction seem indecent. The capacity for positive public action—society's "political muscle," if you will—atrophied. Belief in the possibility that individual action could change anything in the public space reached a low ebb. Since everything meaningful in communist political life happened behind the scenes, people developed a propensity for the paranoid style. This readiness to envision omniscient, omnipresent, and omnipotent forces determining everything through hidden channels did not die with communism; instead, Freemasons and Zionists began to compete with the KGB and the Securitate for pride of place in the conspiratological imagination. At its worst, this postcommunist mentality sees all human efforts as meaningless and impotent; to such a mind, the notions of individual responsibility and public engagement are bound to seem like bad jokes.

Communism produced some of the general modernizational "prerequisites" of democracy, but destroyed or stunted the most crucial mental and social prerequisites. Hence postcommunist transitions, more than any others, depend on an effort in the realm of ideas. The driving force of these transitions has been the understanding, gradually spread by elites, that communism is inferior to capitalism, and that importing Western models is the only way to "catch up." Popular mobilization against the communist regime (and for democracy) was based partly on resentment of the communist bureaucracy and its perks (fed to a large degree by the egalitarian character of communist ideology itself), and partly on nationalism, because everywhere outside the Russian core of the Soviet empire, communism was seen as a system imposed and maintained by a foreign power. In M. Steven Fish's phrase, the postcommunist elites had to craft democracy "from scratch."[11]

The exceptionally difficult tasks that the new elites faced were made even harder by their relative lack of expertise. Their rival, the communist *nomenklatura,* never went fully out of business; it was (with a few exceptions) more resilient and pragmatic than rigidly ideological to begin with, and it claimed (with some justification) superior leadership experience and political instincts. Still, the *apparatchiki* had no more experience of public political action than anyone else, and not all of them were good learners. The new rulers could rely on natural talent (if they had any) and collective recollections of precommunist experience (which made a great deal of difference among different postcommunist countries—as one can see by comparing events in the Baltic states with those in other post-Soviet republics). Crafting democracy takes skill that comes from knowledge and experience, and the postcommunist elites had neither. Their efforts, not surprisingly, were clumsy, which partly accounts for some of the well-publicized problems of "troubled" postcommunist transitions, such as outbreaks of ethnoterritorial strife.

Many of these could have been avoided had the new political elites involved had a better idea of what they were doing.

Postcommunist (A)morality

Another frequently mentioned peculiarity of postcommunist societies is the extreme degree of moral degradation and cynicism that seems to pervade them.[12] The delegitimization of the public sphere implies that decent people should avoid politics, or enter them only grudgingly, on the grounds that "someone has to do the dirty work." And since entering politics means demeaning yourself, perhaps you should reward yourself by being dishonest for your own personal benefit. The term "public good" does not exist and is hard to translate.

The most useful comparison here is to fascism and postfascism. Fascism was nakedly immoral. It aroused and exploited what are, from the modern enlightened perspective, the worst human impulses: raw racism, hatred of foreigners, belief in one's "natural" supremacy. It was an open celebration of evil that might be estheticized, but did not pretend to be moral. It was wicked, but not hypocritical. As a result, the higher qualities of human nature (tolerance, altruism, sympathy, generosity) were suppressed, but not killed or distorted. For liberalism, then, fascism is a clear-cut enemy. Fascism is a terrible malady, but it does not destroy the immune system of the human soul, which remains robust enough to drive out the virus eventually. That is why fascism, however ugly when the infection rages, has proven not to recur easily. The lingering feelings of guilt that it leaves behind are usually strong enough to prevent the rehabilitation of the fascist past. Of course, the total military defeat of the fascist powers in the Second World War and the close supervision applied by the occupying powers were extremely important for the relatively fast and smooth transition to democracy in West Germany, Italy, and Japan. But even the circumstances of total defeat and occupation do not seem to be enough to explain why the moral atmosphere of postfascism seems so much healthier than its more recent postcommunist counterpart.

Unlike fascism, with its stark chauvinism and violent particularism, communism was a kind of delinquent ideological cousin of modern liberalism. It was universalist rather than ethnocentric. It appealed to the "higher," "enlightened" side of human nature and claimed to purge it of everything low and selfish. In contrast to Christianity, it aimed to overcome human vice here on earth through social changes and ideological propaganda. It failed, of course, but not without promoting enormous hypocrisy, even while destroying traditional moral institutions that had been deterring and constraining vice for epochs. The project of communism was to abolish human greed, in contrast to capitalism, which tries to redirect greed into socially productive channels. As a result, we are witnessing the celebration of uninhibited greed in postcommunist society. The project of Soviet communism was to overcome sexual lust (in this, Stalin went further than Marx had projected). As a result, we are witnessing hordes of "liberated" postcommunist citizens frequenting Western-style peep shows. The project of communism was to eradicate ethnicity, contrary to the modern democratic project of rechanneling ethnic loyalties into allegiance to the democratic nation-state. As a result, we have witnessed the celebration of "ethnic cleansing" by leaders who yesterday were proletarian internationalists. It is not only that the "dark" side of human nature has been liberated from the confines of communist hypocrisy; its "noble" side—which was to have furnished the grounds for a better, freer, and fairer world—has already been perverted and discredited by communism.

When listing the tasks of postcommunist democratization, Western political scientists are likely to skip that of *metanoia*—"changing the human mentality." Yet the need to change minds has become a watchword among postcommunist intellectuals. Just as the postcommunist revolution was the reversal of the communist revolution, the postcommunist transition is a mirror image of the communist transition. Communism's central aim was the creation of "new socialist man," who was never born although many died in his name. Postcommunism's task is to cure postcommunist man of the traumatic communist experience.

To say that postcommunist transition is difficult is not to say that it is hopeless. Insofar as democracy today is more a matter of convention than of conviction, it is more safely grounded in Central and Eastern Europe. Unless resentment against the democratic model somehow recruits the deepest feelings of national identity, there will not be any open rebellion against it. Harsh economic realities have already forced people to mature, and there are signs of a generation gap pitting "infantilized" parents formed by communism against "grown-up" children made more self-reliant by capitalism. Reversing the results of moral degradation—and breeding loyalty to law—will be much more difficult, however, and it is much harder to make predictions about that.

NOTES

1. For this debate, see the following articles in *Slavic Review*, vols. 52–54: Sarah Meiklejohn Terry, "Thinking About Postcommunist Transitions: How Different Are They?" (Summer 1993): 333–37; Philippe C. Schmitter and Terry Lynn Karl, "The Conceptual Travels of Transitologists and Consolidologists: How Far to the East Should They Attempt To Go?" (Spring 1994): 173–85; Valerie Bunce, "Should Transitologists Be Grounded?" (Spring 1995): 111–27; Terry Lynn Karl and Philippe C. Schmitter, "From an Iron Curtain to a Paper Curtain: Grounding Transitologists or Students of Postcommunism?" (Winter 1995): 965–78; and Valerie Bunce, "Paper Curtains and Paper Tigers" (Winter 1995): 979–87.

2. Ghia Nodia, "Nationalism and Democracy," *Journal of Democracy* 3 (October 1992): 17–21.

3. Philippe C. Schmitter and Terry Lynn Karl, in "Conceptual Travels" (p. 177), say that a significant number of their interlocutors from the postcommunist world mentioned Spain and Chile as models. Pinochet's Chile was indeed popular—not as a model for democracy, however, but as a model of authoritarian-imposed economic reform that would *precede* democratic transition.

4. See Samuel P. Huntington, "Reforming Civil-Military Relations," *Journal of Democracy* 6 (October 1995): 14–16; and Adam Przeworski, Michael Alvarez, José Antonio Cheibub, and Fernando Limongi, "What Makes Democracies Endure?" *Journal of Democracy* 7 (January 1996): 39–55.

5. "For all its historical geographical ups and downs, diffusion remains a key (nowadays writ large) ingredient of democratic development." Giuseppe Di Palma, *To Craft Democracies: An Essay on Democratic Transitions* (Berkeley: University of California Press, 1990), 14. See also Adam Przeworski et al., "What Makes Democracies Endure?" 43.

6. Samuel P. Huntington, "The Clash of Civilizations?" *Foreign Affairs* 72 (Summer 1993): 22–49.

7. Samuel P. Huntington, "Democracy for the Long Haul," *Journal of Democracy* 7 (April 1996): 8.

8. I say "ostensibly" because it might further be observed that since a society's body and soul are not so clearly separable, communism also did a poor job of building up the body of society. It is widely acknowledged in postcommunist economic transitions, for example, that most of the industrial enterprises left over from communism have to be destroyed or allowed to go under before positive economic development can begin.

9. Here is the flaw in the popular argument that communist systems were "totalitarian" only in their hard-core Stalinist versions, and generally became "authoritarian" (and hence more equivalent to right-wing autocracies) after Khrushchev's de-Stalinization program in 1956. Khrushchev's revolution of 1956 certainly brought about a great feeling of liberation and thoroughly changed many aspects of the regime and social life. The universal fear of Stalinist terror largely lifted, public life became more relaxed, and it became possible to create niches of freedom on the private level. Such a society might be called *post*-totalitarian. Yet inasmuch as the mainspring of communism—the abolition of private property—was retained, it would be a great mistake to include such a society in the category of "authoritarianism" as commonly understood.

10. See Václav Havel's essay "The Power of the Powerless," in his *Living in Truth* (London: Faber and Faber, 1987), 36–122. See also Charles H. Fairbanks, Jr., "Party and Ideology in the Former U.S.S.R.," in Richard Zinman and Jerry Weinberger, eds., *Left, Right and Center: Party and Ideology After the Cold War* (Ithaca, N.Y.: Cornell University Press, 1996); and G.M. Tamás, "Socialism, Capitalism, and Modernity," *Journal of Democracy* 3 (July 1992): 60–74, and "Irony, Ambiguity, Duplicity: The Legacy of Dissent," *Uncaptive Minds* 7 (Summer 1994): 19–34.

11. M. Steven Fish, *Democracy from Scratch: Opposition and the Regime in the New Russian Revolution* (Princeton, N.J.: Princeton University Press, 1994).

12. See Anne Applebaum, "Nice Guys Finish Last," *Freedom Review*, January–February 1996, 24–30.

2

COMPARING EAST AND SOUTH

Valerie Bunce

Valerie Bunce *is chair of the government department at Cornell University and president of the American Association for the Advancement of Slavic Studies. An earlier version of this essay was presented at the University of Wisconsin, the University of Toronto, and the Institute of Economics in Budapest, Hungary.*

Throughout the Cold War era, Eastern Europe (including the former Soviet Union) was the scholarly preserve of regional specialists and was largely excluded from mainstream social-science discourse. With the collapse of communism, however, the region has become a fashionable area to study. The change has been most evident in the burgeoning literature on recent transitions to democracy. Researchers specializing in Latin America, Southern Europe, and even Western Europe have begun to incorporate Eastern Europe into their comparative studies of democratization.

Eastern Europe's sudden leap from the periphery to the core of disciplines like political science and sociology has sparked debate about whether the East can and should be compared with the South. On one side are those who contend that postcommunism is unique in many important respects, and that such cross-regional comparisons are therefore unhelpful at best and misleading at worst. On the other side are those who counter that the uniqueness of postcommunism has been exaggerated, that democratization as a process displays fairly regular contours that allow for comparison across diverse cases, and, indeed, that it is precisely through cross-regional comparisons that we can identify similarities and differences, test hypotheses, and thereby enrich our understanding of democratization.

Embedded in this debate is a time-honored and testy set of exchanges. Defenders of comparison are often quick to charge their opponents with being "typical area scholars." This is a code phrase for such traits as lack of interest in theory, absorption in the "trivial" details of a given country, deficient training as social scientists, and overzealousness in the defense of one's own academic "turf." The response is equally stereotypical. Those who engage in such comparisons, it is often implied, evince the worst sins of the social-scientific endeavor: a superficial grasp of cases, an overeagerness to code and generalize, and a taste for faddish theories that are often entertained with little regard for empirical evidence.

There will always be differences of opinion between "lumpers" and "splitters."[1] Still, there are important intellectual issues at stake in the debate about democratization in the South versus the East. The main questions are as follows: First, how different is the process of democratization in Southern Europe and Latin America from that in Eastern Europe? Second, does that difference matter?

The Decline of Authoritarianism

At the most general level, all authoritarian states share certain common characteristics. By definition, the authoritarian states of Southern Europe, Latin America, and Eastern Europe all featured limits on civil liberties and concentration of political power in the hands of leaders who were not held accountable to the people by means of competitive elections. All of these countries also featured highly protected and inefficient economies. In many of these cases, moreover, leaders employed an economic spoils system in an attempt to attain the political support—or at least the acquiescence—of important groups. Finally, these countries all followed the same general pattern of decline, with the decade preceding the end of authoritarian rule marked in every case by the coincidence of mounting economic difficulties, growing public restiveness, and widening schisms among political and economic elites.

This overview, however, misses a number of crucial details that differentiated the political system operating in Eastern Europe from that seen in Latin America and Southern Europe. These details are not merely of historical interest. They also shaped—and continue to shape—transitions to democracy in these regions.

The first difference relates to the duration of authoritarian rule. The history of Latin America and Southern Europe is, for the most part, a history of alternation between authoritarian and democratic rule. The recent transition to democracy in these countries, then, is more accurately termed _re_democratization. This terminological distinction is important, because it reminds us that authoritarianism in these states was short-lived and always compromised, even in its most despotic moments, by the memory of democratic politics, as well as democracy's residual culture and institutions. This democratic residue also points to a fundamental advantage that these states enjoyed as they embarked on their most recent transition to democracy—not just the existence of trade unions, parties, and other building blocks of civil society, but a sense among political elites of what democracy is, what it requires, and what undermines it.

Eastern Europe has no such democratic tradition. The so-called democratic experiments of the interwar period lasted less than a decade and are best understood, in any case, as authoritarian politics in democratic guise. Even the former Czechoslovakia, the country in the region with the strongest claims to a democratic past, features but 20 years of democratic experience—and that under the leadership of a man who could be called a benign dictator. The consequences for East European politics and the region's transition to democracy are predictable. Without the "feel" for democracy that Latin America and Southern Europe enjoyed, Eastern Europe has faced an especially formidable challenge.

Also differentiating the two sets of cases is the nature of the authoritarianism involved. The state socialism that prevailed in Eastern Europe was a far more invasive system than the bureaucratic authoritarianism and other forms of dictatorship seen in Southern Europe and Latin America. The former system combined extreme goals with substantial means; it featured an ideology of rapid transformation joined with single-party domination of politics, economics, and social life. In short, in Eastern Europe the communist party enjoyed a political and economic monopoly. By contrast, the situation in Latin America and Southern Europe could be termed a political oligopoly: Political elites exerted indirect and very uneven control over what was, we must remember, a capitalist economy. This difference, combined with the above-mentioned differences in the regions' political traditions, indicates that the end of authoritarian rule was a much more profound development in Eastern Europe than it was in Latin America and Southern Europe.

Two other differences are important as well. One concerns the influence of the military. In the South, the military played a strong political role; in the East, the armed forces were subservient to the communist party. Thus Eastern Europe has been free of what is, by most accounts, the major burden on the democratic transitions in Latin America and Southern Europe.[2] The other difference has to do with social structure. Owing to its socialist ideology, Eastern Europe lacked a bourgeoisie and featured a relatively equal distribution of wealth—in contrast to the South, where capitalism resulted in a bourgeoisie and pronounced economic disparities. Clearly, both of these features condition the process of democratization. For instance, democracy in the absence of a bourgeoisie is without historical precedent, and democratization has rarely been accompanied—as it undoubtedly will be in the countries of Eastern Europe—by a dramatic increase in social inequality.

The Process of Collapse

With regard to the actual collapse of authoritarian rule, we can identify at least one similarity between the East and the South—the matter of timing. Transitions in all these countries were part of a global wave of democratization extending from the mid-1970s to the present. Indeed, it is precisely this temporal clustering that has been used to justify inclusion of the East European cases in comparative studies of recent transitions to democracy.

Yet there is little else to indicate that the process of collapse in the two sets of cases was similar. First, students of the Latin American and Southern European transitions seem to agree that, in both regions, political rather than economic and domestic rather than international factors were paramount in the end of authoritarian rule.[3] By contrast, the collapse of state socialism was largely a response to the interaction of two factors: economic decline (with its attendant impact on domestic politics) and the international consequences of the Gorbachev reforms.[4]

Another difference concerns the mode of transition. Specialists in Latin America and Southern Europe make two arguments here. First, they draw a sharp distinction between transitions through pacts—that is, where authoritarian leaders cooperated with opposition leaders in order to orchestrate the transition—and transitions where the key role was played by publics mobilizing against the authoritarian regime. Second, they argue that the former was the dominant mode of transition in the South. When we turn to the East European cases, however, the story is different. Here the contrast between pacted and mass-mobilization transitions breaks down, since the end of authoritarian rule in Eastern Europe tended to involve mass participation as well as elite pacts. In this sense, Bulgaria is the prototypical postcommunist case—its classification in some comparative studies to the contrary notwithstanding.[5] Moreover, other modes of transition are in evidence as well. In some cases, political liberalization resulted from the dictates of powerful actors outside the nation-state. Many of the former Soviet republics fit into this category. We also find cases—most notably Russia—where political liberalization was introduced to "improve" authoritarianism rather than to replace it, but a variety of circumstances, both domestic and international, conspired to push the process in the direction of genuine democratization, even in the absence of pacts or significant mass mobilization.

Finally, there is the question of what "collapse" means. In the South, the overarching political issue was the transition to democracy, which involved a change in political regime. The state itself remained the same. In the East, the situation was far more complex. The events of 1989 and after in the former Soviet Union were at once reformist and revolutionary. It is true that the socialist economy—important both in its own right and in its interdependence with the communist party and the state—was left relatively untouched by the political drama. Indeed, it can be argued that in most of Eastern Europe the socialist economy, while frayed at the edges as a result of economic liberalization and the end of communist-party hegemony, is still basically intact, but with *apparatchiki*

now functioning as "entrepreneurchiki."[6] Thus it is less accurate to
say that socialism has been eliminated than that it has been highly adaptive. This generalization works particularly well for Russia and most of
the successor states. By contrast, we are seeing a sharper break with
socialist economics in, say, Poland, Hungary, the Czech Republic, and
Slovenia.

It is true, as well, that Eastern Europe has exhibited varying *degrees*
of regime collapse. In fully half of the postcommunist countries, communism did not so much collapse as adjust to new circumstances. Indeed, the common denominator of all the former communist countries
is not the end of communist rule or of authoritarian politics, but a more
minimal condition: the end of the political hegemony of the communist
party. In all cases, communists (by whatever name or names) are now in
the position of having to compete—though often, it must be said, with
unfair advantages—for political power.

Clearly, however, the break (or semi-break) with the old order was
still revolutionary. A transition to capitalist liberal democracy is in a
state-socialist setting a process that attacks the very foundations of the
state. This is because of the fusion among party, state, and economy in
Leninist systems. Moreover, we must understand that virtually every
one of the East European transitions amounted to national liberation—
either from the Soviet bloc or from domination by a federal state functioning as a domestic empire. Fully 22 of the 27 states that make up the
former Soviet Union and Eastern Europe are *new* states. Is it any wonder, then, that nationalism is central to the story of the collapse of communism, that nation-building and state-building are central to the story
of postcommunism, and that all the states in the region, new and old,
are weak?

This brings us to a larger question. While democratization clearly is
the central political issue in Latin America and Southern Europe, it is
debatable whether this is also the case in Eastern Europe. Communism
under another name is not democracy. Moreover, if nation-building and
state-building are so central to the postcommunist experience, are we
correct in equating postcommunism with democratization? In short, can
we compare cases in which democratization is an apt summary of the
political moment with cases in which it shares the political stage with
other—perhaps dominant—processes of political change?

Agendas of Transition

If we view Latin America, Southern Europe, and Eastern Europe as
cases of regime transition, we observe a number of similarities. The
items on the common agenda include writing new constitutions, building political parties, and, more generally, constructing the institutions
and culture of a liberal political order.

Two important distinctions, however, quickly emerge. In Eastern Europe, the political tasks of the transition are much more complex than in Latin America and Southern Europe, since the question is one of building rather than rebuilding democratic institutions. Unions, parties, interest groups, the institutions of decision making and representation, the rule of law, and the other foundations of a liberal political order must be constructed virtually from scratch. Moreover, these are not the only items on the agenda. Everything that defines a social system—national identity, social structure, and the state and its relationship to citizens, the economy, and the international system—is a subject for intense negotiation in the postcommunist world. By contrast, in Latin America and Southern Europe most of these issues were resolved long ago and are not part of the current political debate—a fact that augurs well for democratic consolidation in those countries.

The reach of the transitional agenda in Eastern Europe has several implications. As mentioned above, postcommunism is far more than a transition to democracy; it is a revolution extending to politics, economics, and social life. In short, a great deal is in flux—and in flux simultaneously. Second, the items on the postcommunist agenda conflict with one another. It is not easy for politicians accountable to the people to carry out a long and painful economic adjustment; history shows few successful cases of state-building by democratic means; and democracy in situations where national and state boundaries are contested has in general not proved to be viable.

Most important, liberal politics presumes the existence not merely of certain political institutions but of a broad array of social and economic institutions that define interests. In much of the literature on recent transitions to democracy, interests are treated as "givens," with the design of political institutions receiving the bulk of the attention. This is understandable, for Southern Europe and Latin America feature a relatively well established network of economic and social institutions and thus well-defined interests. This is not necessarily the case in the East, where institutions of every imaginable sort are in the process of formation, and interests are accordingly quite fluid. This is one reason why ethnicity is central to identity in much of the postcommunist world. The uncertain social and economic context of these countries invites the use of ascriptive criteria to define oneself and others.[7]

The implications for the process of democratization are enormous. How is a functioning party system to develop if the economy and the social structure—the building blocks of every party system—are not yet in place? How are citizens to define their political preferences and act accordingly if interest groups are weak; parties lack ideological definition, existing instead as temporary followings of this or that leader; interests shift daily in response to major changes in government policy and thus the distribution of power and privilege; and the consequences (individual, group, and systemic) of various policies are difficult to estimate and prone to fluctuate over time? Finally, how are governments to function well if institutions and thus interests are still in the process of formation? The oft-noted uncertainty of the Latin American and Southern European transitions pales in comparison with the multiple uncertainties of the postcommunist experience. If democracy is "organized uncertainty," then Eastern Europe is doing an excellent job of fulfilling half of the bargain.[8]

The Domestic and International Context

The transitions to democracy in Southern Europe, Eastern Europe, and Latin America feature certain contextual similarities. International support for democratization has been crucial in all of these cases (though least so, one could argue, in Latin America). At the same time, the consolidation of democracy has everywhere been accompanied by economic liberalization.

Yet in terms of context as well, the postcommunist experience has been unique. Let us turn first to the domestic side of the equation. The economic stress of the transition from socialism to capitalism is far greater than the stress of further liberalization of an already-capitalist economy. This is clear from comparative statistics on the decline of industrial production, gross national product, and per-capita income in the East versus the South. Moreover, whereas in the South the greatest threat to democratic consolidation is the military, in the East it is probably impatient citizenries. There is also no equivalent in the South of the "red-brown" alliance between communists and nationalists that is currently developing in many postcommunist systems. Party systems also vary between the regions in terms of form, ideological poles, and development. This is not surprising given many key characteristics of postcommunism: the fluidity of the class structure; the central role played in many cases by ethnicity and religion; the well-established and understandable public distaste for the very concept of a political party; and, finally, the continued political influence of a Left that was compromised but maintains popular appeal in times of economic duress and rule by politicians widely perceived as incompetent, corrupt, and isolated. In general, then, civil society is much more in evidence in the South than in the East—though there are important variations along this dimension in Southern Europe and Latin America.

The international context of democratization in Eastern Europe is also unique. Much has been made of the fact that the transitions in the East and the South have occurred roughly within the same time frame. Given the many differences between the two sets of cases, this might suggest that similar international forces have been at work. Yet nothing could be further from the truth—especially if we focus on the international environment after the fall of communism. The transitions in Southern Europe and Latin America took place in the context of a stable international environment. International institutions stood ready to cushion the shocks of transition, and major powers—both regional and global—offered their support. Witness, for example, the economic role of the European Union in the Spanish transition—a role that allowed Spanish elites to stabilize democracy before engaging (some ten years after the death of Franco) in destabilizing economic reforms. Moreover, there was little built into these transitions that demanded a major reorientation of the state in the world system. The alliance structure of Latin America, for example, remained the same, and the integration of Spain and Greece into the international economy was already proceeding apace when authoritarian rule officially came to an end.

By contrast, the fall of communism constituted the end of an alliance system, the sudden dismemberment of a highly integrated regional economy, and the collapse of an international order. This has entailed a radical shift in foreign policy—both economic and politico-military— at a time when the international system and its institutions are in transition as well. Thus transitions to democracy in Eastern Europe, with all their fluidity and uncertainty, are taking place in the context of a fluid and uncertain international environment. Indeed, this uncertainty—rather than the purported "age-old ethnic hatreds"—explains in large measure both the war in the former Yugoslavia and the incapacity and unwillingness of so-called powerful international actors to resolve the conflict.

The transitional character of international politics today is further complicated by relations among states in Eastern Europe. Historically, these relations have been characterized by either isolation or conflict. In either case, the machinations of the Great Powers—most recently the Soviet Union—played a crucial role. Today there are many sources of conflict. These states are in a race to get to the West first; they also suffer from the region's historical legacy of poorly defined state and national boundaries. Indeed, the collapse of communism and the old international order has highlighted the tensions between nations and states. In addition, the revolutionary character of East European transitions could very easily lead to aggressive foreign policies. This is particularly true of Russia, which, though an unstable democracy and a nation-state in formation, is the major power in the region and a country long accustomed to exerting regional and global influence. Thus while it is often argued that promoting democracy is an investment in world peace, democratization in the context of Eastern Europe may be an exception to the rule. It is sobering to realize that the last time Eastern Europe was in transition to democracy in the context of an interna-

tional system itself in transition was the period after the First World
War.

Lessons to Be Drawn

Clearly, then, there are substantial differences between the
postcommunist experience and the transitions to democracy in Southern Europe and Latin America. This is evident whether we focus on the
structure, decline, and collapse of authoritarian rule or on the dynamics
of the transition process that follows. It is not just a matter of details—
for example, such factors as the role of the military, the bourgeoisie,
mobilized citizenries, constitutions, international politics, and economic
reform. Rather, all these details add up to very different processes of
change. Simply stated, recent developments in Latin America and Southern Europe can accurately be termed regime transitions. The transformation of Eastern Europe from 1989 to the present, on the other hand,
is more than a political transition; it is a revolution—in identity, economics, social structure, and the state.

What does this mean for the comparative study of democratization?
It would seem that the most logical comparison to be made is the
comparison of the postcommunist countries with one another. Not only
does this give us a rich database—27 countries at last count—but it is
here where we find the optimal combination of similarities and
differences. These countries have a common authoritarian heritage,
similar agendas of transition, and, owing to timing and situation, similar
arrays of domestic and international circumstances. Where they diverge
is in the details: whether or not socialism was federalized; the extent of
marketization and political liberalization prior to the end of communist-
party hegemony; the method and degree of authoritarian collapse; the
approach taken to the economic transition; the newness of the state; and
the extent of contestation over national identity and state boundaries. In
other words, these countries represent as ideal a base for comparison
with one another as do the countries of Latin America and Southern
Europe.

Comparison of the Southern and Eastern transitions, on the other hand,
does not offer an optimal combination of similarities and differences:
the differences far outweigh the similarities. At the same time, those
who presume a particular postcommunist case to be unique (these are
primarily specialists in Russia) are mistaken. This tendency seems to be
a remnant of the past, when the Soviet Union—like the United States—
was considered to be so important that a single-case analysis was deemed
legitimate and Eastern Europe was dismissed as "those unimportant little
colonies to the west."

Clearly, we must be very careful when viewing the postcommunist
experience through lenses crafted for other cases. Most of the extant

literature on transitions to democracy was developed for a rather circumscribed set of changes. Indeed, the limited character of the agenda
of transition in Southern Europe and Latin America made it easy to adopt
a similarly circumscribed approach—in this case, bargaining between
elites and the opposition. It is hardly surprising that the assumptions
underlying the literature on democratization in these regions are not
applicable to the East European context. In particular, it is often assumed that the transition represents a clear break with the authoritarian
past; that change to a democratic regime is the foremost political issue;
that the building blocks of civil society (for example, capitalism, unions,
parties, and interest groups) are in place; that national and state boundaries are settled; and that elites are the crucial players in both the collapse of authoritarianism and the transition process itself.

If the assumptions of the literature on democratic transitions are problematic in the East European context, then so are the central concepts
involved. The term "transition" is a case in point, as is the distinction—
so commonly drawn in the Southern cases—between transitions resulting from pacts and those featuring mass mobilization.[9] There is also
little evidence to support the common argument that there is a sharp
decline in political mobilization during the transitional period.[10]

Perhaps the best example, however, is the concept of economic reform. Comparativists have been quick to incorporate Eastern Europe
into their analyses of the impact of economic reform on the process of
democratization. Yet economic reform in the East is not the same as
economic reform in the South. While there are institutional implications in both cases,[11] at issue in Eastern Europe is the construction of a
capitalist economy rather than the modification of an already existing
capitalist system. Five other complicating factors also distinguish economic reform in Eastern Europe: the persistence of a basically intact,
albeit unraveling, socialist economic system; the need to move from
socialist isolationism to capitalist international integration; the need to
modernize an inherently primitive economy; the difficulties imposed
by the collapse of the Soviet market (which is now estimated to have
accounted for fully one-half of the 18 percent drop in Polish national
income from 1990 to 1991); and the need in most of these cases to construct a new national economy. The result has been that the economic
reforms in Eastern Europe have been more costly than the economic
liberalization that has taken place in the South. Indeed, Eastern Europe's
economic decline has had more devastating consequences than the Great
Depression.

Finally, the vast differences between the East and the South in terms
of the process of political change call into question the validity of using
the same explanatory factors. At the most general level, application of
the assumptions underlying the literature on transitions to democracy to
the East European countries leads to the conclusion that democratic

consolidation in this region will occur slowly, if at all. This line of reasoning, however, does not take account of situational factors that affect
the process of political change. Democratic consolidation in Eastern
Europe certainly faces many real con-
straints, yet the nature of these constraints
may be very different from what a comparative analysis would lead us to believe. Some
of the so-called problems of the East European transitions—for instance, extensive
public participation in the termination of
authoritarian rule—might very well be assets in the postcommunist context. New
political elites might have to think twice
about engaging in authoritarian practices if
they fear public retribution, and public involvement can under certain
circumstances provide the political capital that elites need if they are to
proceed with the economic reform that is crucial for democratic development.

In postcommunism, political institutions seem to be more a consequence than a cause of political development.

On a more specific level, it appears that the particular mode of
transition—that is, whether mass mobilization or elite pact—goes far
toward explaining the extent to which democratic consolidation succeeds
in the South.[12] In the postcommunist case, however, this factor is
problematic. As noted above, the distinction is not an easy one to make,
and it does not cover all the options. Just as important, the mode of
transition explains very little in Eastern Europe. Most specialists would
argue that the East European countries moving most rapidly toward
democratic consolidation are Hungary, Poland, the Czech Republic,
Slovenia, and Lithuania; these countries run the gamut of transitional
modes. What does seem to have some explanatory power for these and
other cases in the region is an altogether different variable: whether the
first competitive elections produced a win for the communists or for the
opposition.

Another problematic concept is "institutional choice." It is often said
that the particular choices made tend to stick, and that they play a crucial
role in shaping the prospects for democratic consolidation. For example,
it is commonly argued that parliamentary systems are preferable to
presidential systems.[13] In the East European context, however,
institutional arrangements have often changed quickly—through the
establishment of new constitutions, continual tinkering with existing
constitutions, and the elasticity of practice. This can be illustrated with
an update of Arend Lijphart's 1991 comparison of institutional formats
in Poland, Hungary, and Czechoslovakia.[14] What we find four years later
is four countries rather than three; two brand-new constitutions that have
been ratified but feature significant loose ends (the Czech Republic and
Slovakia); one new constitution still in the making (Poland); and one

constitution that has remained intact since 1991, but has been subject to many reinterpretations as a result of conflicting legislation and continuing disagreements over presidential-selection procedures (Hungary). Moreover, if we survey the entire region, we must question whether the oft-posited relationship between institutions and political practice should not be reversed in the East European context. In postcommunism, political institutions seem to be more a consequence than a cause of political developments.

The East European experience complicates the traditional arguments about parliamentary versus presidential government. In practice, the great majority of these new regimes are neither; they are, instead, semi-presidential systems, representing variations on the model provided by the French Fifth Republic. Whether or not this is a constraint on democratic consolidation is unclear. Given the demands of the revolution in economics and foreign policy and the burdens of national diversity and state-building, presidentialism and semipresidentialism may be preferable in the East European context.

The Value of Comparison

This is all by way of saying that the value of comparing the East with the South is limited. The existing research on transitions to democracy does not travel well to the postcommunist world. If the assumptions, concepts, and arguments of this research are problematic, then so, assuredly, are its predictions. Using the experience of the South as a yardstick for the East, as is the proclivity of some "transitologists," is a serious mistake.

Does this mean that we should not compare the process of democratization in Southern Europe and Latin America with recent developments in Eastern Europe? The answer is: It depends. If we focus not on the similarities of the cases but on their differences, such comparisons have much to teach us. In particular, by placing our two sets of cases side by side, we are sensitized to the defining characteristics of each set.

We can also use the comparison to challenge the received wisdom concerning democratic transitions in both the South and the East. The East European experience leads us to question certain common features of the literature—for instance, the beginning of the "transition story" with the decision to liberalize politics, rather than with the evolution of authoritarian rule; the failure to address such variables as federalism (before and after authoritarianism), international politics, citizenries, nationalism, economics, and the role of the mass media in the process of democratization; and the preoccupation with mass mobilization versus elite pacts in explaining patterns in democratic consolidation. We also are led to wonder whether we should not think more in terms of "degrees of transition," particularly when considering the Latin American cases.[15] At the same time, the experiences of Latin America and Southern Europe force us to confront issues that have often been ignored in studies of postcommunist transitions. An obvious example is the role of the military in 1989—the proverbial "dog that did not bark."

Finally, by expanding our observations to include a diverse range of cases, we can enrich our understanding of democratization itself. It is no accident, for example, that the dominant understanding of democratization shifts with each wave of new democracies. What do we learn by comparing Eastern Europe with Southern Europe and Latin America? One lesson is methodological. We can identify the factors crucial to democratic consolidation only if we compare the successes with the failures. Yet much of the literature on democratic consolidation consists of comparisons of successes with successes—a surprising situation, since at least some of these same analysts have also written on democratic collapse.

Cross-regional comparisons also alert us to the sheer diversity of possible paths to democracy. And none of the new democracies in Eastern Europe, despite seemingly calamitous circumstances, has as yet reverted to authoritarian politics, although some countries—among them Romania, Croatia, and rump Yugoslavia—have strayed rather far from democratic ideals. This would seem to suggest that we err when we assume that there are certain standard ways to democratize, with some ways being more promising than others. Democratization, as Guiseppe Di Palma has argued, may be easier and more self-determined than we have often thought.[16] Or, conversely, the reassertion of authoritarian rule may be harder than we have often thought.[17]

The key to the survival, if not the prospering, of democracy has usually been identified as some variant of democratic institution-building—the establishment of the rules of the political game, parties, parliaments, and a democratic political culture. What Eastern Europe shares with Southern Europe and Latin America, however, is the extent to which authoritarian forces have remained divided and weak. In short, the central issue may be not so much building democracy as preventing authoritarianism. Perhaps, then, it is the resources of authoritarians, rather than those of democrats, that should be the primary focus of study.

NOTES

The research on which this essay is based was supported by the National Endowment for the Humanities. The author would like to thank Bela Greskovits, Hector Schamis, and Sidney Tarrow for their comments.

1. These terms are drawn from Gerald Segal, "International Relations and Democratic Transition," in Geoffrey Pridham, ed., *Encouraging Democracy: The International Context of Regime Transitions in Southern Europe* (New York: St. Martin's, 1991), 31–49.

2. See Nancy Bermeo, "Democracy in Europe," *Daedalus* 123 (Spring 1994): 159–78. There are two important exceptions to this general rule. In the former Yugoslavia, the military was an important domestic political actor; this explains, in part, why the breakup of that state was violent. There are also indications that the Russian military is becoming a more important domestic political actor, or at least that some of its units are acting independent of civilian authority. This is, of course, quite out of keeping with Soviet and Russian traditions.

3. See, for example, Guillermo O'Donnell and Philippe C. Schmitter, *Transitions from Authoritarian Rule: Tentative Conclusions About Uncertain Democracies* (Baltimore: Johns Hopkins University Press, 1991).

4. Valerie Bunce, "The Empire Strikes Back: The Transformation of the Eastern Bloc from a Soviet Asset to a Soviet Liability," *International Organization* 39 (Winter 1984–85): 1–46.

5. See Terry Lynn Karl and Philippe C. Schmitter, "Modes of Transition in Latin America, Southern and Eastern Europe," *International Social Science Journal* 128 (May 1991): 269–84, and "What Kinds of Democracy Are Emerging in Southern and Eastern Europe, South and Central America?" (unpubl. ms., Stanford University, January 1992).

6. Jacek Tarkowski, "Endowment of the Nomenklatura, or Apparatchiks into Entrepreneurchiks, or From Communist Ranks to Capitalist Riches," *Innovation* 4 (1990): 89–105.

7. Michael Walzer, "The Idea of Civil Society," *Dissent* 38 (Spring 1991): 293–304.

8. See Adam Przeworksi, *Democracy and the Market* (Cambridge: Cambridge University Press, 1991), 13; and Valerie Bunce, "Elementy neopredelennosti v perekhodnyi period" (Elements of uncertainty in the transitional period), *Politicheskie issledovianiia* (Political Analyses) 1 (1993): 44–51.

9. If we expand our conception of what constitutes democratic transitions to include the weakening, as well as the termination, of authoritarian rule, we discover that many of the pacted transitions in the South were in fact preceded by periods of mass mobilization against authoritarian governance. See, for example, Sidney Tarrow, "Mass Mobilization and Regime Change: Pacts, Reform, and Popular Power in Italy (1918–1922) and Spain (1975–1978)," in Richard Gunther, P. Nikiforos Diamandouros, and Hans-Jürgen Puhle, eds., *The Politics of Democratic Consolidation: Southern Europe in Comparative Perspective* (Baltimore: Johns Hopkins University Press, 1995). This is not to argue, however, that the Southern European and Latin American experiences thereby closely resemble developments in Eastern Europe. What is distinctive about the transitions in Eastern Europe is that 1) pacts were the exception and not the rule; 2) pacts tended to form, then collapse, and then re-form, and therefore lacked the durability of pacts in the South; 3) the temporal lag between mass mobilization and the formation of pacts was very brief; and 4) mass mobilization led directly, in most cases, to the termination of authoritarian rule.

10. See especially the strike data presented by Kazimierz Kloc in "Industrial Conflicts in Poland: The Experience of 90–92" (paper presented at a conference on "The Trials of Transition: Collective Protest in Post-Communist Poland, 1989–1993," Harvard University, 10–12 December 1993).

11. Hector Schamis, "Re-forming the State: The Politics of Privatization in Chile and Britain" (Ph.D. diss., Columbia University, 1994).

12. See Terry Lynn Karl, "Dilemmas of Democratization in Latin America," *Comparative Politics* 23 (October 1990): 1–22.

13. See, for example, Alfred Stepan and Cindy Skach, "Constitutional Frameworks

and Democratic Consolidation: Parliamentarism versus Presidentialism," *World Politics* 46 (October 1993): 1–22.

14. Arend Lijphart, "Democratization and Constitutional Choices in Czecho-slovakia, Hungary, and Poland, 1989–1991," in Gyorgy Szoboszlai, ed., *Flying Blind: Emerging Democracies in East-Central Europe* (Budapest: Yearbook of the Hungarian Political Science Association, 1992), 99–113.

15. This issue is now being confronted to some degree by experts on Latin America. See, for instance, Guillermo O'Donnell, "Delegative Democracy," *Journal of Democracy* 5 (January 1994): 55–69.

16. Guiseppe Di Palma, "Democratic Transitions: Puzzles and Surprises from West to East," in *Research on Democracy and Society* (New York: JAI Press, 1993), 1:27–50.

17. Nancy Bermeo, "Democracy and the Lessons of Dictatorship," *Comparative Politics* 25 (April 1992): 273–91.

3

THE PERSISTENCE OF POSTCOMMUNIST ELITES

John Higley, Judith Kullberg, and Jan Pakulski

John Higley is chair of the government department and professor of government and sociology at the University of Texas at Austin. He has conducted survey studies of elites in several countries and written widely on elite theory. *Judith Kullberg* is a faculty associate in the Center for Political Studies at the University of Michigan–Ann Arbor and is writing a book on Russian legislative institutions. *Jan Pakulski*, professor of sociology at the University of Tasmania in Australia, is currently doing research on postcommunism, social stratification, and new social movements. This essay originally appeared in the April 1996 issue of the *Journal of Democracy*.

A precondition of democratic consolidation is what Giovanni Sartori calls the "taming" of politics so that it "no longer kills" and stops being a "warlike affair."[1] This is first and foremost a question of relations and perceptions among political elites—senior governmental, economic, military, professional, media, religious, and other leaders, including the leaders of opposition parties and movements, who participate in or directly influence political decision making. A nation's politics is "tamed" only when broad support for democratic procedures and institutions, as well as a shared acceptance of norms of accommodation and cooperation, develops among political elites.

The collapse of communism in Central and Eastern Europe has involved dramatic changes among political elites from the relations and behaviors of Soviet-style politics to those of at least nascent democracy. Under communist rule, especially in its early phase, politics was a zero-sum game: Winners took all, and losers lost everything, often including their lives. By examining the extent to which consensual elite support for democratic rules, values, and behaviors has emerged from the inhospitable soil of communism, we can refine ideas about the importance of elites in democratization and make firmer judgments about democracy's progress in the major countries of Central and Eastern Europe.

Many analysts think that the elite patterns necessary for democratic consolidation are produced by deep and wide changes in societies: economic development that gives both elites and mass publics a stake in democracy; the rise of a civil society that channels elite power-wielding in a democratic direction; the flowering of a civic culture that shapes elite and mass behavior alike. Analysts who take a more elite-centered approach to democratic development concentrate instead on continuities and changes in the composition, relations, and behaviors of elites that may or may not be associated with broad economic and social trends. They focus on contingent, explicitly political circumstances and the ways in which previously divided elites may "settle" their most basic disputes or "converge" toward more accommodative relations that make restrained but free and fair democratic contests possible.[2]

The scenarios in which such elite settlements or elite convergences occur are complex. Generally, they take place only after periods of long, costly, and inconclusive conflict reach a crisis that threatens a worsening of strife and induces the leaders of opposing elite camps to look for some better way of conducting politics. If these leaders enjoy enough freedom from cadre and mass pressures, as well as enough authority to drag their followers along, they may be able to settle basic disputes secretly and speedily and thus usher in more cooperative relations and restrained competition. Dramatic historical instances were the sudden and deliberate coming together of Tory and Whig elites in England's Glorious Revolution of 1688–89, and of Hat and Cap elites in Sweden's constitutional revolution of 1808–9; a contemporary instance was the settlement negotiated among Spanish elites in 1978–79.[3] Alternatively, where no settlement has occurred but an unstable democratic regime has nonetheless emerged, the imperatives of electoral contests may over time induce elites to converge toward the shared relations, behaviors, and sense of security that are essential if the new democracy is to be consolidated.[4]

A Gradual Evolution

As in previous historical movements toward democracy, the path of democratization in the former communist countries of Central and Eastern Europe began with a desire among elites for greater security. Under Stalinism, elite status did not confer security; on the contrary, it exposed elite members to the vicissitudes of intraparty strife and to ever-present threats of demotion, purge, arrest, imprisonment, and death. The desire of Soviet elites to achieve greater security after Stalin died in 1953 resulted in a tacit consensus to rein in the internal-security apparatus, to attempt to rule collectively, and to institute a rough "socialist legality" that placed some checks on the use of power. This lowered the stakes of factional struggle in the post-Stalin era: rather than imprisonment or execution, losers faced the comparatively mild penalties of forced retirement or demotion. These changes in Moscow allowed elites in the countries under Soviet domination to effect similar shifts in their relations and relative security.

Gradually, elites in most countries of the region achieved a rough *modus vivendi* featuring more-civilized relations and what often amounted to life tenure in their positions.[5] "*Nomenklatura* communism," of course, could not produce anything like the strong sense of mutual accommodation and security that characterizes relations among elites in consolidated democracies; rather, the public fidelity of elites to Marxist-Leninist tenets, to the communist party's leading role, and to Soviet leadership was blended with pragmatic notions about building socialism by winning consent instead of liquidating opponents. Elite conflicts and insecurity remained substantial, however.[6]

Under "late communism" during the 1970s and 1980s, a further evolution in elite relations and behavior became apparent in some countries of the region. This shift involved a partial decentralization of power; a relative pluralization of elites and their widespread professionalization through intakes of highly educated and specialized personnel; and continued attenuation of the insecurity that had earlier pervaded elite relations. In Hungary, and to a lesser extent in Poland and the Soviet Union, higher-level positions in the party-state were increasingly occupied by younger, better-educated persons who possessed transferable skills and cultural capital. Many among this new breed were critical of communism's economic performance and its political workings. Although the extent of this evolution in the makeup and orientation of elites varied importantly across the region, on the eve of the 1989–91 transitions to postcommunist regimes it was clear that a "taming of politics" was under way.

The evolutionary character of elite change during the post-Stalin era helps to explain important features of elite change during the postcommunist era. To the surprise of most observers, the collapse of communist rule involved no comprehensive turnover of elites. The founding of democratic regimes has instead been accompanied by a marked continuity in elite composition, albeit a continuity whose extent differs importantly from country to country. Comparing the holders of roughly nine hundred top political, economic, and cultural elite positions in Russia, Hungary, and Poland during 1988 with the holders of the same or equivalent positions in each country during 1993, Polish sociologist Jacek Wasilewski finds that about one-third of the 1988 elite position-holders were in the same or comparable elite positions in 1993.[7] In some sectors this top-level continuity was pronounced: 50.7 percent for the economic elite in Poland; 48.2 percent for the political elite and 40.8 percent for the cultural elite in Russia. Wasilewski finds, moreover, that substantial proportions of the "new" holders of elite positions in 1993 had been "deputies" and other influentials located just below the top *nomenklatura* rank in 1988: 49 percent in Russia, 37.4 percent in Hungary, and 26 percent in Poland. Overall, the ratios of "winners" (that is, the 1988 *nomenklatura* elites and sub-elites who kept or moved up to elite positions in 1993) to "losers" (1988 elites and deputies not in 1993 elite positions) were 86:10 in Russia, 23:10 in Poland, and 22:10 in Hungary.[8]

In Czechoslovakia, there was a more extensive turnover of governmental and parliamentary elites as a result of the initial postcommunist elections in 1990. However, most of the old Prague Spring reformers and Velvet Revolution leaders who gained positions in 1990 lost them with the victories of Czech right-of-center and Slovak nationalist parties in the 1992 elections. Since 1992, persons who held sub-elite technocratic positions in the former communist regime have constituted about half of the Czech and Slovak parliamentary and governmental elites.[9] Tabulations of elite continuity in Bulgaria and Romania are not readily available, but most observers agree that elites associated with the former communist regimes remain in the political and economic drivers' seats.[10] Communists, their Agrarian allies, and independents from the old communist establishment dominate the Belarusian parliament, while communists and socialists form the largest group in Ukraine's legislative assembly.

The Survival of the Old Elites

Although perceived by many observers both inside and outside the region as a troubling indicator of the lack of change in postcommunist regimes, or as evidence of the continuing legacy of communism, the generally high degree of elite continuity is better understood as a consequence of how elites were evolving before communism's collapse. Gradual change in the composition and orientation of elites enabled them to adapt to, and even thrive in, the new postcommunist economic and political conditions. A conspicuous example is Aleksander Kwaśniewski, the new president of Poland. Kwaśniewski was a junior minister in Poland's last communist government, but Poles elected him in November 1995 in part because they perceived him as representing the "new," forward-looking, and pragmatic generation of leaders. Interviewed after his election, Kwaśniewski remarked, "From an ideological point of view, I was never a Communist. In Poland I've seen very few Communists, especially since the 1970s. I met a lot of technocrats, opportunists, reformers, liberals."[11] His comment accurately portrays the state of mind not only of Polish communist officials before 1989, particularly the younger ones, but of their counterparts across Central and Eastern Europe by the late 1970s and the 1980s.

This shallow commitment to communism, especially where it had been imposed by the Soviets on subject nations, enabled elites to rapidly reposition themselves to benefit from communism's collapse. Many younger, politically untainted elites were able to retain their influential positions or move to new ones, often in the private sector, during and after regime transitions. Others apparently anticipated communism's collapse, if not its precise form or timing, and made political and commercial preparations through nest-feathering practices that became rife at the elite level. During and after the transitions of 1989–91, communist leaders scrambled to protect their power bases or to create new ones. Their maneuvers were varied. Some negotiated places for themselves in postcommunist regimes through the famous "roundtable talks." Many cashed in the credits they had accumulated through patron-client networks and appropriated large parts of state-industrial enterprises ("*nomenklatura* privatization"); still others colluded in "mafia" activities to profit from weakened state oversight and regulation.

A significant number of political leaders, like Kwaśniewski in Poland, survived regime transitions by repackaging themselves as socialists and social democrats. This did not save them from being trounced in the first postcommunist elections and plebiscites. But protestations that they too are firm democrats and market reformers have enabled ex-communists to capitalize on economic hardships and to stage electoral comebacks and returns to power in Bulgaria, Hungary, Lithuania, Poland, and Slovakia. In Russia's December 1995 parliamentary elections, the somewhat refurbished Communists led by Gennady Zyuganov won more than twice as many votes and seats as any other party and positioned themselves for a serious run at the Russian presidency in June 1996.

Through fancy footwork, in short, the elites who operated the communist regimes largely survived those regimes' collapse. Their survival was greater in the economic and administrative than in the political realms, and it was more pronounced among "deputies" than among top leaders. This helps to account for the generally peaceful nature of the transitions from communist to postcommunist regimes. If one asks why the elites associated with communist rule did not go down fighting against the inroads of democratic and capitalist forces, much of the answer is that they had little need to; their survival was more likely if they did not fight.[12] The most politically visible and discredited leaders of the communist establishments were of course removed quickly and publicly: Todor Zhivkov in Bulgaria, Gustáv Husák and Miloš Jakeš in Czechoslovakia, Mieczysław Rakowski in Poland, Erich Honecker in the German Democratic Republic, Nicolae Ceauşescu in Romania, and Mikhail Gorbachev in the Soviet Union. Lustration laws in the Czech Republic, the "acceleration" of personnel changes following the November–December 1990 presidential election in Poland, and the first round of freely contested elections and plebiscites nearly everywhere caused further turnover in top governmental positions. But these laws and elections did not eliminate the bulk of former communist party and governmental elites.[13]

Although it sounds perverse, the essential continuity of elites is one reason why democracy has been able to progress in Central and Eastern Europe: Democracy has not constituted a dire threat to most established elites. Unlike most previous revolutions, the revolution of 1989 produced no doctrinaire, small, and secretive counter-elite dedicated to the imposition of the democratic order and the liquidation or subjugation of elites associated with communism. Instead of having to fight tooth and nail to defend their power and status, most elites associated with the old order have adapted to democratization without major loss. This suggests the presence of one precondition for democratic consolidation—sufficient security among elites that they do not view democratic competition as jeopardizing their ascendancy.

Yet this is also too simple. In the southern countries of Central Europe and across the vast sweep of the former Soviet Union, very high degrees of elite continuity have gone hand-in-hand with postcommunist regimes that hide the substance of authoritarianism behind a veneer of democratic forms. Beyond a relatively high threshold, in other words, the relationship between elite continuity and democratic progress becomes inverse. Moderate degrees of elite continuity are compatible with, and apparently conducive to, democratic politics in the postcommunist period; really high degrees of continuity are associated with serious shortcomings in democracy.

Specifically, it appears that lack of turnover in top-level political positions during and after transitions has led directly to authoritarian or semiauthoritarian postcommunist regimes. Where top communist leaders remained in power, they did so by transforming themselves not into democrats, but into nationalists and autocrats. Like Ukraine's party boss Leonid Kravchuk, some donned the nationalist mantle, repudiated ties to the USSR, and placed themselves at the head of forces asserting national independence.[14] This nationalist strategy has been especially apparent, with horrifying consequences, in the former Yugoslav republics. In several Central Asian states, top communist leaders have retained control by suppressing opponents, manipulating the media, and engineering long-term tenures in office, with garden-variety authoritarian regimes being the result.

Thus the importance of new top leaders and their contribution to building democratic regimes must not be overlooked. Lech Wałęsa in Poland, Václav Havel and Václav Klaus in the Czech Republic, József Antall in Hungary, Yegor Gaidar in Russia, and others, were not merely decorative new faces. Their actions and credibility did much to launch and legitimate the new democratic orders and also to attract badly needed foreign loans and investments. But important as these top-level changes were, nothing approaching a "revolutionary" circulation of elites occurred; in this key respect, at least, there were no Central and East European revolutions in 1989–91.

Hungarians, Poles, and Czechs

However conducive moderate elite continuity and the relative security it signifies may be to democratization, this is at most only half the story. Fundamental changes in elite relations and codes of political behavior are also a precondition of democratic consolidation. These changes have not occurred in any uniform way across the region, and it is important to consider why this has been so and what the consequences have been for democracy.

Assessment of changes in elite relations and behavior is assisted by a research literature that explores the patterns associated with consolidated democratic regimes.[15] Researchers have found that elites in democracies such as the United States, Australia, and the former West Germany interact through exceedingly complex and dense formal and informal networks of influence and acquaintance. These networks overlap and interlock so greatly as to constitute "webworks" that encompass and tie together all important elite groups. But instead of being subordinate to and reliant upon a party-state, as was the case under communist rule, democratic elites are dispersed across a wide range of organizations and sectors, each of which contains significant power resources.[16] This dispersion fosters and sustains a behavioral pattern of bargaining that works according to the code of *do ut des*—"give in order to get"—in which today's losers can be tomorrow's winners. Winning and losing are therefore relative and partial, rather than absolute, outcomes.[17]

Hungarian, Polish, and Czech elites appear to have completed a shift toward relations and behaviors characteristic of consolidated democracies. By the 1980s, the party-state apparatus of all three societies contained relatively well-articulated hard-line and reformist elite camps. In Hungary, memories of the bloody but failed 1956 uprising against communist rule made quietly dissident, reforming elites careful to maintain personal ties with leaders and cliques in the Hungarian Workers' Party.[18] When Gorbachev's "Sinatra Doctrine" removed fears that the 1956 events might be repeated, factions-cum-parties quickly came into the open. Freely competitive and participatory elections were agreed upon at the National Roundtable between June and September 1989. The first fully competitive elections, held in the spring of 1990, were won by anticommunist forces. Restrained behavior and policy consensus among elites characterized the campaign, and nearly all competing groups had significant numbers of ex-communists in their ranks. The parliament elected in 1990 served its full term, and a Socialist (ex-communist) victory in the May 1994 elections did not undermine accommodative behavior among the elites. Indeed, the decision by the Socialists and their

Free Democrat opponents to share power in a coalition government in order to limit tensions resulting from further reforms indicated that this behavior is well instituted among Hungarian elites.

In Poland under communist rule, there was a protracted standoff between the communist authorities on one side and intellectual, Catholic Church, and eventually trade-union elites on the other. The outward appearance of a strong party-dominated regime was kept up by exclusion and intimidation, but waves of strikes, riots, and protests showed that the regime's power had its limits. A major crisis in the fall of 1981 resulted in the imposition of martial law. During 1988, another wave of strikes and popular declarations of no confidence in the regime signaled the onset of a new crisis, triggering largely secret negotiations between communist elites and their opponents. These negotiations had the earmarks of an elite settlement. In a "historic compromise," Solidarity was granted legal status and the communists agreed to its demands for pluralism, constitutional reform, and free elections. In the controlled parliamentary elections that followed in June 1989, all but two of the communist candidates who had been guaranteed seats in the lower house (Sejm) suffered defeat. A comprehensive power-sharing deal was then struck: Solidarity elites agreed to let General Wojciech Jaruzelski remain president and to accept communist domination of the Sejm, despite the election results, in return for promises that Jaruzelski would be no more than a figurehead and that a host of liberalizing laws would be enacted.

The election of Lech Wałęsa as president in November 1990 and a sweeping turnover of Sejm members in the elections of October 1991 split the Solidarity elites, however. This, plus discontent with economic conditions, enabled the Communist Party's eventual proreform successor, Kwaśniewski's Democratic Left Alliance, to emerge victorious in the 1993 parliamentary elections. Serious disputes over the pace of economic reform, the scope of presidential power, church-state relations, and the extent of welfare rights have kept Polish politics at a boil, but no important elite group has questioned the democratic order, and Kwaśniewski's victory in the November 1995 presidential election occurred after a noticeably pacific contest. Concerted action across the political spectrum defused the danger of serious elite conflict following Prime Minister Józef Olesky's resignation in January 1996 amid spying allegations. The Sejm accepted the report of a special commission that exonerated the intelligence agencies for their role in the affair, President Kwaśniewski proposed a Commission of Public Confidence to screen candidates for high office, opposition leaders (including Wałęsa) called for responsible conduct "within the law," and Olesky was replaced without much difficulty by the pragmatic, somewhat independent, and well-liked deputy speaker of parliament, Włodzimierz Cimoszewicz.

With their country's experience of liberal democratic politics during the interwar period, Czechoslovak elites might well have evolved toward the relations and behavior necessary for democracy before any other country in the region. In fact, this nearly happened with the rapid pluralization of elites that was at the core of the Prague Spring in 1968. But that evolution was cut short by the August 1968 Soviet invasion and the subsequent reimposition of a hard-line regime. The regime's systematic persecution of dissidents, which it dubbed "normalization," hindered the re-emergence of reformist factions within the Communist Party and pre-vented the formation of large and well-organized opposition elites.

Czechoslovakia's Velvet Revolution instituted elite power-sharing in fact if not in theory.

Following signals from Gorbachev that they would have to fend for themselves, leaders of the Husák-Jakeš regime faced fast-growing mass mobilizations during the fall of 1989 as peaceful upheavals rocked the neighboring communist regimes in Hungary, Poland, and East Germany. In the space of three weeks, the de-moralized communist leaders acceded to nearly all the demands that the hastily organized Civic Forum in Prague and Public Against Violence in Bratislava managed to articulate. These included revoking the Communist Party's constitutionally prescribed leading role, appointing a coalition government dominated by anticommunists, Husák's resignation from the presidency, Alexander Dubček's restoration as chairman of the National Assembly, and the election of Václav Havel as president. The Velvet Revolution instituted elite power-sharing in fact if not in theory. Husák and his cronies were driven from power, but less-discredited communist officials, especially in Slovakia, embraced a handful of prominent dissidents who symbolized mass opposition to the communist regime. As indicated by Havel's restrained actions in the presidency and by his appointment of the popular Slovak communist leader, Marián Calfa, as prime minister, accommo-dationist proclivities were strong.

We have already noted that the first free Czechoslovak elections, in June 1990, resulted in a wholesale turnover of parliamentary elites, but that virtually all the democratic leaders who played key roles in the 1989 transition failed to gain parliamentary seats in the June 1992 elections. Instead, nationalists favoring political separation of the Slovak territories made strong showings and set the stage for Czechoslovakia's "velvet divorce" in December 1992. Although the divorce was followed by serious elite conflicts in Slovakia (discussed below), it proved a blessing for Czech elites, because it removed the main source of ethnic tension, attenuated conflicts over economic reform (which many Slovak nationalists opposed), and provided vacancies for younger, more pragmatic elites who in many cases had held middle-ranking positions in the former communist regime. Despite continuing disputes over constitutional questions, a conspicuously restrained politics and a wide policy consensus has since prevailed among Czech elites, with a level of public support for the incumbent government, led by Václav Klaus, unequaled elsewhere in Central and Eastern Europe.

The Less Successful Cases

Elite change has been less substantial in Bulgaria and Slovakia, where coalitions of ex-communist and nationalist elites have resisted power-sharing and accommodations with elites more fully committed to democracy and economic reform. The consequences of winning and losing are therefore more marked in Sofia and Bratislava than in Prague, Budapest, and Warsaw, with a more definite exclusion of losers from political influence. In Bulgaria, communists repackaged as Socialists dominated the regime transition and subsequent politics. Only the threat of a national strike pushed them into desultory roundtable talks during 1990; opposition elites were excluded from the interim governments that followed. Reformist elites clustered under the banner of the Union of Democratic Forces are fragmented and weak, leaders of the sizeable Turkish community are allowed little role in national politics, and the Socialists retain the upper hand, having won a majority of parliamentary seats in the 1994 election. Ideological fissures appear wide and deep.[19]

There is a similar situation in Slovakia. There, nationalist-cum-populist leader Vladimír Mečiar leads a coalition government comprising the neocommunist Alliance of Slovak Workers and the anti-Hungarian Slovak Nationalist Party, as well as his own Movement for a Democratic Slovakia. Opposition parties more firmly committed to democratic and market reforms are fragmented; none has the support of more than 10 percent of the voters. Mečiar and his associates have purged opponents from elite positions and stifled political discourse through control of the media. As prime minister, Mečiar has been engaged in a bitter struggle to drive Slovak president Michael Kováč from office, install himself in the presidency, and make it a more powerful office by altering the Constitution.

To the extent that one can speak of elite change in Romania, Ukraine, and Belarus, it began in each case with a preemptive coup led by actors within the communist party who sought to control the ostensible transition to democracy. Power remains concentrated in the state and the renamed communist party that dominates it, turnover of elite personnel has been restricted to a few executive positions, elite networks appear not to cross the boundary between progovernment and antigovernment camps, and elite behavior suggests anxiety and lack of confidence. Thus the two-session Romanian "roundtable" (a label never used by its participants) at the end of January 1990 was a screen behind which the communist-party and military leaders who had toppled Ceauşescu in the Christmas 1989 coup met to sort out their relations. A plebiscitary presidential election in May 1990 effectively excluded fragmented opposition elites from power. Since the first part of 1995, Romania has been governed by a coalition of populist, "communostalgic,"[20] and ultranationalist parties dominated by President Ion Iliescu's Party of Social Democracy, which speaks vaguely of some "third way" between democratic capitalism and totalitarianism. The government has placed its lieutenants throughout the state administration and in key institutions such as state television and the judiciary, and it has heavily favored those business leaders closest to it.

In Ukraine, local party boss Kravchuk carried out a preemptive "independence coup" against Soviet dominance in August 1991. Kravchuk never bothered to open serious negotiations with the leaders of Rukh and other nationalist elites, which became increasingly disorganized and fragmented. Continued political domination by the ex-communist ruling coalition (the "party of power") has involved a closed elite network running through the executive branch, state-security organizations, and other state institutions.[21] Contested parliamentary elections were delayed until 1994; the presidential voting in July of that year revealed a deep ethnoregional cleavage. Instead of convening a roundtable, the new government of President Leonid Kuchma entered into a short-lived post-electoral pact with opposing parliamentary leaders. Kuchma has since been able to gain only tenuous parliamentary support for his privatization program. Belarus has followed a similar pattern of transition, but with even fewer signs of a meaningfully democratic regime than in Ukraine.

Russia

Broadly speaking, the transition in Russia and subsequent political developments there have also been matters more of coups and power struggles than of negotiation and accommodation. Gorbachev's reforms and maneuvers divided Soviet elites quite fundamentally.[22] The struggle for control involved three dramatic showdowns between August 1991 and October 1993. Two were violent, and featured the military in decisive roles. The failed August 1991 coup, in which the military largely refused to move against Gorbachev and Yeltsin, was the last gasp of the old-guard Soviet elite against the rising power of republic elites, most especially Yeltsin and his parliamentary allies in the Russian SFSR. The second coup, this one peaceful and successful, was led by Yeltsin in collusion with Kravchuk in Ukraine and Stanislav Shuskevich, chairman of the Belarusian parliament. Formally committed to hammering out a new Union treaty with Gorbachev that would specify the relative powers of the Soviet central state and the republics, the three met secretly in Minsk in December 1991 and signed an agreement that dissolved the USSR and established the Commonwealth of Independent States. This put the seal on a seizure of the central powers, resources, and facilities of the Soviet state by Yeltsin and the Russian government.

After eliminating the Soviet state, the Soviet Communist Party, and his rival Gorbachev, however, Yeltsin and his allies began the internecine quarrel that culminated in the third coup—Yeltsin's dissolution of the Supreme Soviet and his ordering of army units to shell and capture the Russian parliament building in October 1993.

Mistrust and conflict among Russian elites have been aggravated by economic decline and the dismantling of the enormous state-run economy. Elites have scrambled to benefit from the opportunities that privatization has created. The result is an aggregate of competing groups whose members see politics as a zero-sum contest. Group leaders continue to accumulate power through patronage and by expanding the administrative hierarchies over which they preside.[23] Sub-elites continue to be rewarded for support and loyalty, and are swiftly punished for disobedience or even for inclinations toward independent action. There is considerable elite insecurity, well illustrated by the significant number of bankers and entrepreneurs who have been murdered, and by noticeable violence against politicians.

In addition, just as Václav Havel's actions were crucial in shaping the character of the Czechoslovakian regime transition and Václav Klaus has been crucial in solidifying accommodation and policy consensus among Czech elites, Boris Yeltsin's leadership has strongly influenced the character of elite relations and behavior in Russia. Unlike Havel and Klaus, Yeltsin sought to implement reform during 1991–93 not through compromise and negotiation, but through decree, expansion of his personal power, and the exclusion of other political actors. Disdaining discussion with his opponents, he even neglected his allies, largely ceasing communications with them and giving them little opportunity to affect the policy-making process.

As a consequence of the reorganization and weakening of representative bodies at all levels that occurred after Yeltsin's confrontation with parliament in October 1993, the power of executives and their administrative apparatuses has increased greatly at federal and local levels. Thus political machines that stifle opposition have developed in many regions of the country, most prominently in Moscow under Mayor Yuri Luzhkov.

Despite these worrisome trends, changes in elite relations and behavior that may facilitate the eventual consolidation of democracy are also occurring. The emergence of coherent groups and political machines anchored in clear interests is propitious for forming wider coalitions through deals and compromises. This will simplify political competition and make elite alignments more durable. Elites still fear the loss of power, and political defeats still cost influence, prestige, and perquisites, but there is virtually universal elite acceptance of the legitimacy and desirability of electoral competition. Although violations of the election law and misconduct on the part of the state election commission occurred, the elections of 1993 and 1995 showed rapid elite adaptation to this competition. Furthermore, attempts by officials to control election outcomes appear to be declining; in contrast to 1993, no parties were arbitrarily barred from competing in the 1995 election, and political manipulation of the mass media was less marked. Despite the many uncertainties, then, the "warlike" character of Russian elite relations and politics may be abating.

Three Possible Outcomes

An elite-centered analysis of democratic development in Central and Eastern Europe leads to conclusions that clash with assumptions about communism's demise widely current among both the public at large and the academic world. First, change in elite relations and behavior was the critical determinant of regime change. Second, continuity of elites from the communist to the postcommunist period has not meant, *prima facie,* an absence of democratic change, but rather a relatively high degree of security that has been conducive to democratic competition in several of these countries. Third, in countries where democracy has taken root, ex-communist elites have on balance contributed to, not undermined, the establishment and strengthening of democratic institutions.

An elite-centered approach also suggests three possible future courses of development, based on current patterns. The least likely is the occurrence of additional elite settlements. These are by definition rare events. Among their preconditions are protracted standoffs between two or three warring but well-organized and well-led elite camps, plus a major crisis that threatens the camps equally and induces secret, speedy negotiations among skilled, authoritative leaders aimed at settling basic disputes and reaching a lasting accommodation. Outside Hungary, Poland, and the Czech Republic, where we think that basic elite accommodations in circumstances approximating these occurred in 1989, current elite lineups are either too one-sided (Romania, Ukraine, Belarus) or too fluid (the fragmented oppositions in Bulgaria and Slovakia) to permit settlements. In addition, no major crises loom. In Russia, on the other hand, fragmented and contending groups appear to be coalescing into camps, but no elite camp is yet clearly dominant and the potential for a major crisis remains high. An elite settlement, possibly triggered by an impending victory of ultranationalist forces, is at least conceivable.

A second possibility is for gradual elite convergences. Further electoral victories by the coalitions of ex-communists and nationalists that rule Bulgaria, Slovakia, and Romania may force their fragmented opponents to coalesce if they are to have a chance of gaining power. The imperatives of electoral contests and the defeats suffered in them may also moderate the ethnic extremists and unreconstructed communists who are waiting in the wings. In this way, all important elites may gradually converge toward a consensus on democratic procedures, restraining their electoral rhetoric and acquiring confidence that solid electoral performances are the best way to defend their interests. More evenly balanced electoral contests producing peaceful alternations in government would be the eventual result.

Finally, where ethnoterritorial cleavages and continued economic decline provide fertile ground for mass mobilizations stimulated by anti-democratic elites, bitter struggles producing instability and authoritarianism may be the pattern indefinitely. Ukraine is particularly susceptible; it is conceivable that Russia will not escape either. All over the world, we should recall, relations among elites are typically characterized by deep division and unremitting conflict. It will be little short of a miracle if the pattern of politics-as-warfare disappears from the whole of postcommunist Central and Eastern Europe.

NOTES

1. Giovanni Sartori, "How Far Can Free Government Travel?" *Journal of Democracy* 6 (July 1995): 105.

2. A seminal statement is Dankwart Rustow, "Transitions to Democracy: Toward A Dynamic Model," *Comparative Politics* 2 (1970): 337–53.

3. Michael G. Burton and John Higley, "Elite Settlements," *American Sociological Review* 52 (1987): 295–307; Richard Gunther, "Spain: The Very Model of the Modern Elite Settlement," in John Higley and Richard Gunther, eds., *Elites and Democratic Consolidation in Latin America and Southern Europe* (New York: Cambridge University Press, 1992), 38–80.

4. John Higley and Richard Gunther, *Elites and Democratic Consolidation in Latin America and Southern Europe*, 24–30.

5. Martin Malia, *The Soviet Tragedy* (New York: Free Press, 1994).

6. G.A. Arbatov, *Zatianuvsheesia vyzdorovlenie (1993–1995gg): svidetel'stvo sovremennika* [The recovery is delayed (1993–95): a contemporary account] (Moscow: Mezh-dunarodnye otnosheniia, 1991).

7. Jacek Wasilewski, *Communist Nomenklatura in Post-Communist Eastern Europe: Winners or Losers of Transformation?* (Warsaw: Polish Academy of Sciences, 1995).

8. Wasilewski's figures conceal the important turnover that occurred among holders of ministerial positions in the government of Russia immediately before and after the Soviet Union's demise at the end of 1991. Of the roughly 145 ministers appointed by Boris Yeltsin between June 1991 and October 1993, about half were "new men" recruited primarily from academic and research institutions who had previously held no significant government or party position. See David Lane and Cameron Ross, "The Changing Composition and Structure of the Political Elites," in David Lane, ed., *Russia in Transition* (London: Longman, 1995), 52–75. Conversely, Wasilewski's figures understate the continuity of Hungarian and Polish elites because they do not take into account the return of former communist leaders to power after parliamentary elections in Poland in 1993 and Hungary in 1994 and after Poland's presidential election in 1995.

9. Lubomir Brokl and Zedenka Mansfeldova, *Czech Political Elites and the Elites of Legislative Power* (Warsaw: Polish Academy of Sciences, 1995).

10. A study of Bulgarian business leaders in 1993 found that 63 percent previously held important positions in the Communist Party. Stephan E. Nikolov, *A Quasi-Elite in Bulgaria* (Warsaw: Polish Academy of Sciences, 1995).

11. *New York Times,* 29 November 1995.

12. Robert Service, "Why the Red Flag Was Furled," *Financial Times* (London), 27–28 May 1995.

13. See Jacques Rupnik, "The Post-Totalitarian Blues," *Journal of Democracy* 6 (April 1995): 61–73. Lustration laws ran into the problem of how to ban former communist leaders from political office without contravening basic precepts of citizens' rights and justice. Thus, attempts to introduce these laws in Poland failed and led to the collapse of Jan Olszewski's government in 1992. In September 1995, the Albanian parliament passed a law barring all those who served in the former communist government or worked for its secret service from holding governmental, parliamentary, judicial, or media positions. But because it would prevent leaders of the opposition Socialist and Social Democratic parties from contesting the March 1996 parliamentary elections, the law was mainly seen as a device enabling President Sali Berisha to consolidate his increasingly autocratic rule.

14. Alexander J. Motyl, *Dilemmas of Independence: Ukraine After Totalitarianism* (New York: Council on Foreign Relations, 1993).

15. Two summaries are Robert D. Putnam, *The Comparative Study of Political Elites* (Englewood Cliffs, N.J.: Prentice-Hall, 1976), and David Knoke, *Political Networks: The Structural Perspective* (New York: Cambridge University Press, 1990).

16. John Higley, Ursula Hoffmann-Lange, Charles Kadushin, and Gwen Moore, "Elite Integration in Stable Democracies: A Reconsideration," *European Sociological Review* 7 (1991): 35–53.

17. Giovanni Sartori, *The Theory of Democracy Revisited: The Contemporary Debate* (Chatham, N.J.: Chatham House, 1987), 214–53.

18. Rudolf Andorka, "Regime Transitions in Hungary in the 20th Century," *Governance* 6 (1993): 358–71.

19. Nikolov, *A Quasi-Elite in Bulgaria,* 7.

20. This characterization was suggested to us by Vladimir Tismaneanu.

21. Marko Bojcun, "The Ukrainian Parliamentary Elections in March–April 1994," *Europe-Asia Studies* 47 (1994): 229–49; see also Motyl, *Dilemmas of Independence,* 159–74.

22. From focus-group interviews conducted with 79 leaders in Moscow in June 1991, Judith Kullberg found that although Soviet elites largely accepted the necessity of reform, they were divided over the character and scope of change. Similarly, from interviews conducted with 116 top ex-Soviet and Russian political leaders in 1993, David Lane found that they were split in half over the "fundamentally sound" or "basically unsound" nature of the Soviet system itself under Gorbachev. See Judith Kullberg, "The Ideological Roots of Elite Political Conflict in Post-Soviet Russia," *Europe-Asia Studies* 46 (November 1994): 929–53; and David Lane, "The Gorbachev Revolution: The Role of the Political Elite in Regime Disintegration," *Political Studies* 94 (April 1996): 4–23.

23. The Russian Federation is estimated to have 1.7 times more bureaucrats than the Soviet Union had in 1989, despite there being 130 million fewer people to administer. *Financial Times* (London), 27 June 1995.

4

CIVIL SOCIETY AFTER COMMUNISM

Aleksander Smolar

Aleksander Smolar is chairman of the Stefan Batory Foundation in Warsaw and senior research fellow at the Centre National de la Recherche Scientifique in Paris. This essay is a version of a paper he presented on 29 August 1995 at a conference on "Consolidating the Third Wave Democracies: Trends and Challenges," held in Taipei, Taiwan. The conference was co-sponsored by the Institute for National Policy Research of Taipei and the International Forum for Democratic Studies of Washington, D.C.

The peaceful revolutions of 1989 in Central and Eastern Europe were carried out in the name of "civil" society, and the related word "citizen" was one of the most frequently used terms in the public discourse of that time. Citizens' committees, citizens' movements, citizens' assemblies, citizens' initiatives, citizens' parliamentary clubs, and citizens' parties all sprang into being. Today, just a few years later, talk of "civil society" is no longer much heard in the streets, and the idea seems to have gone back whence it came, to discussions held among intellectuals on the changing shape of postcommunist countries. The remarkable rise and fall of the concept of civil society is itself worth examining.

As used in Central and Eastern Europe, the notion of civil society never had much to do with the grand theoretical debates that one may trace across two centuries in the works of Locke, Adam Ferguson, Adam Smith, Hegel, Tocqueville, Marx, and Gramsci, among others. To speak of civil society was instead to express a twofold opposition. The first dimension was opposition to authority. Civil society was "us"; the authorities were "them." The second dimension was one in which civil society was held up in contradistinction to "the nation," understood in hereditary, ethnic terms. The potency of ethnic nationalism in Central and Eastern Europe is well known: ethnicity had long furnished the most salient way of dividing "us" from "them," and Marxist class analysis could not rival it for popularity or profundity of influence.

Although the national-patriotic, even nativist, strain of opposition to communism would in time produce its own champions and manifest its own influence, the tone of dissidence during the 1970s and most of the 1980s was set by intellectuals with left-liberal, Western-oriented views. In speaking the language of civil society, they were implicitly challenging the traditionally dominant ethnic conception of the nation with a nonethnic, political concept. By promoting civil society rather than ethnic community, they were not only proposing a wholly different way of defining "us" and "them," but also suggesting a different way of looking at both the past and the future.

The reflections on civil society and the strategy for its self- organization produced by figures such as Czechoslovakia's Václav Havel, Poland's Jacek Kuroń and Adam Michnik, and Hungary's János Kis (to name some of the most prominent) grew out of the oppositionists' reassessment of past failures to overthrow or reform "really existing socialism" in Central and Eastern Europe.[1]

The Hungarian Uprising of 1956 and the Prague Spring of 1968—the former an armed rebellion and the latter a peaceful revolution sparked by the top-down innovations of reform-minded elites—had roused hopes that the communist system imposed on the region by the USSR could be overthrown by force or transformed by nonviolent political change. In both cases, hope was crushed by the tanks of the Red Army. Clearly, any direct challenge to the Soviet empire was doomed.

From 1956 on, there had been numerous efforts to introduce liberalization and democratization by means of gradual reforms. These efforts fell into three categories, each distinguished by its guiding strategy. The first approach, which I call "politics first," was premised on the idea that the reform of party and state institutions was key because, under real socialism, the party-state commanded the economy and society. The reforms begun in Poland in 1956 typified this strategy.

The dominant approach in the 1960s was the "economics-first" strategy. This focused on the economy as the most promising place to start, because economic reform did not seem threateningly political and because officials could more easily be enlisted to support changes designed to increase output and raise living standards. Some proponents of what came to be called "market socialism" hoped that economic change would open the door to social and eventually political change as well.

The third strategy, associated with the era of détente in the 1970s, stressed the influence that economic linkages with the West might come to exert over developments within the Soviet Union and Eastern Europe. The more the countries of the East bloc could be made to depend on flows of Western credit, technology, and trade, went the theory popular in many Western political circles and among some communist reformers, the more they would be induced to respect the human rights guarantees spelled out in the "third basket" of the 1975 Helsinki Agreement, to limit repressive practices, and to liberalize their economies.

The three strategies did help to expand the sphere of social autonomy in the countries of the Soviet bloc, especially Poland and Hungary, but progress was limited and uneven, and gains often precarious. In 1968, armed Soviet intervention against "socialism with a human face" in Czechoslovakia greatly diminished reformist hopes in Eastern and Central Europe. Yet this disillusionment, along with previous progress, paved the way for a fourth strategy, elaborated by independent intellectuals in the region, which I call the "society-first" approach. In the mid-1970s, they seized on what they saw as (to paraphrase Lenin) the weak link of the communist system. Their approach was one of antipolitics, and their discourse was the language of morality.

"Society First"

The "society-first" program, though formulated in scores of articles, can be summed up in a few sentences. Its first postulate, expressed memorably by Solzhenitsyn and Havel, was *living in truth*. This was a genuine moral imperative, and also a way of denying the legitimacy of a public realm that rested on the forced acceptance of an official definition of reality. The second postulate was the value of *self-organization.* Associations formed and acts of solidarity carried out beyond the purview of the party-state were valued in themselves, and as contributors to the reconstruction of authentic social ties. The third postulate was *respect for law.* Hungarian dissident János Kis wrote of the importance of "the conspicuous exercise of rights."[2] The constitutions and laws of the "people's republics" became instruments of the struggle, as did such provisions of international law as the Helsinki Accords.

Under whatever name—"parallel *polis,*" "independent culture," or "independent society"—the idea of civil society remained largely restricted to narrow circles of independent intellectuals in every East and Central European country save one. The exception, of course, was Poland. There, committees for the defense of students, religious believers, and peasants sprang up, as did unofficial "flying universities" and what became the seeds of political parties and, most famously, the Solidarity trade union, which grew out of the Lenin Shipyard strike in Gdansk in the summer of 1980. The society-first strategy was supposed to lead to the gradual rebuilding of civil society, which as it grew was in turn expected steadily and quietly to narrow the terrain over which the party-state actually held sway. The communist parties might never be dethroned, but the substance of their power might be hollowed out to the point where, like the queen of England, they would reign but not rule.

The society-first plan to rebuild islands of social independence soon became the vehicle of even higher ideological hopes. In this gloss, the islands came to be seen as the harbingers of a future society beyond not only communism, but also Western-style capitalist democracy. The civil society taking shape in Central and Eastern Europe would respond not only to the crisis of "real socialism," but to the problems of the West as well. The society-first strategy and its antipolitical approach were taken to portend a worldwide change in human civilization itself.

The first congress of Solidarity spelled out something like this vision in its document on the "self-governing republic," which meant civil society emancipated from the tutelage of the state. Such notions had more than one source: one can see in them a trace of Marx's idea of the withering away of the state, but there was also a strong tincture of traditional Polish antipathy to the state (understandable in a country with a history of foreign rule).

The ideology of civil society had ties to the totalitarian paradigm. In the West, this way of describing communism was associated with authors like Hannah Arendt, Carl J. Friedrich, and Zbigniew Brzezinski. Despite its prestige, most professional Sovietologists and political commentators had rejected the totalitarian model by the end of the 1950s. In some quarters, to speak of totalitarianism was to risk being thought a right-wing "Cold Warrior" with an unscientific, ideological view of communist reality. In the 1970s and 1980s, some Western experts on the USSR and other communist countries rated the differences between the democratic West and these countries as merely secondary. Rather than speak of communism or totalitarianism, these scholars spoke of modernizing, bureaucratic, or corporatist systems characterized by organizational or institutional pluralism.

At the same time, oddly enough, the totalitarian model began to predominate in the thinking of independent circles within the communist world itself.[3] By the 1970s, conditions in Poland, Hungary, and even Czechoslovakia and the USSR were a far cry from what they had been under Stalinism. So in a sense, the description of "really existing socialism" offered by dissidents in the East was as unrealistic as that offered by most Western Sovietologists. The new popularity of the totalitarian model among Central and East European dissidents reflected their increasing alienation and marginalization, their loss of confidence that the system could be reformed from within.

The socialism of the 1970s and 1980s was obviously different from that of the 1940s and 1950s, when communist parties still had genuine revolutionary aspirations. Society was becoming less totalitarian, but the institutions created during the revolutionary period retained their form. To put it another way, totalitarianism as a millenarian movement had long since died, but the set of institutions that it had created was left behind like the fossilized carcass of some extinct beast—the party-state that controlled and corrupted state, society, and economy alike.

Paradoxically, the opposition owed its continued existence to the tacit tolerance of the very state that the oppositionists denounced as totalitarian. This tolerance was scarcely principled, of course, being due mainly to pressure from the West (economic interests plus the Helsinki process, plus the need for respectability).

Although it left much to be desired as a description of reality, the totalitarian paradigm played an important role in mobilizing and integrating independent circles of dissidents. The stark opposition of truth versus falsity, spontaneity versus command, voluntarism versus compulsion, and liberty versus bondage served to set apart the world of the nascent opposition that called itself "civil society" from the official world of the party-state and all its works.

The educational and standard-setting role that the opposition played during the 1970s and 1980s was key: It popularized civic attitudes and the ideal of a rule of law, and undermined the legitimacy of the existing order. The emerging islands of civil society contributed to the elaboration and articulation of alternative collective identities and values in the several countries of Central and Eastern Europe. With the crumbling of the state's monopoly over news, public discourse, and the formulation of visions for the future, dissidents were able to make major contributions to the opening of an authentic public sphere.

These efforts were part of the Central and East European opposition's overall strategy of creating what might be called a "minimal civil society." The word "minimal" is appropriate because even when the Solidarity era was at its height, civil societies in the East bloc had little in common with what is called civil society in developed democracies with long traditions of social autonomy. Similarly, the terms "defensive" and "moral" civil society might also be used, denoting an entity that defined itself in opposition to the state.[4] But a civil society whose essence was radical opposition to the communist state could not survive the disappearance of that state. As the hour of victory over communism arrived, however, this had not yet become evident.

After 1989

A burst of euphoria followed the defeat of the communist state—a defeat that was widely seen as signaling the victory of civil society. Poland's June 1989 elections were won by the Citizens' Committees that had sprung up like mushrooms all over the country. "We don't need to define [civil society]," said the prominent Polish dissident Bronisław Geremek in August 1989, "We see it and feel it."[5] Jiri Dienstbier, a future Czechoslovak foreign minister, spoke of "civil society in power" as Civic Forum became the outgoing communist regime's chief negotiating partner during the Velvet Revolution.

Symbolically, the toppling of the Berlin Wall in 1989 played the same role as the taking of the Bastille had in 1789. In an instant, the "revolutionary civil society" came into being. Yet the feeling of triumph, the holiday atmosphere, did not last. The existence of a civil society of resistance was dependent on the existence of a hostile state that offered no hope for compromise. As soon as this state disappeared, the civil society that opposed it also disintegrated. The revolutionary civil society is by definition a transient phenomenon, even though it remains deeply embedded in the minds of its participants as a myth and an ideal.

The illusion of "civil society in power" and the opposition's antipolitical ideology had certain important, though fleeting, consequences. Dissidents swept into power by the revolutions of 1989 strove vainly to preserve the unity of the amorphous organizations of the moral civil society. Their efforts were spurred by an aversion to parties and partisanship that had its roots in a profound skepticism about traditional political distinctions. Many civil-society activists felt that the division between left and right was an obsolete convention with no relevance to the real choices facing societies emerging from communism. At the same time, they realized that it was no longer tenable to divide their countries' political space into totalitarian and democratic camps. Many of the new leaders' utterances revealed a belief that Central and East Europeans could find new forms of political organization and interest representation that escaped the drawbacks and costs associated with Western-style parliamentary democracy.

The myth of civil society as united, antipolitical, and supportive of radical reform was one of the first casualties of the postcommunist era. As soon as communist authorities showed themselves willing to bargain over the division of power (or even to give it up outright), politics reasserted itself. What had been "moral civil societies" became political blocs—first in opposition, and then, with the decomposition of the old ruling structures, in power. Civil society, it turned out, had been a historical costume; its usefulness disappeared with the times that dictated its wearing. Broad-front organizations broke up when faced with real political decisions, and multiparty systems began to form. Concrete choices and responsibilities cured many of the leaders of moral civil society of their illusory notions about the possibility of a "third way" beyond capitalism and socialism or dictatorship and democracy. What replaced these fancies was the decision to imitate Western arrangements like constitutional democracy, the market, and the rule of law. "Returning to Europe" or "becoming a normal society" became the watchwords of most of the leaders who came from the ranks of the democratic opposition to communism.

Moral civil society suffered blows from all sides. Its activists moved *en masse* into government and business, leaving a plethora of associations, human rights groups, independent publishing concerns, and informal educational institutions without enough people to keep them going. One especially poignant example was the mass recruitment into the Polish Ministry of Home Affairs, including the political police, of young activists from the pacifist group Freedom and Peace.

The greatest shock for civil-society activists, however, was their discovery of society's real condition. The "revolutions" of 1989 happened
not because civil society was tremendously strong, but because
Gorbachev's policies of *glasnost'* and *perestroika* had created a deep-
ening international crisis for the Soviet Union's satellite regimes in
Central and Eastern Europe. It soon became clear that the former oppositionists could command only limited social support, even where there
was profound discontent with the old order. All of civil society's weaknesses had been blamed on the crippling effects of the *ancien régime*.
With the crumbling of the party-state, the hobbles were removed and
the test was at hand. Would the virtues attributed to civil society—a
supposedly greater bent toward idealism and resistance to Western-style
materialism, for instance—come to the fore?

After 1989, leading ideologists of civil society like Václav Havel
and Adam Michnik became severe critics of their own societies. They
painted dark portraits of countries teeming with intolerance, xenophobia, undemocratic tendencies, materialism, and so on.[6] An outpouring
of literature detailed the ravages that the *ancien régime* had left behind.
Just a few years before, many of the same authors had been writing
about popular aspirations for independence, the strength of traditional
values, the signs of passive and even active resistance; now their favorite subject became the peril that postcommunist society posed for political and economic reform. A host of writers detected and decried attitudes and behaviors inconsistent with the values of civil society. Much
ink was spilled describing *homo sovieticus*—the stunted, distrustful
human type produced by real socialism. As one astute observer noted
with a touch of irony: "Somehow, imperceptibly, a magnificent society,
admired by the whole world, has turned into an unpredictable mass posing a danger to its own existence; it can be said in its defense only that,
for a long time, it was subjugated under communism."[7]

Limiting the State

In the 1980s, when there were still no signs of the coming implosion
of real socialism in Central and Eastern Europe, oppositionists used to
ask a waggish question that could not quite conceal the deep anxiety
which lay behind it. "We know that you can make fish soup out of an
aquarium," they would say, "but can you make an aquarium out of fish
soup?" In other words: Can we rebuild a civil society, a viable democracy, and a developed market economy in countries seared by decades
of communist rule? Today, one can risk giving a positive answer, which
implies that the "aquarium," even when communist terror was at its apo-
gee, never quite became "fish soup." At the same time, the experiences
of recent years have laid bare enormous differences among countries
that had long been subject to similar institutions and mechanisms of

control. Differences rooted in remote history and variegated traditions came to the fore, though the great influence of choices being made today is also evident. Thus the current situation and future prospects of the Central European countries (Poland, the Czech Republic, Hungary, Slovenia, Slovakia, and probably Croatia) and the Baltic republics (Lithuania, Latvia, and Estonia) look very different from those of the other former Soviet republics or of the Balkan countries (Romania, Bulgaria, Albania, Serbia, and the other ex-Yugoslav republics aside from Croatia and Slovenia).

Eradicating the communist legacy required action in two main directions: a radical separation of the economic, social, and political realms, and a limitation of the role of the state. Under communism—even in its softer and shrunken version—there was no society, economy, or even state in the strict sense: These domains were strictly integrated and subordinated to a single power apparatus. This was true not only "at the top" but also "at the bottom": In addition to their economic role, enterprises also performed important social, cultural, and other functions. Once communism fell, then, it was necessary to make a clean break with totalitarian indistinction; to separate political parties from the state; to divide power within the state; and to peel the economy, politics, and social life away from one another.

The powers of the state were limited in varying degrees in different postcommunist countries, but it was everywhere streamlined and decentralized. "Public space" was reopened through the abolition of censorship, the provision of greater access to the mass media, and so on. The political police were put on a shorter leash. Old constitutions were replaced or heavily amended. Legislation began to conform to international standards. Political competition became the order of the day. A third sector, nonprofit and nongovernmental, came into being as a result of changes in the laws governing associations, foundations, and social organizations.

Economic life was revolutionized. In many postcommunist countries, including Russia, the private sector now accounts for half or more of GDP. Trade and investment barriers were removed, and extensive privatization and reprivatization has occurred. Real banking sectors and capital markets are taking shape throughout most of the region.

The years after 1989 saw liberal thought become intellectually—if not always politically—predominant in the countries that lead the region in development. Leading liberals like Prime Minister Václav Klaus of the Czech Republic maintained that if artificial restrictions were removed, the totalitarian state was dismantled, and basic rules of the game were promulgated, markets and democracy would follow as a matter of course. In the transformation that he successfully conducted, Klaus's avowed emphasis was on "passive" policies (conscious self-limitation by the state, liberalization, and far-reaching deregulation). Klaus was not rigid about this: In carrying out voucher privatization, for instance, he pursued a more active course. (His government also carried out a highly active policy to protect jobs, delaying enactment of a law on enterprise bankruptcy for two years.) As Klaus himself summed up the work of his government:

> During the last two years, we completed the creation of a pluralistic demo-
> cratic system that guarantees basic civic liberties and enables every one
> of us to benefit from these freedoms. . . . A market economy was also
> instituted, with a small and constantly diminishing role for the state. . . .
> In the political, economic, and civic domains every one of us has ad-
> equate space for taking decisions freely and for individual initiative.[8]

The liberal approach displays a broad streak of optimism about people's adaptive capacities. Change is initiated from the top, but success depends on setting in motion the creative forces of society. The market is a source of strong negative stimuli—the threat of bankruptcy, unemployment, or downward mobility—and of positive incentives—the lure of riches, power, and social prestige. A voucher system neutralizes much of the potential social opposition to privatization. Mythical ownership by the whole people gives way to the aggregate of individual ownerships. The socialist ideol-ogy of equality yields to the liberal ideology of enrichment, and the idea of collective advancement to that of individual prosperity.

The liberal vision of spontaneous social reconstruction is antipolitical. The transformation of economies and societies is described in largely technical terms: The rules of the market and the open society must be grafted into place as quickly as possible so that the patient cannot reject the transplant. Questions are never raised about the social groups at which the reforms are aimed and the social forces on which they rely. Some-times the "middle class" is mentioned, but with little or no acknowledg-ment that in Central and Eastern Europe this group remains a spirit seek-ing a social body.

Initially, the liberal program enjoyed wide social support, mostly because it represented the absolute antithesis of the *ancien régime.* Yet this support waned daily in virtually every country of the region (though it remains highest in the Czech Republic). In fact, the real base of the economic and social revolution lay in government circles (especially the executive branch and its advisors), the new business class, and small groups of intellectuals.

Central and Eastern Europe's liberal reformers have doubts concern-ing the concept of civil society. Prime Minister Klaus spoke freely of the "aberrant idea of civil society," obviously referring to Margaret Thatcher's famous statement that "there is no society, only individuals and their families." He seemed to regard civil society as a stalking horse for collectivism, new bureaucracies, and quixotic searches for the "third way."[9] Clearly alluding to President Havel, Klaus scored critics who were not satisfied with "free citizens" but wanted "better citizens" in the bargain, and warned of "moralizing, elitist, and perfectionist ambitions [that] would create a Huxleyan 'Brave New World.'"[10] Liberal reformers seem especially averse to the idea of interest representation in the economy, seeing it as a potential source of stifling corporatism and a threat to market-based reforms.

Lost in Postcommunism

The ideology of the moral civil society placed its hopes in self-organization, self-help, and citizens' activities. These hopes stemmed from the belief that "totalitarian" restraints had bound potent social forces which were yearning to operate freely. Apart from the sphere of the economy and, to a certain degree, of local government (especially in Poland), however, levels of autonomous social activity have been disappointing.

Of the many reasons for this, the most important (at least at first) was the severe economic recession of the early 1990s. People beset by joblessness and falling real incomes are preoccupied with survival and are unlikely to plunge into social, cultural, scientific, political, and philanthropic activities. State budgetary crises prompted a trimming of all "unnecessary" expenditures, including those that might have supported activities independent of the state. Under pressure from such constraints, and sometimes also for doctrinal reasons, some governments in the region tried to shift a large share of the responsibility for health care, schooling, scientific research, and social welfare to society.

Flight from the public to the private sphere may be regarded as a natural reaction to years of forced participation and mobilization. Everyday life under socialism taught people to survive as individuals and to fear any association with independent collective action. Far from creating a "new socialist man" free of egotism and greed, communism actually bred atomized, amoral cynics good at doubletalk and "working the system," but not at effective enterprise. The shakiness of independent organizations, including political parties, suggests the lack of a culture of free collective activity.

The societies of disintegrating communism were places where civil society, traditions, moral norms, the rule of law, and voluntary organizations had been destroyed or greatly weakened. The more intensely totalitarian the regime, the more dramatic were the consequences of its collapse. In many parts of the Balkans and the former Soviet Union, where communists had ruled traditionally patriarchal societies with an iron hand, the collapse of official control mechanisms had disastrous consequences. As a Russian journalist put it, "In the past there were rules to the game, good or bad or whatever. And there was fear. Now there are no rules, good or bad, and there is no fear."[11]

The countries of Central and Eastern Europe have seen the collapse of much of the network of state-run or formal social institutions that performed functions ordinarily belonging to civil society. In the moribund phase of socialism, numerous social-welfare and income-redistribution tasks were handled by state enterprises rather than by specialized public or private agencies. Today, economic rationality dictates that enterprises relinquish these tasks. The whole system of housing subsidies, employee vacations, sports clubs, health and child care, and so on has disappeared.

The collapse of many social organizations associated with the communist party also helped to weaken social bonds. Although these bodies unquestionably aided the regime's efforts at social control and indoctrination, they also often became the basis of useful social networks. Sports clubs, community centers, summer camps, youth groups, pensioners' clubs, and the like filled a certain void, albeit one that the communist system itself had created by suppressing all autonomous versions of such institutions. Today, tight state budgets, skepticism about old ties of power and subordination, and the conscious liquidation of communist-run institutions have conspired to eliminate this network.

Establishing new institutions for civil society takes time, will, skill, and funds. In the meantime, one gets the paradoxical impression that society today is no less—indeed, perhaps even more—atomized than it was in the final years of communism. People seem to feel "lost" in the new reality of postcommunism. As Elemer Hankiss explains:

> By now, millions of people have lost, or fear that they may lose, their traditional roles and positions in the sphere of production and distribution. They have lost their way in the labyrinths of social and industrial relationships, which are in the midst of a chaotic transformation. People do not know anymore, or yet, what are the rules of the new games, what are their duties and rights, what they have to do for what, what is the cost and reward of what. There is no authority to tell, there are no values to refer to.[12]

Not all the communist-affiliated organizations disappeared from Central and Eastern Europe after 1989, and the ones that remain—including political parties, labor unions, and enterprise associations—are among the strongest influences in the terrain between the state and the individual or family. In the new conditions, to be sure, these organizations have different programs, and often new names and leaders as well. Sometimes they take an ideological line radically opposed to the one favored by their communist-era predecessors, but organizationally they are continuous.

Supporters of radical decommunization cite the failure to break cleanly with the old order as the reason for the institutional strength of the ex-communists. The *nomenklatura* managed to turn its political power into financial capital and retain control over a large part of the mass media and the work of nongovernmental organizations. The successors of communist parties and front groups also succeeded in hanging on to a considerable part of the assets of their predecessors.

It goes without saying that ex-communist parties, unions, and the like had an organizational head start over their newly formed democratic rivals. Still, the decommunizers' argument seems insufficient. The ex-communists adapted themselves ably to democratic conditions because even under communism their organizations had a double role: they not only represented the "authorities," but also filled real social needs. Today, for various reasons, alternative organizations that could fill these needs remain weak. The ex-communists have financial as well as human capital, plus the advantages of continuity; their organizations bring together hundreds of thousands of people who have lost (or not yet found) their bearings in the new postcommunist world.

The New Socialist Civil Society

Real socialism, which has disappeared as a political system and to a lesser extent as a form of economic organization, lives on in the minds of people and in the institutions of civil society. Without delving into the psychological, moral, and attitudinal legacies of real socialism, I would like to point out two of its remnants that have had a direct effect on the formation of new civil societies. One is the surprisingly durable social structure and set of interest groups that formed under it; the other is the similarly durable ensemble of informal social ties (the "shadow society") that people created in order to defend themselves against and cope with the demands of real socialism.

The years just after 1989 were a period of high hopes for independence, democracy, and the "return to Europe"; these made it possible to carry out costly reforms. As reform began to pinch and enthusiasm started to wane, the "politics of values" speedily gave way to the "politics of interests." Faith in a "better future" dwindled, and people focused on protecting their own. In fighting for their interests under postcommunism, the social groups formed under the old system unconsciously fight for the restoration of nonmarket, political mechanisms of shaping the social structure.

The mechanism that produces "socialist civil society" works as follows: Anxiety over the liberal dismantling of the *ancien régime,* plus the awareness—thanks to the free mass media and the network of political and trade-union organizations—of real group interests, spurs protests against reform and support for those identified with the idealized past. This process goes on even after ex-communist parties like those in Poland and Hungary find out, once elected, that they have little choice but to forget their campaign rhetoric and stick with reform.

Some institutions left over from real socialism, like the communist-satellite Polish Peasants' Party (PSL), have become truly independent since 1989. Formally autonomous but quiescent under communism, the PSL today staunchly guards peasant interests—a significant role in a country where more than a quarter of the population engages in small-scale agricultural production and where farming was never collectivized.

The historical joke in all this is that just when it lost political, economic, and spiritual power, real socialism found a refuge in the sphere that it had always tried to suppress: civil society. When real socialism held sway, the "shadow society" was a product of the official world's internal contradictions, ineffectiveness, and red tape—all weaknesses that enterprising individuals exploited in order to gain security, income, or social position. These "operators" fought the system, to be sure, but they also cooperated with it. In mirror-image fashion, the communist authorities tried to suppress such "informal" behaviors, but began to tolerate them as well, in part because they increased the system's own adaptive capacity, bringing it more into sync with the needs of society. The best example is the "parallel economy." This helped the official economy to function, but only because labor, capital, and raw materials were undergoing de facto (and illegal) privatization.

In the 1970s, as repression abated in some East and Central European countries, informal networks began to form out of family ties, friendships, and intimate social circles. These arrangements not only provided practical benefits, but also helped to satisfy needs for belonging and a purpose in life. Society seemed to have two levels: one of artificial official institutions, and another of spontaneous connections formed as a defense against and adaptation to the official world. In time, this mutual adaptation resulted in the integration and corruption of both worlds. Informal society undermined the logic of the official institutions, while the official world intensified the pathological narrowness of informal social bonds. Private and public gradually became intertwined: The state became privatized, while private life became collectivized.

The official society of real socialism disintegrated. The shadow society—its antithesis—has survived in various forms. Even today, studies reveal more confidence in informal ties based on circles of relatives and close friends (or officials who can be bribed) than in the anonymous world of institutions, legal norms, and complicated mechanisms like those of democratic politics.[13] While one can hardly say that the shadow society is "civil" or "civic," it does form one of the concentric circles of social autonomy inherited from the old system. As such, it influences the chances and nature of civil society proper.

Relegitimizing the Open Society

The vision of civil society that the anticommunist opposition in Central and Eastern Europe used in its fight for liberty has lost out as a social program. The moral civil society, an antipolitical, anticapitalist, anticommunist community, could endure as a viable ideal only so long as it remained unencumbered by the need to make real choices. Actual postcommunist civil society, which is rising atop the ruins of the old system, is composed partly of elements left over from this system and partly from the heritage of a more remote past. Civil society is being created in an unfavorable atmosphere of economic recession, withdrawal from public affairs, egotistic individualism, mistrust, and lack of a legal culture. It is arising from expressions of social autonomy that often are far removed from civility, if not their complete opposite. Its rise is also challenging the egalitarian outlook that numerous opinion surveys have shown to be deeply rooted in the minds of Central and East Europeans.

Citizens in Central and Eastern Europe can now form associations, publicly express opinions, vote, run for office, and so on. Yet as far as "social" and "economic" rights are concerned, the situation is different. Many think that liberalization and privatization have dramatically changed social relations and the composition of citizens' rights. The major problem facing postcommunist societies is how to relegitimize private property and the open society, with all the uncertainty that accompanies them. The moral foundations of private property—especially when its ownership is highly concentrated—have always been weak, and have needed support from values associated with religion, tradition, democracy, and human liberty. We cannot assume that this support will be present to legitimize private property and the market economy under the conditions of postcommunism.

Political, social, and economic change means a redistribution of costs and benefits among groups and individuals. The upper and middle classes, old and new alike, stand to benefit from the new shape of citizens' rights. Their biographies and the way they acquired their wealth evoke moral outrage—hardly a boon to legitimation. Meanwhile, those of a humbler sort, whose participation in public life is necessarily limited and who thus benefit less from the recovery of civil and political rights, are also the most affected by the new economic hardships. They do not stand to gain much from privatization, and it is costing them more now in terms of lost jobs and reduced living standards, even if in the long run they too will benefit from joining the modern world.

The civic principle is not just a principle of equality; it also creates the normative basis for the inner integration of civil society as well as its integration with the political system. The development of civil society, the consolidation of democracy, and the closer identification of citizens with state institutions—all these require counteracting the atomizing tendencies that the huge changes of recent years (however necessary and ultimately salutary) have set in motion.

NOTES

1. Václav Havel, "The Power of the Powerless," in John Keane, ed., *The Power of the Powerless* (New York: M.E. Sharpe, 1985), 92, 95; Jacek Kuroń, *Polityka i odpowiedzialnosc* (London: Aneks, 1984); Adam Michnik, *Letters from Prison and Other Essays* (Berkeley: University of California Press, 1985) and *Penser la Pologne* (Paris: La Découverte, 1983); and János Kis, *Politics in Hungary: For a Democratic Alternative* (Highland Lakes, N.J.: Atlantic Research and Publications, 1989).

2. G.M. Tamás, "The Legacy of Dissent: How Civil Society Has Been Seduced by the Cult of Privacy," *Times Literary Supplement,* 14 May 1993.

3. Jacques Rupnik, "Le totalitarisme vu de l'Est," in Guy Hermet, Pierre Hassner, and Jacques Rupnik, eds., *Totalitarismes* (Paris: Economica, 1984), 43–75.

4. Pierre Hassner, "Les révolutions ne sont plus ce qu'elles étaient," in Jacques Semelin, ed., *Quand les dictatures se fissurent . . . Résistances civiles à l'Est et au Sud* (Paris: Desclée de Brouwer, 1995).

5. Quoted in Flora Lewis, "Civil Society: Its Limits and Needs," *International Herald Tribune,* 30 September 1989. See also Bronisław Geremek, "Civil Society Then and Now," *Journal of Democracy* 3 (April 1992): 3–12.

6. See, for example, Václav Havel, "Paradise Lost," *New York Review of Books,* 9 April 1992.

7. Jerzy Szacki, "Polish Democracy: Dreams and Reality," *Social Research* 58 (Winter 1991): 712.

8. Address of 6 December 1994 to the parliament of the Czech Republic, quoted in Václav Havel, Václav Klaus, and Petr Pithart, "Civil Society After Communism: Rival Visions," *Journal of Democracy* 7 (January 1996): 12–23.

9. *Lidove noviny* (Prague), 7 March 1994, quoted from Jiri Pehe, "Civic Society at Issue in the Czech Republic," *RFE/RL Research Report,* 19 August 1994.

10. Address of 17 November 1994 on the occasion of the anniversary of the Velvet Revolution, quoted in Václav Havel, Václav Klaus, and Petr Pithart, "Civil Society After Communism: Rival Visions," *Journal of Democracy* 7 (January 1996): 12–23.

11. Yuri Shchekochikhin, quoted in Margaret Shapiro, "Corruption Threatens to Spill Russia's Economic Brew," *Washington Post,* from the *International Herald Tribune,* 14 November 1994.

12. Elemer Hankiss, "Our Recent Past: Recent Developments in East Central Europe in the Light of Various Social Ideologies and Schools of Scholarly Thought" (address delivered at the Institut für die Wissenschaften vom Menschen, Vienna, Austria, 1994). See also Chris Hann, "Philosophers' Models on the Carpathian Lowlands," in John A. Hill, ed., *Civil Society: Theory, History, Comparison* (Cambridge, England: Polity Press, 1995), 158–83.

13. See Lena Kolarska-Bobińska, *Aspirations, Values, and Interests: Poland, 1989–1994* (Warsaw: IFiS Publishers, 1994); Winicjusz Narojek, *The Socialist "Welfare State"* (Warsaw: PWN, 1991); B. Paqueteau, "La société contre elle-même: Choses vues en Roumanie," *Commentaire* 59 (Autumn 1992): 621–28; and Mira Marody, ed., *What Has Remained from Those Years: Polish Society on the Threshold of Systemic Change* (London: Aneks, 1991).

5

UNDERSTANDING POSTCOMMUNIST TRANSITIONS

Leszek Balcerowicz

Leszek Balcerowicz, president of the National Bank of Poland and professor at the Warsaw School of Economics, was Poland's deputy prime minister and minister of finance in 1989–91 and 1997–2000, and chairman of the Center for Social and Economic Research in Warsaw in 1992–2000. The principal architect of the stabilization and postcommunist transformation of the Polish economy, he has published extensively on economic questions both in Poland and abroad. He has received numerous honorary doctorates and awards, including the Ludwig Erhard Prize, the Transatlantic Leadership Award, and the Friedrich August von Hayek Prize. This essay originally appeared in the October 1994 issue of the Journal of Democracy.

The specific nature of the transition from communism in Central and Eastern Europe becomes clear when we compare it with other major shifts from one stable state of society to another potentially stable state. Other types of transition include: 1) *classical transition,* meaning the extension of democracy in advanced capitalist countries between 1860 and 1920; 2) *neoclassical transition,* referring to democratizations in basically capitalist countries after the Second World War (West Germany, Italy, and Japan in the 1940s; Spain and Portugal in the 1970s; some Latin American countries in the 1970s and 1980s; South Korea and Taiwan in the 1980s); 3) *market-oriented reform* in noncommunist countries (West Germany and other Western countries after the Second World War; South Korea and Taiwan in the early 1960s; Chile in the 1970s; Turkey and Mexico in the 1980s; Argentina in the 1990s); and 4) *Asian postcommunist transition* (China since the late 1970s and Vietnam since the late 1980s). There is, of course, much internal variety, especially within the first two categories. We will, however, disregard it here in order to focus on the fundamental differences *between* rather than *within* the respective types of transitions.

A number of features distinguish the postcommunist transition in Central and Eastern Europe:

First, the scope of change is exceptionally large. Both political and economic systems are affected, and changes in these systems in turn interact with changes in the social structure. All these internal changes in the respective countries came about due to and in the framework of the dissolution of the Soviet Empire. Most of the post-Soviet countries faced the additional transition problems of defining their territorial as well as social and cultural boundaries, and of building their institutional machineries.[1]

In all other cases of radical transition, there was either a focus on the political system while the economic system remained basically unchanged (as in classical and neoclassical transitions), or a focus on the economy while the political regime (usually nondemocratic) was unaffected. The unprecedented scope of changes in Eastern and Central Europe means, among other things, an extreme information overload for top decision makers. Errors and delays are hardly surprising, especially since decision makers must work with a public administration largely inherited from the old regime. Massive administrative turnover proved possible only in the former East Germany after reunification, an option obviously not open to other postcommunist countries.

Second, although the changes in the political and economic systems *started* at about the same time, it is misleading to speak of "simultaneous transitions" in postcommunist Europe. It takes more time to privatize the bulk of the state-dominated economy than to organize free elections and at least some rudiments of political parties. Given the largely simultaneous beginnings of the political and economic transitions, this asymmetry in speed *produces a historically new sequence:* mass democracy (or at least political pluralism, that is, some degree of legal political competition) first, and market capitalism later.[2]

Third, this sequence implies that market-oriented reforms, which must be exceptionally comprehensive because of the socialist economic legacy, have to be introduced under democratic, or at least pluralistic, political arrangements. Most other market-oriented reforms were introduced under nondemocratic regimes (the third and fourth types of transition). Within this group, it is hard to find any case of economic transition that both approached the comprehensiveness of what occurred in postcommunist Europe and was carried out under a democratic regime. Indeed, all the radical economic reforms elsewhere were introduced under clearly autocratic and rather oppressive regimes (Chile in the 1970s, China since the final years of that decade).[3] There were some economic reforms carried out under democracy in the 1980s, including privatization programs in certain developed Western countries and stabilizations and structural adjustments in developing economies. Problems attributable to the democratic political environment did arise during these transitions, perhaps warning of similar hazards lurking in the much more comprehensive and complicated transitions of Eastern and Central Europe.

These complications are, of course, far from sufficient argument for falling back on authoritarian solutions. This is so not only because of democracy's intrinsic importance to human dignity but also because authoritarian regimes do not invariably promote rapid economic development (as they have done in South Korea and Taiwan); many (such as Juan Peron's regime in Argentina) have disastrous effects on the economy.

A fourth exceptional feature of East Central European economic and political transitions is their lack of violence. Other parts of the old communist-dominated East—in particular Yugoslavia, the Caucasus, and areas of what used to be Soviet Central Asia—have seen terrible bloodshed over the last few years even as Eastern and Central Europe have undergone a peaceful revolution, with massive changes in political and economic institutions resulting from negotiations between the outgoing communist elite and the leaders of the opposition. (The only case of violent transition in Eastern or Central Europe took place in Romania, where there were no negotiations prior to the transfer of power.) Negotiations would never have taken place (or, had they taken place, never would have borne fruit) had not the Soviet threat been gradually eliminated by Gorbachev's *glasnost'* and *perestroika*. These negotiated changes were not based on any explicit political pact and contained a large element of surprise for all the main actors. However, they would not have come about if the members of the old elite had felt physically threatened or even if they had not believed that they would be free to seek favorable positions in whatever new system would emerge. In this sense one can speak of a tacit political pact.

The nonviolent nature of the transition in East Central Europe, related to such tacit political pacts, has had important implications for other aspects of the transition. First, the old ruling elites are intact and stand ready to profit electorally from the dissatisfaction of a part of the population—a dissatisfaction which, paradoxically, is likely to be greater in proportion to the economic desolation that these old elites wrought while in power. Second, the newly emerging capitalist class is likely to include many of the former elites, a circumstance that tends to reduce the legitimacy of the whole capitalist transition and may fuel attacks by one part of the former opposition against the part currently in office. Such conflicts within the former opposition are good news for the forces of the old regime.

Differences among Transitions

Any consideration of the political transition in East Central Europe should keep in mind that democracy means the institutionalized practice of peacefully choosing rulers through regular, free, and fair elections based on the principle of one person, one vote. This presupposes freedom of speech and association, which may also exist, however, under certain nondemocratic regimes (for example, constitutional monarchies). In large societies, democracy cannot be direct, but has to be representative. Depending on what proportion of the adult population has the franchise, we can speak of *limited democracy,* in which only a fraction of the populace has the vote, or of *mass democracy,* in which practically all adults can vote. Stable and lasting mass democracy requires mass political parties.

We can isolate a number of peculiarities of the political transition in East Central Europe by comparing it with the classical model of democratic transition. East Central Europe's experience of a sudden shift from a clearly nondemocratic regime to a mass democracy was quite distinct from the classical pattern of democratization, which features a gradual extension of suffrage under limited democracy until mass democracy becomes the new reality. Therefore, these two democratizations differed in both point of departure and speed. The classical model of gradually widening suffrage allowed more time for learning democratic practices than is possible when a sudden shift to mass democracy occurs. The new democracies of East Central Europe are thus likely to require more learning-by-doing than the earlier mass democracies of the West.[4]

This difference may be bolstered by the absence of competitive party systems prior to the postcommunist democratization; the classical model involved the mobilization of previously established working-class organizations into electoral competition with other parties. The exclusive beneficiaries of the gradual extension of suffrage in the West were the subordinate classes, especially the workers; thus they were likely to feel a strong attachment to the democratic system.[5] This may be less true of the postcommunist working classes, who share the suddenly gained mass democracy with all other groups. In postcommunist countries, it is the intellectuals (whose standing in society is much higher than it was in the West a century ago) who are most likely to esteem democracy. The intelligentsia, on average, benefits more than other groups from political opening, which means newfound access to information, foreign travel, and the like.

Two other differences are also of great importance. The classical model of democratization harks back to a time when the idea of using national budgets as engines of economic redistribution was fresh; there was much scope for the inauguration of social programs whose beneficiaries could be enlisted as friends of democracy.[6] The situation today in postcommunist lands is very different. They have inherited an extensive and increasingly inefficient "socialist welfare state" characterized by high ratios of budgetary expenditure to GDP. Successful market-oriented reform, moreover, far from allowing any further increases in budgetary redistribution, actually demands the opposite.

A further difference concerns the role of the mass media, or more precisely the interaction of the mass media's role with developments in the economy and society at large. During the era of classical democratization there was a rather liberal press, no broadcast media, and no fundamental change in the economy. The postcommunist transition, combining both political and economic openings begun under difficult economic conditions, came about in the age of powerful broadcast media (especially television). Under communism—especially before *glasnost'*—the tightly controlled media did not report on negative aspects of the system. When political liberalization freed these media, they naturally focused on once-forbidden negative stories, a tendency strengthened by the generally low level of professionalism displayed by journalists trained under communism. As a result, there was a sudden increase in the public's exposure to negative mass-media coverage, and viewers often mistook the increased visibility of undesirable phenomena like crime and poverty for their true growth. This "visibility effect," absent in classical democratizations, was likely to encourage unfavorable assessments of the whole transition and, consequently, to influence electoral outcomes and the subsequent direction or pace of the economic transition.[7]

If we compare the postcommunist with the neoclassical transition, the visibility effect operates in both cases, but its dangers are smaller in the neoclassical case, which typically presupposes an already established capitalist economy. The economy at the start of the neoclassical transition was usually healthier than a postcommunist economy, while the level of preexisting redistribution in the former was usually much lower than in the latter.

A Web of Interactions

Let us now focus on economic and political transition in East Central Europe. In a fairly simple analytical scheme, economic and political transition can be said to depend on: 1) initial economic and sociopolitical conditions; 2) external developments; and 3) government policies. Initial conditions and external developments are beyond the control of a single country undergoing transition. Policies are potentially controllable, although their content and the degree of their controllability depend on sociopolitical and economic realities. We are dealing with complex interactions containing large elements of chance, which should be analyzed in a dynamic framework: Sociopolitical conditions and chance factors (for example, which officials are charged with planning economic reform) determine the initial policies that, together with uncontrollable external developments, shape the first phase of the economic transition. This first phase in turn influences the subsequent course of economic events up to and including the eventual final outcome of economic transition. This transition is also shaped by political developments, which are partly determined by the initial sociopolitical conditions (consider the visibility effect). Finally, economic developments determined in part by earlier policies (which are influenced by sociopolitical factors) may in turn influence future political developments, and so on.

We can sort out this complicated web of dynamic interactions by focusing first on the economic transition, and then on its interactions with political factors. The post-1989 economic reforms in East Central Europe are fundamentally different from any that the region saw in the past because they go beyond socialism, as defined by the overwhelming dominance of the state sector in the economy. East Central European economic transitions are thus basically in tune with economic reform campaigns in the noncommunist world: The general idea everywhere is to have less state control, more private enterprise, and freer markets. Yet there are important differences between postcommunist and other recent economic transitions. They can best be elucidated by pointing out that in the context of market-oriented reform there are three main types or fields of economic policy:

1) *Macroeconomic stabilization* accomplished by means of macroeconomic policy.

2) *Microeconomic liberalization* designed to remove various state-imposed restrictions on economic activity. This involves both general changes in the framework of economic life (that is, the recognition of property rights) and particular reforms, such as ending price controls and rationing.

3) *Fundamental institutional restructuring* aimed at, for instance, the privatization of state enterprises, the reform of the tax system, or even the creation of wholly new institutions such as stock exchanges. Taken together, microeconomic liberalization and institutional restructuring may be said to constitute *systemic transformation.*

East Central European economic reforms are exceptional because of the unprecedented amount of institutional restructuring that the region's countries require if they are to achieve market capitalism. Under communist rule there, capitalism was destroyed and not merely suspended (as in Germany before 1948) or distorted (as in Latin America and India before their respective rounds of economic liberalization). Moreover, East Central Europe's reforms must also feature an exceptional amount of liberalization, as its economies were not only noncapitalist but also nonmarket, exclusively or predominantly coordinated as they were by the command-rationing mechanism of the communist central plan. The required scope of liberalization can be compared to the dismantling of war-economy mechanisms in Western countries after the Second World War. Recent market-oriented reforms in Latin America have been modest by comparison.

In addition to an unusually large scope of necessary systemic change, all cases of reform in East Central Europe show a common potential for rapid implementation of that part of systemic transformation which depends on the quick, spontaneous learning of specific new skills (in marketing and finance, for example). This potential owes much to the high levels of general education that form one of communism's few positive legacies.

There have also been significant variations in initial economic conditions from one East Central European country to another, however. Some socialist economies inherited extreme macroeconomic imbalances in the form of open or repressed inflation. This group included Poland in 1989 and the former Soviet Union and Albania in 1990–91. There was, by contrast, relatively little macroeconomic instability in Czechoslovakia and Hungary. Bulgaria and Romania were in an intermediate position. Countries with extreme macroeconomic imbalances faced the double challenge of stabilizing and changing the economy at the same time. Countries with much less serious stabilization problems still had to tackle the issue of how to maintain and reinforce macroeconomic stability while liberalizing prices and implementing other systemic reforms.

Every East Central European economy had suffered distortions induced by years of import substitution, centralized investment decisions, and dependence on the Soviet economy for exports as well as petroleum imports. These distortions can be expressed by the notion of *pure socialist output,* meaning that part of total output which could be maintained, if at all, only under a socialist economic order and the related existence of a Soviet-orchestrated trading bloc like the Comecon.[8] The proportion of pure socialist output to total output was exceptionally high in Bulgaria, as well as in most non-Russian republics of the former Soviet Union, because of the great dependence of these economies on the Russian economy for exports. Within the former Czechoslovakia, it was much higher in Slovakia than in the Czech Republic. Poland, Bulgaria, and Hungary inherited large foreign debts, while Czechoslovakia and Romania were largely debt-free. Within the former USSR, Russia has taken over a sizeable Soviet debt.

Three Helpful Propositions

Here are three propositions to provide help in understanding both the challenges that postcommunist East Central Europe faces and the relative merits of various economic policy options:

1) *An extreme case of inherited macroeconomic instability calls for the rapid implementation of a tough stabilization program.* Delay will only worsen the macroeconomic situation, and a gradual or mild stabilization program will most likely fail to overcome inflationary inertia and expectations. A large macroeconomic imbalance, containing elements of hyperinflation, may be compared to a fire: It is very dangerous to delay putting it out, or to put it out slowly.

2) *There are important interlinkages and synergies within the package of market-oriented reforms.* Radical price liberalization is needed to eliminate massive shortages; the elimination of shortages is in turn necessary to ensure the more efficient operation of enterprises. Rapid price decontrol (including substantial adjustments of distorted administrative prices, for example, of energy) is also necessary in order to obtain more rational relative prices. Price liberalization, however, has to be linked to comprehensive foreign-trade liberalization so that increased enterprise autonomy is accompanied by an increase in competitive pressure on the newly freed enterprises. Widespread price controls and other forms of detailed state intervention will tempt enterprises to lobby for hidden or open subsidies, which may threaten macroeconomic stability. Thus liberalization aids stabilization, which in turn is conducive to meaningful institutional change. This is the link between stabilization-cum-liberalization on the one hand, and institutional restructuring on the other. Institutional changes including tax reform, social security reform, privatization, and enterprise restructuring are necessary not only in order to improve efficiency but also to bolster macroeconomic stability. There is, therefore, a link between deep institutional restructuring and the longer-term sustainability of the macroeconomic balance.

3) *Different processes of economic reform have different maximum possible speeds.* Stabilization and liberalization policies, for instance, will bear fruit much more rapidly than institutional changes like reform of the tax system or privatization of a large public sector. Decision makers should remain mindful that the third runs on a slower clock than the first two, and should plan accordingly. Reformers face a choice between quickly stabilizing and liberalizing a still-socialist economy or implementing such changes at a slower pace in order to allow time for the institutional dismantling of socialism to "catch up."

Radical liberalization can be expected to spur a rise in the number of private firms that outstrips the ability to keep pace of the inherited tax system (designed to deal with just a handful of large state firms). A rise in tax evasion is thus an unavoidable by-product of sweeping liberalization. (There may be even more tax evasion if liberalization is limited and the tax system is full of various breaks and preferences.) The danger is that increased tax evasion at a time of unavoidably growing budgetary expenditures will reduce the legitimacy of the capitalist transition and the governments and parties supporting it.

The Timing of Reform

Let us now look at economic policy as a variable that may differ along three dimensions: time of launching, phasing, and pace. Time of launching refers to the interval between a political breakthrough and the start of economic reform; phasing describes the relative timing of stabilization, liberalization, and institutional-restructuring policies; pace describes the implementation rate for each of these main components of reform.

By applying criteria drawn from these three dimensions we may identify many theoretical variants of economic policy, but for brevity's sake we will mention just two general types.[9] The first is a radical and comprehensive economic program, in which stabilizing, liberalizing, and restructuring measures are launched at about the same time and implemented at close to the maximum possible speeds. Such programs may be launched very quickly following a political breakthrough or after some delay. The second type consists of nonradical economic programs, defined here as those in which stabilization, liberalization, and restructuring are not launched simultaneously, or are implemented at a slower pace than they might be, or are even interrupted (for example, stabilization in Russia in mid-1992).[10]

Under the economic conditions existing at the time of communism's demise in East Central Europe, radical economic reforms, resolutely pursued, were the best choice for bringing about disinflation, structural change, and the takeoff into economic growth and market capitalism. Empirical analysis tends to confirm this hypothesis, as there is so far no example of highly successful nonradical reform.[11]

Given the naturally slower pace at which institutional restructuring (including privatization) must proceed, even the most energetically implemented transition to a market economy will require two stages. In the first stage, the economy undergoes liberalization and stabilization but remains more "market socialist" than capitalist. In a second stage— assuming that it is successful—the gains of liberalization and stabilization are consolidated, and the transition to market capitalism is completed and institutionalized.

Given the challenging initial conditions and unfavorable external developments (especially the collapse of trade within the Comecon) that faced each country in East Central Europe during the postcommunist transition, each class of reform measures was bound to generate discontent in some section of the populace. Predictably, the intensity of these currents of discontent was directly proportional to the adversity of initial conditions and external developments. For example, the same set of economic policies produced four times more open unemployment in Slovakia than in the Czech Republic in 1992 because "pure socialist output" accounted for a much higher share of the Slovak economy.

In addition to turning disguised unemployment into open unemployment, radical economic reform also increases discontent simply by broadening the scope of general economic freedom. Since only some people can directly take advantage of the new opportunities, others may feel resentment, especially if they view the new winners as undeserving. Rapid shifts will occur in the relative pay and prestige of various occupations and professional groups as markets replace the planned socialist economy. Miners, heavy-industrial workers, and other groups that see themselves as "losers"—even if only in relative terms—are likely to be dissatisfied. There is an unavoidable trade-off, moreover, between opportunity and security. This hard truth may be poorly understood and bitterly disliked, especially by those who experience a much larger increase in insecurity than in perceived opportunities.

Given the same difficult initial and external conditions sketched above, nonradical reform will also produce discontent, though in different ways. If the initial macroeconomic situation is highly unstable, nonradical economic reform will find itself immediately bedeviled by high and growing inflation, which produces its own version of severe economic insecurity. Nonradical reform programs do this by preferring hidden over open unemployment. Hidden unemployment is less psychologically painful to the persons concerned, but it must be financed through fiscal or quasi-fiscal subsidies, which in turn spur inflation.[12] The result is inflation-bred insecurity and disaffection. Moreover, it must be kept in mind that any future attempts at macroeconomic stabilization will flush hidden unemployment out into the open.

Nonradical programs, which typically feature less liberalization and correspondingly more state intervention, also give rise to new economic inequalities, with the "winners" being those who can successfully lobby the government. In practice, this means members of the old communist elite, who are more experienced, better organized, and better connected than others. The inequalities generated by their lobbying are less justified by economic performance than those that stem from radical reform programs, and rankle the "losers" even more. Finally, by channelling entrepreneurial and managerial energies into rent seeking and corruption rather than the search for greater efficiency, nonradical programs that avoid liberalization destroy the prospects for economic development. Anyone willing to take the longer view, then, should realize that the discontents and drawbacks associated with nonradical reform outweigh the problems brought by sustained and radical efforts at comprehensive liberalization, stabilization, and institutional restructuring.

The Period of "Extraordinary Politics"

The key to understanding the interaction between the political and economic dimensions of postcommunist transitions is to realize that any great political breakthrough in a country's history is followed by a period of "extraordinary politics" that soon gives way to "normal politics."

Figure 1 on the following page presents this two-stage model in highly simplified form. The function $r = r(t)$ expresses the level of readiness to accept radical economic measures, starting at the moment immediately

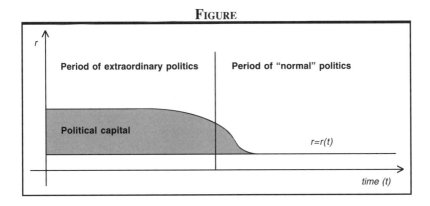

FIGURE

following the epochal political change—in this case, the fall of communism. It is based on the assumption that liberation from foreign domination and domestic political liberalization produce a special state of mass psychology and corresponding political opportunities: the new political structures are fluid and the older political elite is discredited. Both leaders and ordinary citizens feel a stronger-than-normal tendency to think and act in terms of the common good. All of this is reflected in an exceptionally high level of r.

Extraordinary politics, however, quickly gives way to the more mundane politics of contending parties and interest groups (as described, for instance, by Nobel laureate James Buchanan and other theorists of the public-choice school). It is in this second period that certain features of political contention which are common in established democracies become much stronger (parties searching for an agenda and an ideological profile, the ensuing politicization of major issues, and so on). These features superimpose themselves on the developments typical of a new democracy—the visibility effect, the appearance of an inchoate party system, and the like—and then normal politics in the fledgling democracy comes to seem unattractive and levels of r drop sharply.

Variations in sociopolitical characteristics from one country to another can be reflected in the initial level of r, the duration of "extraordinary politics," the downward slope of $r = r(t)$ after this period, the subsequent level of r persisting under "normal" political conditions, and so on.

The brevity of the exceptional period means that a radical economic program, launched as quickly as possible after the breakthrough, has a much greater chance of being accepted than either a delayed radical program or a nonradical alternative that introduces difficult measures (for example, price increases) in piecemeal fashion. Bitter medicine is easier to take in one dose than in a prolonged series of doses.[13]

Each of the clearly radical economic programs in postcommunist East Central Europe was the handiwork of a government representing new political forces. This is true of Poland, the former Czechoslovakia, Bulgaria, Estonia, and Latvia. Yet new political forces did not launch such programs everywhere that they were in control. Lithuania in 1992–93 was radical with regard to privatization but hesitant with regard to stabilization, while Hungary in 1990–94 pursued a "gradualism" that was partly due to the weight of previously accumulated changes and partly deliberate.

By contrast, whenever the political system remained dominated in the first phase of transition by the forces of the past, only nonradical economic options were pursued. The clearest examples are Belarus and Ukraine, and to a lesser extent Romania. In each of the two former cases (as in Russia), the post-Soviet legislature erected formidable barriers to radical economic reform.

Countries that did not take advantage of the period of "extraordinary politics" to launch a radical economic program still face the challenge of making the transition to market capitalism, but now under more difficult political and economic conditions. From the point of view of economic development, the radical strategy is the best option, regardless of when it is deployed. Yet countries that have missed the first period are in danger of going from one kind of nonmarket economy (central planning) to another characterized by pervasive macroeconomic instability, detailed but chaotic state regulation, and related massive rent seeking. This is especially likely if the legislatures in these countries continue to be dominated by industrial and agricultural interest groups even after the second cycle of free elections.

Given the evanescence of "extraordinary politics," time-consuming institutional reforms (for example, privatization, social security reform, health reform, and the like) are likely to meet more resistance than quickly implemented stabilizing and liberalizing measures. One must therefore expect delays in institutional restructuring, for reform of this nature is simply out of sync with the brevity of the "extraordinary" interval.

If a country has been operating under difficult initial and external conditions, it is a mistake to blame social discontent on a particular type of economic program. Attributing widespread dissatisfaction to "shock therapy," for instance, is erroneous because under conditions grave enough to elicit such radical measures, *any* economic policy package will generate discontent. There is no *a priori* reason to expect that the dissatisfaction attendant upon radical reforms will be greater than that attendant upon nonradical ones.

Indeed, the reverse could well be the case. Even cursory examination of the East Central European experience shows no clear link between the intensity of displays of social discontent (strikes, demonstrations, and so on) and the type of economic program pursued. Poland, Bulgaria, and Romania have seen the worst displays of discontent, yet the former two countries pressed radical reforms while Romania followed a stop-and-go gradualism. Hungary, Czechoslovakia (and later the Czech Republic and Slovakia), Estonia, and Latvia have had few manifestations of discontent. Hungary never adopted a radical economic program, while all the others did.

The Importance of Initial Conditions

The foregoing suggests that one should seek to explain differences in social discontent and political instability from one country to another by first of all examining the conditions present as the transition got underway. A paucity of open unemployment during the transition is a great help, as officials in the Czech Republic can testify. The intensity of labor unrest seems to depend on the presence of militant workers like the miners of Poland and Romania, as well as on the existence of influential trade unions that played a large role in toppling communism only to turn increasingly populist (Solidarity in Poland, Podkrepa in Bulgaria).

The character of the country's political class is also relevant. Demagogues presumably exist everywhere, but clearly they are not equally mobilized and vocal in all countries. The relative extent of their presence, along with the intensity of the visibility effect, may have a serious impact upon popular attitudes and behavior in different countries during the economic transition.

If it is erroneous to blame unrest on this or that type of economic reform, it is equally mistaken to attribute the electoral defeats of the political forces that ruled during the first stage of postcommunist transition to one sort of economic program. Such defeats happened in 1993 in Poland—a radical reformer—but also in Lithuania, Russia, and Hungary, where radical reform never came close to being adopted. Thus causes other than the type of economic program must underlie these outcomes. Among these causes are phenomena that are present everywhere but operate with varying force depending on circumstances.

The visibility effect is one such phenomenon; it strengthens the usual tendency of a part of the electorate to blame problems on whatever government is in power. In reality, the magnitude of these problems as well as the prospects for quickly solving them depended on a given postcommunist country's initial situation, and this varied greatly across the region. Another important variable is the type and composition of the political class, especially the relative importance of its populist component. Also significant is the extent to which opposition to the government's economic policy becomes linked to the popular position on certain emotional issues such as the loss of empire in Russia, the status of the Hungarian minority in Romania, or the role of the Catholic Church in Poland.

Finally, the preelection strategies adopted by the various political forces matter as well. For example, in Poland in 1993, the ruling parties of the moment committed the grave mistake of going through the elections separately even as their chief rivals, the ex-communists, were agreeing to run together under the banner of a single coalition. With help from a new electoral law, the ex-communists obtained about 21 percent of the vote and 33 percent of the seats in Parliament, making them Poland's single largest political force.[14]

Even if for some of the aforementioned reasons the political forces that launched radical economic reform suffer an electoral defeat, the economy is likely to be in much better shape than would have been the case had other approaches been adopted. Furthermore, radical reform tends to leave behind certain legacies—currency convertibility, an independent central bank, a large private sector—that even ostensible opponents are likely to respect.

From our analysis, a clear conclusion emerges. Given the typical initial conditions of a socialist economy, a country will be better off politically and economically in the medium-to-long run if it adopts a radical and comprehensive economic reform program as quickly as possible after the political transition, implements as much of this program as possible during the brief period of extraordinary politics, and then stays the course of reform by implementing far-reaching institutional changes.

NOTES

I am grateful to Christopher Giessing for research assistance and to Marek Jaskiewicz and Edmund Wnuk-Lipinski for useful comments. This essay was completed while I was a visiting fellow at the Institute for Human Sciences in Vienna, where Kelly Musick assisted me in editing the final version.

1. See Claus Offe, "Capitalism by Democratic Design? Democratic Theory Facing the Triple Transition in East Central Europe," *Social Research* 58 (Winter 1991): 865–902; and Philippe C. Schmitter, "Dangers and Dilemmas of Democracy," *Journal of Democracy* 5 (April 1994): 57–74.

2. Valerie Bunce and Maria Csanadi, "Uncertainty in the Transition: Post-Communism in Hungary," *East European Politics and Societies* 7 (1993): 240–75.

3. The case that comes relatively close to a comprehensive economic reform conducted under democracy is Argentina since 1989. Even there, however, the amount of needed economic change was much less than in the postsocialist economies, as capitalism in East Central Europe was destroyed, not merely distorted as in Argentina and other Latin American countries.

4. An exception to this hypothesis may be those countries that have strong traditions of well-functioning democracy dating back to before the Second World War. In East Central Europe, only the Czech Republic meets this condition.

5. This is pointed out by Dietrich Rueschemeyer, Evelyne Huber Stephens, and John D. Stephens in their *Capitalist Development and Democracy* (Chicago: University of Chicago Press, 1992).

6. For a summary article investigating to what extent the growth of public expenditures has been related to the expansion of suffrage and to what extent to other factors, see Dennis C. Mueller, "The Growth of Government," *IMF Staff Papers*, March 1987, 115–49.

7. The visibility effect may be conceived in economic terms as a mechanism producing false utility information and thus pointing to wrong decisions. False utility information is still supplied by most economists in postsocialist countries, as official economics was heavily politicized. Some Western experts and politicians also unwittingly engage in the provision of false utility information.

8. The economic structure in East Central European countries was, on average, worse than that in China with respect to the difficulty and costs of economic transition. The former contained a very high share of distorted socialist industry, while the Chinese economy had a high share of technologically simple and, therefore, easily privatized agriculture. Besides, the Chinese economy at the start of the reforms in the late 1970s displayed relatively little macroeconomic instability.

9. For a more comprehensive typology of economic policy options in the transition economies, see Stanisław Gomułka, "Economic and Political Constraints During Transition," *Europe-Asia Studies* 46 (1994): 89–106.

10. But the actual rate of implementation may differ between two countries because of differences in their starting conditions. For example, substantial previous price liberalization or an initial macroeconomic balance may require only limited further price decontrol or macroeconomic tightening. This was the case in Hungary.

11. See, for example, Leszek Balcerowicz and Alan Gelb, "Macropolicies in Transition to a Market Economy: A Three-Year Perspective," *Annual Bank Conference on Development Economics* (Washington, D.C.: World Bank, 1994); Andrew Berg, "Does Macroeconomic Reform Cause Structural Adjustment? Lessons from Poland" (unpubl. ms., International Monetary Fund, Washington, D.C., 1993); and Jeffrey D. Sachs and Wing Thye Woo, "Structural Factors in the Economic Reforms of China, Eastern Europe, and the Former Soviet Union," *Economic Policy* 18 (April 1994): 101–45.

12. Another way to finance increased hidden unemployment is to accept reduced average productivity of labor, but this means a corresponding reduction in average real wages, and falling wages cut buying power as surely as do rising prices.

13. From the point of view of the probability of acceptance of difficult economic measures, the "political capital" existing during the period of "extraordinary politics" may be regarded as a counterpart to the use of force in the authoritarian regimes that implemented radical economic programs. Given the relatively short duration of this period, however, some of these regimes (that is, procapitalist autocracies) may have a comparative advantage in sustaining and completing such reforms.

14. On Poland's September 1993 elections, see the essays by Aleksander Smolar and Marcin Król gathered under the title "A Communist Comeback?" in *Journal of Democracy* 5 (January 1994): 70–95.

6

ESTONIA'S SUCCESS STORY

Mart Laar

Mart Laar, *Estonia's prime minister, serves as chairman of the Pro Patria Union party and chairman of the board of the Jaan Tönisson Institute in Tallinn. He also served as prime minister from 1992–94, and is the founder of the Estonian Christian Democratic Union. This essay is based on remarks he gave at the Fifth World Conference of the National Endowment for Democracy in Washington, D.C., on 2 May 1995.*

No one ever said that making the transition from communist totalitarianism to democracy would be easy. No guidelines were marked out; no textbooks were available. For countries like Estonia that made the change, it was truly a leap into the unknown and untried. Even though we landed on solid ground, we had no guarantee of success, while the costs we faced were certain.

A mere four years ago, coming out from under a half-century of Russian occupation, Estonia was a land in ruins. Today, it is usually classed with Slovenia and the Czech Republic as having gone the farthest down the road away from socialist authoritarianism and toward democracy and a market-based economy. When we regained our independence, 92 percent of our trade was with Russia. Our industry and agriculture were a shambles, quite unable to compete on the world market. Inflation was running at the rate of 1,000 percent a year, and in 1992 alone our GDP fell by 30 percent. Basic goods like bread, milk, and fuel were strictly rationed. On top of all that, we faced challenges to our political stability from extremists of the right and left, while rising tensions between the native population and a largely Russian community (that immigrated during the period of Soviet occupation) seemed for a time as if they might spill over into open conflict.

Today, all these problems are receding so rapidly that our troubles of just a few years ago seem like distant memories. It is hard to believe that they ever happened. Estonia has changed beyond recognition. We have reoriented our economy, going from dependence on the East to trade with the West. Inflation has dropped, and exports are increasing at a clip of 60 percent per year. Our per-capita level of foreign investment is higher than that of Latvia, Lithuania, Russia, Belarus, Ukraine, Romania, and Bulgaria combined. Our state budget is balanced, and the official unemployment rate is a minuscule 2 percent. The International Monetary Fund expects our economy to show a 6 percent rate of GDP growth in 1995.

Things have also changed greatly for the better on the political front. Extremists from both ends of the spectrum have been sidelined, and today democracy really is "the only game in town." Ethnic tensions have greatly decreased, and a large majority of those residents who are not ethnically Estonian now supports Estonia's independence. We deserve the moniker that *Newsweek* magazine gave us in one of its headlines: "The Little Country That Could."

The Primacy of Politics

How did Estonia manage to accomplish all this? First, we tried to learn from the experiences of other countries that had undergone a similar transition. Two main lessons emerged. One was to take care of politics first, and then to proceed with economic reform. The other is summed up by the well-known advertising slogan: "Just do it." In other words, be decisive about adopting reforms, and stick with them despite the short-term pain they bring. Politics has to be dealt with first, because to initiate and sustain radical reforms, there must first be a legitimately formed consensus for change. This is possible only through democracy, using regular, accountable institutional structures and free and fair elections.

The first item on the political agenda was to devise a new constitution. The process was an open one. In September 1991, a 60-member Constitutional Assembly was chosen to do the work of drafting. The Assembly determined that the best route to stability lay in a shift away from presidentialism and toward a parliamentary form of government. The largely ceremonial president is directly elected, but in the event that no candidate gains a majority, the 101-member parliament chooses between the top two finishers. The president also nominates the premier, but a cabinet cannot form without majority support in parliament. The new election law laid down a 5 percent threshold for representation in parliament, which has helped to promote a workable two-party system.

The constitution was ratified by popular vote in June 1992, and in September of that year Estonia held its first free and democratic elections since the beginning of the Second World War. Parties supporting radical reform did well in this balloting, but soon learned that profound and sweeping changes are easier to talk about than to enact. Pondering the experiences of our neighbors in Central and Eastern Europe, we saw that the only way to achieve real change was quickly, and with a definite plan. To hesitate was to be lost. We knew that any talk of a "third way" between capitalism and socialism was bound to be idle: "The 'third way,'" as Czech prime minister Václav Klaus has said, "is the quickest way to the Third World." Speed was crucial because, as experience has shown, the period of "extraordinary politics" following the downfall of dictatorship can last only a short while. Once that window of opportunity closes, widespread popular support for rapid, radical change begins to erode, and the "ordinary politics" of who gets what, when, and how reasserts its dominance. Reformers who miss this window may have to wait a long time for another chance.

The first step in radical economic reform was the introduction of a national currency—the kroon—pegged to the deutschmark at a fixed exchange rate of 8 to 1. A tight monetary policy (designed to prevent inflation) was combined with a dramatic liberalization of trade and economic life in general. The new government, for example, abolished *all* tariffs at a single stroke.

In order to make liberalization meaningful, we needed to establish the institutions that are vital to the rule of law. Parliament quickly passed a bill reforming the court system and then enacted a new civil code and trade code. The guiding idea behind these codes was to reduce the role of the state so that private enterprise and civil society could flourish free of the stifling detritus left behind by a command economy and "socialist legality."

Hearts and Minds

The most basic and vital change of all, however, had to take place in the hearts and minds of Estonia's people. Without a major readjustment of attitudes, the postcommunist predicament would become a trap, and the nation would never move forward to become a "normal" country with free government and free markets under law. In the era of Soviet-imposed socialism, most people withdrew into a kind of private quietism; associations seldom extended beyond small circles of relatives and close friends, and the public realm was dominated by the communist party-state and its enforced conformities. People were not used to thinking for themselves, taking the initiative, or assuming risks. Many had to be shaken out of the illusion—common in postcommunist countries— that somehow, somebody else was going to come along and solve their problems for them. It was necessary to energize people, to get them moving, to force them to make decisions and take responsibility for themselves.

The project of paring back the overgrown state and getting people to step up to greater responsibility entailed the shifting of various public functions from the centralized state apparatus to local governments. It also entailed the fostering of nongovernmental organizations, independent print and electronic media, local cultural activities, and national-minority institutions such as schools, churches, and cultural groups. Ready to help those who showed a concrete readiness to help themselves, the government in many cases assisted in financing such efforts.

Between 1992 and 1994, bankruptcy cut a huge swath through the ranks of the big, old-fashioned Soviet military factories that had once employed so many. About 25 to 30 percent of Estonians found themselves jobless at some point during this period. We decided that the best way to use our scarce resources was not to make high unemployment payments to people who had lost their jobs, but rather to spend the money on retraining those interested in learning new skills. Many of the unemployed decided to take things into their own hands by establishing small independent enterprises. To help them, we set up a special fund to underwrite long-term small-business loans at modest rates. The private sector boomed, with the number of private businesses in the country going from 2,000 in 1992 to 70,000 just two years later. Many new jobs were created; long-term mass unemployment was averted. By the close of 1994, unemployment was a mere 2 percent.

With the intention of supporting the free and productive activity of our people, we introduced a proportional, flat-rate personal-income tax in 1993. As Estonians saw that hard work was going to be rewarded rather than punished by confiscatory taxation, their attitude really began to look up.

The success that we have achieved did not come without difficulty. Reforms of the magnitude and intensity that I have been describing are never easy. In the year or two immediately after independence, living standards dropped rapidly. Only a strong sense of patriotism and shared hardship helped Estonians to make it through this time of trial without strikes or other major conflicts. Predictably, there were strong pressures to slow down or soften reform. To resist them, and to stay on the challenging path that we had chosen, the parliamentary consensus for reform had to remain broad and solid. Gauging the difficulty of such a feat might be easier if one imagines a government elsewhere in Europe completely abolishing farm subsidies, almost completely eliminating unemployment insurance, and at the same time allowing the once-subsidized price of gasoline to rise to world levels (meaning, in this case, an increase of 1,000 percent).

This is certainly shock therapy, with the early emphasis on shock. Yet the therapy worked, even if it took a bit longer to show its effects. After falling living standards bottomed out in 1992–93, they began to rise again in 1994 and even more in 1995. Today, Estonians enjoy a clearly higher standard of living than do the people of nearby Lithuania, where the option was for "soft" economic reform. Indeed, recent polling done across Central and Eastern Europe by the Gallup organization shows that Estonia ranks first in the proportion of the population that believes it is living better now than it did under socialism.

Overcoming Electoral Setbacks

Surprising as it may seem in light of the foregoing, the free and democratic election held this past March saw Estonia's reform government toppled from power as a new left-of-center coalition gained a majority of seats in parliament. The rise of this coalition, whose core is a party run by members of the old *nomenklatura* and other ex-communists, closely parallels what has happened in other countries of postcommunist Central and Eastern Europe.

Has reform, and perhaps even democracy itself, been decisively repudiated in the region? I do not think so. The pace of reform can be slowed somewhat, but cannot be stopped. Any return to the communist system is now out of the question. More than 60 percent of Estonia's GDP is produced by the private sector; the new constitution, the rule of law, and free institutions are all secure. There is really no way back. Its populist campaign rhetoric notwithstanding, the new government has mostly stuck with the reform policies laid down by its predecessor.

This raises the question of why, in Estonia and elsewhere, reform governments lost at the polls. First, we must remember that the peaceful alternation of governments is itself an important sign of a healthy democracy. For decades, people in Central and Eastern Europe had no say in how they were ruled. If reform, necessary though it may be, begins to pinch, it is understandable that voters in such a region would exercise their right to "throw the rascals out." Then, too, part of the legacy that communism left behind is a distrust of government as such. In the early 1990s, the countries of Central and Eastern Europe had a mix of right-wing, left-wing, and centrist governments. Some aggressively pursued radical reform; others did not. Yet virtually all these governments were quite unpopular.

Turning from attitudinal to more objective reasons for these electoral outcomes, we might note first the surprising resourcefulness and resiliency that the ex-communists have displayed. Many of them found clever ways to retain a grip on power and resources. In countries where they were not clearly and publicly condemned, former communists often found the political-comeback trail a fairly easy hike. As of this writing, the Czech Republic—which adopted the region's most radical and controversial anticommunist laws—is the only country in Central and Eastern Europe whose prime minister does not have a communist background.

Second, let us not underestimate the role that the reform parties' own mistakes played in their defeat. The democratic parties in Eastern and

Central Europe are young institutions. They have little in the way of traditional support bases, and are prone to splinter easily. The resurgent ex-communists would have had a much tougher time everywhere had reform parties been able to meet them with something resembling a united front. In Poland, for example, all the pro-reform parties combined garnered more than 50 percent of the total vote in the 1993 elections, yet got only 15 percent of the parliamentary seats. The reformers disarmed themselves by fragmenting into too many parties. Something similar happened in Estonia in 1995.

> *The underlying tide in Central and Eastern Europe is clearly pulling in the direction of democracy and the market.*

There is no point in trying to assign blame for these errors. Democracy takes time—time and tradition. Whatever eddies may appear on the turbulent surface of events, the underlying tide in Central and Eastern Europe is clearly pulling in the direction of democracy and the market. Indeed, the ex-communists' turn at the top of the parliamentary seesaw may soon be over. Lithuania was the first country in the region to witness an electoral comeback by a renamed communist party, and if the results of its 1994 local elections are any guide, it may be the first to vote the communists back out again. For now, the most critical concern for the countries of this region is preserving positive international conditions for their own normal development. Concretely, this means that Central and East European countries that successfully continue reforms should be able to receive full membership in NATO and the European Union. This is the only effective guarantee against negative developments in the region.

If favorable trends continue, with democrats in Central and Eastern Europe pressing through thick and thin for economic reforms and the consolidation of democracy, and with Western democracies opening doors for them, the region's proreform parties may be set to stage a comeback of their own.

7

THE POSTCOMMUNIST WARS

Charles H. Fairbanks, Jr.

Charles H. Fairbanks, Jr. is director of the Central Asia–Caucasus Institute and research professor of international relations at the Paul H. Nitze School of Advanced International Studies of Johns Hopkins University. This essay was first presented at a conference on civil-military relations co-sponsored by the International Forum for Democratic Studies and the George C. Marshall European Center for Security Studies in Washington, D.C., in March 1995.

We are living through what may be the twilight of an era, several centuries long, during which the use of force became ever more closely associated with the state. There are probably no symbols more strongly tied to the state than the flag and the military uniform, both of which date back only to the late seventeenth century. Everywhere that modern nation-states have arisen, one of their key tasks has been to restrict the scope of private fighting and to make themselves the sole legitimate wielders of force within their respective borders.

In much of the postcommunist world today, however, one encounters a reality that challenges all of our standard assumptions about the relations between armed forces and civilian governments. This essay will focus on the nature and role of armed forces in the new states and largely unrecognized ministates that have formed since 1991 on the territory of what used to be the Soviet Union and Yugoslavia. I will note only in passing the case of Russia; for present purposes, it shows great continuity with the state identity of the old Soviet Union. I will have much to say, however, about the 11 breakaway ministates that have arisen (and sometimes vanished again) since the dissolution of the Yugoslav and Soviet federations: Srpska Krajina in Croatia; Republika Srpska and Croat-ruled Herzeg-Bosna in Bosnia; Kosovo (which has rival ethnic-Serb and ethnic-Albanian governments, only the former of which has an army) in Serbia; the Transdniester Republic in Moldova; Abkhazia, the Adzhar Republic, and South Ossetia in Georgia; Chechnya in Russia; Nagorno-Karabakh in Azerbaijan; and Gorno-Badakhshan in Tajikistan.

Widely differing processes have governed the evolution of armies in the various states that emerged after the collapse of communism. The old Yugoslav National Army (JNA), for example, rested on a delicate ethnic equilibrium maintained by quotas; it disintegrated along with the Yugoslav Federal Republic in the winter and spring of 1990–91. Thus all the new nations emerging from Yugoslavia had to construct new armies. The Soviet army, on the other hand, had an officer corps recruited primarily from the three Slavic nationalities (Great Russians, White Russians, and Ukrainians). Russia, Belarus, and Ukraine all inherited organized units from the old army that had been stationed inside their respective borders at the time of independence. The other post-Soviet states had to devise new armies. Most of these non-Slavic nations had no indigenous officer cadres, since Soviet citizens who were not Slavs generally did not follow military careers. The professional identity of the Soviet officer corps, moreover, was strongly infused with Russian nationalism, and such non-Slavs as did make their way into its ranks tended to be assimilated to that ethos.

Of the inherited Belarusian and Ukrainian armies, little need be said; what is true of the Russian army broadly applies to them as well. Like their Russian counterpart, they are subject to considerable civilian control, though civilian supremacy was stronger still in Soviet days. They suffer even more from inadequate funds than the Russian army does, because of their countries' slower-reforming economies. As in Russia, military life is riddled with corruption, most of it having to do with illegal trafficking in arms, supplies, and equipment from military stockpiles. Finally, both Ukraine and Belarus, like Russia, display a growing tendency to develop new military formations identified with particular officials or agencies of government.

Two differences between the Russian army and its "inherited" counterparts are worth mentioning. First, most of Ukraine's and Belarus's officers still identify with Russia—indeed, many are Great Russians remaining with former Soviet units that became Ukrainian or Belarusian by virtue of their geographical posting at the time of the USSR's collapse. In the event of conflict with Russia, the loyalty of these officers would be in question. The second difference somewhat offsets the first: Belarus and Ukraine do not toil under Russia's burden of wondering whether to play an imperial role in the "near abroad," and have thus been spared the border adventures, politicization, and factionalization that plague the Russian army.

The remaining recognized states of the former Soviet Union and Yugoslavia, as well as all the unrecognized ministates, have had to improvise military forces quickly in a dangerous environment, usually without trained officer cadres or adequate funds. In the non-Serb states of former Yugoslavia, the Baltic states, Moldova, and the Caucasian republics, the organization of informal armed forces preceded independence, going forward against the will of Moscow or Belgrade and often of local authorities as well.

The ministates had to create armed forces even more quickly in order to fight wars of independence. Indeed, in Herzeg-Bosna, Srpska Krajina, Republika Srpska, and Chechnya, the armed force created the state. In all these areas, trained enlisted manpower and Soviet or Yugoslav military bases, equipment, and unit structures were ceded to or seized by the new authorities, although crime, general chaos, and Yugoslav or Russian interference usually prevented new units from being built directly on the foundation of old Soviet or Yugoslav units. In Georgia, for instance, the looting of military bases was so common that one sees in the countryside windmills made from aircraft propellers and pigsties made from the pontoon sections of Soviet bridging equipment.

Armenia, Nagorno-Karabakh, Serbia-Montenegro, and Croatia are special cases. Armenia and Nagorno-Karabakh (the mountainous Armenian-majority enclave in Azerbaijan) had high national morale, felt an imminent threat from the Azeris, deployed large numbers of officers with experience in the old Soviet army, and enjoyed substantial Russian help (including generals sent as military advisors). Yet even though Armenia and Nagorno-Karabakh have been able to field forces comparable in efficiency to the Soviet army, there are "armed groups" in Nagorno-Karabakh that the government has attempted to disarm, and the victories over Azerbaijan have been followed by massive looting and burning of villages.

Serbia-Montenegro started out ahead in the army-building game because more than three-fourths of the officers in the ground forces of the JNA were ethnic Serbs, and Belgrade managed to get control of most of the JNA's modern equipment as Yugoslavia broke up. With this edge in expertise and materiel, Serbia-Montenegro has created an efficient, powerful army of the familiar modern type. Croatia's swift rout of the Krajina Serbs in August 1995 demonstrates that Croatia has rebuilt a modern army in the face of far greater difficulties. Reasonably modern and well-organized forces are also being slowly constructed in the Baltic states and Slovenia. Elsewhere, however, things are fundamentally different.

Militiamen, *Condottieri,* and Brigands

When we speak of an army or military forces, we usually mean a group or groups of armed men, raised, trained, and commanded by the state, with a fixed organization and terms of service. Such armed forces normally have disciplinary rules and a clear chain of command. At least some of the commissioned and noncommissioned officers, moreover, are highly trained career soldiers. Although there may be multiple services, as well as police, security, border-patrol, or "paramilitary" forces, it is understood that the government controls all the large-scale "means of coercion." Hunters, target shooters, and criminals operating alone or in groups may legally or illegally possess firearms, but all are sharply distinguished from official forces and are normally much weaker.

The new states that I am discussing are full of armed men, some with weapons as large and sophisticated as tanks and armored personnel carriers, but many of these men do not belong to modern armies. They are not regular soldiers, but irregulars or militiamen. Their characteristic type of organization is not the modern military formation structured by impersonal commitment to the state and the chain of command, but rather a loosely bound group—often with a charismatic personality at the center—that one joins or leaves spontaneously.

The only place where I have seen this summed up in print is the Helsinki Watch *Report on the War in Abkhazia,* which notes:

> These fighters are not real soldiers in the professional sense. Typically, they serve in loose units out of personal loyalty, or for booty, or revenge on specific individuals, or a desperate hope of protecting or regaining their territory. These are, significantly, armed formations without noncommissioned officers, the disciplinary backbone of professional armies. There are no sergeants in these ranks, no one to insist on discipline among the ordinary soldiers even of a strictly military, prudential nature—to sandbag positions, dig trenches, safeguard bivouacs. . . . Actual aiming of artillery, mortars and rockets in a standard military manner is minimal because neither side is known to have employed forward spotters or fire control systems—a major factor in the extraordinary indiscriminateness of this and similar wars in the former Soviet republics.
>
> The result is a "disordered warfare" . . . high technology coupled with improvisation, weapons of great firepower which yet lack adequate control mechanisms from both the military and humanitarian points of view.[1]

Wandering through their camps and battlefields, you see that these formations, even if they are units of nominal "regular" armies, are either ignorant of or have abandoned the technical skills and routines that modern armies ordinarily employ. High-technology weapons, for instance, are used in ways that would astonish any professional military man. Because there are usually no forward observers and no fire control, artillery is used either for direct bombardment, in the eighteenth-century manner, or for terror against civilians. Rockets and jet aircraft are used in the same way.

Many of these new states defy the standard categories of civil-military relations that one finds in Western books and journals. The simple tandem of "the soldier and the state," to borrow a phrase from Samuel P. Huntington, is replaced by a spectrum including nongovernmental irregular formations, nongovernmental formations with official patrons, and armed formations that move in and out of the government's ambit like Dzhaba Ioseliani's Mkhedrioni ("Horsemen") in Georgia. Finally, there are nominally official forces, like Surat Huseinov's 709th Brigade in Azerbaijan or Davit Zeikidze's police force in Georgia, that actually follow a party or warlord rather than the government.

Even forces that have inherited the standard organization of modern militaries tend to sink toward the level of the militias. This was apparent in the Western press accounts of the Chechen War. I witnessed the phenomenon firsthand in Bosnia, where I observed the routines of ethnic-Serb, ethnic-Croat, and Bosnian Government forces. They were all rather similar. The higher Serb commanders are all professionals from the JNA, and have the bearing of veteran, highly trained officers. Nevertheless, even their units did not dig latrines outside their living areas and did not mark mine fields or mineswept areas—both omissions that would make a conscientious military man blanch. Against regular armies, as in Chechnya and the Croatian Krajina, militias usually lose.

The nebulous, ill-disciplined character of these forces can embroil the nations that they supposedly serve in conflicts with groups of their own people, thereby exacerbating disloyalty and secessionism. In conflicts with other peoples, their plundering, vandalism, sexual predation, ethnic cleansing, and general disregard for human rights can turn low-level conflicts into bitter wars of survival. By the same token, these forces frequently lack the military competence to settle the trouble they start: They are too inefficient to impose order internally or to win wars externally.

This problem is particularly acute in the unrecognized ministates, which have to rely for assistance on criminals or intelligence agencies, operating clandestinely and not always with the full approval of their governments. As a result, the ministates are becoming magnets for outlaws and other elements marginal to normal societies. As a perceptive Russian reporter has recently written of the Transdniester Republic: "This 'zero' land is a distinctive state that draws into itself romantics, adventurers, and soldiers of fortune, with their unthinkable ideas and fantastic projects, like some enormous funnel."[2]

New Realities

Scholarship and public discussion alike are still struggling to catch up with these new realities of armed forces after communism. In the 1994–95 edition of its authoritative annual handbook *The Military Balance,* the International Institute for Strategic Studies in London mentions irregulars only in the sections on Georgia, Moldova, and Azerbaijan. Yet my own reckoning, based on somewhat uneven knowledge of the 20 newly recognized states and 11 unrecognized ministates in the former USSR and Yugoslavia, reveals a much more complicated picture. Of these 31 new political entities, 12 contain party or movement militias, 11 contain ethnic or regional militias, 8 contain armed criminal groups sufficiently powerful to be discussed in the context of military affairs, and 6 have independent warlord units that nominally operate as parts of their armies. The scale of what we are dealing with is vast. A quick survey of readily available sources on Georgia, for instance, reveals 21 armed organizations that can be listed by name, as well as others (whose number can only be guessed at) that are called simply "illegal armed formations" or "bandit formations."

The larger "militias," which usually consist of between 500 and 4,000 men arrayed in groups of 5 to 30 (a number roughly corresponding to a military platoon), tend to have a two-tier structure. There are "platoon-level" leaders or officers, who may be elected or self-appointed. Then there is the overall leader of the militia, with a small entourage that might charitably be called a staff. In many cases, there are no noncommissioned officers and nothing corresponding to field-grade officers. Recruits are drawn through family, clan, local, or professional connections; through pay or promises of plunder; or through displays of awe-inspiring equipment. In many cases the leaders are without professional officer training. Loti Kobalia, who commanded former president Zviad Gamsakhurdia's militia in western Georgia, was a truck driver; his deputy Tengiz Bulia was a roofer. Ioseliani and Tengiz Kitovani, the leaders of Georgia's most important militias, were artists with criminal records. (Wags in Tbilisi used to call the capital's devastated downtown "Kitovani's latest sculpture exhibit.") The Serb commander in the now-reconquered enclave of Srpska Krajina who was going by the *nom de guerre* of "Captain Dragon" ran a successful bordello in Australia before returning home to join his people's 600-year-old crusade against Islam and popery.

As the outstanding televised coverage of the Chechen war illustrated, militia troops often do not wear uniforms. In Georgia, Mkhedrioni leaders wear Armani suits bulging with guns, while rank-and-file members wear distinctive civilian jackets and neck medallions. I once asked a Mkhedrioni member why he and his fellows did not wear uniforms. "We prefer American clothes," was his reply.

In most cases—including many "regular" armies—fighters serve at their own discretion; they can go home when they want to. Accordingly, such forces tend to melt away almost completely after a defeat. Mobilizations, conversely, are often accomplished through the broadcasting of televised messages about times and places of assembly.

It might be useful to sketch one militia unit, a Serb outfit involved in the fighting over Vukovar, Croatia, whose history I learned through numerous interviews in Serb-occupied Bosnia during August 1993. The leader and founder was an unemployed actor from Belgrade whom his men called simply "Chief." His best friend served as second-in-command. During the confusion surrounding the breakup of Yugoslavia and the disintegration of the JNA, the Chief got hold of a twin-barreled, 23-millimeter antiaircraft gun that he used against people and buildings, in the manner common to these ethnic wars. The Chief's command of this fearsome-looking weapon and its firepower attracted ten other young Serb nationalists.

The Chief and his crew received general strategic directions from the senior Serb commander in Vukovar, a JNA veteran and Serbian army general sent from Belgrade. Tactical decisions, however, were made on the spot without consulting higher authority. Thus when the upper ranks signed a truce with the Croats, the Chief impressed his men by declaring: "I didn't sign it, so I'm not going to obey it!" The group was not linked to any organized logistical system. They received food from friendly Serbs or took it from Croats. When they needed ammunition, they would go to a JNA supply dump and say, to take one example, "Please give us 12,000 hand grenades." Members left the unit when they "couldn't take it anymore" and wanted a respite from the front.

The complex relationships of these voluntary organizations to the state and society, to decency and crime, have been perfectly captured by the Bosnian journalist Tihomir Loza:

> Some of the gangs were created and are partly controlled by the government. But there is no absolute control, and some of them have outgrown the government. Some gangs are loyal to one faction or another within the regime, while some are independent and interested only in money. In fact, there are very narrow lines between the regular police, the military forces and the private militias.

The anti-official mentality which has always been present in Bosnia, especially in Sarajevo, is a partial explanation. Power, even when it is not criminal, does not circulate through usual, legal ways, but through the intricate network of private or semi-private connections. The position of minister or member of the presidency does not in itself guarantee power. Furthermore, the fact that a powerful man acts as a criminal in one field does not necessarily mean he might not be completely honest and well-intentioned in another. Many gangs and militias steal and profit on the black market, but fight bravely on the front.[3]

Dubious Loyalties

If the identification between these armed forces and the nation-state is so tenuous, to what are they loyal? The tendency to break and run that many of these forces have shown, especially in the Abkhaz, Nagorno-Karabakh, Bosnian, and Krajina wars, bespeaks poor cohesion and suggests that irregular fighters are loyal mainly to themselves. Individual fighters and whole units, moreover, have been known to change sides in midcampaign.[4]

To the extent that these *Freikorps* display loyalty, it seems to be *abstract* allegiance to an ethnic group that is not identified with a specific

state, or *personal* allegiance to particular warlords or *condottieri*. Sometimes these groups are based on subethnic ties (many hard-core
Mkhedrioni members, for instance, belong to Ioseliani's ancestral
ethnolinguistic group); regional bonds (the case in Croatia, Bosnia,
Ukraine, Georgia, Azerbaijan, Tajikistan, Chechnya); or political parties. In Russia, Georgia, Azerbaijan, and Serb-occupied Bosnia and
Croatia, many political parties or movements sponsor their own armed
groups.

The relation of these informal armed forces to the state is thus complex and volatile, all the more so because of the presence of mercenaries, adventurers, volunteers, or foreign formations in at least 15 of the
new states or ministates. The war that raged through the winter of 1994–
95 in the breakaway North Caucasian region of Chechnya, for example,
was not exclusively an affair of Russian regulars versus Chechen regulars. Instead, it also drew the participation of Chechens fighting on the
Russian side; Russians fighting on the Chechen side; Ukrainians fighting on both sides; Abkhazian and other North Caucasian mercenaries;
plus Azeris, Afghans, Lithuanians, Arabs, Turks, and Belarusians.

In Chechnya, however, mercenaries and foreign elements had little
effect on the course of the fighting. By contrast, in the wars in the
Transdniester Republic, Abkhazia, South Ossetia, Nagorno-Karabakh,
and Tajikistan, mercenaries, volunteers, and foreign forces and equipment have had a major and at times even decisive effect. In the Abkhazian
war of secession from Georgia, for instance, the majority of "Abkhaz"
forces were probably from outside Abkhazia, most had no ethnic-Abkhaz
blood, and their commander at the turning point of the war was a Chechen
acting under Russian sponsorship—the same Shamyl Basayev who in
June 1995 led the most successful anti-Russian terrorist operation in
history at Budyonnovsk.

The tendency to mix armies and nationalities in the former Soviet
Union is exacerbated by the Russian army's practice of recruiting people
from other republics for service in the "near abroad." In Tajikistan, for
example, the Russians are recruiting Tajiks to fight Tajiks. In Armenia,
the Russian forces are recruiting Armenians. The Russian peacekeeping
force on the Georgian-Abkhazian border is recruiting Georgians.

While governments may pay some of the units that we are discussing, many make money on their own by stealing, selling their arms,
dealing drugs, or soliciting subsidies from wealthy businessmen and
foreign countries. Russian mercenaries in Abkhazia, in several attested
cases, were paid by the government of the Transdniester Republic.[5]

In some of the places most wracked by militia activity (Bosnia, Georgia, Azerbaijan, and Moldova), there now seems to be a real movement
away from militias, turning them into armies or "dissolving" them by
decree or disarmament. Although Russia, Tajikistan, and Chechnya have
moved in the other direction, one should not dismiss the possibility of

further professionalization or reprofessionalization there as well. But the militia phenomenon is due to underlying structural conditions that may be submerged or come to the surface depending on the circumstances. The fading of most (though by no means all) militias from public view in Moldova, Georgia, and Azerbaijan is connected with the success of ethnic insurgencies, so that many militias turn into "armies." With relatively stable truces holding in all three cases and a tenuous political stability in the rump states, there is no need or excuse for militias and they subside into a state of latency. They can, however, come to the surface again in favorable conditions.

Regulars and Irregulars

In addition to militias, almost all of the new states also have ordinary armies with traditional standardized, numbered units. But closer examination shows that these conventional formations have many times actually been under private control. In the case of Surat Huseinov's 709th Azeri Brigade, mentioned in passing above, a wealthy and well-connected individual twice used a private army disguised as a regular formation to mount coup attempts against the president of his country.

Around his brigade—which consisted mostly of fellow townsmen plus Russian paratroopers, all paid with money made through corrupt activities—Huseinov grouped a number of organizations within the Azeri government that were loyal to him rather than to their official superiors.[6] The governments of other new countries are right to fear that elements of their official hierarchies could be subverted into privatized and militarized organizations dangerous to the state. Without habits of loyalty to states that are new and governments with weak legitimacy, and in the absence of money to reward obedience or a functioning judicial system to punish disobedience, it is hard to erect safeguards against the danger.

Drawing a clear distinction between public and private military forces in the post-Soviet and post-Yugoslav context is difficult for five reasons:

1) The chain of command linking bureaucratic units had already begun rusting under Brezhnev and Tito. When *glasnost'* sapped the legitimacy of the communist state and rapid political change disorganized the already-shaky governing apparatus, its component bureaucracies began to turn into independent organizations controlled by their old bosses. The bureaucratic division of labor, which the modern state had created, now turned on its maker, becoming a source of loyalties outside or even *against* the state. Military forces and security agencies, despite their special characteristics, are also bureaucracies. They were scarcely exempt from this dynamic.

2) In revolutionary periods, public armed forces are often used for

partisan or private ends rather than public purposes. This is how the Russian intelligentsia interprets the armed suppression of the Supreme Soviet in October 1993 and the Chechen War. Even if these are misinterpretations, they cause public armed forces to be seen as private.

3) Even when the bonds among them fray, the various fragments of the old state apparatus can still wield enormous power in their own right. Even if they cannot or will not enforce the law, they can still confer favors. Thus public power can be used to create private military forces such as the Moscow bankers' security services, which Yeltsin approved because they would fight for him. Indeed, private military power usually develops with the complicity of certain bureaucracies.

4) Bureaucratic units increasingly depend not on their appropriations in the state budget, but on "nonbudget funds"—that is, resources the unit acquires in exchange for services rendered to private clients. This little-understood mechanism is transforming the fundamental structure of the postcommunist states. "Nonbudget funds" are the equivalent of medieval fiefs: sources of revenue given to units of the government in order to support their operations, in a financially stringent environment, and in recompense for favors rendered. Like fiefs, such funds render bureaucratic units partially but not totally independent of their official bosses. Georgia's security minister until September 1995, Igor Giorgadze, commanded a force far excelling the regular army in efficiency and morale, because he paid the enlisted men several times as much. The money came from giving protection to private businesses and shipments.[7]

5) The most elusive but perhaps the most powerful factor blurring the distinction between public and private military forces comes to light through a revealing paradox about the popularity of military service. Almost every one of the militias fighting for ethnic groups contains numerous mercenaries or volunteers from other areas. But the armies fighting for their own nations under the direction of the state are unpopular, as is shown by the high rates of draft evasion and desertion found in many former communist states, whether they were at peace like Russia or at war like the republics of the Caucasus and the former Yugoslavia.

The great difficulty facing transitions to democracy in the postcommunist East is a lack of basic social cohesion. Democratic institutions, political parties, and branches of the state itself, such as regular armies, all find it hard to function in such a highly atomized environment. Here is another consequence of communism's collapse that we failed to anticipate. Many of us foresaw great difficulties, but we tended to locate them in some sort of authoritarian "political culture"—that is, in too much cohesion rather than too little.

The postcommunist world has witnessed the emergence of a kind of "antipolitics" that is more radical than antipolitics elsewhere; it goes beyond trying to replace one form of politics with another, and even beyond trying to reduce the importance of politics.[8] At its core is a near-total flight from the public world as such.

There are many signs of this flight, including the crime and corruption that are so rampant in postcommunist countries, but the one that concerns us here is the character of armed forces in this world. Their amorphousness flows from a horror of any organization that is not spontaneous or voluntary, of any obedience that is expected or compulsory, or simply of any and all forms of "political obligation."

What is causing this flight from the public world? At its root, I believe, it is a reaction against the overwhelming experience of communist rule. After decades and decades of communism's discipline and regimentation, people dread the idea of being subjected to any kind of authority that comes from outside them.

This argument about the unpopularity of armies and the state might seem to contradict what everyone knows from the evening news: The biggest new fact about the postcommunist world is the emergence of violent nationalism, bent on carving out ethnically pure states. Yet this nationalism, for all its passionate intensity, has somehow failed to build strong states. Indeed, it seems to have actually *replaced* the state after the latter lost its legitimacy. The *ethnos* functions as a surrogate for the state, which is withering away. Nationalism gives people an identity and preserves a link with some felt community without making too many demands. Indeed, what the state and its laws deny to you, the new nationalism permits and excuses: Theft, rape, and crimes of revenge are central features of the wars of ethnic cleansing.

As for the forces that fight these wars, they are more dangerous to their own countrymen than to enemy states. These new armies have left great cities like Sarajevo, Tbilisi, or Baku undefended, like so many fat cattle tethered out for the hyena and the crocodile. Azerbaijan, with its vast oil and gas reserves, is ripe for conquest by the first force that seriously wants to try.

Implications for Civil-Military Relations

For reasons that should be clear by now, saying anything cogent about civil-military relations across much of the post-Soviet and post-Yugoslav worlds is exceedingly difficult. How can one discuss civilian control of the armed forces if the civilian government does not even raise or organize the armed forces? Nevertheless, it is possible to venture a few generalizations.

First, weak as the governments of many of the new states are, they are still able to confer important privileges and benefits. In the high feudal age, kings were weak but the barons still sought many things from them. Militias and political elites in today's postcommunist world often find each other useful. But the relationship differs from "normal" civil-military relations in that it is totally unstructured. It is not "constitutional," even in a broad sense; there is no "sovereign."

My second generalization describes a great paradox of postcommunist politics that has yet to be explained. Governments do not control militias, and militia-driven secessions, coup attempts, or rebellions have occurred in Croatia, Bosnia, Moldova, Georgia, Chechnya, Azerbaijan, and Tajikistan. But unlike Africa, the Middle East, and Latin America, where military regimes are a familiar phenomenon, the post-Soviet and post-Yugoslav worlds have seen no full-blown military dictatorships. I am not sure why this is so, although it is tempting to speculate that military leaders, themselves affected by the flight from the public world, want money and power more than glory and responsibility.

The result is that civilian governments are often the prisoners of militias. In Georgia, for example, President Eduard Shevardnadze had to rely on Tengiz Kitovani and Dzhaba Ioseliani in order to take power. The president managed to outmaneuver Kitovani, but Ioseliani remains so formidable that Shevardnadze has long tolerated the Mkhedrioni and their lawlessness.

Of all the items on the postcommunist political agenda, none is more urgent than the creation of serious, publicly controlled military power. So far, however, neither the citizens of the new states nor interested Westerners have been very helpful in this regard. Most of the democrats in these states are unsympathetic to the use of force; their roots are in nonviolent dissidence, not armed struggle. They have little acquaintance with the military world or military personnel: officers in Soviet-style armies were generally either upwardly mobile peasants or the sons of officers, and formed a separate professional caste. After communism fell, many democrats paid lip service to the need to refound national armies and intelligence services on a democratic footing, yet showed little interest in or enthusiasm for the actual work of doing so. Because military life, whether in militias or armies, seems *déclassé* and in many countries has been penetrated by the world of crime, the military career's lack of respectability has deepened even further.

We in the West have not helped. We admire revolutions only as long as they are "velvet," without strife or disruption. We talk about economic reform and democracy-building but never about army-building, which is the indispensable foundation of both. We are half-aware of how important the military realm is, but are prudishly reluctant to discuss it. The same is true of our attitude toward nationalism, another potentially strong state-forming force. We approach the postcommunist world with peremptory expectations of lasting change, but can barely bring ourselves to acknowledge the forces that could produce it.

This is folly. When the respectable and high-minded shun the military world, it is left open to vengeful neocommunists, criminals, crackpots, and fascists. The current state of affairs resembles Machiavelli's account of Renaissance Italy: Good men are so weakened by their goodness that they relinquish their states to the wicked. Enter Ratko Mladić, Dzhaba Ioseliani, and Surat Huseinov. What is sadder still is that even these brutal characters are trivial figures with base aspirations: They are usually driven by the desire for money or raw power or by pointless grudges rather than by the ambition that builds states.

The Last Argument of Kings

It is astonishing that the chaotic former Soviet world, so similar in its disarray and corruption to Revolutionary France in 1799, has not yet given rise to a Napoleon. Perhaps this is an unlooked-for consequence of the illegitimacy of military life and the flight from the public world, or perhaps it is an underpublicized achievement of postcommunist governments building on the useful communist tradition of generals obeying commissars.

Yet even if no men on horseback appear, the absence of stable democratic institutions, genuine party systems, and legitimate ideologies means that the political destiny of many a postcommunist state is likely to be decided by "the last argument of kings," armed force. It appears that many future governments will come to power through civil wars and coups or partial coups that will change governments or policies without actually putting the military in power.

With all apologies, I will play devil's advocate for a moment and ask if this is really so bad. Looking back at history, it is hard to regret the American Revolution (which was a harsh civil war as well as an anticolonial rebellion), Ataturk's victory over the Ottomans, or the Meiji Restoration. The military intervention that brought Charles de Gaulle to the presidency of France in 1958 seems pretty clearly to have been a good thing. And to take on a much knottier question, even Napoleon's seizure of power might be defended on the ground that he gave events a new direction after the French Revolution had foundered in a way that is reminiscent of what is now happening to some postcommunist reforms. Napoleon was the creator of that enduring synthesis of revolutionary utopianism (equality before the law, religious toleration, human rights) and tradition (monarchy, religion, the appeal to honor) that made the nineteenth century a haven of relative order and decency between two agonies of war and terror. Without the amazement created by Napoleon's personal subjugation of Europe, there would have been no energy for this new departure. Conquest and usurpation have been the motor of history up until now. Are we trying to end history by pretending that it is already over?

Since 1989, the new states we are considering have seen 13 secessionist or ethnic rebellions, 5 civil wars, and 6 armed coups or quasi-coups. Eleven or twelve of the ethnic rebellions were broadly success-ful (as seen from the perspective of the ethnic group making them, of course). Only one of the civil wars—the first civil war in Georgia—drove the incumbents from power, and all were disastrous in the long run to most of the forces that initiated them. Of the coups or quasi-coups, only two—both mounted by the Tajik opposition against Presi-dent Rahman Nabiyev in 1992, first forcing him into a coalition and then ousting him—were successful, and then only at first. In Azerbaijan, Surat Huseinov forced out President Abulfaz Elchibey, only to see power stolen by Heydar Aliyev. Military men in the postcommunist world, and those who arm and educate them, ought to know this striking record.

These facts enable us to see the other side of the argument. We have been discussing the possible utility of military intervention in politics in a situation of disintegrating states, poorly established institutions, and weak legitimacy. If the military forces that do the intervening are themselves suffering from low morale, loyalty, and competence, their involvement will just make things worse. Consider, for example, the chaos and bloodshed that followed the overthrow of President Zviad Gamsakhurdia in Georgia—an act that weakened the already-feeble in-hibitions against political action outside democratic limits. Ukraine, by contrast, remained patient under a president whose incompetence was comparable to Gamsakhurdia's, but replaced him according to law and suffered no civil strife.

Democracy's prestige in the postcommunist world is not based on any lived experience of democratic governance, but rather on a widespread sense that democracy and the market are the normal way that civilized life is conducted. Where this sweet illusion has not been shattered, it is better not to touch it.

For the present, at least, the case for military activism in post-communist politics is still unpersuasive, but the conventional Western model of civil-military relations also is not easily applicable. In this model, the armed forces as an institution are resolutely apolitical. They understand themselves as professional managers of coercion, prepared to follow the lawful instructions of the duly constituted political authorities.

This model, unexceptionable as it is in the West, does not translate well to the very different circumstances of the postcommunist world. To begin with, as Andrew Bacevich has pointed out, the conventional Western model of civil-military relations emerged out of the experience of the West in the three and a half centuries between the end of the Thirty Years' War (1618–48) and the fall of the Soviet Union, when there were fairly clear distinctions between war and peace, war and politics, war and economic life, warrior and civilian. Such distinctions are much harder to draw amid the brutal but low-intensity ethnic wars of the postcommunist world today, a world that in some ways eerily resembles early-modern Europe during the dynastic and religious wars of the sixteenth and early seventeenth centuries: Civilians are both combatants and victims; soldiering and brigandage overlap; and war looks like peace, peace like war.

Another problem with the Western ideal of civilian supremacy is that it presupposes decent, law-abiding civilian government. Such supremacy becomes questionable when, as in the postcommunist world today, governments are neither liberal nor democratic and see the armed forces as potential tools of domestic repression. In Russia, various parts of the former Yugoslavia, Tajikistan, Azerbaijan, Georgia, South Ossetia, Abkhazia, Moldova, and Chechnya, rulers have used armed force to crush political opponents or to settle ethnic questions within their own borders. Is it wise to encourage militaries to give unstinting loyalty to corruption-riddled governments that came to power irregularly and lack democratic accountability? Civilian supremacy is not very appealing if the supreme civilian turns out to be someone like Vladimir Zhirinovsky.

Given the probable character of some future governments and the disorder amid which they will be functioning, there will be many dubious orders, many temptations and excruciating dilemmas. So the officers who face them, unlike Western officers, desperately need an education in political judgment. Many of them will be faced again with dilemmas like those that have recently confronted Russian generals. In October 1993, Russian generals had to decide whether to allow extremist militias to dominate Moscow streets or to disperse the elected parliament by tank fire. The generals obeyed orders then, but the disappointing outcome may have moved General Ivan Babichev, at the start of the invasion of Chechnya on 11 December 1994, to defy the hasty orders that would have begun—against the judgment of most public opinion and of the officer corps—the killing of Russian civilians. Babichev's initiative having sunk, on New Year's Eve his fellow officers received instructions from a civilian favorite of Yeltsin's for a tactically preposterous armored assault on Chechen president Dzhokar Dudayev's skyscraper headquarters, thrown together to give the defense minister, born on the first of January, a fiery birthday celebration. Those professionals faced, again, a choice: whether to send thousands of half-trained youngsters to their deaths, or to throw the country, by an open act of mutiny, into unknown waters.

Some Provocative Suggestions

The best counsel that one can offer in such bleak circumstances is that armed forces work toward *isolation* from civilian government and from crime and corruption—that is, from economic life—except in the gravest crises. For now, armed forces are wise not to respond to every civilian order to use force, but to comply only with orders for routine, nonpolitical crime prevention and measures to guard the community (as opposed to the state narrowly understood) against urgent threats to its survival. In Bosnia, Nagorno-Karabakh, and Abkhazia the armed forces were right to respond to such threats.

Because many existing "armies" are more dangerous to their countries than to the enemy, the question of civil-military relations cannot be separated from wider defense policy. Under present conditions, there are forces *both* in society and in government that are acting to privatize military power. There are grave dangers in spontaneously raised volunteer forces, but also sometimes in "professional armies." In practice, these can mean collections of autonomous legions tightly controlled by particular officials and isolated from society, like the Kremlin guard commanded by General Aleksandr Korzhakov. This force has a factional identity so strong that it took to the streets to attack a banker's security force aligned with the mayor of Moscow.

Militias of the existing type have been disastrous, but systematically recruited reserve armies of the Swiss type based on universal service have both disadvantages and advantages. On the one hand, they continue the existing diffusion of arms and military skills; on the other, they can still act—as they have done so often in history—as a check on despotism and the exploitation of society by narrow armed groups. Media coverage of the postcommunist wars has given us glimpses of so many able-bodied citizens, of both sexes, looking on helplessly as their countries writhe in the grip of militia depredations and ethnic cleansing. Student training for reserve service, like the Reserve Officer Training Corps in the United States, is worth considering. It is particularly important to involve the new middle class, which has so many other opportunities, in military service.

If armies are to protect their peoples rather than plunder them, it may also be important to work gradually to restore the prestige of military organizations and the use of force. The post-Soviet world is in a situation that is virtually without historical precedent. In most epochs of disorder, the profession of arms and the use of force have been glamorous, often too glamorous. This was the experience of tribal societies, of the Middle Ages, and, more recently, of the postcolonial Third World with its guerrilla chic. Now the profession of arms has little prestige beyond the strange glamor which, in the postcommunist world, seems to attach to criminality, plus the glamor of group defense. Both types of glamor are fading.

These suggestions, which have been formulated to be provocative, will not persuade everyone. Any policy toward military affairs must be adapted to the circumstances of individual countries, which vary enormously. Whatever the choices citizens and leaders make, they must choose in the knowledge that decisions about armed forces, more than anything else, will mold their future.

NOTES

1. Human Rights Watch Arms Project and Human Rights Watch/Helsinki Reports, *Report on the War in Abkhazia*, vol. 7, no. 7 (1994), 11.

2. Aleksey Chelnokov, "Azartnye igri v strane 'zero'" (Games of chance in country "zero"), *Izvestia*, 12 November 1994.

3. Tihomir Loza, "A People with Tolerance, a City Without Laws," *Balkan War Report*, August–September 1993, 11.

4. In August 1993, on the eve of the most decisive phase of the Abkhazian war, the commanders of the Sukhumi brigade and the Gali battalion—both units of Georgian president Eduard Shevardnadze's militia—announced that because of the "disgraceful" truce agreement with the Russians and Abkhazians, they were joining Loti Kobalia's militia then rebelling in the name of former president Gamsakhurdia. See *Georgian Chronicle*, August 1993, 6.

5. Human Rights Watch, *War in Abkhazia*, 43.

6. On Huseinov and his activities, see Thomas Goltz, "Letter from Eurasia: The Hidden Russian Hand," *Foreign Policy* 92 (Fall 1993): 111–12; and Baku Radio and Television broadcast of 11 October 1994, *FBIS-SOV*, 12 October 1994, 61.

7. Author's interview with a U.S. government official, 19 June 1995.

8. I draw here on the more complete exposition in two book chapters: "Post-Communist Antipolitics," in Andreas Schedler, ed., *The End of Politics? Explorations in Modern Antipolitics* (New York: St. Martin's, 1997); and "Party and Ideology in the Former U.S.S.R.," in M. Richard Zinman and Jerry Weinberger, eds., *Left, Right and Center: Party and Ideology After the Cold War* (Ithaca, N.Y.: Cornell University Press, forthcoming). I have drawn upon the insights of G.M. Tamás, especially "Irony, Ambiguity, Duplicity: The Legacy of Dissent," *Uncaptive Minds* 7 (Summer 1994): 19–34.

II

The East European Experience

8

THE POSTCOMMUNIST DIVIDE

Jacques Rupnik

Jacques Rupnik is director of research at the Fondation Nationale des Sciences Politiques in Paris and professor at the College of Europe in Bruges. He is author of Le Déchirement des nations *(1995) and editor (with François Fejtö) of* Le Printemps tchéco-slovaque: 1968 *(1999) and* International Perspectives on the Balkans *(2002). This essay originally appeared in the January 1999 issue of the* Journal of Democracy.

Ten years after the collapse of the Soviet empire, one thing is clear: The word "postcommunism" has lost its relevance. The fact that Hungary and Albania, or the Czech Republic and Belarus, or Poland and Kazakhstan shared a communist past explains very little about the paths that they have taken since. Indeed, it is striking how vastly different the outcomes of the democratic transitions have been in Central and Eastern Europe. Nonetheless, certain patterns do emerge. A new tripartite political geography of formerly communist Europe is emerging: a new Central Europe (the so-called Visegrád group, the Baltic countries, and Slovenia) as a clear "success story"; the Balkans, where the democratic transition has often been derailed by the priorities of nation-state building or undermined by the legacies of communism and economic backwardness; and Russia, in search of a postimperial identity and teetering on the brink of economic disaster. (The fate of democratizaton in Ukraine, Belarus, and Moldova will to a large extent depend on what happens in Russia.)

Shortly after the collapse of the communist system, Ralf Dahrendorf identified three interrelated areas of change with different "timetables": political democracy and the rule of law (six months), the conversion to a market economy (six years), and the emergence of a civil society (six decades). Almost a decade later, it appears that so far the new political elites in Central Europe have successfully met the challenge posed by the disjunctive time spans of these three processes of change. They have established parliamentary democracy as the only game in town, creating a constitutional framework and political institutions that are seen as legitimate by all political actors; moreover, the formation of a relatively stable party system, allowing for smooth alternation in power, by now has taken place everywhere in Central Europe. A market economy has been established, with more than half of GNP produced in the private sector and over three quarters of trade now conducted with the OECD countries. A civil society is developing, with both its economic dimension (emerging new strata of entrepreneurs) and its networks of nongovernmental organizations (NGOs).

This picture contrasts not only with the former Soviet Union (the Baltic states excepted) but also with the Balkans. The most extreme case of a "derailed" transition, of course, is former Yugoslavia, because of the war and the breakup of the Federation into several successor states whose legitimacy and viability are still being questioned. The legitimacy of the territorial framework clearly remains the first prerequisite for a democratic transition.

To be sure, the situation in the Balkans should not be seen solely through the prism of the Yugoslav war and ethnonationalist conflict. There have been encouraging developments over the last year or two in both Bulgaria and Romania. In the former, the winter of discontent (1996–97), culminating in the ransacking of Parliament, forced the incompetent and corrupt ex-communist government to step down and call for an early election, opening the way for much delayed economic reforms. In Romania, a belated alternation in power ("We have lost seven years," said President Constantinescu when taking over from Iliescu) saw the ex-communists replaced by a right-wing coalition, although after two years in power it has produced little or no reform. If the contrast between the Central European and Balkan models can be summed up as that between democratic consolidation and the rise of "illiberal democracies," then Romania and Bulgaria (as well as Slovakia) are in an intermediate position.

There is, of course, no single factor that accounts for this process of differentiation. One can only point to a combination of factors, explanations, or hypotheses that can help make sense of the uneven progress of the democratic transition in the region.

1) The legacies of communism. More important than the manner of the changeover in 1989–91 (gradual or sudden, negotiated from above or imposed from below) in influencing the longer-term prospects for democratic success are the nature of the old communist regime and the depth of its imprint on society. The harshest totalitarian domination in the postwar period tended to be in the Balkans (Albania, Romania, Bulgaria), whereas a greater degree of reform and accommodation was characteristic of the post-1956 regimes in Poland and Hungary. Of course, the contrasting cases of relatively liberal Yugoslavia (since the 1960s) and of "normalized" Czechoslovakia after 1968 show the limits of such a generalization.

Nonetheless, it is instructive to examine the nature of the pre-1989 crises of communism in the two regions. In Central Europe, communism experienced three major crises (the 1956 Hungarian revolution, the Prague Spring in 1968, and the rise of Poland's Solidarity movement in 1980–81) that posed primarily the issue of democracy and civil society, and only in a second phase (under growing external constraint) that of national independence. By contrast, the three major crises of communism in the Balkans (Tito's 1948 break with Stalin, Hoxha's 1961 switch of allegiance from Moscow to Peking, and Ceauşescu's 1968 bid for foreign policy independence) all stressed the autonomy of the national communist apparatus vis-à-vis Moscow, while reinforcing the totalitarian features of the regime. The origins of the rebirth of civil society in Central Europe go back to the region's three major crises, as well as to the dissident movements of the 1970s and 1980s. The origins of "nationalism as the final stage of communism" (Adam Michnik's phrase) in the Balkans owe a great deal to the legacies of Tito, Hoxha, and Ceauşescu. Similarly, the emergence of alternative political elites during and in the immediate aftermath of 1989 in Central Europe owes a great deal to the existence of organized democratic opposition movements. These were largely lacking in Southeastern Europe, where the first free elections were all won by the ex-communist parties.

2) *Market and civil society.* "No bourgeoisie, no democracy." Barrington Moore's famous phrase provides a second clue for a comparative assessment of the democratic transitions in Central and Eastern Europe. There were, of course, differences due to the uneven level of economic development dating back to the precommunist period or the degree of economic reform pursued in the decaying phase of communism (here Hungary and Poland were the frontrunners, while Romania and Bulgaria lagged behind). The most striking contrast, however, is between those who after 1989 embarked on radical market reforms and those who chose gradualism or simply the postponement of market reforms and privatization.

The results are fairly clear, not only in terms of the relative size of the private sector, but also in foreign trade, growth rates, and the level of foreign investment (nearly half of direct investment in Central and Eastern Europe went to Hungary alone). There are one million registered private entrepreneurs in the Czech Republic and over 800,000 in Hungary. The emergence of new middle classes is also related to the progress of the "information revolution" and the formidable expansion of the service sector, areas where "human capital" is rewarded. (Before 1989, less than a third of Czechs believed that education was related to success; today almost two-thirds do.) The development of these middle strata, along with the conversion (through the privatization process) of part of the old *nomenklatura* into the new bourgeoisie, provides the backbone of the new market.

As for civil society, a term that emerged within the dissident movement in the late 1970s, it was originally understood as a self-organizing alternative society (a "parallel polis," as Václav Benda put it in 1978) in opposition to totalitarian rule. After the collapse of the latter, the concept acquired two new meanings relevant to the democratic transition. The first, prevalent in Central Europe among "liberals on the right," tended to identify it with the above described economic revolution. This is civil society as *Bürgergesellschaft,* secured by the market economy.

The second definition of civil society, prevalent among "liberals on the left," divorced the term almost completely from the market economy and identified it with the so-called third sector, that is, NGOs. According to this view, civil society is distinct from both state and market. The NGO is doubly pure, corrupted neither by power (that is, politics) nor by money (that is, the market). Civil society understood in terms of the first definition is more developed in Central Europe, while the NGO sector has been relatively more important to the transition in Southeastern Europe, where it can help compensate for the weakness of both the middle class and of political opposition to semi-authoritarian rule (Romania under Iliescu, ex-Yugoslavia). In the recent elections in Slovakia, which after 1993 seemed to be drifting away from the Central European model, the "third sector" demonstrated how effective it can be in mobilizing society and helping the opposition to overcome the "democratic deficit."

3) The rule of law and the "Habsburg factor." The recent debate about "illiberal democracies" has usefully reemphasized the crucial importance of the rule of law for democratic consolidation, a relationship that is underscored by the experience of the past decade. Although all generalizations are also exaggerations, one can say that the rule of law, constitutionalism, and the existence of an independent judiciary are undoubtedly more developed in Central Europe than in the Balkans. Explanations for this fact can be sought in specific political circumstances and in the degree of receptivity of the new elites to Western models of the separation of powers.

There is another factor, however, that warrants mention in this connection: the legacy of the Austrian as opposed to the Ottoman empire. It may be going too far to call the Habsburg empire liberal, but neither was it an autocracy like Czarist Russia. It was a *Rechtsstaat,* that is, a state run by the rule of law. Indeed Austrian turn-of-the-century literature (from Musil and Roth to Broch and Kafka) is dominated by the question of the law, the tension between legitimacy and legality. That Habsburg legacy of the rule of law has influenced several of its Central European successor states, as reflected in their legal scholarship, public administration, and political culture more generally. It was already being rediscovered in the last phase of communism, as the rulers began to accept some limitations on their powers and the opposition began to challenge their rule in the name of accepted domestic and international legal commitments. The 1990s have confirmed the trend. The weakness of the rule of law in the former Habsburg domains of Slovakia and Croatia qualifies but does not invalidate the general argument.

4) Nation-state building and "homogeneity." The return of democracy in 1989 was inseparable from the return of the nation: Popular sovereignty and national sovereignty became indistinguishable. In this respect, 1989 followed in the footsteps of 1848 and 1918, reaffirming the idea that the nation-state is the natural and most favorable framework for democracy. The demise of federalism inherited from communism in the Soviet Union, Yugoslavia, and Czechoslovakia seemed to validate this conviction. But a preoccupation with building the nation-state can also work against democracy and the rule of law, as we have seen in the former Yugoslavia. This classic dilemma was described by the Hungarian thinker István Bibo at the end of World War II in his essay on *The Misery of the Small Nations of Eastern Europe:* "Fascism exists in germ everywhere where, following a cataclysm or an illusion, the cause of the nation separates from that of freedom." The fear that freedom and democracy will "threaten the cause of the nation" was a major impediment to democracy during the interwar period and has no doubt been an important factor in the sidetracking of the democratic transition after 1989 in the Balkans.

One reason why Central Europe has been less troubled by the national question than Southeastern Europe is that today its populations are more homogeneous (and where they are not, as in Slovakia, is precisely where the transition has been least successful). Poland, where minorities once comprised a third of the population, today is a homogeneous state; this dream of Poland's old nationalist right was realized with the help of Hitler and Stalin. Similarly, the Czech Republic today is without Jews, Germans, and now even Slovaks. Alone at last! Slovenia, the only Yugoslav successor state where the democratic transition fits the Central European pattern, also does not have a significant minority population. In short, in Central Europe "ethnic cleansing" was completed half a century ago, whereas in the Balkans the process of "homogeneous" nation-state building is still under way. This, as Ernest Gellner once put it, is purely a description, not a prescription. It would be absurd to suggest that ethnic "homogeneity" is a prerequisite for democracy. Yet the contrasting situation in this respect of Central Europe and the Balkans accounts at least in part for the different fates of their democratic transitions.

5) Culture. This is one of the oldest arguments about the development of democracy, going back to Max Weber's classic thesis about the Protestant ethic and the spirit of capitalism. In looking at the balance

sheet of the democratic transition in Central and Eastern Europe, is there
a case for pushing the Weberian thesis one notch further and suggesting
a correlation between Western Christianity and democratic success (Central Europe), or between Orthodox Christianity and difficulty in achieving democratic and market-oriented change? The argument revolves
around the issue of whether the subordination of the Church to the State
and the close identification between religion and ethnicity in Orthodox
Christianity poses a significant obstacle to the emergence of a democratic public space and a civil society.

This whole subject has become politically loaded since the publication of Samuel Huntington's thesis about the "clash of civilizations,"
which has many ardent disciples in the Balkans and has been widely
used and abused in analyzing not only the war in Bosnia but the goals of
Western policy. Fortunately, democratic difficulties in Catholic Slovakia
and Croatia (as well as encouraging developments in Orthodox Romania and Bulgaria) tend to disprove Huntington's thesis. My response to
this controversy is both to reject cultural determinism (especially when
reduced to its religious dimension) as misleading or politically dangerous, but also to avoid the kind of political correctness that would make
Max Weber's classic sociological question taboo.

6) The international environment. The international environment,
at least so far, has been exceptionally favorable to the democratic transition in Central Europe: Russia is weak and its sphere of influence
shrinking; Germany is powerful but democratic and integrated in both
the EU and NATO; and there are no significant regional conflicts. This
favorable combination of factors, unprecedented in Central European
history, contrasts with the instability in the Balkans—not merely the
wars in the former Yugoslavia, but the collapse of the Albanian state at
the very moment that the Kosovo issue is intensifying, and the latent
Greek-Turkish rivalry.

This divergence is reinforced by the prospects of "Euro-Atlantic" integration, the Central European code word for the double enlargement
of NATO and the EU. Both institutions insist on democracy as a condition for membership (and, as the case of Slovakia showed, they mean
it). On the whole, it can be argued that both these institutions embody-
ing democratic Western values have been preoccupied primarily with
the integration of Central Europe. No Balkan country is high on the list
of candidates for either NATO or the EU. It remains to be seen what
impact the noninclusion of Romania and Bulgaria will have on the democratic process in those countries. Thus far the differentiation in the enlargement process between the "ins" and the "outs" has largely been a
consequence of the relative success of their democratic transitions. In
the future, however, the enlargement process itself could help to undermine the democratic transition precisely where it is most fragile.

9

EUROPE TRANSFORMED

Richard Rose

Richard Rose, director of the Centre for the Study of Public Policy at the University of Strathclyde, Glasgow, is the senior author of Democracy and Its Alternatives: Understanding Post-Communist Societies *(1998). This article, which originally appeared in the January 1999 issue of the* Journal of Democracy, *draws on New Democracies Barometer surveys that he has conducted since 1991 as international scientific advisor to the Paul Lazarsfeld Society in Vienna, and parallel CSPP surveys in Russia and the Baltic states.*

The fall of the Berlin Wall and its consequences are transforming a continent that had been divided for 40 years. Western Europe was the "ideal" Europe; freedom and prosperity could be found there. The lands behind the Iron Curtain had a better claim to be the "real" Europe, for authoritarianism and oppression by an alien ruler could be found there. While intellectuals sometimes speak of the Czech Republic, Hungary, or Poland as returning to a golden age, ordinary people in postcommunist societies do not want to return to the dictators, wars, and poverty that characterized earlier European history.

Ten years into this transformation, what kind of a Europe is emerging at the start of the new millennium? Central Europe—which includes Sweden, Germany, the Czech Republic, Austria, Slovenia, Poland, Hungary, and even parts of Italy—is once again central to the continent. The fall of the Wall has created a *Drang nach Östen* (drive toward the east), of which the movement of Germany's capital to Berlin this year is an apt symbol. The new German parliament will meet in the new Reichstag; the old building has been transformed by the design of a British architect. The problems of the reunified Germany—in the Rhineland as well as along the Elbe—are a reminder that transformation has costs as well as benefits.

Ten postcommunist countries have already reoriented their attention from Moscow to Brussels, applying to join the 15 member states already in the European Union (EU). The five leading candidates are the

Czech Republic, Estonia, Hungary, Poland, and Slovenia; Bulgaria, Latvia, Lithuania, Romania, and Slovakia make up the second flight. Russia, Ukraine, and Croatia are still outside the pale.[1] If these ten countries gain membership, Europe's population center—the point equidistant from the population of the entire continent—will be Ulm, a pleasant town in Southern Germany with the tallest church spire in Europe and the birthplace of a quintessential modernist, Albert Einstein.[2] The river that runs through it does not flow toward Bonn or Berlin; it is the Danube, on its journey to the Black Sea.

Achievements of a Decade

Whereas England and Sweden took centuries to evolve into democracies and Germany stabilized democratic rule only under foreign occupation, many of the new regimes in postcommunist Europe have shown substantial evidence of becoming normal democracies in a single decade. In all ten countries, there has been at least one change of government through the ballot box, and often two. For example, in 1990, anticommunist governments were elected in Hungary and Poland. The ex-communists then showed their consistency—"Once an opportunist, always an opportunist"—and won elections campaigning as social democrats. The ex-communists, in turn, have been defeated at the polls and replaced by right-of-center governments.

Voters have consistently rejected undemocratic alternatives. In Hungary, the radical right-wing party of István Csurka cannot be sure of winning enough votes to gain any seats in the parliament. In the autumn of 1998, Slovak voters rejected Vladimír Mečiar, who had led the country to a peaceful separation from the Czech Republic but has subsequently shown antidemocratic tendencies. In Latvia, a popular referendum rejected proposals that, in effect, would have prevented most of its Russian residents from ever becoming citizens. Only in Romania does the total vote for fragmented antidemocratic parties begin to approach the vote won in established democracies by parties with dubious democratic credentials, such as Jean-Marie Le Pen's National Front in France or Jörg Haider's Freedom Party in Austria.

The costs of economic transformation have been substantial; establishing a market economy where none had existed for over 40 years is much harder than ending a recession in a country with well-developed market institutions. Still, these costs have been much exaggerated. In the days of the command economy, shortages were frequent, choice was nonexistent, and bribery and party favoritism often determined who got what. People learned to augment their standard of living by household production or by working in second economies; these skills have helped tide them over the worst of the move to the market.

The benefits of transformation by trial-and-error are now evident throughout most of postcommunist Europe. Most countries where GDP declined and inflation raged in the early 1990s have now reversed their course. Poland and Slovenia have already surpassed their 1990 GDP levels, and the Czech Republic, Hungary, and Slovakia will soon do so. Estonia, Latvia, and Lithuania suffered severe dislocations, but in each of these countries the economy is now growing. Only Bulgaria and Romania have yet to demonstrate consistent growth. All of these economies have far better prospects today than they had a decade ago, because Moscow and the edicts of bureaucratic planners no longer determine what happens. Instead, realistic prices, foreign imports, and consumer choice are rewarding efficiency.

The breakup of multinational communist regimes has reduced a classic source of political conflict in the region by creating successor states that are much more ethnically homogeneous. Czechoslovakia broke up through a "velvet divorce," not bloodshed. In Estonia and Latvia, the attitudes of ethnic Russians, legal residents but not citizens, are far more moderate than those of their self-appointed spokesmen in Moscow and elsewhere. What Russians in the Baltic states value most is the right to work and to draw social security benefits. The right to vote and to participate in politics is a lower priority—more ethnic Russians see their future as best secured by living in a Baltic state than by integration with the Russian Federation. Ethnic minorities are now just that, a small percentage of a country's population, and the threat they pose to peace and security is diminishing. In 1992, New Democracies Barometer surveys in seven postcommunist countries found that an average of 40 percent were concerned that ethnic minorities could be a threat to order. By 1998, the proportion expressing anxiety had fallen to 25 percent.[3]

The bloody conflict in the former Yugoslavia is no more representative of Europe than Albania (under communism or today) is a typical "European" country. The European Union recognizes this. Slovenia, the one Yugoslav successor state that has peacefully moved toward democracy, is negotiating for EU membership, while the other post-Yugoslav states, for the indefinite future, are still outside the pale.

Catching Up

Most people are inclined to make comparisons with their own national past. By this standard, a majority of citizens in every postcommunist country see themselves as enjoying much more freedom than they did under communist rule. This is the view of ethnic Russians in the Baltic states, of the Baltic peoples themselves, and of most citizens in such imperfect democracies as Bulgaria and Romania too. While none of the postcommunist countries receives the top score in Freedom House's *Comparative Survey of Freedom,* the five countries furthest ahead in joining the European Union are given the same high rating as Belgium, Germany, Italy, Spain, and the United Kingdom, and rank above Greece.[4]

No postcommunist country has achieved the standard of living of Luxembourg or Denmark, the countries with the highest living standard in the EU. But 13 other EU countries have also "failed" to match that level; the living standard in Greece and Portugal is barely half that of the richest EU countries. It is only a matter of time until continuing economic growth pushes countries such as the Czech Republic and Slovenia past the current level of the least prosperous EU member states. Other postcommunist countries will follow. And since postcommunist countries grow faster than established market economies, the gap will close quickly.

Health provides another way to evaluate welfare. While health improved in every communist society over 40 years, the noncommunist countries of Central Europe improved at a much faster rate: Hungary lagged behind Austria, and health in East Germany improved more slowly than in West Germany. While transformation caused some initial disturbances in health, postcommunist countries are beginning to catch up to, or even surpass, some established market economies. The Czech Republic, for example, now has an infant mortality rate (six deaths per thousand live births) lower than some EU countries, and substantially lower than the United States, where there are eight infant deaths per thousand.

People in postcommunist countries would like an American standard of living, a Swedish welfare state, and British democratic institutions overnight. But life under communism has taught a lesson in keeping expectations low and being patient—that is, suffering in silence. Today, time horizons are long-term. When Central and East Europeans are asked how long it will be before they have reached a standard of living with which they are content, the median person says "ten years," and two in five either say they don't know or think they will never be content. The same pattern is found when people are asked how long they think it will take the government to sort out the economic problems of their country as a whole.

The biggest problem that postcommunist countries face is escaping the legacy of 40 years of communist rule. In the late 1940s, Stalinist regimes disbanded competing political parties; imprisoned, exiled, or executed opposition politicians; and made adherence to the party line (whatever it was at the moment) a condition of appointment to leading positions in universities, the media, and trade unions. As a result, representative institutions such as political parties, trade unions, and even parliaments are widely distrusted or viewed with skepticism today. People find it easier to name a party that they would never vote for than to name a party they like. At election time, the median voter casts a ballot for a party he neither trusts nor identifies with.[5]

Under communism, the old Central European ideal of the *Rechtsstaat* (a state that rules by right, not might or ideology) was replaced by "socialist legality." Courts did not have to weigh evidence to arrive at a verdict; the party-state knew what the "correct" verdict was. A maze of bureaucracies combined the worst features of party control and Kafkaesque indifference. Individuals became highly skilled at bending, evading, or breaking the law. While communist parties have lost their leading role, the personal networks that they created have encouraged *nomenklatura* privatization; the currency for getting things done has changed from a party card to dollars or deutschmarks.

The level of corruption varies greatly in postcommunist countries, as it does in established democracies. Among the 85 countries covered by the 1998 Transparency International Index of Perceived Corruption, Poland, the Czech Republic, Hungary, and Estonia all rank in the upper half for honesty, equal to or above three EU member states, Belgium, Greece, and Italy. Russia is among the world's ten most corrupt countries, ahead of Pakistan and not far behind Indonesia.

New Members, New Club

The European Union is an inclusive club; it must admit any applicant that is a democracy and adheres to the laws and practices of a market economy. The consideration of ten postcommunist countries for membership shows how far transformation has come; this would have been unthinkable a decade ago. While transforming a communist system requires more time than it took Spain and Portugal to move from dictatorship to EU membership, by the end of the next decade, the EU will be transformed into a union of more than 20 states.

The current member states disagree over how fast the EU should be enlarged and on what terms. Hesitancy can be motivated by national interest, such as a desire to protect the status quo in agricultural subsidies, which are so high that they could not possibly be paid to new members like Poland too. It can reflect realistic political anxieties about an inrush of job-seekers from neighboring countries, given the free movement of labor within the single EU market. Before any new member states can be admitted, existing members must give up the right of any one to veto an EU decision, and decide what voting rights small new member states will have vis-à-vis big states. Here, the interests of Germany, France, Italy, and Britain diverge from those of Belgium, the Netherlands, Denmark, and Ireland.

Loss of sovereignty, a major issue among the neo-Thatcherites in Britain and neo-Gaullists in France, is not a major concern in postcommunist countries. They all experienced this during World War II, and their postwar history left them far more fearful of Moscow than of any directive from Brussels. By pooling sovereignty in the EU, small postcommunist countries will gain the right to sit on decision-making councils with larger countries and sometimes set the agenda for meetings. EU enlargement will fundamentally change what it means to be a European democracy. English critics who mutter "But they are not like us!" are correct insofar as the abrupt postcommunist route to democracy follows centuries of undemocratic rule. But it is Britain, not the Czech Republic or Poland, that is the exception here. Only six of the EU's 15 current member states have made an English-style evolutionary transition to democracy. In an expanded EU, countries that have abruptly returned to democracy or have "bootstrapped" their way to this goal will be the vast majority. Just as West Germans who lived through the Third Reich broke with their history of authoritarian rule, the peoples of the postcommunist countries, after centuries of war and undemocratic rule, are anxious to live together in peace and freedom.

NOTES

1. See Richard Rose, William Mishler, and Christian Haerpfer, *Democracy and Its Alternatives: Understanding Post-Communist Societies* (Baltimore: Johns Hopkins University Press, 1998), especially ch. 10.

2. See Richard Rose, *What is Europe?: A Dynamic Perspective* (New York: Addison Wesley Longman, 1996), 290.

3. Survey results for Central and Eastern Europe are from the multinational New Democracies Barometer, conducted by the Paul Lazarsfeld Society in Vienna, and for the Baltic states from the New Baltic Barometer, conducted by the Centre for the Study of Public Policy at the University of Strathclyde. For further details, see www.strath.ac.uk/Departments/CSPP.

4. See *Freedom in the World: 1997–1998* (New York: Freedom House, 1998), 605; and Richard Rose, "Freedom as a Fundamental Value," *International Social Science Journal* 145 (September 1995): 457–71.

5. See Richard Rose and William Mishler, "Negative and Positive Party Identification in Post-Communist Countries," *Electoral Studies* 17 (June 1998): 217–34.

10

REASSESSING THE REVOLUTIONS OF 1989

Vladimir Tismaneanu

Vladimir Tismaneanu, *professor of government and politics at the University of Maryland at College Park, is the editor of the journal* East European Politics and Societies. *He is the author, most recently, of* Fantasies of Salvation: Democracy, Nationalism, and Myth in Post-Communist Europe *(1998) and the editor of* The Revolutions of 1989 *(1999). This essay originally appeared in the January 1999 issue of the* Journal of Democracy.

Ten years have passed since the momentous series of events in Eastern and Central Europe known as the revolutions of 1989. In that year, what appeared to be an invulnerable system collapsed with breathtaking speed, not from an external blow (although external pressure did play a role), but due to inner tensions that could not be resolved. The Leninist systems were terminally sick, and the disease affected above all their capacity for self-regeneration. After decades of flirting with the idea of internal reform, it had become clear that communism did not have the resources for readjustment and that the solution lay not within, but outside, and even *against* the existing order. The implosion of the Soviet Union itself, which took place before the eyes of an incredulous world in December 1991, was intimately related to the previous dissolution of the East European "outer empire" provoked by the revolutions of 1989. The historical cycle inaugurated by World War I, the Bolshevik seizure of power in Russia in October 1917, and the long European ideological warfare (some call it the "European civil war") that followed had come to an end.

The importance of these revolutions cannot be overestimated. They represented the triumph of civic dignity and political morality over ideological monism, bureaucratic cynicism, and police dictatorship. Rooted in an individualistic concept of freedom and skeptical of all ideological blueprints for social engineering, these revolutions were (at least at the outset) liberal and nonutopian. Unlike traditional revolutions, they did not originate in a chiliastic vision of the perfect society and they rejected any role for a self-appointed vanguard in directing the activities of the masses. No political party guided their momentum. In their early stage, they insisted on the need to create new political forms unlike traditional ideologically defined parties. The fact that these revolutions have been followed by ethnic strife, unsavory political bickering, rampant corruption, and the rise of illiberal parties and movements does not detract from their generous message and colossal impact. Where such revolutions did not occur (Yugoslavia) or were derailed (Romania), the exit from state socialism has been convoluted, tentative, and much more problematic.

These facts must be kept in mind when we face arguments that question the success of the revolutions of 1989 by emphasizing their ambiguous legacies. This "reactionary rhetoric" is designed to delegitimize change per se, by making it look impossible or undesirable.[1] According to such arguments, either: 1) the postrevolutionary environment has unleashed long-dormant ugly features of national political cultures, including chauvinism, residual fascism, ethnoclerical fundamentalism, and militarism, and is therefore more dangerous than the *status quo ante;* or 2) nothing has really changed, and the same people have remained in power, simply donning new masks; or 3) contrary to the wishes of those who made the revolutions, the results have turned out to be extremely disappointing, opening the way for political scoundrels to exploit the new opportunities to establish their domination.

It is therefore politically, morally, and intellectually useful to remember the real message of these revolutions. We should not forget that at the beginning of 1989 the end of Sovietism was only seen as a remote possibility. It is true that some dissident thinkers (Ferenc Fehér, Agnes Heller, Václav Havel, János Kis, Leszek Kolakowski, Jacek Kuroń, and Adam Michnik) thought that the system was slowly decaying and had no future, but even they did not think that the collapse was imminent. The philosophy of dissidence was predicated on a strategy of long "penetration" of the existing system and restoration of the public sphere (the independent life of society) as an alternative to the omnipresent ideological party-state.[2]

Although a number of thinkers anticipated the inevitable collapse of Sovietism, hardly any thought that it would come so quickly and with so little violence. Leninist regimes had never accepted negotiations with the opposition, let alone the peaceful transfer of power. Thus one of the most surprising developments of 1989–90 was the willingness of communist elites in Hungary and Poland first to share power and then to give it up entirely. In so doing, they abandoned the cherished Leninist dogma regarding the communist party's "leading role" and allowed democratic transitions to unfold gradually and peacefully. In other countries, reforms were rejected in the name of defending the "socialist gains of the people," but this confrontational line could not save the ruling elites. Veteran observers of the Soviet bloc—historians, political scientists, and journalists alike—were amazed by the extraordinary dynamics that, in less than 12 months, brought a peaceful, nonviolent end (except in Romania) to Leninist tyrannies in Central and Eastern Europe.[3]

The initial scholarly reaction to the events of 1989 was to regard these revolutions as part of a global democratic wave and as a confirmation of the ultimate triumph of liberal democratic values over collectivist attempts to control the human mind. Few analysts called attention to the illiberal and neoauthoritarian components of the anticommunist upheaval in the East. Most observers preferred to gloss over the fact that not all those who rejected Leninism wanted to replace it with an open society and liberal values. Among the revolutionaries were quite a few *enragés,* ill-disposed to compromise and negotiation. There were also populist fundamentalists, religious dogmatists, and those who were nostalgic for precommunist dictatorships. Only after the disintegration of Yugoslavia and the "velvet divorce" that led to the breakup of Czechoslovakia did scholars and policy makers realize that the liberal promise of these revolutions could not be taken for granted, and that it was not inevitable that communism would be succeeded by liberal democracy. In the early 1990s it became increasingly clear that the postcommunist era was fraught with all sorts of threats, including bloody ethnic conflicts, social unrest, and the resurgence of populism and tribalism in both old and new forms.

An Irreversible Transformation

What happened in Eastern and Central Europe has had a long-term impact on international stability. Not only did the Soviet zone of influence and the Warsaw Pact come to an end as a result of these events; they also led to the fall of the Berlin Wall, the reunification of Germany, and victory for the liberal West in the Cold War. Nowadays, all this seems normal, even banal, but ten years ago, such an end to the East-West confrontation would have seemed surreal.

It is therefore extremely important politically and intellectually to rethink the main implications of these fascinating developments in recent European and world history. Why did these revolutions take place? Is it true, as some writers have argued, that they were nothing but an effort to "undo" the failed communist experiment—in other words, just an attempt to restore the precommunist *status quo ante?* Were these revolutions primarily a consequence of the failure of the command economy to meet the challenges of the postindustrial age? How does one account for the nonviolent and limited nature of these revolutions and the absence of large-scale vindictive attempts to punish the former communist leaders? What was the real popular attitude toward the dissidents, and how can one make sense of the transition from "velvet revolution" to "velvet restoration"? Indeed, it was the end of communism in

Eastern and Central Europe that accelerated centrifugal and disintegrative processes in the USSR, catalyzed national-patriotic movements in the Baltic states and Ukraine, and ushered in a new post–Cold War and post-bipolar world. This in turn has created a fundamentally new and dangerous situation where the absence of norms and predictable rational behavior could result in global chaos. Without being nostalgic for the pre-1989 arrangements, we must recognize that these revolutions, and the end of Leninism, have placed all of us in a radically new situation.

A crucial question to be addressed is whether the events of 1989 were genuine revolutions. If they were, then in what respect did they differ from similar previous events (the French Revolution or the Hungarian Revolution of 1956)? If they were not (as some today like to argue), then what were they? Were they simply mirages, or the results of obscure intrigues on the part of beleaguered bureaucracies that mesmerized mankind but did not fundamentally change "the rules of the game?"

In my view, the upheavals in the East, especially in the Central European core countries, were indeed a series of *political revolutions* that transformed the existing order decisively and irreversibly. They replaced autocratic one-party systems with emerging pluralist polities. They allowed the citizens of the former ideologically driven despotisms to recover their principal human and civic rights and to build new open societies.[4] Instead of centrally planned command economies, these societies have begun to create market economies. Some have succeeded better and faster than others in creating political pluralism, a market economy, and a civil society, but throughout the former Soviet bloc the once-monolithic order has given way to political and cultural diversity.[5] While we do not yet know whether *all* these societies will become functioning liberal democracies, we do know that in all of them, the Leninist systems based on ideological uniformity, political coercion, dictatorship over human needs, and suppression of civic rights have been dismantled.[6]

Ironically, the revolutions of 1989 were a vindication of Lenin's famous definition of a revolutionary situation: Those at the top could no longer rule in the old way, and those at the bottom would no longer accept it. These were more than simple revolts; they attacked the very foundations of the existing systems and ushered in a complete reorganization of society. Communist parties had not come to power as a result of legal or rational procedures. No free elections had brought them to their ruling positions. Whatever legitimacy they had, they derived from their claim to represent the "vanguard of the proletariat" and, consequently, to have a universal emancipatory mission. Once this ideology ceased to be an inspiring force and influential members of the *nomenklatura* lost their emotional commitment to Marxist doctrine, the Leninist castles were doomed to crumble. Here, what is often called the

"Gorbachev effect" came into play. It was the international climate generated by the shockwaves of Gorbachev's policies of *glasnost'* and *perestroika* that permitted an unprecedented degree of open dissent and political mobilization in Eastern and Central Europe. Gorbachev's denunciation of the ideological perspective on international politics fundamentally changed the nature of Soviet–East European relations.

The revolutions of 1989 have transformed the political, economic, and cultural map of the world. They have made possible the rediscovery of democratic participation and civic activism. After decades of state aggression against the private sphere, these revolutions have reinstituted the distinction between that which rightfully belongs to government and that which must remain private. Emphasizing the importance of political and civic rights, they have created a space for the flourishing of liberal democratic values. In some countries, these values now provide the foundation on which the institutions of an open society can be safely built. In others, the adherence to pluralism remains somewhat perfunctory. But even in countries where the transition to democracy has been less successful (Albania, Bulgaria, or Romania), the revolutions have succeeded in their most important task: The old Leninist order, based on suspicion, fear, and mass hopelessness, is gone forever, and the citizens of these countries are now free to shape their own destinies.

NOTES

1. See Albert Hirschman, *The Rhetoric of Reaction: Perversity, Futility, Jeopardy* (Cambridge: The Belknap Press of Harvard University Press, 1991).

2. See Miklós Haraszti, "The Independent Peace Movement and the Danube Movement in Hungary," in Vladimir Tismaneanu, ed., *In Search of Civil Society: Independent Peace Movements in the Soviet Bloc* (New York: Routledge, 1990), 71–87.

3. On ideologically driven modern despotisms, see Daniel Chirot, *Modern Tyrants: The Power and Prevalence of Evil in Our Times* (New York: Free Press, 1994).

4. See Ivo Banac, ed., *Eastern Europe in Revolution* (Ithaca, N.Y.: Cornell University Press, 1992).

5. See Claus Offe, *Varieties of Transition: The East European and East German Experience* (Cambridge: MIT Press, 1997), especially 29–105.

6. See Ferenc Fehér, Agnes Heller, and György Márkus, *Dictatorship Over Needs* (New York: St. Martin's, 1983).

11

THE TRANSFORMATION OF CENTRAL EUROPE

Bronisław Geremek

Bronisław Geremek *served as foreign minister of Poland from 1997–2000. A medieval historian by training, he was a key advisor to Lech Wałeşa from the earliest days of Solidarity, and spent over a year in prison during the period of martial law. He chaired the Committee for Political Reform during Solidarity's 1989 "roundtable" talks with the leaders of Poland's communist regime. From 1989 until his appointment as foreign minister in 1997, he was chairman of the parliament's Foreign Affairs Committee. This essay is based on a lecture that he delivered at George Washington University on 22 April 1999.*

Only ten years ago, the political world that we live in today would have been considered a bold, futuristic vision. The reality of those bygone years had been shaped by many decades of the Cold War, during which a huge part of Europe had been ruled by communist regimes. Central and Eastern Europe was separated from an integrating Western Europe by the "Iron Curtain," and both the economic gap and the civilization gap between the two halves of Europe continually widened. Although the weaknesses of the so-called people's democracies were clearly visible, almost no Western experts were predicting the rapid downfall of the entire Soviet system.

Against this backdrop, ten years ago representatives of Poland's democratic opposition sat down at a negotiating table in Warsaw with the hierarchy of the country's communist regime. Within that same year there followed the fall of the Berlin Wall and the Velvet Revolution in Czechoslovakia. Soon other societies awoke—and that was the end of communism in Europe.

Central European societies paid the price of their struggle for freedom on the streets of Budapest in 1956, in Czechoslovakia in 1968, and in Poland in 1956, 1968, 1970, and 1981. In 1989, however, Poles chose dialogue instead of confrontation as a means to overcome a political deadlock. The "roundtable" talks, sometimes called the "negotiated revolution," marked the beginning of the end of the struggle against communism for Poles and other peoples of Central and Eastern Europe.

I would like to present some thoughts on our transition to democracy and a free market, but I also wish to call attention to some of the hazards of that process. I believe that today we are at a very particular moment in European history. Our perception of the successes and failures of the last 10 years is heavily influenced right now by pictures from Yugoslavia, pictures that call into question the view that Europe is becoming a single entity. This view has been advanced for the past few years by Central Europeans contending that the notion of a separate and distinct Central and Eastern Europe had lost its validity.

The term "Central Europe" has sometimes been considered as an expression of nostalgia for the old Austro-Hungarian Empire. The term also implied a special intellectual atmosphere, which was often seen as a privilege for those born there. In the 1960s, 1970s, and 1980s, the notion of Central Europe could also be associated with the dream of freedom and the aspiration to membership in a community of free nations.

Nowadays the notion of Central Europe is associated with rapid economic and social transformation, albeit not without high social costs. This transformation, firmly based on the premises of democracy and human rights, allowed many nations in our region to claim that we belong to a single European family. The crisis in Kosovo is a severe test for that family, and at the same time proof that the ghosts of nationalism are still alive in parts of Central and Eastern Europe.

The roots of the nationalism that has destroyed so many lives in the Balkans over the last eight years are not to be found only in remote history. Those roots grew very quickly during the decadent phase of communism. When I think about the success of Poland, I now can see very clearly that in Yugoslavia the postcommunist elites rejected democratic change, and the Central European model of transformation was not applied there. This is a painful lesson for those of us involved in democratic change in the region, as well as for the entire European family of nations.

Everyone now acknowledges that communism was economic nonsense. By wasting capital reserves and human resources, by overburdening society with arms production, and by suppressing the spirit of entrepreneurship and innovation, it finally bankrupted itself. On a philosophical level, however, communism inflicted upon itself an even greater defeat. Unable to convince society to believe in their ideology, communist leaders restricted the rights of their citizens and built their empires on a foundation of violence, terror, and lies.

But these pillars of power proved inadequate to the task. Alexis de Tocqueville was correct in stating, "There is no end which the human will despairs of attaining through the combined power of individuals united into a society." The power and the will of the Polish nation were welded together by the spirit of Solidarity. This spirit united proponents of diverse ideological views in a fight for the rights of the oppressed, a call for human dignity, and a drive to remind those in power of their role as servants to the people.

The core of the great Solidarity movement was the dream of freedom and democracy, understood as an innate right of every human being to decide his or her own fate and to share responsibility for the fate of the nation.

The core of the great Solidarity movement was the dream of freedom and democracy, understood as an innate right of every human being to decide his or her own fate and to share responsibility for the fate of the nation. Thus the opposition movement in Poland was not just a rebellion against a constraining system, but a positive force shaping an attractive new alternative in the form of democracy, free markets, and a bond with European and Euro-Atlantic structures. As a result, Poles, at the brink of regaining their independence, knew not only what they rejected, but also what they wanted. This was a critical factor in the transition.

At the beginning of our transition, we introduced as the basis of our democracy the principles of human rights, constituent-oriented government, legally based means of conflict resolution, and guarantees of the right of ethnic minorities to their identity. We quickly established good relations with our neighbors, making our borders open and friendly. We made an historic effort at reconciliation with Germany, which is not only our largest economic partner but also an important ally in promoting European unity. We have opened a new chapter in relations with Ukraine—we were the first country to recognize its statehood. In the past, our relationship with Ukraine had often been beset with conflicts. Today, however, Ukraine is our strategic partner, and we share a community of interests. Our countries and peoples have understood that only together can they be independent and secure: One cannot imagine an independent Poland without an independent Ukraine, and vice versa. Partnership between these two countries is a cornerstone of peace and stability in Europe. We have continually supported Lithuania and the other Baltic States in their efforts to integrate with Western structures. Another example of our commitment to regional cooperation is the Višegrad Group, composed of Poland, Hungary, Slovakia, and the Czech Republic, which has overcome some past animosities in favor of a close partnership. We are building relations with Russia in a spirit of mutual respect, and we hope that Russia will become a member of the European community of democratic states.

We are committed to our role as a friendly and reliable partner in the region, for we are determined that new walls should not be raised in Europe. Now that the "Iron Curtain" has vanished, we cannot let another curtain descend, one that would divide peoples not by political beliefs but by economic performance. This kind of curtain might not be made of iron, yet it could be as cruel as the old one. We think that regional cooperation will help prevent such an evolution. This outlook is also a legacy of the Solidarity movement.

I have enumerated with some pride these accomplishments on the international scene. Thanks to them, Poland is looked upon as a country that plays a vital stabilizing role in the region. This also helps to explain why we have exceptionally good relations with the United States, with which we share many political interests and a common view of the values that are essential to the proper functioning of the international community.

Overcoming the Past

During the last 10 years, Poland has laid the foundations for a stable free market economy. A large portion of our GDP—70 percent—is produced by the private sector, and by the year 2005 we intend to raise this ratio up to 92 percent. Despite the unfavorable global economic environment generated by the effects of the recent crises in Asia, Latin America, and Russia, the Polish economy is still expanding. Politicians might be suspected of exaggerating Poland's economic success, but nearly $30 billion in Western investment is an irrefutable testimonial to the confidence of the global market in Poland's stability and prospects for future growth.

The accomplishments that I have noted were possible only through the hard work of the Polish people. To achieve these results, we had to overcome the fear of the unknown future that lay ahead of us, such as life under a free, competitive market. We also have had to discard the burden of historical prejudices and stereotypes. It was essential to get used to criticism and to plurality of thought and ideas, and also to leave behind our nostalgic attachment to the illusory benefits of a *paternalistic* socialist state. Although echoes of the past are still with us, I am certain that they will not deter us from reaching our destination.

We are delighted that other Central European states besides Poland have also been successful in their transformations. This can be easily confirmed by noting their participation in the process of integration with European and Transatlantic structures. Unfortunately, however, some countries in Eastern and Southeastern Europe are still bedeviled by problems characteristic of the transition period.

The emergence of democratic political, social, and economic institutions is initially marked by the coexistence of old and new elements. The process of reform frequently suspends society between the expiration of the old system and the genesis of the new. It is a time of uncertainty and frustration, with a shortage of quick answers to pressing questions. Sometimes the sheer magnitude of the necessary changes is so great that a temptation arises to find a "third way" that can offer a panacea for current problems. Yielding to this temptation often leads to delays in reform—an ideal situation for influential interest groups that seek to turn the process of change to their own advantage. This can produce understandable bitterness in transitional societies, which have a tendency to accept the false explanation that the free market is the *cause* of the negative social and economic phenomena that appear. The real truth is that it is precisely the absence of stable institutions and of honest and fair free-market rules that is responsible for the impoverishment of some societies in transition.

The bankruptcy of communist ideology and the downfall of its power have produced a moral vacuum that can pose a clear and present danger to democracy. Sometimes advocates of primitive and shallow slogans use fear as a tool to promote nationalism. If they obtain power, they use it for destruction, not creation. Their unhappy countries, instead of participating in integration processes, often drift into alienation, increasing the risk that they will develop an aggressive policy toward internal and external enemies (many of whom are totally imaginary).

The only countries in Central Europe that have succeeded in their transformation are those which have shown determination in pushing through free-market reforms and which have built their public institutions on strong democratic foundations. Democracy and the free market are complementary: There is no lasting democracy if the economy is in chaos, and corruption can hinder the development of truly democratic institutions. It is also impossible to build a free-market economy in the long run unless the government has the support of the people. Otherwise, the fear of an uncontrolled display of popular dissatisfaction frequently forces regimes to impose costly economic restrictions. Some may argue that the compromises required in modern democracies are too time-consuming and inefficient for building a modern economy, but Poland has proven that this is not the case.

I look forward to the twenty-first century with optimism. Central Europe is becoming a part of the transatlantic zone of security and prosperity. The North Atlantic Treaty Organization (NATO) has already embraced new members from our region, and soon the European Union will also be enlarged. Thus there is now an expanding area that Zbigniew Brzezinski has called the "bridgehead of democracy" in Eurasia. I believe that this process marks a new policy direction for the entire Euro-Atlantic community during the coming century, a period in which Poland and the entire Central European region will have a vital role to play in further extending the bridgehead of democracy.

For this to happen, a united Europe must develop a common vision for the future of the continent, including the parameters within which the Euro-Atlantic community will function. The continuation of NATO expansion is a vital element of this process. The "Open Door" policy must provide concrete opportunities for those Central and Eastern countries that have expressed the desire and possess the capabilities to join the Treaty. As a Treaty member, Poland will be an active advocate for these countries. We know the price of freedom, and we know how valuable security is in a region that suffered more than any other as a result of this century's wars.

The European Union needs vision and courage. Those two elements have been the cornerstones of its success since the beginning of European integration in the 1950s. We in the candidate countries may feel that those elements are sometimes lacking. Discussion of the future of a united Europe cannot be limited to functional matters, no matter how important these may be. There must also be room for a deeper debate on the shared values that are the philosophical basis of European integration. The Union must not be like Tarzan, with strong muscles, but problems in communication. It must enlarge and promote a community of values, which include democracy, free markets, the rule of law, and the centrality of human rights. Only such a Union, fully conscious of its identity and its goals, can fulfil its role as the agent of stability, peace, and prosperity in Europe.

In some Central and Eastern European countries, one may hear doubts about whether the difficulties of the transition period can be overcome. Many look back nostalgically to the "good old days" and doubt that the future will be as good. We hope that NATO and the European Union will support the process of transformation. The readiness of these organizations to include new members will motivate the countries of our region to work harder. Our common goal should be to counteract the threat of a new wall dividing the democratic and affluent countries of Europe from those sunk in political chaos and economic stagnation.

In closing, let me once again quote Tocqueville: "It cannot be repeated too often that nothing is more fertile in prodigies than the art of being free; but there is nothing more arduous than the apprenticeship of liberty. . . . Liberty [unlike despotism] is generally established with difficulty in the midst of storms; it is perfected by civil discord; and its benefits cannot be appreciated until it is already old." We accept these words with humility, but we cannot wait for the fruits of freedom to age. On this point, at least, we hope to prove this great visionary wrong.

12

VICTORY DEFEATED

G.M. Tamás

G.M. Tamás was E.L. Wiegand Distinguished Visiting Professor of Democratization at Georgetown University's School of Foreign Service in 1998–99. He was one of Hungary's leading dissidents and wrote extensively in samizdat; he was also among the founders of the Free Democratic Alliance and served in parliament during 1990–94. He is the author of L'Oeil et la main, Les Idoles de la tribu, Másvilág (The Nether World), *and other books. This essay originally appeared in the January 1999 issue of the* Journal of Democracy.

A Hungarian émigré historian, Miklós Molnár, professor at the University of Geneva, called his important book on the 1956 uprising *Victoire d'une défaite.* In his view, although Hungary was defeated by the Red Army, the world communist movement was robbed of its most precious asset, its legitimacy: The purest proletarian revolution in history had been directed *against* the heirs of Lenin. The tide turned. The mesmerizing ideological force of radical socialism was broken. It became morally impossible for Enlightenment humanism to remain in cahoots with the butchers of Budapest. Sooner or later, radical socialism would have to lose the historic battle.

Is it possible to argue that what we now see, ten years after 1989, the *annus mirabilis,* is the moral exhaustion of liberal capitalism brought about by its global victory?

To offer at least a partial answer to this alarming question, we must first clarify the difficulties apparent in the Western understanding of the so-called new democracies, difficulties that have a perverse impact on the self-understanding of East Europeans themselves (by East Europeans I mean people from the former Warsaw Pact countries, including the former Soviet Union). It also has to be taken into account that East Europeans do not understand one another's languages, and are aware of one another only *via* the West, usually the United States and France. That, by the way, has always been the case. I read T.G. Masaryk in German, not in Czech.

The role assigned to East Europeans in the retelling of their own story is *bearing witness*. Our job is to furnish anecdotal evidence, the raw material of the *analysis* supplied by Westerners. I, for one, was more than happy to play the role of the *native informant* in the period when—due to censorship—Eastern Europe did not have its own voice. But now that it has got one, "martyrology" (*martyr* means "witness" in Greek) ought to stop. The voluminous political literature on contemporary Eastern Europe, with a few exceptions, pretends that East Europeans do not think about the changes in their own countries, that no theories are presented and no debates and quarrels are taking place. Once upon a time, the slightest stirrings in the Central Committee and the Institute for the Scientific Study of Marxism-Leninism were reported in excruciating detail by myriads of Kremlinologists; the infinitesimal signs of nascent baby heresy were scrutinized as portents of great events. Since the demise of communism, however, East Europeans have given up cerebrating altogether—at least as far as Western observers are concerned.

Yet the most interesting phenomenon in Eastern Europe today is the *new press*. Irreverent, raucous, passionate, invective-laden, pugnacious, it is perhaps the most revolutionary aspect of the new democracies. While in New York there is only one quality broadsheet and two tabloids, Budapest has six broadsheets and three tabloids and Bucharest about thirty dailies, and people are queuing up to buy them. Hungarian intellectuals publish their theoretical-cum-polemical essays in national weeklies with a readership of around 100,000 (in a country of 10 million). Of all this, not a whisper is heard in the West.

It seems that things keep happening to East Europeans, but they are totally passive and do not think about them. Events in Eastern Europe seem to be either economic in nature (that is, "objective" in some sense) or "ethnic" (again, a tragedy arising from what is "given" [race], that is, something "objective"). East European parliaments do not seem to legislate. There do not seem to be left-wing or right-wing governments, only promarket "experts" and antimarket lunatics. Skinhead-style (that is, marginal) antisemitic incidents are reported, but the centrality of the Jewish question (as Leo Strauss said, *the* social problem *par excellence*) is ignored. Western political scientists do not read novels, although the paramountcy of literature in Eastern Europe is unchanged; it is still the best source for understanding the region, far better than collections of footnoted scholarly articles by the usual suspects.

In general, the parts of the story where East Europeans play an active and central role are relegated to the background. A bit player like Mikhail Gorbachev (who was an important but incomprehending and passive figure, indeed somebody to whom things kept happening) occupies center stage, while Solidarity is slowly forgotten. It is characteristic that the name itself by which the events of 1989 are known, to wit, "the collapse of communism," conveys passivity (the building just crumbled), while the crowds taking over civic edifices, smashing the Wall, remain unexplained. The sheer chronological fact that the story begins in 1976 in Poland has disappeared.

Also, the ideas that preceded the changes get short shrift. Imagine a history of the French Revolution without a mention of Voltaire, Rousseau, Linguet, Dom Deschamps, Condorcet, Turgot—we do not have anything of comparable magnitude, of course, in Eastern Europe, but this does not mean that Rudolf Bahro and Robert Havemann in East Germany, for example, have not lived. The thinkers and orators who inspired and harangued the more or less peacefully rebellious masses are still with us, but apart from the half-true cliché of bearded, impractical, bumbling dissidents (and I am all that), not much is known about their ideas. Yet, for better or worse, their ideas were the ones people had at their disposal when faced with the daunting task of mapping out some new arrangements in the novel, astonishingly free world. Aleksandr Zinoviev, Aleksandr Solzhenitsyn, or Igor Shafarevich may not enjoy the respect of Western liberals or, indeed, of their own compatriots right now, but at the time they were people's inspiration and hope.

It is rather telling, I think, that the greatest success story of the region, Poland, is so much ignored. Poland is different from the rest because what happened there, both good and bad, was the result of a genuine and profound revolution—one that was extremely original, full of flashes of political genius and authentic heroism, as well as authentic skulduggery and *Schweinerei*. Poland showed us that the Soviet threat was not absolute; that Soviet power was tired, lacking in energy and self-confidence; that the absence of strong local democratic traditions was not fatal; that the germs of liberty under communism could be transformed into a lush vegetation of modern, original civic initiatives conducive to democracy; and more recently, that the controversy about the market economy need not be fatal to a new democracy and its governance. The great media stories in the West were about Yeltsin and the Stasi files. These are sideshows.

The "collapse of communism" or *die Wende* ("the turn") was the outcome of a treble exhaustion: an exhaustion of ideas, of economic efficiency, and of integrative power in the societies of "really existing socialism." Communist tyranny, unlike hidebound military dictatorships, saw itself as and, to a certain extent, really was the embodiment of a utopia. The obsolescence of utopian faith proved fatal, since the legitimacy of the regime depended on the realization of a prediction and on the veracity of a doctrine—the consequence of communism's enduring Enlightenment legacy. When the promised state of affairs failed to materialize, the specifically communist claim of authority was rendered void, and it was clumsily and awkwardly replaced by Brezhnevite borborygms of the status quo. Beginning in the late 1970s, the Soviet bloc underwent an economic crisis more severe than the Great Depression of the 1920s and 1930s. The East European economy still has not

completely recovered. (Unfortunately, many people see the present predicament as a result of, rather than the reason for, "the turn.") Ethnic
conflicts within and between communist states demonstrated that the
regime was no longer capable of integrating society; people sought other
foci of identity than what the system was willing to offer. The new
ethnicity and proletarian protest, the mass emigration of Soviet Jewry,
the flight of the intellectuals, the sudden rebelliousness of popular culture, and the ever-bolder human rights groups were all signals that the
communist party had lost the initiative.

The exhaustion of the old order is naturally always a cause for change,
but the exhaustion of a regime of revolutionary origins is a different
kettle of fish. For distaste for a utopian-revolutionary regime means distaste for utopia and revolution. Resistance to late communism meant
antipathy, not hope: The language of joyous hope and radical change
was exhausted too. East Europeans thought not that capitalism and liberal democracy were excellent, but rather that the publicly professed
ideas of Bolshevism had failed—ideas like "equality," "community,"
and "civic duty."

The "delegitimization" of "real" socialism succeeded without the
onset of a new legitimacy because the very language or discourse of
legitimacy had become unacceptable; it was irredeemably tainted by
decades of mendacity. The majority was glad to be rid of one-party rule,
gagged speech, servility, and fear. But what most people—minus an
enthusiastic but vocal fraction of the population—thought about the new
dispensation soon became painfully clear: It was something alien, perhaps efficacious and comfortable, but also bewildering; one had to put
up with, adapt to, become accustomed to the unusual logic of the new
victors, the West and its local allies.

In other words, what we *did* was to do away with the remnants of the
old regime—and what *happened* to us, in the absence of a new social
idea of our own, was capitalism, which is supposed to be the even older,
presocialist regime. Modernity in the East European imagination is linked
to socialism—the whole area, including Bohemia, Moravia, and eastern
Germany, was pretty backward prior to 1945—and capitalism is linked
to the past. At the same time, this return to the past was not a return to
tradition (which is local and happened to be more rural and feudal than
bourgeois and capitalist) but to the historic past of the West, which is
also its present. The warmly welcomed defeat of the "radiant future," of
"les lendemains qui chantent," ushered in something certainly fitter for
human consumption, but woefully mundane, prosaic, materialistic, and
selfish.

In the autumn of 1989, just after I had been "reintegrated" to the
university (which caused a stir, especially as I was running a parliamentary election campaign at the same time), a beautiful young student told
me, "What do you want, Professor? Morality is finished, we'll have to

face real life." I asked her, "But what *is* real life, my dear?" "Don't you know? Well, I guess, money, power, and sex." Of course this was mostly reverse youthful romanticism, nothing more; nevertheless, this is what we have been hearing ever since. There is a sense of sobering up, of lost illusions, and this is strange since nobody had seemed to believe the old communist bromides any longer. If you would like to coin the most successful slogan in Eastern Europe, surely it would be, "No slogans!"

If you would like to coin the most successful slogan in Eastern Europe, surely it would be "No slogans!"

This is why even ethnic nationalism, the bogeyman of the early 1990s, has ultimately failed—at least in the sense of a desire for a new, autonomous political community as opposed to sheer *pogrom.* It failed because nationalism, too, is an idea. "Real" socialism insisted on an absolute, unconditional commitment, on loudly affirmed loyalty and duty-driven conformity. Hence the total demise of commitment. Ideas requiring actions are utterly unpopular. Politics by other means usually means no politics at all. People do not turn up when drafted into the army, do not pay their taxes, and do not give to charity. These three fundamental varieties of social or national solidarity cannot function when an ultranominalist doubt concerning institutions is dominant.

Belief in the impersonal fairness of institutions (the "rule of law," *Rechtsstaat,* and their cognates) is possible only if you are willing to make a leap of faith, to believe that there is a Church in spite of your delinquent vicar, to believe in science in spite of your bibulous schoolmaster, in literature in spite of Danielle Steel and Barbara Taylor Bradford. Not many people are willing today—anywhere—to make that leap; Eastern Europe has joined the "free world" at a particularly unpropitious, although quiescent and prosperous moment. East Europeans, make no mistake, are eager to learn the rules of the new dispensation; they want to make the most of it and wish to succeed. After all, they tried to use the old regime too for their own personal purposes, and even that unyielding, rusty, obsolete machinery quite often had to give.

But accepting and using a set of circumstances when there does not seem to be any alternative is not the same thing as believing it to be right or just. A phrase like "You can't do this here, this is a free country," would be greeted with derision. At the same time, East Europeans will sue if their privacy or their rights are violated. It is always difficult to draw the line between healthy skepticism and rampant nihilism. Post-Soviet political attitudes have a big dose of both, I think. Institutions adorned with grand principles invariably calling for sacrifice have traditionally been distrusted by peasant populations uninvolved in and unconsulted about decisions taken "at the top." My compatriots do not believe the leopard called the State will ever change its spots, but they still will cast their vote, mostly to chase away incumbents and to annoy "the leadership." "They" should not feel too secure—and "they" do not, which is delightful. The *negative* side of democracy, like the ingrained distrust of modernity, works like magic.

As to the positive side, there is little encouraging to report. The problems facing post-Soviet democracies are nothing new. Poverty, corruption, abuse of power, chauvinism, and lack of sympathy for the unfortunate are not unknown in older free societies either. But it is one thing to believe, as Marxists did (and do), that this set of facts is endemic in class societies but will disappear under socialism, or to think (as does the worldwide liberal establishment, from social democrats to neo-conservatives) that these are matters for reform and moral betterment reconcilable with the system. Well, in Eastern Europe there is no doubt that all this is the price we are paying for the only genuine novelty perceived there—that we no longer have to shut up. Any state of affairs that can be designated as economic and political inequality (that is, there are leaders and there are those who are led) is construed as proof that freedom is a joke, and the mere existence of political power is interpreted as evidence that "nothing has changed" (the single most frequent political utterance in Eastern Europe, a hyperbole immediately followed by the second most frequent one, namely, "We never had it so bad"). So we can confidently assert that the validity of radical anticapitalism and antimodernism is not doubted. Capitalism is accepted as the honest and straightforward application of original sin as a political blueprint.

Liberal democracy in Eastern Europe is on sufferance. There is no radical alternative, like, say, militant Islam on the horizon. But it is clear that what began as an exhaustion continues as an exhaustion. This has its nice sides. There is a refreshingly unsentimental view of the human and political condition, bereft of seriousness concerning obligations and patriotism. The political talk is often very funny, disrespectful, savagely satirical. One cannot, however, fail to notice the accents of despair.

I was once asked on Hungarian public radio whether I, as a former dissident, would say I am happy now. I replied, democracy is rather an odd thing to be glad about all on one's own.

13

THE INTERNATIONAL CONTEXT

Jacques Rupnik

Jacques Rupnik, *director of research at the Fondation Nationale des Sciences Politiques in Paris and professor at the College of Europe in Bruges, is author of* The Other Europe: The Rise and Fall of Communism in East-Central Europe *(1989) and* Balkans: Paysage après la bataille *(1996). He was executive director of the International Commission on the Balkans, whose report,* Unfinished Peace, *was published by the Carnegie Endowment in 1996. An earlier version of this essay was presented at a June 1998 conference in Warsaw cosponsored by the International Forum for Democratic Studies, the Stefan Batory Foundation (Warsaw), and the Institute for National Policy Research (Taipei).*

The democratic revolutions of 1989 in Central and Eastern Europe have been described as the culmination of the "third wave" of global democratization that began in Spain and Portugal in the mid-1970s. It is indeed tempting to see the disintegration of the Soviet empire as part of a worldwide crumbling of dictatorships. This view certainly influenced how the democratic transition in East-Central Europe has been perceived in the West (as the "end of history") as well as by some of its protagonists. Ten years later, however, despite extensive Western efforts at democracy promotion, the democratic tide has somewhat retreated, leaving a picture of successes in Central Europe (as well as in Latin America and parts of Asia) offset by setbacks in the former Soviet Union and the Balkans (but also in China and most of Africa).

In no other region of the world has the impact of international factors on democratization been as apparent as in Central and Eastern Europe. The revolutions of 1989 were characterized by two important features: First, they were made possible by the lifting of the Soviet imperial constraint. The Soviet bloc imploded, rapidly and peacefully. The falling dominoes of Soviet hegemony in East-Central Europe seemed to complete the triumph of the periphery over the center of the empire. To be sure, the roots of the ideological, political, and economic decay of the communist system go back at least to the post-1968 "restoration of order" and to continuing resistance and dissent in Central European societies, most powerfully exemplified by the Solidarity movement in Poland. Western policies, both public and private, also no doubt played a part in undermining the old order. Future historians will establish the proper weight to be attributed to each. Yet at the critical moment, the victim was a consenting one: Gorbachev's decision not to back the communist regimes in East-Central Europe with military force marked the beginning of the end.

Until Gorbachev came to power, the countries of East-Central Europe hardly featured in the discussions about prospects for democracy. In a 1984 article entitled "Will More Countries Become Democratic?" Samuel Huntington argued that "the likelihood of democratic development in Eastern Europe is virtually nil. The Soviet presence is a decisive overriding obstacle, no matter how favorable other conditions may be in countries like Czechoslovakia, Hungary, and Poland."[1] That constraint was gradually lifted under Gorbachev, finally opening the possibility for a successful transition to democracy.

Second, the revolutions of 1989 were unique in that they proposed no new model of society. Imitation of existing Western models and reconnection with the precommunist past were seen as the quickest path to democracy and prosperity.

The Cold War came to an end in 1989 with the triumph of the Western liberal democracies. The scale of the changes that followed the fall of the Berlin Wall was every bit as great as those that followed either of the two world wars, with one major difference: After the Cold War, there was no victor willing or able to impose a "new international order." Neither the United States, the sole superpower, nor the European Union (EU) was willing to play that part. Instead, they served as an inspiration, a pole of attraction ("Magnet Europa," to use Adenauer's phrase) for the new democracies in East-Central Europe. It was only later that the prospects of integration into Western institutions began to act as an external democratizing force.

1919 and 1989

In examining the relationship between the international system and democracy-building in East-Central Europe, the most relevant historical comparison is with the situation after World War I. Then, as after 1989, liberal democracy was seen as the most desirable form of government. Then as now, the victory of the Western powers was widely presented as the victory of democracy over autocracy. This triumphalist view is reflected in the writings of Tomás G. Masaryk, the founder of Czechoslovakia (and is in many ways echoed by his post-1989 successor as "philosopher-king," Václav Havel). In his book *World Revolution: The Triumph of Democratic Revolution* (published in English under the more sober title *The Making of a State*),[2] Masaryk puts the making of a new Europe of democratic nation-states in the context of World War I, which he interprets as a conflict pitting the forces of Western democracy and humanism against a backward, semifeudal order of authoritarian theocracy. The phrase "end of history" was not used then, but the confidence in the forces of democratic progress echoes the democratic euphoria of the "velvet revolutions" of 1989.

The new democratic states in post-1919 East-Central Europe were created in this spirit. Then as now, the new democracies borrowed much from existing Western models. The constitution of the French Third Republic was widely imitated in Central Europe (including the Baltic states), while constitutional monarchies were established in the Balkans (Romania, for instance, adopted a copy of the Belgian constitution). Western guarantees to the new states created by the Versailles Treaty went hand in hand with the promotion of Western constitutional models. Yet few of these democratic regimes survived into the early 1930s. Understanding why the interwar attempts to promote democracy failed can be of relevance in assessing the chances of success today.

In the aftermath of World War I, critics of the democratic triumphalism of Wilson and Masaryk raised three questions that would have a crucial bearing on the success of democratization in East-Central Europe. The first issue was raised by Oskar Jaszi, the Hungarian democrat, historian, and political figure, who identified the proliferation of unviable small states as a major obstacle to the development of democracy in Central and Eastern Europe. The problem of national minorities (between a quarter and a third of the population) in the newly created states made them internally weak and also prone to conflicts with hostile neighbors. The Hungarian political philosopher Istvan Bibo, in what remains the best work on the subject, *The Misery of the Small East European States* (1944), identified the authoritarian or fascist threat to would-be democracies arising from the tension or conflict between "the cause of the nation and the cause of freedom."[3]

The second reason for the failure of the new Central European democracies in the interwar period was the rise of Nazi Germany or, more generally, the imbalance between the political fragmentation of East-Central Europe and the "weight" of an undemocratic Germany. The French conservative historian Jacques Bainville, in a book published in 1920 entitled *The Political Consequences of The Peace,*[4] predicted the collapse of the new democracies and of the system established by the Versailles Treaty ("written by Bible readers *for* Bible readers"): "Amid this mix of nationalities, religions, and races, Germany alone remains concentrated, homogeneous, and relatively well-organized. Its weight, hanging over the void of Eastern Europe, threatens to shake the entire continent one day."

The third issue of importance for the fate of the interwar democracies was raised by French liberal sociologist Elie Halévy. In a lecture delivered at Oxford in 1920,[5] he questioned the wisdom of redrawing the map of Europe exclusively on the basis of the principle of nationalities: "Simple ideas are revolutionary ideas and lead to war." A stable order in Europe, he argued, required that the principle of self-determination be matched by that of maintaining a balance of power in Europe.

These three issues provide a useful point of comparison with the post-1989 transitions.

1) The viability of the Central European nation-states. Unlike their Balkan counterparts, the Central European states of the 1990s have become much more homogeneous than their predecessors of the 1920s. As Ernest Gellner once noted, Central Europe in the interwar period resembled a painting by Kokoschka, full of subtle touches of all shades. Today it has come to resemble a painting by Modigliani made up of single-color blotches. Poland and the Czech lands are, for the first time in their history, virtually homogeneous states. The absence of major minority or border issues at least partly accounts for the relative weakness of nationalist forces and for the lack of conflict among neighboring states. Slovakia has been the exception that confirms the rule: Priorities of nation-state building (vs. Prague) and tensions with Budapest over the Hungarian minority issue were major ingredients of Vladimír Mečiar's authoritarian populism (1991–98).

In contrast to the quasi-permanent tensions among Central European states in the interwar period—described by Hugh Seton-Watson as a "private civil war"—the 1990s were marked by a modest degree of cooperation. The Visegrád group (Czechoslovakia, Hungary, Poland), launched in February 1991, had a triple goal: to de-Sovietize Central Europe, to encourage regional cooperation, and to coordinate the process of integration into the EU. This cooperation remained limited, partly because the members had different definitions of Central Europe and different expectations. An understandable reaction against the legacy of Soviet-sponsored cooperation also played its part: After 1989, everybody was looking to the West rather than at their neighbors. Unlike the 1980s, when the rediscovery of the idea of Central Europe was important to dissident intellectual elites, the 1990s were marked in the region by a denial of identity. The Czecho-Slovak separation at the end of 1992 reduced Visegrád cooperation to a minimum—a free-trade association (CEFTA). Yet even if the Central European environment did not make a significant contribution to the democratic transition, it certainly did not hinder it—a major contrast with the situation between the wars.

2) The role of Germany. A superficial analogy would stress the contrast between a reunited Germany and an East-Central Europe even more fragmented than it was in 1919. Czechoslovakia and Yugoslavia are no more. The revolutions of 1989 meant the end not just of Yalta but of

Versailles as well. This gives rise to a question that evokes memories of hegemony rather than prospects of democratic transition: Is a new version of *Mitteleuropa*—a German sphere of influence—in the making? Germany (both East and West) was where the interplay between Western influence and change in East-Central Europe was most obvious. It was the collapse of communism in Central Europe that helped to bring down the Berlin Wall and thus brought about the reunification of Germany. Conversely, German reunification (the change of an internationally recognized border in the name of the principle of democratic self-determination) established a precedent for those in East-Central Europe who considered the territorial status quo inherited from World War II to be unjust or even an obstacle to democratic transition.

As important as German influence has been in the 1990s, however, it has been primarily economic rather than military, and exerted through the Bundesbank rather than the Bundeswehr. Between the wars, East-Central Europe was divided into two camps: 1) authoritarian, "revisionist" regimes (Hungary, Bulgaria, Albania) that turned to Nazi Germany as the challenger of the Western-imposed Versailles system; and 2) would-be democracies (mainly the Little Entente: Czechoslovakia, Yugoslavia, and Romania) that looked to the West for support and inspiration. After 1989, by contrast, Germany was seen as a model for the democratic transition, mainly because the postwar Federal Republic was widely regarded as a successful exit from totalitarianism to democracy. Historically, Germany had been seen in East-Central Europe both as a modernizing influence and as a potential threat to national identity. After 1989, however, for the first time Germany also appeared to its Eastern neighbors as a model of democracy. This points not only to a different European context but also to a different kind of German reunification: While Bismarck's unification was, to use A.J.P. Taylor's phrase, "the conquest of Germany by Prussia," Kohl's reunification was essentially the "conquest" of Prussia by West German federalism and the "Rhineland model." No longer an obstacle to Central Europe's integration into the democratic West, Germany has become an agent of that integration.

3) Self-determination, democracy, and the European order. In 1989, democracy returned to East-Central Europe together with national sovereignty, thus reinforcing the strong historical connection between democracy and the nation-state. Today, the counterweight to national self-determination is no longer the concern for the balance of power in Europe but the process of European and Euro-Atlantic integration. While the former was a potential constraint on the new democracies in the interwar period, the latter has, on the whole, acted as an external democratizing force in postcommunist East-Central Europe.

In sum, the three-part comparison with the failed democratic transitions of the interwar period suggests that the regional and international environment in the 1990s has been exceptionally favorable to the democratic transition in East-Central Europe. Russia is weak, its influence in the lands of the former Soviet bloc is shrinking, and it seems to have understood (at least under Yeltsin) that it could not democratize and remain an empire. It has given up Central Europe and now concentrates its attention on the former Soviet republics—the so-called "near abroad." The question for the Central Europeans thus becomes: How near *is* Russia's "near abroad"? Germany is more powerful but also more democratic and anchored in the West. Its influence has thus become a strong force for integration in the democratic European and Atlantic communities. Today there are no significant regional conflicts within Central Europe. A degree of regional cooperation is now seen by all the countries concerned as part of the process of "Euro-Atlantic" integration, and consolidating democracy in each country is seen as part of the shared goal of regional stability.

The Central European regional environment contrasts with that of Southeastern Europe in all these respects. Paradoxically, it is the countries that were the most independent of Moscow (Yugoslavia, Albania, Romania) that have been the least successful in their transition to democracy. The "independent" or "national" communism asserted by Tito (and later, by Enver Hoxha in Albania and Nicolae Ceauşescu in Romania) proved to be an even greater handicap than sovietization, allowing postcommunist national elites to sidetrack the democratic transition. As for Germany, it has so far shown less interest in promoting the enlargement of the European Union and NATO to the Balkans than to Central Europe. Finally, the regional environment in the Balkans has proven to be much less favorable to democratic transitions than in Central Europe. Over the past decade, it has been marked by instability and tensions between neighboring states: the "Wars of Yugoslav Dissolution," the collapse of the Albanian state, the fragility of Macedonia, and, last but not least, the rivalry between Greece and Turkey.

A decade after the fall of communism, a clear distinction can be made between the relative "success story" of Central Europe and the problems in the Balkans, where democratic transitions have been derailed by nationalist agendas, economic backwardness, and an unstable regional environment. It remains difficult to assess the extent to which this difference is due to external factors (including Western policies). Other factors, such as the legacies of communism, the economic situation, the state of civil society, and the degree of "homogeneity" of populations, not to mention older historical or cultural legacies, may in most cases have been more influential.[6]

Integration and Democratic Consolidation

The post–Cold War predicament in Europe can be summed up as follows: The continent's geopolitical center of gravity has shifted eastward, to the center of Europe, while its institutional center of gravity has moved to the west. NATO and the European Union have become the only game in town. It is in East-Central Europe that this tension (some would call it a contradiction) is being confronted. Joining both institutions has been identified in most of postcommunist Europe as the prime foreign-policy goal of the transition, and both institutions consider the consolidation of democracy to be a prerequisite for membership. European and Euro-Atlantic integration is therefore a unique case of a foreign-policy goal that requires internal (legal and institutional) democratic change as a precondition.

Since the cases of NATO and the EU are different, let us examine each of them in turn.

1) NATO enlargement and "democratic security." The revolutions of 1989 heralded the "return to Europe," which was widely identified with the European Union. Ten years later, three Central European countries (Poland, Hungary, and the Czech Republic) have already joined NATO, while the EU enlargement process is still moving slowly, with no established target date. The European dream has begun to materialize under the auspices of the Atlantic Alliance. How can we account for this paradox, which also coincides with the candidate-members' own priorities?

First of all, it can be explained by the primacy of security concerns. Allowing East-Central Europe once again to become a security void, a no man's land, would not bode well for the stability of the new democracies. As the situation in the former Yugoslavia has demonstrated, security is the precondition of a successful transition. Democracy, in turn, is the best way to enhance security, since democracies tend not to go to war with each other. Democratic transitions are unlikely to be consolidated if they do not establish proper socioeconomic foundations by integrating into Western economies and institutions. That, however, requires . . . security. Following this logic, joining NATO takes precedence over joining the EU.

Second, Central Europeans perceive the United States as the guarantor of European democracy. The democratic order imposed at Versailles did not survive long after America withdrew from Europe. America's staying in Europe after World War II allowed democracy to survive in the West and eventually created the conditions for its return to the East. Unlike some West Europeans, Central Europeans have no problems with the primacy of American power and (particularly in the case of Poland) see their own role in the region or in the Alliance as closely connected to it. They see their membership in NATO and the U.S. presence in Europe not only as a counterweight to their relationship with Russia but also as providing a framework for their new relationship with Germany. While NATO debated its new strategic concept, the East European newcomers would have been quite content with the old one: "To keep the Americans in, the Russians out, and the Germans down."

Third, NATO is perceived in East-Central Europe as a more "value-infused institution" (to use Aleksander Smolar's phrase) than the EU, which (rightly or wrongly) is seen as primarily an economic institution with complicated bureaucratic procedures—a political project disguised as a currency device. Paradoxically, when in March 1999, barely a week after Poland, Hungary, and the Czech Republic joined the Alliance, NATO embarked on its first military intervention in half a century in defense of what it considered to be Western democratic values, the new members (particularly the Czechs) were anxious and perplexed. Instead of escaping Balkan instability by joining the democratic club, they had been drawn closer to it than ever.

Finally, joining NATO is less demanding than joining the EU. There is, of course, an important element of democratic conditionality, but the actual preparation for enlargement concerns civilian control over the military and an official secrets act, along with the restructuring of the military itself, including English-language courses for officers. That explains why there was little public debate in the candidate countries about what the shared values and responsibilities of NATO membership entailed: The Poles (rightly) assumed overwhelming support anyway, and the Hungarians were concerned not to compromise the results of the popular referendum on membership, while the Czechs simply trusted Václav Havel.

Although some objections were voiced to NATO expansion on strategic grounds, few doubted that NATO membership would enhance democratic stability in Central Europe. The only democracy-related objection concerned Russia: Would NATO enlargement undermine the (already tenuous) prospects for democracy in Russia by playing into the hands of the nationalists and the communists? The *New York Times* feared that expansion would be "a mistake of historic proportions"[7]: America (or the West) should not seek to isolate Russia or treat it as a threat but should help make it democratic, just as it did with Germany and Japan after World War II.

This argument is unconvincing on several grounds. First, since Russia, unlike Germany and Japan, had not been militarily defeated, democracy could not be introduced or imposed there from outside. Moreover, the argument that small democratic gains for the West in Central Europe could jeopardize bigger democratic gains in Russia raises serious doubts about the latter: What kind of democrats would feel "threatened" by the consolidation of a Western, democratic anchor in Central Europe? More importantly, the persistence in Russian political culture of non-Western institutions and anti-Western attitudes casts doubt on the assumption that, except for the issue of NATO expansion, Russia is on a course of democratic convergence with the West. "Who lost Russia?" Certainly not the Central Europeans.

2) The European Union—from reluctant model to democratizing force. Joining the European Union has generally been viewed as the ultimate goal of the East-Central European transition. The post-1989 hopes for reuniting the continent became identified with the enlargement of the EU. Central Europeans, driven by a moral-superiority complex mixed with resentment, emphasized the shared European culture, civilization, and democratic values that had survived crumbling ideologies. A divided Europe, they claimed, is a Europe emptied of its substance. From Milan Kundera's famous article about Central Europe as the "kidnapped West" to the Polish Pope's vision of a united Christian Europe, we can find both secular and Christian variations on this theme. The West Europeans responded with embarrassment (there is nothing to make you doubt your own democratic principles more than the discovery that several hundred million of your neighbors have suddenly converted to them!) and with concern that precisely through enlargement Europe could be "emptied of its substance." Although the EU may have been a model for the Central Europeans, it was a reluctant one.

Beyond cultural identification, the aspirants to EU membership also had a political motive. They saw integration into the EU as an indicator of the success and irreversibility of their democratic transitions. In other words, they hoped that the European Union could do for the Poles, the Czechs, and the Hungarians what it had done successfully for democratic consolidation in Spain, Portugal, and Greece.

There were also economic reasons for integration—the EU was seen as a club not only of democracies but also of prosperous countries. Central Europeans looked forward to the expected benefits of the principle of solidarity and redistribution that has worked so well over the last 20 years for the benefit of the EU's less-developed members. Moreover, as the bulk of East-Central European trade shifts to Western Europe, pressure is increasing for East-Central Europe to adopt its legal norms and institutions. No less importantly, one can argue that if economic dependency on Western Europe is Eastern Europe's likely future, it will be acceptable to the societies concerned only if there is a parallel process of political integration among European democracies. Otherwise, the backlash of economic nationalism is always possible.

Finally, there is the "democratic security" motive already mentioned in connection with NATO expansion. While NATO has a "curative" function, in that it can intervene in response to latent threats or actual conflicts, the EU has a more "preventive" (or indirect) security purpose—to create such a web of interdependence among member states as to make conflict unthinkable. Just as the EU was the fruit of Franco-German reconciliation, it should now provide the impetus to consoli-

date Polish-German or Czech-German reconciliation. It can also provide the proper framework for bilateral or regional efforts to deal with
the problem of national minorities. Hungary's dealings with its neighbors "in Europe's name" is the most successful case in point.[8]

Obviously, the appeal of the "European model" and the strength of the
incentives for EU membership vary considerably across the postcommunist
landscape. They are strong for Polish or Hungarian elites, marginal in
most of the former Soviet Union, and nonexistent for Milošević. In other
words, the attraction of the EU depends on a mixture of factors such as
geographical proximity and the orientation of postcommunist elites. The
EU did not play the decisive role in whether a country followed a democratic (Central European) or authoritarian/nationalist ("Balkan") pattern
of exit from communism; its influence was most effective where the domestic commitment to democratic reform was already strong.

Democratic Conditionality

The magnitude of the international influence on the transition is related not only to the strength of the candidate's motives for joining the
"club" of Western democracies but also to the plausibility of its prospects for being admitted. The relationship in the 1990s between the East-
Central European candidates and the Union went through three main
phases: an initial euphoria over the "return to Europe"; the disappointment that followed the first association agreements of 1991 and the realization that membership remained a distant prospect; and a third, more
"realistic" phase once the accession negotiations with the five leading
candidates began in March 1998. This latter stage is where we move
from indirect influence to direct leverage or *democratic conditionality.*

Democracy is the first condition for EU membership, as was made
clear in the criteria spelled out at the June 1993 EU summit in
Copenhagen: 1) democracy and human rights; 2) economic readiness to
join the single market; and 3) the capacity to implement EU legislation.
The degree to which prospective candidates met these conditions was
assessed by the EU Commission in the ten *avis* ("opinions") published
as part of Agenda 2000 in July 1997. Five countries (Poland, the Czech
Republic, Hungary, Slovenia, and Estonia) were recommended for negotiations on accession. Romania, Bulgaria, Latvia, and Lithuania were
not included, primarily on economic grounds. Slovakia was the only
country excluded on explicitly political grounds—for failing to meet
the democratic criteria. "A democracy cannot be considered stable," the
Commission said about Slovakia, "if respective rights and obligations
of institutions such as the presidency, the constitutional court or the
central referendum commission can be put into question by the government itself and if the legitimate role of the opposition in parliamentary
committees is not accepted."[9]

The subsequent role of the EU as an external democratizing force must be analyzed in terms of its effect on two distinct groups of countries: those on the fast track to EU membership and the others. The first group has entered into an Accession Partnership with the EU that clearly spells out the specific requirements for membership and provides assistance to the candidates in meeting them. Thus the PHARE (Poland and Hungary Assistance for the Restructuring of the Economy) program, which used to be "demand-driven" (that is, assistance was provided according to the needs of the transition, as established by the recipient) is now "accession-driven" (that is, assistance is now designed to help candidates reach the goals set by the EU as criteria for acceptance of new members). The "screening" process, with annual reports released by Commission experts, monitors each candidate's progress in adopting the required reforms and legislation. In the fall of 1999, for instance, the progress of Hungary and, to a lesser extent, Poland was evaluated fairly positively, while that of the Czech Republic and Slovenia was considered inadequate (reform of public administration and of the judiciary are considered the main weak points). The procedure is tedious, sometimes almost humiliating, but it has been accepted, primarily for two reasons: 1) Most of these reforms (such as the establishment of an independent judiciary or civil-service reform) would be necessary for a liberal democracy even if it did not wish to join the EU. The EU constraint, in fact, can be an effective tool for governments in forcing through unpopular measures over the opposition of lobbies or established bureaucracies. 2) Even when they resent the intrusiveness of the process, Central European political elites are well aware that the domestic political costs of failure on the EU accession issue (and relegation to the second group of candidates) would be potentially high. The result is clear enough: Although Poland has had eight different governments in ten years, it has basically followed the same reform-oriented economic policy and Western-oriented foreign policy. Much the same can be said about Hungary. The accession process considerably restricts the room to maneuver of would-be members.

That is precisely what some leaders in the second group of countries wished to avoid. Mečiar in Slovakia, Iliescu in Romania, and the former communists in Bulgaria all thought they could pay lip service to the goal of rejoining Europe while ignoring its constraints at home (as in their treatment of the media or of ethnic minorities). In late 1996 in Romania and in the spring of 1997 in Bulgaria, a mixture of economic unrest and external pressure helped democratic, reform-minded coalitions topple the former communists, but these democratic changes came too late and were too fragile to have a decisive influence on the NATO and EU enlargement process. Lack of progress on the latter front could well undermine reformers in both countries.

Slovakia is certainly the clearest case so far of the effectiveness of

EU democratic conditionalities. The decision in July 1997 to exclude Slovakia from the first wave of enlargement came as a shock to Slovak society and was widely seen as a verdict on Mečiar's nationalist authoritarian regime. There was some concern before the September 1998 Slovak elections that the opposition's use of the "European" card could backfire. Mečiar repeatedly rebuffed European interference, while accusing the opposition of damaging the country's image abroad. But external pressure (mainly from Europe) combined with pressure from Slovak civil society helped to compensate for the weaknesses of the coalition of democratic opposition parties. In fact, the issues of EU and NATO enlargement have been a major unifying factor in an otherwise weak and divided post-Mečiar government (better described as a coalition of coalitions). Since 1998, on issues ranging from respect for the rule of law to the new language law accommodating the aspirations of the Hungarian minority, Slovakia's desire to catch up with its Central European neighbors on the road to Europe has been a powerful incentive for democratic reforms.

These conditionalities, however, can be effective only as long as the prospect of joining the EU is considered a realistic one. To a great extent, the legitimacy of several governments in the region (Slovakia, Bulgaria, Romania) depends on the EU enlargement issue. Including Slovakia in the first group would stabilize the moderate reformist government there and would also be a major boost to Central European cooperation (within the Visegrád Group). The Bulgarian and Romanian cases are no less important, since the current governments, despite their limitations, are more committed to democratic, Western-oriented reforms than any of their successors are likely to be in the foreseeable future. Both countries are in danger of being ignored by the West, because while they do not fit the Central European pattern of the first wave of enlargement, they are not conflict-ridden disaster areas requiring the imposition of an international protectorate (as in Bosnia or Kosovo-Albania-Macedonia). Neglecting Bulgaria and Romania could prove counterproductive for the West, since it is precisely the success or failure of countries like these, which might go either way, that could have a "snowball effect" on the rest of Balkans.

The Balkan wars and their consequences challenge the hitherto prevailing concept of EU enlargement. Paradoxically, the failed states in the Balkans, where protectorates are being established, could find themselves more closely associated with the EU than are the Central European candidates for enlargement. This would mean integration not through shared democratic and market institutions but through conflict and protectorates. Such a development could have two unfavorable consequences: First, it could slow down even further the EU enlargement process in Central Europe, simply because political and financial priorities would be shifted toward the emergencies in Southeastern Europe. Second, it could make the task of democratic consolidation even harder for countries like Bulgaria and Romania, which are being asked to cooperate in the EU-sponsored Balkan Stability Pact launched in the summer of 1999 while waiting patiently—perhaps for more than a decade—for EU membership. Such a policy risks widening the gulf (already apparent during NATO's Kosovo intervention) between the pro-Western political elites now in power in these countries and the rest of society and may thus inadvertently prepare the return of nationalist populists. If there are no tangible dividends from a policy course identified with the democratic West, there could well be an authoritarian, nationalist, anti-Western backlash.

History moves faster than politics, which moves faster than institutions. The war in Kosovo, and more generally the Balkan crisis, should lead the European Union to rethink its enlargement policy. Democratic conditionalities will create a positive dynamic of "democratic contagion" only if the prospects for integration remain credible—that is, if they are seen as moving forward. Granting political membership promptly to the consolidated democracies of Central Europe (while working out a schedule for the continuation of economic reform and legal harmonization) could be a powerful incentive to democratic reforms in the countries of the "second circle" (from Lithuania and Latvia to Bulgaria and Romania).[10]

The EU and the New Democracies

The interplay between EU integration and the democratic transformation of East-Central Europe presents three large issues. The first concerns the relationship between democracy, sovereignty, and the nation-state in East-Central Europe and the specific nature of the EU as a political entity. After a history marked by the discontinuity of statehood and four decades as satellites of the last colonial empire, the nations of East-Central Europe have recovered their sovereignty and democracy. Yet they are told that their democratic future in the EU requires them to abandon part of that sovereignty to an institution whose democratic *modus operandi,* transparency, and accountability are not always obvious, even to citizens of its current member states. This is more than simply a matter of a democratic model confronting its own "democratic deficit." The EU was built on the principle of consensus, not that of majoritarian democracy. Its culture derives from a permanent process of negotiations among member states whose aim is to create a community built on interdependence and trust. Hence the confusion between the means and the ends, the process and the goal, the journey and the destination. Hence also the concern voiced by critics within the EU about creating a political void where legal procedures substitute for political content. The question posed by the EU to its candidates for membership is this: Can they endorse and internalize this culture of negotiation, compromise, and the pooling of sovereignties? The question reopened by the enlargement of the EU to include the new democracies is: Does the nation-state remain the framework *par excellence* of democracy? If it does not, then what is the supranational (European) or subnational (regional) dimension of democracy?

Second, after a decade of democratic transition, there are already clear signs, even in the Central European countries considered "success stories," of democratic fatigue—low election turnout, diminishing trust in the institutions of representative democracy, and contempt for political parties. The new democracies of the Eastern part of the continent already seem to be suffering from the same ills as the established democracies of Western Europe. The crisis of political representation, the gulf between political elites and the electorate, and the rise of populist parties (from the Italian Northern League or Jörg Haider's Freedom Party in Austria to their Slovene and Slovak counterparts) are all now trans-European phenomena. Democracy is not the only "contagion" that could spread to East-Central Europe.

Finally, we must note the distinction between the borders of European democracy (the EU) and the borders of Europe itself. The European Union can be considered in some respects as a functional equivalent in Central Europe of the Habsburg Empire—it is meant to neutralize tensions among the Central Europeans, but also to provide a balance and a framework for their relationship with Germany. Yet there is an essential difference as well; the EU is a reluctant "empire" that grows through the expansion of democracy and the market economy. A new map of the continent has been in the making since 1989, the contours of which remain uncertain. The new dividing lines are drawn not by imperial or great-power ambitions but by a differentiation process among postcommunist transitions. These transitions, as has become clear in most of the Balkans and the former Soviet Union, do not always lead to democracy. Hence a series of questions arises: How far can, or should, democratic Europe expand? What do the new, enlarged borders of democratic Europe imply for the future fate of democracy beyond those borders?

Every inclusion is by definition also an exclusion. The EU enlargement process thus raises the question about its relationship with Russia and Turkey,[11] two semi-European countries too large for comfort, which are unlikely any time soon to become Western-style democracies acceptable for membership. What kind of relations or partnerships can be established to help democratic change there? The EU is unlikely to be decisive in either case. It can, however, make a difference on the periphery of Central and Southeastern Europe. The relations that will be established between the "ins" and the "outs" in the EU enlargement process will, therefore, be of utmost importance. Will a "soft" border concept prevail, making the Central European newcomers to the EU a factor in promoting democracy further east and south? Or will "hard" borders (such as the "external" borders created by the 1993 Schengen Accords) be imposed on the new members (who perceive them as a reallocation of risks and constraints upon the weakest members of the Union), thus creating *de facto* a new dividing line further east. Such a policy not only risks reinforcing the feeling of exclusion, it also could become a self-fulfilling prophecy, actually hastening the destabilization or failure of the democratic transition on Europe's eastern periphery.

Nobody can yet tell what the eastern borders of democratic Europe will be, and that is for the best. It is crucial that the democratic enlargement of the European Union remain an open process where it is the nature of the project that shapes the borders, and not the other way around.

NOTES

1. Samuel P. Huntington, "Will More Countries Become Democratic?" *Political Science Quarterly* 99 (Summer 1984): 217.

2. Tomás G. Masaryk, *The Making of a State: Memoirs and Observations, 1914–1918,* Henry Wickham Steed, ed. (New York: Frederick A. Stokes, 1927).

3. Istvan Bibo, *Misère des petits états d'Europe de l'Est* (Paris: L'Harmattan, 1986), 115.

4. Jacques Bainville, *Les conséquences politiques de la paix* (Paris: La Nouvelle Librarie Nationale, 1920), 19.

5. See the reprint of Elie Halévy's lecture in *Commentaire* (Spring 1992): 125–27.

6. These internal factors are spelled out in more detail in Jacques Rupnik, "Eastern Europe a Decade Later: The Postcommunist Divide," *Journal of Democracy* 10 (January 1999): 57–62.

7. "NATO and the Lessons of History," *The New York Times,* 29 April 1998.

8. After 1919, Hungary sacrificed democracy for the goal of changing borders. After 1989, Hungary opted for a European democratic strategy that aimed at a devaluation of borders as a means of establishing closer ties with Hungarian minorities in neighboring states.

9. Heather Grabbe and Kirsty Hughes, *Enlarging the EU Eastwards* (London: Royal Institute of International Affairs, 1998), 46.

10. At the December 1999 EU summit in Helsinki, these countries were included as "candidates" and the two groups were merged. Each candidate will be assessed on its "merits."

11. In December 1999, the EU acknowledged the legitimacy of Turkey's application to join the organization. Although it has been reluctant to expand into Central Europe, it now suggests the possibility of expanding into the Middle East, with prospective borders with Iran, Iraq, and Syria.

14

A DIVERGING EUROPE

Richard Rose

Richard Rose, director of the Centre for the Study of Public Policy at the University of Strathclyde, Glasgow, is the director of the New Europe Barometer surveys. He is the senior author of Democracy and Its Alternatives: Understanding Post-Communist Societies *(1998). His most recent books are* The International Encyclopedia of Elections *(2000) and* Elections Without Order: Russia's Challenge to Vladimir Putin *(2002). This essay originally appeared in the January 2001 issue of the* Journal of Democracy.

Whatever its boundaries and in whatever century, Europe has never been unified. Nor has Europe ever been stable politically. In the past century, democratic and undemocratic regimes rose and fell and national boundaries were twice reshuffled. The fall of the Iron Curtain further transformed the map of Europe: Czechoslovakia and Yugoslavia broke into seven new states; the breakup of the Soviet Union enabled Estonia, Latvia, and Lithuania to regain their independence; and the Russian Federation, Ukraine, Belarus, and Moldova became independent with boundaries adjoining historic European states. Given the lives lost in the destruction of World War II and the establishment of the communist bloc, the opening of this new era in European politics has been surprisingly peaceful.

Europe has never been completely democratic. For most of its history, undemocratic rule has been the norm. Challenges to old regimes were as likely to come from undemocratic nationalist politicians as from proponents of democracy. Textbook examples of democratization such as England and Sweden, in which a modern rule-of-law state gradually expanded the franchise to become a twentieth-century democracy, have been the exception rather than the rule. Of the 15 member-states of the European Union (EU), a majority have had recent experience of undemocratic rule. Four—Germany, Austria, Italy, and Finland—came to democracy after the military defeat of authoritarian or totalitarian regimes in World War II; three—Spain, Portugal, and Greece—dismissed undemocratic regimes in the 1970s; and the Fifth French Republic was established in the aftermath of a military coup. Citizens of EU states often argue that their systems of government are still not completely democratic, but debates about electoral reform in Britain are minor compared to the absence of free elections in Belarus, and corruption in France or Germany does not threaten state and market as it does in the Russian Federation.

Today, democracy is the critical qualification for European countries. Unlike NATO, which has always had nondemocratic members, the European Union makes democracy a necessary condition for membership, and a member state that shows signs of departing from such standards is threatened with isolation.[1] Negotiations to enlarge the European Union give practical as well as academic bite to the question: What does democracy mean in the postcommunist states of Central and Eastern Europe?

Democracy requires the rule of law as well as free elections and the enjoyment of political rights and civil liberties. An electoral democracy without the rule of law is an incomplete democracy, just as a rule-of-law regime without free elections is not democratic. In European history, the *Rechtsstaat* (rule-of-law state) came centuries before universal suffrage was granted. Given the rule of law, advocates of democracy could concentrate on campaigning for the right of all citizens to vote: Political parties, the media, and interest groups were able to participate in elections, the conduct of elections was free and fair, and the ruling powers accepted that they were accountable under the constitution, whether democratic or undemocratic.

The new regimes of postcommunist Europe, however, have started democratization backwards.[2] With hardly any exceptions, they hold free elections. Competitive elections and turnovers of power have been a regular feature of the political landscape since 1990. NATO bombs could not topple Slobodan Milošević, but Serbian voters could and did. Yet the legacy of "socialist legality" and communist-style corruption means that the rule of law cannot be taken for granted. In order to complete the democratization process, countries such as Russia and Serbia must create in the twenty-first century what they failed to create in the twentieth: a modern state that enforces laws preventing rulers from arbitrarily violating political and civil rights or exploiting public office for the private profit of themselves, their families, and their cronies.

The great obstacle to the completion of democracy in postcommunist Europe is the absence of the rule of law. Citizens of postcommunist countries not only want to be free to say what they think and to vote for or against the government of the day; they also want a government that obeys the laws it lays down and is not steeped in corruption. The completion of democracy is of immediate concern for EU countries because corruption and crime now have a transnational dimension. Cars can be stolen to order in Germany and Austria for delivery in Poland or Ukraine, and new businesses and banks in Eastern Europe cannot attract investment from Western Europe if those receiving the money divert it to Swiss bank accounts. Although elections are common to postcommunist Europe, there are big differences among states in the extent to which corruption flourishes. Countries are diverging: Some are moving toward completing the process of democratization and entering the EU, while others, because of deficiencies in the rule of law, remain outside the pale.

Freedom in Electoral Democracies

In European history, the state was oppressive; it was not the democratic instrument of "we the people." Political reformers demanded freedom from the state; the right to vote was often seen as a guarantee of freedom rather than as a means of positively influencing government action. In established democracies such as Britain and the Scandinavian countries, the state granted substantial freedoms to citizens a century or more before it granted the right to vote.

By contrast, the communist regimes established under Soviet tutelage in half of Europe after World War II were totalitarian in aspiration. Unlike previous undemocratic regimes, where elites got on with governing and the masses were left to themselves as long as they did not challenge authority, totalitarian regimes were intrusive. The communist party-state sought to compel individuals to think and act as the government commanded. Party *apparatchiki* produced 99.9 percent turnout in one-party elections, and subjects were encouraged to spy on friends and relatives.

Freedom from the state. Whereas electoral democracy focuses on an activity that involves citizens less than once a year, freedom affects what people are able to do and not to do in their daily lives—to say what they think, to join organizations of their own choice, or to decide whether or not to go to church. Unlike social-welfare benefits, these freedoms do *not* require government to spend large sums of money and take positive action; Isaiah Berlin has characterized them as "negative freedoms," that is, freedom *from* the state.[3] For individuals to enjoy these freedoms, the state had to stop doing what it had customarily been doing under communist rule. The collapse of the old regime has meant the end of the security police, censorship, and compulsory indoctrination in Marxist-Leninist doctrines in schools, the media, and the workplace.

Newly gained freedom from the state means that today researchers can use familiar social-science methods of sampling public opinion to survey the mass response to transformation in Central and Eastern Europe and the former Soviet Union. This essay draws on New Europe Barometer surveys from 16 postcommunist countries, including all ten countries currently negotiating membership in the European Union (Bulgaria, the Czech Republic, Estonia, Hungary, Latvia, Lithuania, Poland, Romania, Slovakia, and Slovenia), as well as countries where progress toward European standards has been slower (Croatia, Serbia and Montenegro, Russia, Ukraine, Moldova, and Belarus, the one country where the governing power rejects democracy as a goal).[4]

In postcommunist Europe, adults have lots of first-hand experience of living without freedom. Therefore, we can measure the extent to which people have achieved freedom from the state by asking whether they think their new regime is better, much the same, or worse in granting them the right to do things taken for granted in established European democracies. Across postcommunist Europe, an average of 84 percent of citizens feel freer than before to decide whether or not to follow a religion; 80 percent feel freer to join any organization that they want; 77 percent feel freer to say what they think; and 73 percent feel freer to decide for themselves whether or not to take an interest in politics. Across the region, an average of 79 percent feel they have gained greater personal freedom thanks to the collapse of communist regimes. Most of the remaining fifth say their situation was much the same as before; very few say that conditions have worsened.

The priceless character of freedom is emphasized by the fact that people appreciate it even when they see themselves worse off economically as a result of the transition from a planned to a market economy. The median postcommunist citizen feels freer than before, but also poorer. An average of 62 percent say that they are worse off now than before the economic transformation commenced nearly a decade ago. It is arguable whether this statement is correct—for example, 83 percent of households now have a color television, 44 percent a car, and 36 percent a video cassette recorder, levels of consumer affluence unknown in the communist era. People may be better off materially yet feel worse off, if only because they are now comparing themselves with West Europeans rather than with the living standards of a stagnating planned economy.

Citizens are almost as likely to feel free under governments that do not fully recognize citizen rights as under governments that do. Postcommunist countries are divided into two broad categories by Freedom House according to the extent to which they respect political rights and civil liberties. All ten countries negotiating entry to the European Union are described as Free in the annual Freedom House ratings. Eight are ranked equal with Britain and Germany, while Bulgaria and Romania have a rating similar to Greece, the least highly rated EU country. In these ten countries, an average of 80 percent say that they feel freer than before. The new regimes in five countries—Croatia, Serbia and Montenegro, Russia, Moldova, and Ukraine—are categorized as Partly Free and Belarus as Not Free. Yet even in these countries, 73 percent feel freer in their personal life than under the previous regime. In Russia, where the media are under pressure from the government, 81 percent feel freer than in Soviet times, and in Belarus, where the regime does not allow free elections, an average of 69 percent say the new regime gives them more scope for freedom in everyday life. Although these Partly Free regimes are incomplete democracies, people who have lived most of their lives under communist rule nonetheless find them better than what went before.

Distancing the state. The importance of freedom *from* the state is underscored by the fact that a big majority of citizens in postcommunist regimes do not view the state's influence in favorable terms. When the New Europe Barometer surveys ask people to compare the fairness with which their new government treats people with the behavior of the old regime, only 27 percent say that everyone is treated more fairly now than before. The median citizen—and 40 percent of the total—believe that they are just about as likely to be treated unfairly now as under the communist regime, and 33 percent see the government as acting less fairly than before.

Citizens in postcommunist Europe do not see their new regimes as civic democracies open to their influence. When asked whether they have more influence on government today than before, 46 percent see no difference, 31 percent think that they have more influence, and 23 percent actually think that they have less influence. The evaluation of the government's responsiveness is only 11 percentage points higher in countries that Freedom House characterizes as Free than in countries labeled Partly Free. In other words, the introduction of free elections has not bridged the "us versus them" gulf between bureaucratic officials of centralized hierarchical ministries and people at the grassroots.

The feeling that government is unresponsive to public opinion can also be found in the established democracies of Western Europe,[5] but the context is radically different. In Western Europe, freedom from the state is taken for granted, including the freedom to criticize government for not caring. Electoral competition encourages opposition politicians to stir up dissatisfaction with the government of the day and to promise to "feel your pain." The failure of politicians, once elected, to deliver as promised can add to dissatisfaction. In established democracies, complaining that the government is out of touch is a harmless recreation, for people know that their freedom to complain is secure. In the new regimes of postcommunist countries, however, freedom to complain represents a major step toward democracy.

Freedom from the state is personal and nonpolitical, because it is defined by the explicit absence of government involvement. It is thus in marked contrast to the idea of government reflecting the will of the people, or Tocqueville's ideal of a civic democracy in which people cooperate to influence government, and government responds positively to their demands. The philosophical distinction between freedom from the state and positively influencing the government of a civic democracy is borne out by the New Europe Barometer surveys. People in the postcommunist countries may not feel able to influence government but nonetheless feel that government is now less likely to influence them.[6]

Two, not three cheers. Theories of popular government are ambivalent about the attitude that people ought to take toward their governors. The U.S. Constitution has an elaborate system of checks and balances because its authors *distrusted* governors. Schumpeter based his theory of democratic electoral competition on the assumption that dissatisfied citizens ought to be able to "turn the rascals out," and that often a majority would want to exercise this right. Churchill characterized democracy as "the worst form of government, except all those other forms that have been tried from time to time," and E.M. Forster thought democracy was worth two cheers, "one because it admits variety and two because it permits criticism."

How do people evaluate a new regime if it does not respond to their wishes and is often unfair, yet allows much greater freedom than before? The countries surveyed by the New Europe Barometer differ substantially in the extent to which they may be considered democratic. It would be misleading to ask people how well they think democracy is working when (as in Belarus) it is not even in operation or its presence is contestable. Instead, people are asked to evaluate the current system of governing their country, with free elections and many parties, on a "heaven/ hell" scale that runs from plus 100 to minus 100, with zero as a neutral midpoint.

Across the full range of 16 postcommunist regimes, only 47 percent of citizens positively endorse their new system of government. Since 10 percent are typically neutral, those who are positive about their new regime outnumber those who are not. The character of the regime influences the extent to which people endorse it. As one would expect, in the ten electoral democracies of this region that Freedom House classifies as Free, 55 percent of citizens are positive about their new regime, 12 percent neutral, and a third negative. In the six countries where government falls short of full democracy, about one-third approve of the system and an absolute majority are negative. In the extreme case of Ukraine, only 22 percent are positive about their system of government. This low rating is not a sign that Ukrainians have no desire for democracy but rather that they strongly disapprove of the very defective system of government supplied by Ukrainian elites.[7]

Within every postcommunist country, up to a quarter of citizens are skeptics, disapproving of both their current regime and the old regime.

TABLE 1—SUPPORT FOR UNDEMOCRATIC ALTERNATIVES

	(PERCENT ANSWERING "YES")			PERCENT AGAINST ALL THREE
	RETURN TO COMMUNIST RULE	MILITARY RULE	STRONGMAN RULE	
FREE COUNTRIES				
Slovenia	14	1	13	78
Czech Republic	16	3	13	75
Hungary	25	1	18	68
Poland	15	6	27	67
Latvia	2	4	39	62
Romania	20	18	26	60
Slovakia	29	6	23	57
Bulgaria	24	12	29	56
Lithuania	10	4	58	40
MEAN	17	6	27	63
PARTLY FREE & NOT FREE				
Croatia	14	4	11	76
Serbia	30	12	41	48
Belarus	33	10	38	46
Russia	39	15	40	37
Ukraine	51	14	55	24
Moldova	n/a	13	64	30
MEAN	33	11	41	43

Source: New Europe Barometer Surveys. Estonia omitted for lack of comparable data. Countries grouped by Freedom House ratings.

In the extreme case of Croatia in the last days of Franjo Tudjman, 42 percent were skeptics. While skeptics have doubts about how their country is currently governed, they are also optimistic about the future. When the New Europe Barometer surveys ask people what they expect their new system to become in five years, the proportion who are positive goes up substantially. In Free electoral democracies, an average of 69 percent are positive about the future of their government and an additional 14 percent are neutral. In the Partly Free countries, optimism is lower, but the hope for improvement is greater still. Whereas less than one-third are positive about a regime with lots of political deficiencies, 58 percent have positive expectations of what their system of government will be like in five years.

Given significant disapproval of the present system of government, optimism about the future could reflect hope for a new undemocratic regime to be established. To test the demand for undemocratic rule in societies where it is a familiar form of government, the New Europe Barometer asks people whether they would like to see their country governed differently. Three choices are offered: a return to communist rule, military rule, or rule by a dictator. The replies show that nine-tenths or more of citizens reject a military takeover, and rejection is high even in Croatia and Serbia, where the army has been important in battles between Yugoslav successor states (see Table 1 above). Returning to communist rule is rejected by five-sixths of respondents in Central and Eastern Europe. In any event, a return to the old communist days is impossible, because the basis of the old regime—Soviet dominance—has disappeared, and many former communists have responded to the opportunities created by free elections by becoming democrats. Among those who endorse the principle of rule by a strong man without the trappings of democracy, there is no agreement about just who that person should be. In all but one country in Central and Eastern Europe, a clear majority reject all three undemocratic alternatives.

In the successor states of the Soviet Union, however, a different picture emerges. There, a majority endorses one or more undemocratic alternatives. In part, this is due to the conflating of communist rule with the existence of the Soviet Union; a return to a multinational Union is attractive to Russians outside the Russian Federation. But there is also substantial support for the idea of rule by a strongman (albeit least in Belarus, where such a person is already in power). The survey data suggest that the Partly Free electoral democracies of Soviet successor states may, up to a point, be consistent with the wishes of a significant minority of citizens who have little regard for democratic institutions.

Even though both Croats and Serbs had similar experiences of communist and strongman rule, the 1998 Barometer survey showed substantial differences in their reactions. Croats rejected undemocratic alternatives as consistently as did Czechs or Slovenes, but Serbs and Montenegrins were as ready as Russians to endorse strongman rule, and a large minority was in favor of communist rule in a context where that was identified with Milošević. Taken together, the evidence showed the Serbs divided almost equally, with 52 percent favoring at least one undemocratic alternative and 48 percent rejecting all of them.

The introduction of an undemocratic regime does not depend on a popular vote and can happen against the wishes of a majority of citizens. To ascertain how secure people think their new regime is, the New Europe Barometer asks people whether they think there is any chance that their parliament might be closed down and parties abolished in the next few years. In the Free democracies, only three percent think it *likely* that this could happen, and in Partly Free countries only five percent think so. More—14 percent in Free systems and 24 percent in Partly Free countries—think that the parliament *might* be suspended. In most countries of postcommunist Europe, dejected authoritarians, wanting to see the parliament suspended but thinking it unlikely to happen, outnumber optimistic authoritarians, who would like to see it happen and think it actually could happen in their country. Those anxious about the undermining of the legislature are a potential asset for democracy, because they are likely to be on guard against attacks on representative institutions. But no matter how people view their new re-

gime, a very large majority expects it to be around for the foreseeable
future.

Governing Without the Rule of Law

Labels such as "partly free" or "incompletely democratic" are useful
cautions against assuming that all countries holding competitive elections are governed by the democratic standards that apply in Sweden or
Australia, but they do not specify what is missing. The answer is: the
rule of law.

In twentieth-century Europe, the characteristic violation of the rule
of law was the abuse of rights through bureaucratic arbitrariness, unjust
imprisonment, and political terror and violence. Today, corruption is
the main cause of departures from the rule of law by European governments. The problems of minorities (such as the Roma) or immigrants
are real but affect only limited groups in the population. By contrast,
corruption affects most citizens through petty exactions and delays in
the delivery of public services, along with the costs that it imposes on
the national economy as a whole.

Making money by breaking laws. Corruption was endemic in communist countries, for the minority in the party's *nomenklatura* enjoyed
great privileges. The peculiarities of a Marxist political economy made
power, not money, the currency with which privileges were obtained.
Ordinary citizens who were exploited politically had opportunities to
break or bend the law by making use of *blat,* a system of informal social
capital in which gifts and favors were exchanged among friends. The
one-party state's control of the media enabled governors to expose corruption selectively, but it prevented society from uncovering wrongdo-
ing.

Postcommunist states are different, as money has replaced power as
the currency of privilege. The wholesale transfer of state assets to private hands created great one-time opportunities for insiders who previously had exploited public assets without owning them. They could put
their names on the title deeds of newly privatized companies and use
their insider knowledge to buy favors from public officials.

Across postcommunist Europe, Barometer surveys find that an average of 72 percent believe that their new regime is more corrupt than its
predecessor; 23 percent believe that the level of corruption is much the
same as before; and only 6 percent believe that corruption has been
reduced by political change. These judgments differ very little according to the political character of the regime or national living standards.
In every country, most citizens see their national government as corrupt. Part of the explanation is the achievement of media freedom; the
media can now show the country's new governors and their friends driving expensive Mercedes or enjoying holidays in elegant hunting lodges

or on the Mediterranean. But such activities are also indications that the rule of law is deficient.

While Europe's postcommunist regimes are alike in holding competitive elections, they differ in their readiness to curb corruption and govern by the rule of law. Transparency International (TI) publishes the best-known index of corruption, one that averages a multiplicity of corruption indicators to produce a "perception of corruption" index covering 90 countries, assigning each country a position on a scale from 1 to 10.

Among the EU's 15 member-states, the Nordic countries are the most honest; on a 10-point scale, Finland has the top mark of 10. The median EU country is Austria, with a score of 7.7. Two EU countries—Greece (4.9) and Italy (4.6)—fall below the midpoint of the scale. Among the 29 countries belonging to the Organization for Economic Cooperation and Development (OECD), the variability of corruption is even greater than within the EU. Mexico has the lowest rating in the OECD—3.3. The median OECD countries are Germany and Ireland, with ratings just below the U.S. score of 7.8.

None of Europe's postcommunist governments has the integrity of the Nordic countries, but three—Estonia, Slovenia, and Hungary—have higher TI Index scores than Greece and Italy. In addition, eight postcommunist countries have a higher rating than Mexico. The assessment of the Czech Republic, Lithuania, Poland, and Belarus is closer to Italy than to Mexico, while Croatia, Bulgaria, Slovakia, and Latvia are just above Mexico on the TI Index. In eight postcommunist countries—Romania, Moldova, Albania, Bosnia-Herzegovina, Macedonia, Russia, Ukraine, and Serbia-Montenegro—corruption is more comparable to China, Venezuela, or Nigeria than to the median country of Europe. TI scores there range from Romania (2.9) to Ukraine (1.5) and Serbia-Montenegro (1.3).

Completing Democracy—and the Obstacles

The weakness of the rule of law is the biggest obstacle to completing democracy in Europe today. Barometer surveys show that an overwhelming majority of people in postcommunist Europe appreciate their newly gained freedom from the state: Big majorities reject undemocratic alternatives, and majorities are positive about their future and sometimes even about the current political system. Yet big majorities of citizens also see their new governors as more corrupt than their predecessors. The higher the level of corruption, the less worthy a new regime is of support—and the less support it receives from its citizens.[8]

A complete democracy requires the rule of law plus free elections. There is a significant relationship between electoral democracy and honest government, but the correlation is not perfect.[9] Between the extremes of Finland, which is completely democratic and completely hon-

TABLE 2—POSTCOMMUNIST REGIMES AS RULE-OF-LAW DEMOCRACIES

	FREEDOM HOUSE[1]	TRANSPARENCY INT'L[2]	RULE-OF-LAW DEMOCRACY[3]
	INDICES		
Estonia	1.5	5.7	74
Slovenia	1.5	5.5	73
Hungary	1.5	5.2	72
Czech Republic	1.5	4.3	67
Poland	1.5	4.1	66
Lithuania	1.5	4.1	66
Slovakia	1.5	3.5	63
Latvia	1.5	3.4	62
Romania	2.0	2.9	56
Bulgaria	2.5	3.5	56
Moldova	3.0	2.6	46
Macedonia	3.0	2.1	44
Croatia	4.0	3.7	39
Ukraine	3.5	1.5	37
Albania	4.5	2.3	32
Russia	4.5	2.1	31
Bosnia-Herzegovina	5.0	2.5	29
Serbia	5.5	1.3	19
Belarus	6.0	4.1	19

[1] Freedom House score 1999–2000. See Adrian Karatnycky, "The 1999 Freedom House Survey: A Century of Progress," *Journal of Democracy* 11 (January 2000): 187–200.
[2] Transparency International Perception of Corruption Index 2000 (see *www.transparency.de*).
[3] Rule-of-Law Democracy score; an average of the Freedom House and Transparency International indices, with the Freedom House rating standardized on a 1-to-10 scale, set so that 100 is the maximum score.

est, and very corrupt and undemocratic countries such as Angola, there are many possible permutations.

Freedom House ratings for the presence of political rights and civil liberties and Transparency International scores for corruption can be averaged to create a measure of *rule-of-law democracy* (see Table 2 above). On such a scale, Finland and other Scandinavian countries remain at peak positions in Europe, but other countries with a long history of free elections but also a long record of corruption drop substantially. Although Belgium has had competitive elections for more than a century and a half, it has a worse rating on the TI corruption index than Japan. In France, corruption detracts from democracy more than the unusually lengthy seven-year term of office of the president. Taking corruption into account lowers the EU minimum standard for democracy, because of the extent of corruption in Italy and in Greece.

Six postcommunist countries are at or above the minimum level of EU rule-of-law democracies. The achievement of a high level of electoral democracy enhances the position of the Czech Republic, Lithuania, and Poland, countries where corruption is more prevalent than in Greece but civil liberties are more respected. Corruption pushes four Free electoral democracies—Slovakia, Latvia, Bulgaria, and Romania—below the minimum standard of European Union countries.

All the countries that have not achieved the standard of a Free electoral democracy also fall short of the European Union minimum for integrity in government. Countries that Freedom House groups together as Partly Free differ substantially in their level of corruption. Russia is one of the ten most corrupt of the 90 countries assessed by Transparency International. Croatia is credited with being more honest than Slovakia under Vladimír Mečiar. While Ukraine holds more or less free elections, it is the third most corrupt country assessed by TI, surpassed only by Serbia-Montenegro and Nigeria. Belarus is exceptional in that it is undemocratic but not especially corrupt—or at least, corruption is not evident. Its TI score is 4.1.

What is to be done? The composite index of rule-of-law democracies calls attention to differences in the obstacles facing postcommunist regimes that have yet to complete the process of democratization. The idealist prescription to improve government is that the people should vote the rascals out and put the good guys in. The bad guy was voted out in Slovakia, where Mečiar, who was threatening to deprive Slovaks of political rights and civil liberties, was defeated in 1998. Where this prescription is most needed, however, it is sometimes impossible to apply, because the governing regime does not allow free elections. In principle, a free election could remove Belarus's democratic deficit by removing its dictator Alyaksandr Lukashenka from office. But Lukashenka is trying *not* to promote free elections but to make Belarus a stable dictatorship, closer in political spirit to post-Soviet Central Asian states than to its geographical neighbors, such as Poland.

Getting rid of a dictator is much easier than getting rid of corruption. The former requires a quick, sharp, and effective blow, whether from the electorate, an external source, or an internal coup. Getting rid of corruption is less dramatic and more impersonal. It requires what Max Weber describes as "the slow, patient boring of hard boards."[10]

The aftermath of war leaves successor regimes with big systemic obstacles. Today, there appears to be little disposition on the part of the military to take power in troubled countries and there is certainly no popular demand for them to do so. The threat to democracy comes from people with guns turning to criminal pursuits for their livelihood once a war ends, and corrupting the state apparatus in the process. Serbia had massive corruption while Milošević was in power, and criminal gangs and some of their powerful friends remain in place even though he has gone. In the former battlefields of Bosnia-Herzegovina and Albania, the casual attitude toward the rule of law bred in times of civil war threatens the integrity of civil administration. It is one thing for international supervisors to monitor free elections in the cantonal successor regions of the former Yugoslavia. It is another for outsiders to enforce the rule of law when winners want to enjoy what they see as the deserved spoils of office. Corruption is a greater problem than electoral democracy in

Macedonia, which has been flooded with refugees from warring neighbors, or Moldova, where Russian troops remain in the Transdniester
region.

In Russia and Ukraine, free elections are periodically held, but the
media, financial, and administrative advantages of the "party of power"
mean that electoral competition does not take place on a level playing
field. After a decade of administering an almost worthless national currency and offering favors in exchange for hard foreign currencies, the
government of Ukraine appears even more trapped in ways that leave it
far from European standards of governance. If the Russian Federation
and Ukraine were to be as (partly) honest as they are (partly) democratic, then the integrity of government, as measured by the TI Index,
would rise by half or even double. President Vladimir Putin has talked
about using his authority to deal with corrupt officials and businessmen, but it remains to be seen whether his actions meet the standards of
the *Rechtsstaat* or those of the KGB. An impartial campaign against all
major corruptors of government risks being overwhelmed by the massed
opposition of corrupt organizations, and a selective anticorruption campaign can easily become a means of intimidating opponents while shel-
tering friends.

Corruption is the greatest obstacle to progress in postcommunist countries. The longer a regime uses free elections as a facade while those
inside government use elected office to enrich themselves, the greater
the divergence will become between those countries making progress
toward the completion of democracy and those going nowhere. Moreover, the longer corruption persists at the elite level, the greater the
likelihood that the mass of the electorate will become indifferent to dis-
honesty, or decide that the only way to deal with a corrupt state is to
benefit from lawbreaking oneself, whether in the form of avoiding taxes,
smuggling, or corrupting civil servants and elected representatives.

Corruption is also the biggest obstacle to European unity today. The
European Union is promoting the eastward expansion of its boundaries,
but not at any price. The longer the governors of an incomplete democracy continue to scoff at the rule of law, the greater the divergence will
be between the countries that will join the EU and those that remain
outside the pale. The European Union is not only a political union; it is
also a unified market with free movement of goods, money, and people.
For markets to work, contracts and property rights must be enforced by
the courts, and factory and tax inspectors must go about their work hon-
estly. Furthermore, the boundaries of a single market must be secure
against smugglers of merchandise, or of drugs, or of human beings pro-
cured for prostitution or exploitation as cheap workers. New Europe
Barometer surveys show that where governments have regard for the
rule of law and representative institutions, popular support is higher.
Where governors are less ready to be accountable to the electorate or to

their own laws, popular support is lower, and rightly so. To extend the boundaries of rule-of-law democracy further eastward in Europe does not require a transformation in the political culture of the population as a whole; it requires changes in the behavior of the governing elites.

NOTES

1. Following the abortive attempt of EU member states to isolate Austria when it admitted the right-wing Freedom Party of Jörg Haider into government, the EU Council of Ministers is now considering procedures so that it can act with due process and full knowledge of the facts if a member state develops in an undemocratic direction. See Richard Rose, "The End of Consensus in Austria and Switzerland," *Journal of Democracy* 11 (April 2000): 26–40.

2. Richard Rose and Doh Chull Shin, "Democratization Backwards: The Problem of Third-Wave Democracies," *British Journal of Political Science* 31 (2001).

3. Isaiah Berlin, "On Liberty," in *Two Concepts of Liberty* (Oxford: Clarendon Press, 1958), 6ff.

4. The year 2000 surveys in the four successor states of the Soviet Union were funded by the British Economic and Social Research Council through grants to Richard Rose and Stephen White. Year 2000 surveys in the three Baltic states were funded by grants to Rose from the Bank of Sweden Jubilaumsfond and the Swedish Ministry of Foreign Affairs. Surveys in Central and Eastern Europe were conducted in 1998 by the Paul Lazarsfeld Society, Vienna, under the direction of Richard Rose and Christian Haerpfer, with funding from the Austrian National Bank and the Austrian Ministry of Science. All surveys involve face-to-face interviews with nationally representative samples. Total number of respondents: 17,424. For further details, see *www.cspp.strath.ac.uk.*

5. See Russell J. Dalton, *Citizen Politics: Public Opinion and Political Parties in Advanced Industrial Democracies* (Chatham, N.J.: Chatham House, 1996); Susan J. Pharr and Robert D. Putnam, eds., *Disaffected Democracies: What's Troubling the Trilateral Countries?* (Princeton, N.J.: Princeton University Press, 2000).

6. Factor analysis shows that the "freedom from" attitudes reported above are empirically separate from the "civic" attitudes. See Richard Rose, William Mishler, and Christian Haerpfer, *Democracy and Its Alternatives* (Baltimore: Johns Hopkins University Press, 1998), 147ff, 238.

7. There is a significant correlation (0.57) between the level of popular support for a new regime and the extent to which its Freedom House score is democratic.

8. The correlation between approval of the current regime in the New Europe Barometer surveys and its score on the Transparency International Index is -0.63.

9. The correlation between the Freedom House score of a country and its TI rating is -0.61.

10. *From Max Weber: Essays in Sociology,* H.H. Gerth and C. Wright Mills, eds. (London: Routledge, 1948), 128.

15

HISTORY AND MEMORY: THE REVOLUTIONS OF 1989–91

Aleksander Smolar

Aleksander Smolar *is senior research fellow at the Centre National de la Recherche Scientifique in Paris and chairman of the board of the Stefan Batory Foundation in Warsaw. He served as a political advisor to Polish prime ministers Tadeusz Mazowiecki and Hanna Suchocka. This essay, which originally appeared in the July 2001 issue of the* Journal of Democracy, *was translated from the Polish by Magdalena Potocka.*

During the years 1989–91, people had the impression that they were living through political events comparable in scope and importance to the French and American Revolutions. With the downfall of communism, decades of Cold War and the threat of global annihilation came to an end, and the bipolar world was consigned to the past. For some, this meant "the end of history" in a philosophical sense: the disappearance of a plausible alternative to a liberal democratic order. For others, by contrast, it meant that history was just opening its doors, enabling previously suppressed countries, nations, and continents to regain their ability to shape their own destiny. Still others feared that the political changes would lead to cataclysms: chaos, anarchy, civil war, ethnic conflict, and the threat that "rogue states" or terrorist gangs would use weapons of mass destruction. The bipolar world, it was noted, had at least brought a certain order and predictability. Articles appeared prophesying the return of the demons of the past. It was recalled that World War I, World War II, and the Cold War had all begun in that part of Europe that lies between East and West, the meeting point of great empires and great religions: Western Christianity, the Orthodox Church, and Islam.

The peaceful revolutions of a decade ago fascinated the entire world. Their heroes were "the people," "the nation," and "civil society," along with intellectuals who invoked the language of "truth," "morality," and "human rights." It seemed that an old dream was about to be realized—that of the "rule of philosophers," or of a democracy capable of creating and respecting true elites. Men such as Václav Havel, Jacek Kuroń,

Tadeusz Mazowiecki, Adam Michnik, János Kis, Bronisław Geremek, Gyorgy Konrad, Jiri Dienstbier, Andrei Sakharov, Vytautas Landsbergis, Vyacheslav Chornovil, Zhelyu Zhelev, Arpád Göncz, and Sergei Kovalev occupied the front ranks of public life and the front pages of the world press. As far back as the 1970s, Jean-François Revel, citing Karol Wojtyla's elevation to the papacy and the publication of Aleksandr Solzhenitsyn's *Gulag Archipelago,* entitled one of his articles: "Ex Oriente Lux" ("Light Comes from the East"). There were more and more reasons, it seemed, to think so.

The fall of communism also had a ricochet effect, unblocking politics in the democratic West. The reunification of Germany quickened the pace of European integration. The expansion of democracy around the world was accompanied by political upheavals in many of the older democratic countries. With the disappearance of their systemic rival, democratic countries had to fall back on internal sources of legitimacy and to meet internal criteria of success or failure. Today citizens evaluate much more strictly phenomena that they might have tolerated during the Cold War, such as corruption or lack of transparency. Alongside politics and the economy, ethical concerns seem to assume a continually growing importance in public life. The international community reacts ever more strongly against massive violations of human rights, and the "right of intervention" in the domestic affairs of other countries in response to mass crimes against civilian populations is challenging the traditional concept of national sovereignty. The results include the war in Kosovo, the creation of tribunals to prosecute crimes committed in the former Yugoslavia and Rwanda, and finally the decision to create the International Criminal Court itself. Directly or indirectly, all of these changes had their sources in, or were substantially accelerated by, the revolutions of 1989–91.

Yet on the tenth anniversary of 1989, even the most serious international newspapers and journals published relatively little about the events that had shaken the world, and it is unlikely that the tenth anniversary of the 1991 collapse of the "evil empire" will evoke greater interest. In the autumn of 1999, two *Washington Post* columnists wondered why the tenth anniversary of the great changes seemed to resonate so weakly in American public life.[1] Charles Krauthammer pointed to the character of certain elites in the United States who had been shaped by their struggles against the Vietnam War and President Reagan's anticommunist policies, and thus found it difficult to celebrate their own intellectual and political defeat. His colleague E.J. Dionne, on the other hand, cited the general decrease in American interest in international issues. During the Cold War, interest in world affairs was sustained by the sense of being threatened by what was happening even in remote corners of the globe. Paradoxically then, at a time when we speak constantly of globalization, people's interests are becoming more centered on local

issues. This is true not only of America. While there may be growing
interest in global economic and ecological matters, the sentiment among
peoples that their destinies are interconnected is much fainter than it
was during the Cold War.

The End of the "Grand Narrative"

This decreasing interest in the world, however, is not the only reason
for widespread indifference toward the successive anniversaries of the
fall of communism. Such inattention is also related to the fact that the
"grand narrative" of the twentieth century, encompassing the two World
Wars, the Great Depression, communism, fascism, Nazism, the Cold
War, and decolonization, seems to have reached its end. This history
defined the direction of events and gave them meaning and dignity; it
touched the life and destiny of everyone. Time appeared to have direction and evoked hope; it was leading us somewhere. Emmanuel Levinas
noted that the "fall of communism has hit at the very concept of the
laws of history. . . . Our time all of a sudden turned out to be deprived of
a future."[2] François Furet wrote in a similar spirit: "History again becomes a tunnel where man enters as in the darkness, without knowing
where his actions will lead, uncertain of his destination, dispossessed of
the illusory sense of security about what he is doing."[3] Czesław Miłosz
stated: "Looking back . . . one could begin to see Marxism as a revolt
against European nihilism, against the inner emptiness first diagnosed
by Dostoyevsky and Nietzsche. To fill that void, communism had given
European culture a vision of man overcoming nature and himself, and
restoring meaning to historical time. Now that Marxism had sunk back
into the nihilism from which it had emanated, what would take its place?
Where would men and women find their hope?"[4]

How, then, can we give order and meaning to today's events and
inscribe them into history? In 1998, Timothy Garton Ash wrote about a
discussion in Davos devoted to determining those events of the twentieth century that would have the greatest meaning for future generations.[5]
The renowned intellectuals and politicians taking part concluded that
communism, fascism, the World Wars, the Holocaust, and the Gulag
had played an insignificant role. The more consequential developments
were the advances in biotechnology and genetic engineering and the
revolutionary developments in transportation and communications that
have shrunk the distances separating people and created our current global order. From this perspective, the political events of a decade ago
seem outdated and anachronistic. They bring to a close the "grand narrative" of the past. Although they appeared crucial ten years ago, today
the transformations of 1989–91 seem to belong to a distant era, to a
world that has vanished.

Despite the great role of intellectuals in the revolutions of 1989, surprisingly little serious intellectual reflection on the character of the changes has come from the postcommunist countries themselves. The lively, if brief, discussion carried out in the West partially explains why those events have rapidly been pushed onto the back pages of memory. Jürgen Habermas saw in the changes of 1989 a "rectifying revolution," one that "clears the ground in order to catch up with developments previously missed out on." He wrote about "its total lack of ideas that are either innovative or oriented towards the future."[6] His conservative opponent, Ernest Nolte, saw in 1989 a fulfillment of the program of Joseph de Maistre, for whom the counterrevolution was not to be a revolution against the revolution but the opposite of revolution ("*ne sera point une révolution contraire, mais le contraire de la Révolution*").[7]

The events of 1989 have most often been seen as a revolution of freedom, a revolt against violence and oppression at the individual, societal, and national level. Lord Dahrendorf, along with many others, has written about "liberal revolution" and the "confirmation of old ideas of democracy, pluralism and citizenship."[8] He saw the originality of the events of 1989 in their openness, their nonideological character. Let us also recall the assessment of François Furet, the renowned historian of the French Revolution, who denied the events of 1989 the dignity of being a "revolution." In his view, the fundamental, defining element of revolution is the creation of a new social order, an explosion of collective creativity.[9] This cannot be said of 1989, which was all about a *return* to private ownership, equality before the law, guarantees of freedom, the independence of the Church, free elections, and constitutional government.

There has been a much wider discussion of the meaning of 1989 as a turning point in the history of Europe and the world. Many have seen 1989 as bringing to a close the period that began with the Ribbentrop-Molotov Pact, and thus marking the real conclusion of the Second World War. It has also been described as "the end of the European civil war" that had begun in 1914. Others have emphasized that the events of 1989–91 closed the era of totalitarian systems that had begun with the Bolshevik Revolution of 1917. Still others have seen these events as ending the whole period of modern revolutions initiated by the French in the memorable year of 1789, and with it the revolutionary vision of history and the romanticism of "the new beginning." Poland's Solidarity movement broke away completely from that tradition and its semantics and symbols. It sought to avoid the dynamics of 1789 and the revolutionary radicalization that it initiated. That which for two centuries had been a fascinating example for millions was now viewed as a dangerous nemesis. (People brought up on the history of revolution often had an exaggerated reaction to what they saw as the dangers of "right-wing bolshevism"; in Poland, Adam Michnik's voice was often heard on this theme.) The *annus mirabilis* of 1989 was also interpreted in many other ways:

as the gravedigger of the socialist tradition and of Marxist messianism; as a break with the faith in radical egalitarianism and the dominant role of the state; as the end of the Enlightenment tradition; and even as the death of modernity.

The wealth of opinions regarding the character, causes, and consequences of the revolutions of 1989–91 resulted from the conviction that their effects extended far beyond the central and eastern parts of Europe. Outside a narrow circle of specialists, however, the problems of East Central Europe very quickly ceased to be the subject of major intellectual debates. It is as if the sterility of communism has been matched by the sterility of postcommunism. Those revolutions turned out to lack—in Hannah Arendt's words—the "pathos of novelty," and the expectation that new ideas and new energy capable of changing the world would come from the East quickly faded.

Hopes and Myths

There were, however, three ideological camps, of unequal weight and influence, that saw a universal and creative influence in the East European opposition movements and revolutions. These were small circles of the liberal-left intelligentsia, a part of the new Western right, and influential circles in the Christian world.

Intellectuals from the liberal-left found inspiration in the phenomenon of the "self-limiting revolution" and in the experiences of "civil society." The focus of their analyses was the "extraparliamentary forms of public activity" that drove the revolutions of 1989. Civil society was perceived here as the ideal of a voluntary community opposing the coercion of the state, as the arena of the democratic formation of collective will, and as a space for freedom, dialogue, and communication. It was not hard to discern in this vision, in a new guise, the old utopian desire for societal self-government and social emancipation from the domination of the state.

The idea of "civil society" introduced by the East Central European opposition also had an influence on Western conservatives, who saw it as a basis for the critique of liberal individualism. They saw the strengthening of civil society as a way to fight the moral crisis of the contemporary era and to rebuild communities confronted by weakening social bonds and an erosion of traditional values. For the conservatives, the idea of civil society also offered a tool for attacking the bureaucratized welfare state, opposing to it the ideal of virtuous individuals, healthy families, and a society that encourages mutual assistance, solidarity, and care for our neighbors.

Various Christian circles placed great hopes in the postcommunist revolutions. Such hopes were strongly present in Russian religious and social thought, which frequently looked back to the nineteenth-century tradition of anti-Western Slavophilism. Aleksandr Solzhenitsyn's famous speech at Harvard University in June 1987 still remains a classic presentation of the ideas and aspirations at its core. In addition to his wholesale condemnation of communism, Solzhenitsyn radically criticized the West, claiming that it was in decline and experiencing a moral and spiritual void. He attacked American democracy for its soulless materialism, its cold and mechanical dependence on law, and its lack of moral restraint. For Solzhenitsyn, the moral and spiritual superiority of the East, and above all Russia, could not be doubted: "Multiple and deadly pressure" was conducive to the creation of characters that are "stronger, deeper, and more interesting" than those in the wealthy, ordered West. "If East becomes West, it will lose something very valuable."

Among some Catholics, great hopes were tied to a spiritual revolution expected to come from liberated Europe, especially from Poland. In a famous interview given to Italian journalist and politician Jas Gawronski in 1993, John Paul II spoke of the greater moral maturity of countries that had lived through the experience of communism.[10] In response to a question about which part of Europe would benefit most from integration, he said: "I may not be far from the mark in saying that it is Eastern Europe that has more to lose—in the sense of identity—because, thanks to the experience of totalitarianism, it is Eastern Europe that has achieved greater maturity." According to John Paul II, the countries of the East had been able, despite the pressure of communism, to maintain their identity and even to strengthen it. How close this opinion is to that of Solzhenitsyn!

The impressive influence of the Polish Church during the communist period, its tradition of resistance, and its contribution to the spiritual nurturing of the Solidarity movement and the events of 1989 all awakened the hope that Poland could play an important role in the rebirth of Christian Europe. George Weigel, who later published a biography of the Pope, wrote in a book dedicated to Solidarity, "Poland is currently facing a challenge of potentially great historical consequences: how can a liberal democratic state and a free economy be built on a foundation of intact Catholic culture?"[11] The Pope himself also spoke frequently on this theme. On a June 1991 visit to Warsaw, he declared: "Poles can either simply enter into consumer society and, if they are successful, take up the rear before it closes its gates forever to new arrivals; or else they can contribute to a rediscovery of a great, deep, and authentic European tradition, proposing an alliance between the free market and solidarity."[12]

The Pope wanted Poland to search for a synthesis that had not succeeded in the West: a synthesis of spirituality and materialism, community and individualism, religion and secular life. He told Poles that they could choose a Western model of "practical materialism" and thereby condemn themselves to the second rank, or they could dare to take part in the great task of renewing Europe's Christian roots by seeking a reconciliation between the market and solidarity, between the Church and democracy.

Václav Havel has been another famous spokesman for the hope for an original, as well as intellectually and spiritually deep, path for a new Europe. Expressing a Heideggerian revolt against the soullessness of the modern world, he thought he glimpsed a preview of a new world in the dissident "islands of freedom" and the citizens' initiatives that were formed in the 1970s and 1980s. Central and Eastern Europe was to provide a systemic alternative not only to collapsing totalitarianism but also to what Havel perceived as the mechanistic, materialistic civilization of the West, with its democracy dominated by market logic. Havel thought that the greatest treasure the East could offer the West was its experience of totalitarianism and resistance. Central and Eastern Europe was to be a beacon of truth and responsibility in a world governed by "the dictatorship of money, profit, and incessant economic growth and, because of this, the necessity to rob natural resources." Yet today the president of the Czech Republic seems to be filled with doubt: "I am not sure whether we are fulfilling our historical mission correctly. Maybe we did not have this historic task, and taking credit for it was only a manifestation of reprehensible revolutionary pride?"[13]

Faith in the spiritual rebirth that was to come from the East quickly gave way to often exaggerated visions of the moral and spiritual collapse of societies that had been subject to decades of totalitarianism. The term *homo sovieticus,* popularized by Aleksandr Zinoviev to characterize the degraded man of "really existing socialism," seemed more appropriate than any invocation of Christian virtues to describe the condition of the societies emerging from Sovietism. Today one can see that the faith in Europe's new evangelization, which was to come from the East, was excessively optimistic. No one has spoken of it for a long time.

Certain elements of the revolutionary myth that were present in embryonic form in the movements of 1989 and in the democratic opposition of the preceding decade have also been forgotten, including a faith in the fundamental unity of society, in the possibility of overcoming the tensions between the sacred and the profane, state and society, and politics and morality. In Poland there was also the hope, currently forgotten, that the Solidarity movement could overcome the tensions between the elites and the people, the intelligentsia and the nation, and the workers and the middle class.

The democratic opposition awakened the hope of a citizenry that would actively participate in public life. It was believed that the new democracy would overcome the tension identified by Benjamin Constant between the "freedom of the ancients" and the "freedom of the moderns," that it would succeed in reconciling self-government by virtuous republican citizens with the enjoyment of personal independence. There was a strong conviction that democracy would be the natural fruit of a liberated society. The collision between these idealized expectations and the less-than-aesthetic practices of the democracy that actually emerged has weakened the authority of democratic institutions and political parties.

The myth of Central Europe, which at a certain moment had a strong influence on the elites of the region and on opinion in the West, has almost been forgotten. Milan Kundera, Gyorgy Konrad, Czesław Miłosz, and others who made the notion of Central Europe so attractive wanted the world to recognize a separate historical and cultural existence for their part of Europe. The myth of Central Europe meant something more than just a turning away from the Soviet East; it contained an implicit distancing from the West, an affirmation of a different tradition and an alternative direction. It was a geographic representation of the myth of the "third way." Before the changes of 1989–91, the opposition in all the countries of the region was dominated by the conviction that their future was to be located beyond both Soviet socialism and Western capitalism. This myth was quickly buried in 1989, when the slogan "The Third Way Leads to the Third World" appeared simultaneously in many countries, and a full identification with the West won out. The liberated countries of Central Europe looked only to the West and quickly lost interest in their neighbors.

"A Return to Europe"—the last great myth of the revolution of 1989—was the idea of a brotherly meeting of two forces, two separated parts of the continent, to achieve Europe's unification. The basis for unification was to be a thousand years of a common destiny, cultural kinship, and shared values and faith. In this return to a common home, the West obviously had quite a lot to offer: security, democratic and market institutions, and the prospect of economic development. But the other Europe also had something to give: its spirituality tempered by fire, its living Christian faith, its willingness to defend European culture and traditions, its experience of the struggle against totalitarianism, and its attachment to the idea of Europe. Timothy Garton Ash wrote that Europe was divided between those who *believed in* it and those who *possessed* it.[14] So the mission of Central and Eastern Europe was also to restore the faith of West Europeans in the value of what they already possessed.

There was, of course, a great deal of myth in this vision, beginning with the widespread conviction that Yalta alone had divided the destiny of Europe—as if a deep gulf, running almost exactly along the same line, had not separated the civilizations of Europe since the time of Charlemagne. (Istvan Bibo, Jeno Szucs, and Jerzy Jedlicki, among others, have described this.) It very quickly became apparent that we would experience not the reunification of Europe but the very different process (probably the only realistic one) of the enlargement of the European Union. Instead of the dreamed-of union of equals, Central and East Europeans are faced with a laborious fulfillment of conditions from Brussels, a rigorous application of the EU's commandments spelled out in 80,000 pages of regulations (the so-called *acquis communautaire*). European unification resembles the unification of Germany, except that in Europe as a whole the West lacks the same sense of profound ties with, and obligation toward, the East.

An Imitative Revolution?

It has been frequently stressed that the revolutions of 1989–91 were not driven by any sort of utopianism and did not possess their own ideology. After the experience of communism, the opposition forces in Central and Eastern Europe were allergic to ideologies. These revolutions were original only with respect to the nature of the system against which they rebelled, their peaceful character, and the importance that they ascribed to human rights and to the principle of self-organization of society. Whatever timid hopes there were for a distinctive model of development, for originality based on a particular historical experience, were quickly abandoned. The countries that have achieved the greatest success—Central Europe, the Baltic States, Slovenia—all have chosen to imitate the West and its democracy, market economy, and rule of law. They have done so deliberately, confining their creativity to the choice among the Anglo-Saxon, French, and German models. Tadeusz Mazowiecki, the first noncommunist prime minister in the former Soviet bloc, spoke of a "return to economic institutions that have been known and tested for a long time. . . . Poland cannot afford to experiment." This last sentence was almost an exact repetition of Konrad Adenauer's famous words: *"Keine Experimenten!"* (No experiments!) In countries that had experienced the tragic results of great historical cataclysms, there was a natural aversion to any kind of experimentation.

The choice made by most of the pro-Western countries was basically the right one, and it proved successful for their societies. The transformation of Central and Eastern Europe took place to a great extent with help from, and under the supervision of, the West. The process by which the European Union is expanding is a fascinating and unprecedented example of institutional engineering. Even postwar Germany and Japan, supervised directly by the conquering Allies, were not subject to as radical an "imitative revolution" as the countries of East Central Europe are undergoing. Obviously, in the latter case "imitative revolution" was freely chosen, even if the status of the European *ossis* brings about frustrations and tensions. It is also true that political, social, and economic imitation can itself be a creative process. For it is an attempt to put down roots, to adjust policies to fit local conditions; it is filtered through local culture and subject to the test of popular resistance. In the future, however, we in the East will repeatedly ask the question of whether we could have "negotiated" better terms with Western modernity by retaining and thus introducing into this common heritage a little bit more of our own distinctiveness, character, and identity.

At a time when the countries of our Europe have chosen to try to catch up with the West by imitating its institutions, policies, constitutions, stock exchanges, and banking systems, the West's interest in us has waned. We are therefore faced with a peculiar paradox. Thanks to open borders, pluralism, democracy, and the free market, the countries that are making the difficult journey toward the European Union have never been closer to the West. At the same time, however, our countries seem to be becoming more distant from the consciousness of the elites and societies of the West. We were much more interesting as rebellious subjects of the Soviet Union than as poor relations who want to be like their more fortunate cousins. One proof is the ever-lessening enthusiasm for the expansion of the European Union in many member countries (especially France, Great Britain, Germany, and Austria), even though the governing circles of the EU realize that expansion to the East is necessary in the near future to prevent the destabilization of Europe.

The West's decreased interest in the postcommunist countries, even Russia, does not require any proof. It has found evident expression in the first steps of George W. Bush's administration. The fears that Russia previously raised have receded, but the hopes for Russia's rapid Westernization have also diminished.

The changes in the West's attitude toward the new democracies began shortly after the 1989 revolutions. It very quickly turned out that political and economic transformation was much more challenging than had previously been thought. The West's picture of the East became dominated by news of ethnic conflict, xenophobia, antisemitism, authoritarian tendencies, populist movements, and the like. Dozens of articles have recycled the formula according to which the West is moving toward a postnational twenty-first century while the East is sinking ever more deeply into nineteenth-century nationalism.

The desire to form a new state, even by so large a nation as the Ukrainians, was often perceived (as in the speech of President Bush in 1991 in Kiev) as an anachronistic nationalist aspiration. *"Europe contre les tribus"* (Europe against tribes) was the amazingly arrogant title of an international conference organized with great flourish in Paris under the patronage of President Mitterrand in 1991. Lord Dahrendorf was not alone when, in his *Reflections on the Revolution in Europe,* he expressed his concern about the appearance of fascist tendencies in the new democracies. This seemed to be a likely result, given the prevailing social disorganization and the inevitable clash of modernity with the nostalgic, traditional attitudes of societies with strong authoritarian features. Fortunately, this kind of pessimism turned out to be largely groundless. The tragic events in the former Yugoslavia and in the Caucasus were due primarily to local factors and should not be used as the basis for generalizations about the postcommunist countries as a whole.

It is worth noting that the anniversary of the events of 1989 was celebrated in only two places: Berlin and Prague. In Berlin, the guests of honor were George Bush, the former president of the United States, and Mikhail Gorbachev, the former general secretary of the Communist Party of the Soviet Union. Other speakers at the Bundestag were Helmut Kohl, Germany's "Chancellor of Unification," and his successor, Gerhard Schroeder. The original version of the program did not even include any speakers from the former German Democratic Republic, but the indignation of the *ossis* resulted in the program's modification. In Prague, in addition to Bush and Gorbachev, Margaret Thatcher was also present, as well as the widow of former French president François Mitterrand. Among the invitees, only Lech Wałęsa symbolized the aspirations and achievements of the nations of Central and Eastern Europe.

It is not, I think, an exaggeration to treat both these celebrations as a reflection and symbol of a change in the way that the events that shook Europe and the world a decade ago are perceived today. The events of 1989 are no longer perceived as the *revolution in Europe:* the fall of dictatorships, the mobilization of the masses, the peaceful departure of communist elites from power, the recovery of national independence, the creation of new democratic governments, or the radical transformation of polity, society and economy. Instead, 1989–91 represents above all profound geopolitical changes—the end of the "Evil Empire," of a world divided into two blocs, and of the threat of nuclear annihilation.

The question that preoccupies international opinion today in discussions about 1989–91 is "Who deserves the credit for winning the Cold War?" not "What were the domestic and external causes of the democratic revolutions?" The radical changes of a decade ago are viewed not as eruptions of political, social, and economic revolution, driven by the energy of nations enslaved for decades, but rather as an earthquake set off by the greats of this world: the Americans and, to a lesser extent and unknowingly, the Soviets. Today we can see that 1989–91 marks above all the end of yet another war, just like 1918 or 1945. And just as after those earlier wars, it is the victors who redraw the borders, dictate the conditions for peace, define the spheres of influence, and write the histories of their own heroic actions and of their enemies' fall.

Ambivalence in the East

An ambivalent attitude toward the revolution of a decade ago is by no means limited to the West. After ten years, Central and East Europeans' attitude toward communism and the developments of the decade following its fall are not conducive to anniversary celebrations. The proof of deep disappointment can be seen everywhere. An extreme example is provided by Romania, where the most severe and irrational communist dictatorship reigned to the very end. In 1999, neither Romania's democratic government nor President Constantinescu, who came from the anticommunist camp, planned any celebrations of the revolution's tenth anniversary: "They were afraid that just one spark could cause a revolt."[15] According to public opinion polls, over 60 percent of Romanians viewed life as having been better under Ceaușescu than at present. An ambivalent attitude toward communism and democracy is evident even in those countries in which communism was associated with national enslavement and in which considerable successes were achieved after 1989. The regaining of freedom has not outweighed the sense of fear, uncertainty, and degradation. This does not mean that these countries want to return to the past. Even in Russia or Ukraine, where support for the current economic and political system is very weak, communist parties regularly lose elections. (The former communist parties in Central Europe that returned to power through elections have undergone a deep democratic transformation.)

The refusal to accept the current situation and the fear of the future in the postcommunist countries make it difficult to appreciate the magnitude of the achievements of ten years ago. This refusal is not only found among the large social groups that paid a high price for the changes; it is also evident among the anticommunist elites in Poland and in Prime Minister Victor Orban's governing party in Hungary. In 1989, neither of these countries experienced a revolutionary takeover of power. Anticommunist radicals find this hard to admit, however, and it is even more difficult for them to accept that the negotiations and concessions that weaned the communists from power were inevitable. Thus, reluctant to acknowledge the greatness of these events, they more or less openly accuse of betrayal, or at least of stupidity, the more liberal leaders of the former democratic opposition who were at the helm at the crucial moment of transformation. Further proof of disillusionment can be found in numerous pronouncements on the part of intellectuals regarding the vulgarity, the brutality, and, worst of all, the banality of postcommunist developments. This mood is clearly reflected in the quasi-religious language of the Hungarian writer Gyorgy Konrad: "A solemn feeling of redemption in the period of great systemic changes has given way to discouragement. Something has changed, but we lack salvation."[16]

The difficulty in embracing the changes of 1989–91 has its source above all in the huge material, social, and psychological costs that resulted from the breakdown of the old system. Instead of blaming the departed communists, from whom one can no longer expect anything, the bill has been issued to democratic institutions and the new economic rules and elites. The chaos left behind by the *ancien régime* and the failure of the new model of development to fulfill the promises made by the democratic opposition have led to a moral rejection of the present in the name of an ideal of equality and justice. The tradition of paternal egalitarianism and social protection during the time of "really existing socialism" has provided a symbolic cultural standard for interpreting the postrevolutionary changes as a "tragic narration."[17] The fact that there have been no revolts against the postcommunist elites and conditions may be attributed partly to satisfaction, at least in some countries, with the new freedom and democracy, but also to the lack of systemic alternatives ("it is the same way in the West") and to fear of the specter of violence.

> *It can be said of Central Europe that, with laborious efforts and surprising speed, we are following in the footsteps of developed Europe. That is the true face of normalization.*

It is true that history is written by the victors. Yet Central Europeans are also winners, even if our victory does not match our expectations, even if we did not discover the Promised Land. We have not become the Chosen People, leading humanity across the Red Sea to new shores. It can be said of Central Europe that, with laborious efforts and surprising speed, we are following in the footsteps of developed Europe. That is the true face of normalization.

In an essay written by a Polish author, it is difficult to avoid discussing the role of Solidarity in this history. This unprecedented movement of ten million Poles demanded freedom and democracy and aspired to bring about a moral revolution. Solidarity certainly played a very important role in the fall of communism. It proved to be an excellent and deadly tool. Millions of workers, together with other social groups, rose up against the communist authorities who pretended to be their representatives. Solidarity also helped to transform millions of working people from slaves into citizens. It created a consciousness that, between the individual in his solitude and the unity of all men in God, there can and should exist a political community of citizens.

Solidarity has historic significance for one more reason, in this case limited to Poland itself. In 1981, Lech Wałeşa compared his relationship to the revolutionary masses with how one should approach a startled horse. In order to avoid misfortune, he said, you must first run alongside the horse for some time, then jump on its back, and only then, when you are firmly in place, slowly spur it to gallop in the right direction. Surprisingly, a similar metaphor was offered by Daniel Manen, the leader of the 1848 revolution in Venice: "The people are a horse that one must know how to ride" (*"Il popolo è un cavallo che bisogna saper caval-*

care"). Solidarity allowed the horse to "be saddled," making it possible to impose a discipline that the government of communist Poland was never able to secure, even with the use of violence.

In Solidarity's romantic vision of 1980–81, Poland was supposed to become a completely different country than the one that is now being created. It was supposed to combine what were perceived as the good sides of both capitalism and socialism, of both individualism and collectivism. Generous visions can combine contradictory values and opposite interests, but the confrontation with reality inevitably leads to their breakdown. Faced with real constraints, revolutionaries always have a choice: to try to impose, even through terror, beautiful projects that run counter to real human aspirations, or to accept the tensions, contradictions, and conflicts of real life. Was the procapitalist choice of the new democratic elites a "betrayal" of Solidarity's original dream? The majority of the Polish people understand that it was the only way out of backwardness, dependence, isolation, poverty, and provincialism. Perhaps using the horse metaphor to describe how the Polish people were finally pushed in that direction is too cynical, as is another of Lech Wałęsa's metaphors: "In order for the potatoes to grow, you need to plant them in shit." Let us reach instead for the Holy Bible:

> And it came to pass, when Pharaoh had let the people go, that God led them not through the way of the land of the Philistines, although that was near; for God said, Lest peradventure the people repent when they see war, and they return to Egypt: But God led the people about, through the way of wilderness of the Red Sea: and the children of Israel went up harnessed out of the land of Egypt. (*Exodus,* 13:17,18)

Solidarity was the Polish road to independence, democracy, and capitalism—a capitalism that is individualistic and competitive, a break with the solidarity of the community and with egalitarian culture. It was the Polish road to a "normal" modernity. Today this goal has almost been reached. For the first time in its history, Poland has a chance to join the prosperous and stable countries at the forefront of world civilization. Yet the price that Polish society has paid and is paying is very high. Is this a great achievement, or is it a sin that should be repented?

NOTES

1. Charles Krauthammer, "Reluctant Cold Warriors," *Washington Post,* 12 November 1999, A35; E.J. Dionne, Jr., "After the Cold War: A Healthy Normality," *Washington Post,* 9 November 1999, A25.

2. Interview by Roger-Pol Droit, *Le Monde,* 2 June 1992, reprinted in Emmanuel Lévinas, *Les imprévus de l'histoire* (Paris: Ed. Saint-Clément-la-Rivière, 1994).

3. François Furet, "Democracy and Utopia," *Journal of Democracy* 9 (January 1998): 79.

4. Czesław Miłosz, quoted in Michael Ignatieff, "The Art of Witness," *New York Review of Books,* 23 March 1995.

5. Timothy Garton Ash, "Co nam uczynil XX wiek?" (What has the twentieth century done to us?), *Gazeta Wyborcza,* 21–22 February 1998.

6. Jürgen Habermas, "What Does Socialism Mean Today? The Rectifying Revolution and the Need for New Thinking on the Left," *New Left Review* (September–October 1990): 4, 5.

7. Ernest Nolte, "Die unvollendete Revolution. Die Rehabilitierung des Bürgertums und der defensive Nationalismus," *Frankfurter Allgemeine Zeitung,* 24 January 1991, 27.

8. Ralf Dahrendorf, *Reflections on the Revolution in Europe: In a Letter Intended to Have Been Sent to a Gentleman in Warsaw* (New York: Times Books, 1990).

9. François Furet, "La désagregation communiste," *Le Débat* (November–December 1990); and "Fin d'un empire, fin d'une époque," in Stephan Courtois, Marc Lazar, and Shmuel Trigano, eds., *Rigueur et passion: Mélanges offerts en hommage à Annie Kriege* (Paris: CERF, 1994).

10. *La Stampa,* Polish translation in *Tygodnik Powszechny,* no. 46 (1993).

11. George Weigel, *Ostateczna rewolucja: Kościół sprzeciwu, a upadek komunizmu* (Poznań: W Drodze, 1995), 20, Polish translation of *The Final Revolution: The Resistance Church and the Collapse of Communism.*

12. *Rzeczpospolita,* 30 June 1991.

13. *Gazeta Wyborcza,* 17 May 1999.

14. Timothy Garton Ash, *The Magic Lantern: The Revolution of '89 Witnessed in Warsaw, Budapest, Berlin, and Prague* (New York: Random House, 1990), 153–54.

15. Donald D. McNeil, Jr., "Romanians Grimly Mark Anniversary of Revolution," *International Herald Tribune,* 23 December 1989.

16. *The Great Challenge* (Warsaw: NOW, 1994), 66.

17. J.C. Alexander, "Civil Society I, II, III: Constructing an Empirical Concept from Normative Controversies and Historical Transformations," in J.C. Alexander, ed., *Real Civil Society* (London: Sage, 1998), 1–19.

III

The Post-Soviet Experience

16

ONE STEP FORWARD, TWO STEPS BACK

Michael McFaul

Michael McFaul *is associate professor of political science and a Hoover Fellow at Stanford University. He is also a senior associate at the Carnegie Endowment for International Peace, and author of* Russia's 1996 Presidential Election: The End of Polarized Politics *(1997). This essay originally appeared in the July 2000 issue of the* Journal of Democracy.

Russia's March 2000 presidential election represents one step forward and two steps back for Russian democracy. For the first time in Russia's history, power within the Kremlin has changed hands through an electoral process. The election not only took place but was conducted as constitutionally prescribed, no small achievement for a country with Russia's authoritarian history. More than two-thirds of the eligible voters participated, and they appeared to make informed choices among a range of candidates who offered competing platforms, policies, and leadership styles. The election, however, was not contested on a level playing field. The winner, acting president Vladimir Putin, enjoyed tremendous advantages that tainted the process. Although weak in some arenas, the Russian state still enjoys too much power with respect to the electoral process, while nongovernmental forces—political parties, civic organizations, trade unions, and independent business groups—remain too weak to shape the outcomes of elections.

Does this latest election represent a fundamental turn away from democratic practices or merely a temporary setback for democratic consolidation in Russia? It is too early to tell. Putin may turn out to be Russia's Milošević. Or he may develop into a weak leader presiding over a feudal order, dominated by oligarchs and regional barons, in which the people have little say. Yet it is also possible that he will lead Russia out of its chaotic, revolutionary, and anarchic recent past into a more stable decade of economic growth and political stability—and economic growth and political stability can help consolidate democratic institutions. Thus far, Putin has provided mixed signals about the direction in which he wants to take Russia and has demonstrated a real indifference to democracy. Consequently, the only honest assessment to be made at this stage is that democracy in Russia is not lost, but its future remains uncertain.

Why Putin Won

The first step in coming to grips with post-Yeltsin Russia is to understand why Putin won. The election reveals much about the evolution of Russia's political system and the mood of Russian society.

The simple explanation goes like this: Putin was chosen by Yeltsin and his band of oligarchs as a loyal successor who would keep them out of jail and preserve the existing system of oligarchic capitalism, in which oligarchs make money not by producing or selling goods and services but by stealing from the state. To boost Putin's popularity in order to get him elected, they had to provoke a war with Chechnya. Some assert that this cabal was even responsible for blowing up apartment buildings in Moscow and elsewhere last fall—crimes that were attributed to Chechen terrorists—as a way to bolster support for the war and Putin. This "popular" war, however, could sustain Putin only for so long. Therefore Yeltsin resigned on 31 December 1999 to allow the presidential election to take place three months earlier. As acting president, Putin had at his disposal all the resources of the Russian state, which he wielded to win a convincing election victory.

There is much truth to this simple account, but it is only part of the story. To see the fuller picture, one must reexamine the role of the war in Chechnya and bring other actors into the analysis, including the voters and the other presidential candidates.

1) The Chechen war. Why do we always think that the people in the Kremlin are so smart and everyone else in Russia is so dumb? In the summer of 1999, no one believed that a quick little war with the Chechens would be the formula for delivering electoral success the following year. On the contrary, when Yeltsin ordered the Russian military to respond to the Chechen incursion into Dagestan in August 1999, most electoral analysts in Russia thought that the counteroffensive would result in another unpopular military debacle.[1] If the entire event was staged to assist Putin's electoral prospects, then Shamil Basaev—the Chechen commander who led the military intervention in Dagestan aimed at freeing the people there from Russian imperialism—must be either a traitor to his people or a fool. Basaev, it should be remembered, is the same Chechen commander who in August 1995 led the raid on Budennovsk in southern Russia, killed hundreds of Russian citizens, seized a Russian hospital, and then escaped. His record in the field suggests that he is neither a traitor nor a fool.

Basaev did, however, overestimate the anti-imperial sentiment in

Dagestan and underestimate the determination of the Russian state to respond. Putin, then prime minister, acted decisively, with the blessing of Boris Yeltsin. Everyone who has discussed the Chechen war with Putin personally will tell you that he expresses real passion only about his resolve to "destroy the Chechen terrorists." Last summer, for the first time since 1941, a military force invaded Russia. It is excessively cynical to argue that the Russian military response to this incursion was motivated solely by electoral calculations. Terrorist attacks on apartment buildings in Moscow and elsewhere shortly after the invasion made the Russian people feel like a nation under siege. Society demanded a response from its leaders, and Putin responded.

What was different about this particular response was its apparent "success." In the first Chechen war, the Russian forces appeared to be losing the war from the outset, in part because they performed so miserably and in part because the rationale for the war was not embraced by either the Russian army or the population as a whole. Independent media, led by NTV, a nationwide television network owned by Media-Most, reported on military setbacks and questioned Russia's war aims. After several months of fighting, a solid majority in Russia did not support the war.[2] Compelled by electoral concerns, Yeltsin called for a ceasefire in April 1996 and then allowed his envoy, Aleksandr Lebed, to broker a temporary settlement with the Chechen government. The second war started under very different circumstances. First, the Russian military and the Russian people believed that the rationale for this war was self-defense. A majority of Russian citizens supported the counteroffensive from the very beginning and have continued to support the invasion of Chechnya throughout the military campaign. Second, the Russian army used different tactics in this campaign, relying on air power to a much greater extent than in the first war. The complete demolition of Grozny is the gruesome result of this change in tactics. Third, coverage of the war in the Russian media has been much less critical. The Russian state has exercised a greater degree of control over media coverage of this war; at the same time, it has learned the value of conducting its own propaganda war on the airwaves to help sustain the military offensive on the ground. Over time, NTV has become more critical of Russia's war aims and the means deployed, but not nearly to the same degree as in the last war. All other major media outlets supported the Kremlin's position in the months leading up to the presidential vote.

Consequently, this second Chechen war has been a popular one in Russia. During the 2000 presidential campaign, public support remained steady at roughly 60 percent; it did not waver, as many had predicted, when Russian casualties increased.[3] Popular support for the war translated into positive approval ratings for Putin. Opinion polls conducted in the fall of 1999 demonstrated that people were grateful to Putin for accepting responsibility for the security of the Russian people.

He looked like a leader who had taken charge during an uncertain, insecure time and had delivered on his promise to provide stability and security. By the end of 1999, he enjoyed an astonishing 72 percent approval rating.[4]

2) A vote for the future. Putin's decisive response to the sense of insecurity that prevailed in Russia in the fall of 1999 is the reason why he initially rose in the polls. Yet his Chechnya policy is not the only factor that enabled Putin to maintain a positive approval rating throughout the spring of 2000. In fact, our polls of Russian voters in December 1999–January 2000 showed that 28 percent of those planning to vote for Putin believed that Chechnya should be allowed to leave the Russian Federation—almost as large as the proportion of Putin voters (35 percent) who believed that Russia should keep Chechnya at all costs.[5] This distribution of opinions roughly reflects the distribution of opinion on this question among *all* Russians. Thus other factors—more psychological than material in nature—also must have come into play. First, Putin symbolized for voters the end of revolution. For the first several years of the past decade, Russian politics was polarized by the struggle between communists and anticommunists. In contrast with the more successful transitions from communist rule in Poland or Hungary, in Russia the debate about communism as a political and economic system continued for many years after the Soviet collapse. A period of volatile and unpredictable politics resulted. In his last years of power, Yeltsin further fueled political instability by constantly changing prime ministers. Putin's coming to power signaled for many an end to this volatile period and the advent of the "Thermidor" of Russia's current revolution.

Putin's youth and energy also provided a striking contrast to his old and sick predecessor. Voters welcomed this generational change. In focus groups that we commissioned in December 1999 and March 2000, Russian voters uniformly stated that Putin's youth was a positive attribute. Ironically, Putin's rise to power reminds many Russians of that of Mikhail Gorbachev.

Second, Putin's lack of a record as a public leader allowed voters to project onto him their wishes and desires for the future. With the exception of his policy toward Chechnya, he was a *tabula rasa* on which voters could write what they wanted. In focus groups that we commissioned on the eve of the presidential election, participants had a long and diverse list of expectations about Russia's future under Putin's leadership, which included everything from order in Chechnya, respect for Russia on the international stage, and a crackdown on crime to higher pensions, a better educational system, and more job opportunities for young people. In other words, his supporters were casting their votes for Putin as a future leader, not supporting him for his past achievements, ideological beliefs, or policy positions. Understanding this mood in the Russian electorate, Putin and his campaign managers deliberately refrained from articulating a program or set of policies before the election.[6]

This motivation on the part of Putin voters was radically different from what we had witnessed among Yeltsin supporters in 1996. In that election, voters knew exactly what they were getting with Yeltsin and had no illusions about a more promising future. Yeltsin won 54 percent of the vote in the second round of the 1996 election, even though his approval rating was only 29 percent at the time. In 1996, people were voting against communism, supporting the lesser of two evils. In the spring of 2000, Putin supporters had a much more positive assessment of their leader and were much more optimistic about the future. They were motivated more by this emotional feeling about the future than by individual material interests, ideological beliefs, or party identification. For instance, when asked in a January 2000 poll about their attitudes concerning Russia's political future, 41 percent of respondents believed that the new year would be an improvement over the previous year, while only 9 percent believed that the political situation would worsen. Similarly, 39 percent of respondents believed that the economy would improve in 2000, while only 12 percent believed that it would worsen.[7] The last time that Russians were so optimistic about the future was the fall of 1991.

Strikingly, Putin's support was national in scope and not influenced by age or even by income level. He did just as well in rural areas as in urban areas and won as many votes from the poor as the rich. Amazingly, he carried 84 out of Russia's 89 regions. His chief opponent, communist leader Gennady Zyuganov, won in only four regions, and Aman Tuleev received the highest number of votes in the region where he is governor, Kemerovo Oblast. By contrast, Zyuganov had carried 25 regions in the second round of the 1996 presidential vote.

3) The lack of an effective opposition. A third important reason why Putin won was the weak competition he faced. Though often forgotten in analyses of Russian politics, the real story of the 1990s is not the Kremlin's cleverness but the ineptitude of its opponents. The Communist Party of the Russian Federation (KPRF) continues to dominate the space of opposition parties in Russian electoral politics, yet it has not generated new leaders or a new image. To be sure, the KPRF's economic platform in the 1999 parliamentary election and 2000 presidential election was considerably more market-friendly than the communist ideas the party had advocated in 1995 and 1996. Zyuganov tried to look and sound more modern, and even appeared on a campaign poster with young people. So far, however, the makeover has had only limited success. The contrast between the modern, Western-oriented, and young leader of the left in Poland, Aleksander Kwasniewski, and his traditional, anti-Western, and elderly Russian counterpart could not be more striking.

Years ago, well before anyone had even heard of Vladimir Putin, all experts on Russian electoral dynamics knew that whoever emerged as the candidate of the "party of power" would win the 2000 election. The reasoning is simple when one keeps in mind the solid and consistent electoral support for Zyuganov and Russia's two-ballot electoral system. Zyuganov was virtually assured of a second-place showing—and possibly a first-place showing—in the first round no matter who ran against him. His voters have supported him and his party consistently for the last decade. There was no reason to doubt that they would do so in 2000. At the same time, however, polls have also shown for years that Zyuganov would lose to almost anyone in a runoff. The only presidential contender he could beat would be Vladimir Zhirinovsky. Consequently, Putin and his associates were eager to see the KPRF do well in the parliamentary vote to ensure that Zyuganov would decide to run in the presidential election.

We also knew that Grigory Yavlinsky, the leader of the liberal Yabloko party, would run for president in 2000. Yet no serious analyst ever believed that Yavlinsky stood a chance of making it into a second round. Yavlinsky also has his loyal core of supporters, but his share of the vote has never exceeded 10 percent.

The only real question, then, was who would emerge from the so-called party of power. In 1998, Moscow mayor Yuri Luzhkov looked poised to assume this mantle, but in 1999, former prime minister Yevgeny Primakov emerged as a more likely candidate. When Yeltsin fired him as prime minister, Primakov's popularity soared. Many regional leaders and part of the Moscow elite rallied to his cause. As a symbol of stability in a time of uncertainty, Primakov skyrocketed in the polls. Having navigated Russia out of a financial crisis that began in August 1998, Primakov earned a reputation as a pragmatist who would chart a slow, "centrist" reform course, somewhere between radical reform and communist restoration. He originally joined the Fatherland–All Russia electoral bloc as a means to jump-start his presidential bid and as a strategy for building parliamentary support for his presidency.

These plans proved premature. In fact, Primakov's participation in the December parliamentary elections actually damaged his prospects as a presidential candidate. During the runup to the parliamentary elections, the Kremlin's media empire launched a full-scale negative campaign against Primakov and his bloc. With varying degrees of truth and evidence, the Kremlin's media accused the former prime minister of being a feeble invalid, a lackey of NATO, a Chechen sympathiser, a closet communist, and a destabilizing force in international affairs who had ordered the assassination attempt against Georgian president Eduard

Shevardnadze. This smear campaign, in combination with Putin's spectacular rise in popularity, helped to undermine popular support for Fatherland–All Russia, which won only 12 percent of the popular vote, while the Putin-endorsed Unity bloc won 24 percent.

In effect, the parliamentary vote served as a presidential primary for the party of power. Primakov lost this primary and pulled out of the presidential contest. With Primakov out of the race, there was never any doubt that Putin would win the presidential election. The only real question was whether Putin could win more than 50 percent in the first round and thus avoid a runoff. He did, capturing 52.9 percent of the vote in the first round, compared to Zyuganov's 29.2 percent.

4) The early election. By resigning on 31 December 1999 and thereby moving the electoral calendar forward three months, Yeltsin gave Putin the most important campaign present of all. According to Putin's own advisors, his popularity peaked in mid-January, when 55 million eligible voters were prepared to vote for him. On election day on 26 March 2000, only 40 million voters cast their ballot for the acting president. In other words, between January and March, Putin lost the support of five million voters each month. Putin's "no-campaign" campaign strategy was viable only in a short campaign season. If the vote had not been held until June, Putin most certainly would have faced a runoff.

Winners and Losers

Putin was the clear winner of this election. He will now serve for a fixed four-year term, and the ebbs and flows of his approval rating will matter very little for the next three years. The fact that he managed to escape a runoff by only a few percentage points will also fade in importance over time. Instead, he is now enjoying a honeymoon period in which everyone—oligarchs, governors, parties, the Duma, and the people—is supporting him and seeking his favor. No one in postcommunist Russia has ever enjoyed this level of support.

Putin's small majority, however, does have a few immediate political implications. Because Putin just squeaked by in the first round, he and his team are much less likely to dissolve the Duma and call for new parliamentary elections anytime soon. In the wake of the pro-Putin Unity bloc's strong showing in the December 1999 parliamentary vote and Putin's skyrocketing support in the polls in early 2000, some of his allies, including Unity's new leaders, had called for new Duma elections immediately after the presidential vote, believing that Unity could win an even larger share of the parliamentary seats. Such a move became very unlikely after Putin's weaker-than-expected showing, since most observers concluded that a new parliamentary vote would yield basically the same result as last December. This is a positive outcome that should result in stable relations between the president and the legislature for the foreseeable future.

Putin's narrow majority is also likely to make him more cautious in taking steps against his election allies. Before the election, for instance, Putin's advisors spoke brashly about removing "difficult" governors from office. With a smaller mandate, however, Putin is now less likely to move aggressively against regional leaders. He must tread especially lightly in those places where regional leaders may have falsified the results to help push Putin over the 50-percent threshold. For the same reasons, Putin will now be reluctant to take action against the oligarchs who helped him win election. He is also less likely to pursue constitutional amendments, such as extending the presidential term to seven years.

Gennady Zyuganov and the KPRF must be satisfied with their performance in the first round, even if they were unable to force a second round. Citing the results of their own parallel vote count, KPRF officials claim that the results were falsified and that Putin did not win 50 percent in the first round. They did not pursue this issue vigorously, however, perhaps because Zyuganov believes that the KPRF can cooperate with Putin. On election night, Putin made very conciliatory comments about Zyuganov and the communists, remarking that their strong showing demonstrates that many Russian citizens are dissatisfied with the status quo. Boris Yeltsin would have never made such a comment.

Putin did not include communists in major positions in his new government. He understands the importance of creating an ideologically unified team. At the same time, however, he is likely to continue to consult and cooperate with the communists on a long list of issues where they hold similar positions, including the war in Chechnya, greater support for the military-industrial complex and intelligence services, and the building of a stronger state. Unlike Yeltsin, Putin has never seen Russian politics in bipolar terms. More generally, Putin is much more of a nationalist than Yeltsin and therefore shares the worldview of many prominent KPRF leaders.

For Zyuganov personally, his strong showing—five percentage points above his party's total just three months earlier in the parliamentary vote—ensures that he will remain the leader of the KPRF for the foreseeable future. Compared to 1996, he increased his vote totals in many large cities and even outpolled Yavlinsky in both Moscow and St. Petersburg. This new strength in urban regions, combined with a drop in support in traditionally communist rural areas, suggests that the KPRF's electorate may be gradually changing. Although it is dangerous to generalize based on one election, economic concerns and the resentment over hardships associated with market reforms may be replacing age and nostalgia for the Soviet Union as the most important motivators for KPRF supporters. With the threat of a communist restoration having faded, protest voters may believe it is now safe to vote for Zyuganov.

Russia's liberals suffered a major setback in this presidential election. The Union of Right Forces (SPS)—a coalition of liberals headed by former prime ministers Sergei Kirienko and Yegor Gaidar, former deputy prime ministers Anatoly Chubais and Boris Nemtsov, and a handful of other prominent figures such as Samara governor Konstantin Titov and businesswoman Irina Khakamada—emerged from the December 1999 parliamentary vote with real momentum. To everyone's surprise, they placed fourth in that election, winning 8.5 percent of the popular vote and outpolling their liberal rival Yabloko by more than two percentage points. Many thought their strong electoral showing marked the rebirth of Russian liberalism. Yet SPS squandered this momentum through their indecision regarding the presidential election. They failed to endorse a presidential candidate, even though one of their founding members, Governor Titov, was on the ballot. Some SPS leaders, such as Kirienko and Chubais, backed Putin while others wavered. In the end, SPS had no impact on the presidential vote.

Yavlinsky, however, fared no better, despite the fact that his campaign was flush with money.[8] Without question, he spent more on campaign advertising than any other candidate. In contrast to previous elections, he also enjoyed access to all the major television networks. He did endure some slanderous attacks from ORT, the largest television network, only days before the vote,[9] but few experts believed that these attacks had any effect. Yavlinsky ran a very professional campaign, his best performance to date. Yet despite an excellent and well-funded campaign, very little harassment from the state authorities, and the absence of serious competitors for the liberal vote, Yavlinsky finished with only 5.8 percent, well below his 7.4 percent showing in 1996 and only a fraction above Yabloko's share of the December 1999 parliamentary vote. This constituted a major defeat for Yavlinsky personally and for Russian liberals as a whole. In the mid-1990s, running as a "third-way" alternative to both the retrograde communists and the extremely unpopular Yeltsin and his "radical" reformist allies, Yavlinsky seemed to have real electoral potential. In 2000, however, running against a popular prime minister who was not firmly identified with "shock therapy" (or even with Yeltsin himself) and a communist candidate who no longer advocated a Soviet restoration, Yavlinsky's "third way" seemed less attractive, even stale.

The election was also a setback for nationalist leaders and parties independent of the Kremlin. Vladimir Zhirinovsky, the head of the Liberal Democratic Party of Russia, fared very poorly, winning a paltry 2.7 percent. None of the other nationalist hopefuls won more than 1 percent of the vote. This is in marked contrast to 1996, when General Aleksandr Lebed took third place a strong double-digit showing, which enabled him to deliver a critical endorsement to Yeltsin in the second round.

In several respects, the first round of the 2000 vote resembled the runoff in the 1996 presidential race. Third-party candidates played a much smaller role in 2000 than in the first round in 1996. In fact, the biggest losers in 2000 were liberal and nationalist parties, whose candidates performed so poorly that one has to wonder if they will be able to survive as political movements in Russia in the future.

Implications for Russian Policy

Because Putin ran an issue-free campaign, we learned very little about what he intends to do as president. Putin himself probably is still forming views on the thousands of issues that he now must address. This is not a man who spent decades preparing to become president. After all, this was the first time he had ever run for political office! Yet we do have some clues regarding his priorities.

We know that Putin is committed to preserving Russia's territorial integrity at any cost. In addition to continuing to support a military solution to the Chechen crisis, Putin will attempt to strengthen the center's control over the regions more generally. In his first weeks in office, Putin moved aggressively to weaken the powers of the governors by creating seven new supraregional district administrators who will report directly to the president. He also announced plans to introduce direct elections to the Federation Council, the upper house of parliament. (Currently all oblast governors and republic presidents hold seats in this body.) The battle to reign in the regions and change the composition of the Federation Council will be a protracted one. Proposals for change are not the same as real changes. Nonetheless, it is clear that Putin has assigned the highest priority to the task of strengthening the authority of the federal government.

Regarding economic reform, Putin's initial signals have been clear and positive. Putin called upon a young team of economists, many of whom formerly worked for former prime minister Yegor Gaidar, to draft a comprehensive reform program.[10] In his first major new appointment to his economic team, he invited Andrei Illarionov, Russia's most ardent and principled proponent of radical market reforms, to be his economic advisor.[11] Putin's new program, still in draft at the time of this writing, covers all the right subjects, including tax reform, a new land code, deregulation, social-policy restructuring, and new bankruptcy procedures. Yet his new government, under the leadership of Prime Minister Mikhail Kasyanov, is not composed entirely of people dedicated to this radical program. The new finance minister, Aleksei Kudrin, and the new minister of the economy and trade, German Gref, are dedicated liberals, but the rest are not. It remains to be seen if Putin has the will and the political skill to execute far-reaching reforms. Paradoxically, short-term economic growth fueled by devaluation and rising oil prices might make the new government complacent about undertaking the painful structural reforms necessary for sustained long-term economic expansion.

Regarding foreign policy, the initial signals have been less clear, but mostly positive. Putin does not speak fondly of "multipolarity" or use the tired language of balance-of-power politics. Instead, he claims to want to make Russia a normal Western power. During the presidential campaign, he even entertained the possibility that Russia might someday join NATO. His international heroes come not from the East or the South, but from the West.[12] In his short time in office, he has devoted particular attention to England, meeting twice with Prime Minister Tony Blair before holding his first summit with President Clinton in June 2000. He appears to want to put greater emphasis on Europe and less on Russia's relations with the United States. Yet Putin appears ready to cooperate with the United States on key issues. Even before his inauguration, he pushed the new Duma to ratify Start II and the Comprehensive Test Ban Treaty and urged his diplomats to begin negotiations on Start III and modification of the Anti–Ballistic Missile treaty. At the same time, Putin has emphasized the need to expand Russian arms exports and trade more generally with all comers, a new initiative that could include the transfer of nuclear technologies to countries like Iran and renewed trade ties (in violation of UN sanctions) with Yugoslavia and Iraq.

Putin's views on democracy are less clear. Although he has expressed his admiration for past Soviet dictators such as Yuri Andropov, Putin has expressed no desire to restore authoritarian rule in Russia. He has pledged his loyalty to the constitution and has not (yet) supported calls for the creation of new authoritarian regime like that of General Augusto Pinochet in Chile as a means for jump-starting market reform. Yet neither is he a passionate defender of democracy. In his first several months in office, Putin has demonstrated a willingness to use the power of the state and to ignore the democratic rights of society in pursuit of his objectives. For Putin, the ends justify the means.

In the realm of electoral politics, Putin wielded the power of the Russian state in ways that have caused considerable damage to democratic institutions. After Putin and his allies created the Unity party out of thin air in October 1999, state television incessantly promoted it and destroyed its opponents with a barrage of negative advertising never before seen in Russian politics. As a result, Unity won nearly a quarter of the vote in December. Putin then used national television to broadcast his "anti-campaign" for the presidency.

More gruesome has been Putin's indifference to the human rights of his country's own citizens in Chechnya. Russia has a right to defend its borders, but the egregious violations of human rights in his pursuit of this cause reveal the low priority that Putin assigns to democratic principles. Independent journalists, leaders of nongovernmental organizations, and academics also have felt the heavy hand of the Russian state under Putin. Reporters like Radio Liberty's Andrei Babitsky and national television networks like NTV have suffered the consequences of reporting news from Chechnya that inconveniences the Kremlin. Babitsky was arrested and then handed over to the Chechens; the offices of Media-Most, the owner of NTV, were raided by the Federal Security Service (FSB). Commentators and columnists critical of Putin report that many newspapers are unwilling to carry their articles. Self-censorship has returned to Russia. Environmental groups and human rights organizations also have reported increased monitoring of their activities by the FSB in the Putin era.

Many of Putin's proposed political reforms also sound antidemocratic. His advisers speak openly about changing the electoral law to eliminate the requirement that half of the Duma's deputies be elected by proportional representation—a revision that would virtually keep Russia's prodemocratic political parties out of parliament. Putin and his aides also have expressed support for the highly antidemocratic idea of appointing governors rather than electing them. Putin has even hinted that he would like to extend the term of the Russian presidency to seven years. None of these innovations alone would spell the end of democracy. In combination, however, they could resurrect a system dominated by a single "party of power," the Kremlin.

Despite all of these ominous signs, it would be wrong to conclude that Putin is an "antidemocrat." He is simply too modern and too Western-oriented to believe in dictatorship. Rather, Putin is indifferent to democratic principles and practices, perhaps believing that Russia might have to sacrifice democracy in the short run to achieve "more important" economic and state-building goals. He will continue to allow an independent press, elections, and individual liberties as long as they do not conflict with his agenda of securing Russia's borders, strengthening the Russian state, and promoting market reform. What will happen, however, when democracy becomes inconvenient for him?

Implications for Russian Democracy

The fate of democracy in Russia does not depend solely on Putin's views on the subject; if it did, Russia could not be considered a democracy. In fact, it has now become fashionable both in Russia and the West to assert that Russia is not a democracy, and the rise of Putin is cited as the latest confirming evidence. Some assert that Russia has never been a democracy, contending that the current regime in Russia is at best comparable to that of the late Soviet period, with a small group of people at the top making all the political decisions. Others have even likened contemporary Russia to feudal Europe, a system in which a handful of nobles—now called oligarchs and regional barons—decide everything.[13]

Such historical analogies, however, are dangerously distorted. They suggest that no change has occurred in Russia over the last decade or the last 400 years. They imply cultural continuity in Russia. Russian leaders are authoritarian and the Russian people support them because Russian leaders and Russian society have always favored dictatorship. This line of argument suggests that there is no threat to Russian democracy today because there is no democracy to be threatened.

To be sure, Russian democracy is weak and unconsolidated. Russia is not a liberal democracy. Pluralist institutions of interest intermediation are weak, mass-based interest groups are marginal, and the institutions that could help to redress this imbalance—parliament, the party system, and the judiciary—lack strength and independence.[14] The weakness of these institutions means that Russia's electoral democracy is more fragile than a liberal democracy would be.[15] In addition, a deeper attribute of democratic stability—a normative commitment to the democratic process on the part of both the elite and society—is still not present in Russia. Although all major political actors and Russian society as a whole recognize elections as "the only game in town" and behave accordingly, antidemocratic attitudes persist. A 1999 public-opinion survey revealed that solid majorities think it "impermissible" to ban meetings and demonstrations (66 percent), cancel elections (62 percent), or censor the mass media (53 percent),[16] but these numbers should be much higher ten years after the collapse of communism. Qualitative elite surveys show stronger support for democratic institutions and values.[17] Yet the marks given for the practice of Russian democracy to date are very low. Only 2 percent believe that Russia has achieved a democracy, while 46 percent believe that Russia has failed to do so.

Finally, the rise of a leader with Putin's background and the process by which he was elected are not positive signs for democratic consolidation. No one who welcomed the destruction of the Soviet police state can be happy that a former KGB officer has now become the president of Russia. And what does it mean for democratic consolidation when the electorate supports antidemocratic policies such as the slaughter of innocent people in Chechnya?

When assessing Russian democracy and its prospects, however, the real question is: Compared to what? Compared to American or even Polish democracy, Russian democracy has a long way to go. Yet compared to other states that emerged from the Soviet Union or to Russia's own authoritarian past, Russia does appear to have made progress in building a democratic political order. Czarist-era peasants did not vote, did not read independent newspapers, and did not travel freely. Neither did Soviet citizens. Princes and Communist Party secretaries were not removed from power by the ballot box, as were four out of nine regional leaders and hundreds of Duma deputies in the

December 1999 election. Moreover, two-thirds of an extremely well-educated population freely opted to participate in presidential and parliamentary elections. If these elections were meaningless, then why did these people bother to show up? Even societal reaction to some of Putin's early antidemocratic moves has been encouraging. For instance, in response to the FSB raid on Media-Most, the Communist Party, the Union of Right Forces, Yabloko, human rights groups and media monitoring organizations, and even several business tycoons united to denounce the intimidation.

The more interesting question is not whether or not today's Russia is a democracy, but what its future trajectory will be. Putin's victory and the way that victory was achieved are not positive steps. Yet it would be premature to generalize about the long-term future of Russian democracy from this one election. Even in established democracies, the same party can remain in power for decades. Only time will tell if Putin's election is the beginning of the creation of a one-party state or just a rather accidental consequence of a popular war and a weak opposition.

The fact that a man like Putin, whose credentials and proclivities are not prodemocratic, could be elected president of Russia nearly ten years after the collapse of the Soviet Union suggests that the future of democracy in Russia is highly uncertain. At this moment in history, after years of revolutionary turmoil, the Russian people clearly want a leader with a strong hand who promises to build a stronger state. But neither popular desires for stability and security nor Putin's lack of commitment to democracy need necessarily translate into authoritarianism. Russia today is a large, divided, and multilayered society. Consequently, reestablishing dictatorship would be difficult and costly, especially if Putin and his team are serious about wanting to integrate Russia into the Western world. But if their new government does try to move toward dictatorship, would the Russian people be willing to sacrifice their democratic freedoms for more order? Or would they be willing to fight for these freedoms? After a decade of transition, these unfortunately are still open questions.

NOTES

1. The author convened a seminar of Russian electoral analysts at the Moscow Carnegie Center shortly after the counteroffensive, and this was the consensus at the time.

2. Fond "Obshchestvennoe mnenie" (FOM), "Klyuchevye problemy predvybornoi kampanii v zerkale obshchestvennogo mneniya," *Rezul'taty sotsiologicheskikh issledovannii* 29 (10 May 1996): 4–5.

3. See the tracking polls conducted by the Russian Center for Public Opinion and Market Research (VCIOM) at *www.russiavotes.org.*

4. Agentstvo regional'nykh politcheskikh issledovanii (ARPI), *Regional'nyi Sotsiologicheskii Monitoring* 49 (10–12 December 1999), 39. Sample size: 3,000 respondents in 52 Federation subjects.

5. This survey project of 1,900 Russian respondents, directed by Timothy Colton and Michael McFaul and executed by Polina Kozyreva and Mikhail Kosolapov of DEMOSCOPE, was conducted shortly before the parliamentary vote.

6. Author's interview with Mikhail Margelov, Putin's campaign manager (February 2000).

7. FOM, *Soobshcheniya fonda "Obshchestvennoe mnenie,"* 536 (12 January 2000), 30.

8. Author's interviews with senior Yabloko leaders (March 2000).

9. ORT commentators asserted that Yavlinsky and Yabloko were funded by German and Jewish organizations. They also showed clips of homosexuals announcing that they planned to vote for Yavlinsky and intimated that Yavlinsky himself was gay.

10. This team of economists and lawyers, under the direction of German Gref at the Strategy Center formed by Putin last year, in many ways represents the most liberal thinkers in Russia. The list of specialists includes Vladimir Mau, Aleksei Ulukaev, Sergei Sinelnikov (all former Gaidar aides and deputies), Oleg Vyugin, Andrei Illarionov, Mikhail Dmitriev, and their chief mentor, Yevgeny Yasin.

11. For a snapshot of his views, see Andrei Illarionov, "The Roots of the Economic Crisis," *Journal of Democracy* 10 (April 1999): 68–82.

12. See *Ot pervogo litsa: razgovory s Vladimirom Putinym* (Moscow: Vagrius Books, 2000).

13. See the comments by Thomas Graham in "A New Era in Russian Politics," *Meeting Report* 2 (Washington, D.C.: Carnegie Endowment for International Peace, 30 March 2000).

14. For the author's own assessment of these institutions and the causes of their weakness, see Michael McFaul, "The Perils of Protracted Transition," *Journal of Democracy* 10 (April 1999): 4–18; "Party Formation and Deformation in Russia," working paper, Carnegie Endowment for International Peace (May 2000); "Russia's 'Privatized' State as an Impediment to Democratic Consolidation: Part I," *Security Dialogue* 29 (June 1998): 191–200; and "Russia's 'Privatized' State as an Impediment to Democratic Consolidation: Part II," *Security Dialogue* 29 (September 1998): 315–32.

15. On the differences between electoral and liberal democracies, see Larry Diamond, *Developing Democracy: Toward Consolidation* (Baltimore: Johns Hopkins University Press, 1999).

16. The survey was conducted by ROMIR in July 1999.

17. See Sharon Werning Rivera, "Explaining Elite Commitments to Democracy in Post-Communist Russia," unpubl. ms., September 1999; Arthur Miller, Vicki Hesli, and William Reisinger, "Conceptions of Democracy among Mass and Elite in Post-Soviet Societies," *British Journal of Political Science* 27 (April 1997): 157–90; and Judith Kullberg and William Zimmerman, "Liberal Elites, Socialist Masses, and Problems of Russian Democracy," *World Politics* 51 (April 1999): 323–58. Kullberg and Zimmerman, however, find a real gap between elite and mass values, with the latter exhibiting more illiberal ideologies.

17

THE PRIMACY OF HISTORY AND CULTURE

Zbigniew Brzezinski

Zbigniew Brzezinski, U.S. national security advisor during the Carter administration, is professor of U.S. foreign policy at the Paul H. Nitze School of Advanced International Studies of Johns Hopkins University and counselor to the Center for Strategic and International Studies. This essay is based on an interview he gave to the Journal of Democracy *on 9 July 2001.*

When speaking of the plight of democracy in the lands that once made up the Soviet Union, we must remember that we are talking about 15 different states, and that no common answer will cover all of them.

That said, I think we can sort these states into three basic categories. In the first category are the most advanced countries, clearly on their way to becoming stable and secure democracies. These include the three Baltic republics of Latvia, Lithuania, and Estonia, which have become increasingly difficult to think of as belonging to the same political context as the other former Soviet republics. The elements of culture and history mark these three as fundamentally different from the others.

Turning to the remaining dozen, we may say that nine are countries where democracy exists only nominally or as a slogan that the local rulers reluctantly feel they must mouth, given their economic and financial dependence on the West and its sensibilities. To this class belong the five Central Asian states (Kazakhstan, Turkmenistan, Uzbekistan, Tajikistan, and Kyrgyzstan) plus Azerbaijan, Armenia, Moldova, and Belarus.

In between these nine essentially nondemocratic states and the democratic group comprising the three Baltic states, we find the third and most ambiguous category, which contains Ukraine, probably Georgia, and Russia itself. Theirs are unstable authoritarian and yet also semi-anarchic political systems, in which democratic institutions operate at some levels but are absent at others. In these countries, the movement toward democracy on a societal level must contend with counterpressures that are driving the country in the direction of a more stable and authoritarian form of government.

In Ukraine and Russia, especially, there are genuine elements of democracy at work in segments of the mass media, in the widespread freedom of personal expression, in the confidence with which many people exercise that freedom, and in terms of access to external sources of information. But all of this is still vulnerable to political pressures emanating either from the desire to create a powerful state, as is the case in Russia, or simply from the desire of entrenched interests not to be challenged and constrained in their quest for self-enrichment, as in the case of Ukraine.

Although in Russia there has lately been a narrowing of the scope of what we would normally call democracy, some of that has been a consequence of the reduced scope of internal anarchy. This in turn should remind us that much of what we would wish to call Russian democracy has not resulted from the establishment of an institutionalized, constitutional, law-abiding system, but is more a function of the collapse of the state and the open-ended, anarchic competition for power, influence, and information which that collapse triggered. I am not trying to exonerate Russia's President Vladimir Putin and his associates. Their democratic credentials are suspect. But I do think that some restoration of what might be euphemistically called "law and order" in Russia did require constraints on certain aspects of the chaotic freedom that opened up in the wake of the Soviet downfall.

We do not yet know what the terminal point of these changes in Russia will be—of course, there are no such things as terminal points in politics, anyway. But over the next decade or two, we may witness Russia turning into a kind of authoritarian democracy reminiscent of, say, pre-1914 Germany. Russia will not quite be a democracy in the full modern meaning of the word, but at the same time it will not be as arbitrary or brutal or dictatorial as one might fear. Certainly it will be difficult to reimpose on Russian society the kind of effective authoritarianism that some graduates of KGB schools might desire deep in their hearts, even as they publicly mouth democratic slogans.

The Russian political elite is finding it very difficult to digest the fact that Russia's empire and status as a world power are gone forever. Nostalgia still dominates this elite's outlook and inhibits its ability to accommodate the West. But this elite will be passing from the scene. So perhaps we should be somewhat pessimistic about Russia's short-term prospects but more optimistic about its longer-term prospects, insofar as a genuine accommodation with the West is concerned.

Russia's current elite would like to have its cake and eat it too. It wants Russia to be included in the West, thereby relieving potential problems with China to the east and the Muslims to the south. Yet it wants this inclusion to take place on terms that would allow Russia to cling to such imperial baggage as its war against the Chechens and its unwarranted desire for continued recognition as a world power.

As this elite fades, however, more and more Russians will realize that, by the year 2020, the number of Muslims living along Russia's southern border will have risen from 300 million to 450 million. (Russia's population is currently 147 million and falling.) In the meantime, Russia's brutal wars against Chechnya will have thoroughly antagonized the Muslim peoples. And to the east will be a China that *already* has an economy five times larger than Russia's, and a population nine times as big.

The best historical analogue of Chechnya is Algeria. France would not be what it is today if de Gaulle had not cut loose from Algeria, even though this step was very difficult for many Frenchmen to accept, given their deep attachment to the notion of *Algérie française*. The war in Chechnya will either go on poisoning Russian political life and inhibiting Russia's entry into the West, to the detriment of Russia, or at some point the Russians will realize that the Chechens are not Russians, just as the French eventually realized that the Algerians really were not French. It is as simple as that. It seems absurd today, but 40 years ago the majority of Frenchmen thought that the Algerians were French.

Once the Russians realize that the Chechens are not Russians, and therefore are entitled to some distinctive and separate status of their own, the two sides can work out a solution (there are many innovative formulas available) for bridging the gap between Russia's territorial integrity and Chechen national sovereignty. But learning to acknowledge that the Chechens are not Russians will be a *sine qua non* of Russia's true integration into the West.

A growing sense of geopolitical reality should help Russia to understand that it must accommodate the West on Western terms or else suffer isolation and be condemned to increasing difficulties. This led me to say in one interview with the Russian press that if the Russian elite does not wake up, if it does not shed its nostalgic delusions, we may end up, geopolitically, with what General de Gaulle once grandly described as "Europe from the Atlantic to the Urals"—but this time quite literally.

History and Culture Matter

In asking what sets our three categories of post-Soviet states apart from one another, I think that we must look primarily to history and culture. Not only were the Baltic republics under communist domination for a shorter period (50 rather than 70 years), they also belonged to the European tradition, with its feudal history of decentralized authority, with its restricted concept of political power, with the institution of private ownership, and so forth. Russia, by contrast, never had these attributes.

All of that contributed to a different cultural outlook. The Baltic states culturally were part of Western Europe, of West European Christendom, and later of West European Protestantism (with the exception of the Lithuanians, who are actually more Central European than properly Baltic). In contrast, in Russia we see the traditions of absolute state power, of religion totally subordinated to the state, of the absence of a property entitlement and the political implications it brings. All of these historical and cultural differences make for fundamentally different contexts whose significance is not captured in abstract discourse about this or that set of political institutions.

This does not mean that I accept the view that one can make useful generalizations about entire civilizations. In Russia, for instance, I think that the history of Mongol domination, followed by the emergence of a supreme state to which everything in society, including property ownership and the church, was fully subordinated, created a different cultural context, not only from Western Europe, but even from other parts of Orthodox Europe such as Bulgaria, Romania, and Serbia, where the church was never as fully subjected to state authority as it was in Russia.

The fault lines that we see among the post-Soviet states today are thus the combined products of historical accident and cultural evolution. In some cases, these lines map neatly onto ethnic distinctions. In others, they run right through ethnic communities. In Ukraine, for example, there are remarkable political differences between Ukrainians from west of the Dnieper and those from east of it—and this includes Orthodox on both sides. Generalizations about Islam are probably just as dubious as generalizations about Orthodox Christianity. Both the Orthodox world and the vast "Islamic crescent"—which extends from Nigeria in the west right through to Indonesia in the east—contain more internal variety and cultural diversity than most casual observers recognize.

In the light of history and culture, institutional choices such as parliamentarism or presidentialism—to mention a type of explanation much beloved by political scientists—are more a consequence than a cause of the different levels of receptivity to democracy that we find in various countries.

To put this point another way, a country cannot just adopt a parliamentary system and make it work without the necessary cultural and historical underpinnings. We have seen this in Russia. There, the conflict between President Boris Yeltsin and the Duma, which culminated in the use of armed force, exemplified the difficulty of making either a democratic presidential system or a parliamentary system work, or even coexist.

The choice of institutions can reinforce certain tendencies, but it cannot replace the causal role of historical experience and cultural formation, which create a predisposition for certain mechanisms to work or not work in this or that particular case.

In a similar fashion, economic reforms worked in certain countries—most notably, Poland, Estonia, and Hungary—because of a favorable combination of subjective and objective realities. The subjective reality was the predisposition of the public to support these reforms, to respect them, even to make sacrifices in order to help them succeed. The objective conditions were some of the historical factors that I have already mentioned, which were then favorably matching the requirements of the subjective conditions and interacting with them.

Economic Reform in Russia

Russia has seen no large-scale political movement uniting great numbers of people in subjective readiness to pursue market-based reform. Nor were objective conditions conducive to smooth and effective privatization or economic transformation. Instead, the Russian situation was one in which a lack of commitment to any alternative vision of society interacted with a catch-as-catch-can experimentation in the dismantling of state-owned industry to the benefit of a small cluster of individuals who had the savvy and initiative to manipulate the mechanics of privatization to secure their own self-enrichment.

I was skeptical early on, as my writings document, of the prospect that shock therapy would succeed outside Central Europe. While I doubt that delayed or more orderly reforms would have worked much better elsewhere in the postcommunist world, I was inclined to feel that they stood a better chance of being moderately successful than the pell-mell simultaneous adoption of rapid economic privatization and rapid political democratization.

Many blame Yeltsin and the corruption that he encouraged or tolerated for what went wrong in Russia, but that is only part of the story. Responsibility also rests with the Western "consultants" who rushed in encouraging Yeltsin and his associates to do what they did, while in the process partaking of some of the spoils themselves. We all know about the rich oligarchs in the former Soviet Union; we have paid much less attention to the rich Westerners who became rich because they partook in ravaging the former Soviet economy.

Western governments bear less blame for the ills associated with economic reform in Russia, if only because their control over the situation was so limited. The nearest cognate to what happened in the post-Soviet world in the 1990s was what happened in Germany and Japan after the Second World War. Both countries benefited from large-scale Western economic assistance, including the much-admired Marshall Plan. But both Germany and Japan had been defeated in a shooting war, and then subjected to years of military occupation and government, which imposed both discipline and norms of conduct.

This was not the case in Russia. It was not a case of reform imposed from above and outside. Reform in Russia was part of the messy after-math of the collapse of a system in which successor domestic elites were interacting with often-predatory Western advisors who were helping them, not for the sake of reform as such, but for personal profit.

Yet in the absence of direct—really direct—Western control over the reform process, could it have gone any differently? Perhaps the exploi-tation of the opportunities that opened up might have been less cynical and more restrained. But it remains doubtful that the West, by adopting some set of enlightened policies, could have produced in Russia what took place in Estonia, Hungary, or Poland. And the West certainly was in no position to try to duplicate in Russia what Deng Xiaoping and company were able to do on their own in China.

In brief, a certain fatalism is in order, though it need not rule out distaste for Western hypocrisy, to say nothing of the self-delusions that were fostered so actively by Bill Clinton and the architects of his Russia policy, with the American public being misled into believing that Rus-sia was already a successful market economy and a successfully func-tioning democracy.

Geopolitics and the Future

Looking to the future, I believe that the Soviet Union's successor states will remain independent. Most of them are relatively weak and politically underdeveloped, but with a commitment to independence strong enough in each case to ensure that survival as an independent state is not in doubt. Ukraine, as things settle down, will begin to gravi-tate more toward the West. Ukraine is too big to be easily reabsorbed by Russia, and there are too many Ukrainians who, whatever their other dissatisfactions, are gratified by being cabinet ministers, generals, or ambassadors of an independent Ukraine, and prefer that to being pro-vincial officials in an empire ruled from a foreign capital.

If Russia moves toward the West, Ukraine will certainly move to-ward the West. And if the Russians do not move toward the West, the Ukrainians will still have every reason to want to become more Western in their orientation. In the first instance, if Russia moves toward the West, it is inconceivable for the Ukrainians not to do so. In the second instance, if the Russians do not move toward the West, they will stag-nate and be in dire geopolitical difficulties, and the Ukrainians will have no interest in joining them in that condition. It is not irrelevant to note that Ukrainian mothers are delighted that their sons do not have to pur-sue Russian imperial nostalgia in Chechnya.

Belarus is likely to be a serious problem, with President Alyaksandr Lukashenka perhaps becoming a candidate to join Slobodan Milošević in the dock at The Hague. Since Russia has been sponsoring his re-gime, Russia's willingness to bring him to account also has to be considered a test of Russia's readiness to become part of the democratic West.

Whether or not Russia itself moves toward the West will depend mainly on the speed with which the present Russian elite is replaced, hopefully by a more open-minded successor generation that is less driven by nostalgia for the imperial past and more aware of Russia's geopolitical dilemmas. Russia will not again be, in our lifetime, a major world power. Either it will begin to remedy some of its internal weaknesses by closer association with the West—and again, this must be on Western terms—or it will become increasingly beleaguered by conflicts with Muslim societies to the south, even as it struggles to contain Chinese encroachments in the Far East.

That is Russia's strategic choice. The path that it chooses will decisively influence not only the geopolitics of Eurasia but also the prospects for democracy in Russia itself.

18

THE IMPACT OF NATIONALISM

Ghia Nodia

Ghia Nodia is chairman of the board of the Caucasian Institute for Peace, Democracy, and Development (CIPDD) and professor of sociology at Tbilisi State University. This essay was originally published in the October 2001 issue of the Journal of Democracy.

Observers who comment on the slide toward "de-democratization" across much of what used to be the USSR often neglect another development that is just as interesting: Why is it, just ten years after all of them were born from the same Soviet institutional womb, that these 15 countries have become so different from one another?

Take Estonia and Turkmenistan. The former is a consolidated democracy with a liberal market economy. It belongs, or will soon belong, to all the "best" international clubs: NATO, the World Trade Organization, the Council of Europe, the European Union, and so on. The latter is run by a dictatorial (though not very ideological) strongman, and in some respects may be even farther from democracy than it was at the end of the Brezhnev era.

These may be extreme cases, but they are not exceptional. In the widely cited annual Freedom House survey, post-Soviet states can be found in each of the three major categories: "Free" (meaning securely democratic), "Partly Free" (semi-autocratic or democratic with serious flaws), and "Not Free" (autocratic).[1] That is, differences among post-Soviet countries are almost as big as those among any other sample of states in the world.

To scholars of the influential "constructivist" or "institutionalist" school, who try to explain political realities through elite-led institutional arrangements, this is abnormal. Rogers Brubaker, a champion of this approach, has shown persuasively how Soviet policies that institutionalized nationality on both the territorial and the personal levels helped to foster nationalism and the eventual breakup of the USSR.[2] But this theory cannot begin to explain why the emergent countries differ so widely from one another in various ways, including their respective manifestations of nationalism.

Far from confirming the claims of social constructivism, the story of the Soviet Union, its demise, and the varying plights of its successor states suggests precisely the opposite. Indeed, it is tempting to see the entire Soviet and post-Soviet experience as a gigantic historical experiment designed to cast doubt on the notion that explanations built around "institutional engineering" can go far toward explaining why polities and societies develop as they do.

Although the USSR was formally quasi-federal, Soviet institutions were essentially the same everywhere. Moreover, the communist ideological desire—unprecedented in human history—to shape and control every area of life did not leave much room for regional or local exceptionalism. If any regime could impose conformity across all the areas of a large country, this was it.

Since the fall of communism and the Soviet breakup, all the newly independent successor states have felt the same globalized pressures to adopt markets and democracy. With varying degrees of sincerity, almost all of them swear fealty to democratic capitalism. In their efforts to shape market-friendly and democratic institutions, all have received advice, assistance, and sometimes pressure from the same international organizations, Western governments, foundations, NGOs, and so on.

In other words, the lands of the old Soviet world are like so many fish that have long swum in the same institutional sea. Looking at this situation, an "institutionalist" would predict that these countries should begin to converge on a single model of polity and society. But a funny thing happened on the way to uniformity. Despite coming out of the same Soviet institutional environment, and despite following (or trying to follow) the same democratic-capitalist path since independence, these states persistently display glaring differences while they have in common little more than what is vaguely referred to as a "shared postcommunist mentality."

Are there other explanations that can succeed where the institutionalist framework fails? Might economics hold the key? After all, countries that were more prosperous at the moment of the breakup (such as the Baltics) are doing better now, ten years after, in terms of both the economy and democracy. This seems to make sense, but it only relocates the problem by making us ask why some regions within the single, centrally planned Soviet economy were better developed than others in the first place.

Another possibility is one that I call the argument from cultural geography. As Michael Mandelbaum puts it, "The most successful postcommunist countries are those closest to the part of the world from which the definition of success comes."[3] The more "Western" you are, the more likely it is that you will be both more prosperous and more democratic. It is as simple as that.

Why is this so? Perhaps the West cares more about countries that are physically closer to it, and helps them more. Or maybe democracy spreads like a bodily contagion, reaching nearby places first. There is probably some truth to both of these suggestions, but they are hardly sufficient. Many undemocratic countries receive lots of Western support and assistance, and democracy does not spread concentrically across the map like ripples on a pond. Belarus lies farther west than Russia (and on roughly the same longitude as the Baltic states), but it is much less democratic.

This brings us to the controversial issue of culture. In the former USSR, as elsewhere, democracy has fared better in countries that are culturally "Western" than it has in countries that are not. If we take "the West" to coincide with the world of "Western Christianity," then only the Baltics among all the post-Soviet states belong to it—and they are the only ones that we can now confidently categorize as "consolidated democracies." Those that belong to Eastern Christianity (Orthodox Russia, Ukraine, Moldova, Georgia, Apostolic Armenia) cannot be called democracies in the full sense. Each is either a flawed democracy or a relatively mild autocracy.

The Islamic Belt formed by the five Central Asian republics plus Azerbaijan is on the whole closer to full autocracy: Either there is hardly any space for independent public activity (as in Uzbekistan and Turkmenistan), or this space is a good deal smaller than it is even in the incompletely democratic states. Belarus does not fit neatly into this picture, but even this most autocratic of the Eastern Christian countries still has much more free public space than Uzbekistan or Turkmenistan.

"Fit" for Democracy?

Precisely because the cultural argument is a powerful one, it is crucial that we correctly interpret the correlation on which it rests. One line of interpretation sees cultures or civilizations as fixed, self-sufficient entities that supersede all other social realities, and may "clash" (if we are pessimists) or "enter into dialogue" (if we are optimists), but otherwise have nothing to do with one another. By this token, some civilizations may be considered "fit" for democracy, others not. For instance, the West could be said to be fit, the world of Eastern Christianity at best partly fit, and the Islamic world largely unfit.

One can try to base this judgement on a specific set of cultural preconditions, understood as objectively measurable features that make democracy possible. Examples could include a tendency to privilege abstract rules over personalistic ties; a propensity to form large-scale organizations rather than small groups; a habit of long-term rather than short-term thinking; and the like.

In *The Moral Basis of a Backward Society,* his 1958 study of the southern Italian region of Calabria, Edward C. Banfield argued:

> There is some reason to doubt that the non-Western cultures of the world
> will prove capable of creating and maintaining the high degree of orga-
> nization without which a modern economy and a democratic political
> order are impossible. There seems to be only one important culture—the
> Japanese—which is both radically different from our own and capable of
> maintaining the necessary degree of organization.[4]

The global "third wave" of democratization that began in Southern
Europe in the mid-1970s defied such expectations and undercut the
notion that certain sociocultural preconditions absolutely must be
present if democratization is to occur. But the totality of the post-Soviet
experience—as summed up by the Estonia-Turkmenistan gap mentioned
at the outset of this essay—should caution us against throwing out the
preconditions thesis altogether. A wiser course would be to qualify and
reinterpret this thesis in a more flexible and dynamic way. The way in
which Adam Przeworski and his collaborators have handled arguments
about the role of economic factors in democracy-building is a good example of how to do this.[5]

According to Przeworski, promising economic performance may make
a young democracy more likely to last, but it does not explain why democratic transition was chosen in the first place. To account for that, we
must look at the specific choices of real political actors under definite
circumstances and, above all, at the incentives and legitimating grounds
that drive and support these choices. In this regard, Przeworski and his
colleagues find that "contagion" counts for more than the level of economic development.[6]

Since we have seen that democratic contagion does not simply follow physical or spatial laws, we should revisit the argument from culture, but with a twist. For this time we will not approach the matter from
the essentialist standpoint of a search for objectively measurable cultural features. Instead, we will think about civilizational choices or cultural factors that help to incline a given country or region toward one or
another model of development.

To acknowledge that the modern blueprint of democracy originated
in the Western and indeed the Protestant world, and only afterwards
spread around the globe, is not to say that the West was predestined to
invent this form of government. We might instead agree with Montes-
quieu, as interpreted by Pierre Manent: It was by chance that the English
found the magic formula of modern democracy—the unity of liberty
and commerce. This formula cannot be logically deduced from the
previous development of Western civilization.[7]

Other metaphysical interpretations might be adopted as well, but the
point stands that the inception of democracy within a certain cultural
and geographical area holds the power of an accomplished fact. Democracy (along with other traits of "modernity") arose first in the West.
In light of that fact, democracy appears in history as something "West-

ern," and a choice in favor of democracy assumes a cultural as well as a political character. Thus feeling culturally close to the West will tilt a country toward political democracy. Conversely, a country where the West is seen as alien will be a country that is less likely for that reason to choose democracy. This is not to say that cultural (dis)affinity must always be the sole or most potent factor, but it does matter.

As democracy spreads, so grows the number of countries that can serve as models for potential democratizers, and there are greater opportunities to justify a choice for democracy in cultural terms. As scholars of "third wave" democratizations have convincingly argued, the victory of democracy on the Iberian peninsula had a strong effect on Latin America: For these Spanish- and Portuguese-speaking societies, democracy ceased to be alien.[8] Likewise, the consolidation of democracy in Greece since 1974 may one day prove to have made a deep impression on Eastern Orthodox countries, while upon the fate of democracy in Turkey may hinge the prospects of democracy throughout the Islamic world.

Belonging and Choice

Precisely how does the sense of cultural belonging converge with political choices? It depends on the kind of nationalism that predominates within a given country. Nationalism requires an aversion to the other. This other can be internal or external. The internal other is usually an ethnic minority; mistreatment of such minorities is the main reason why nationalism is often said to be inherently illiberal. But normally it is an external other that is more important in determining the basic political choices that a country makes. The target of this "outbound" nationalism is usually a current or former imperial power, but it can also be a great power that nationalists blame for imposing its will on their country. Unlike inbound nationalism, with its air of ethnic animosity, outbound nationalism tends to be more civic, not least because great powers themselves tend to be more civic than ethnic in behavior and ideology.

Another important dimension of nationalism is whether its gaze at the other is directed "up" or "down." The criterion is usually closeness to the West, the wellspring and homeland of modernity. Thanks to postimperial guilt and pressure from the left, avowals of cultural superiority by Westerners are now taboo, and Western scholars and officials hasten to distinguish between "modernization" and "Westernization." No such sensitivities constrain public discourse in ex-communist countries, where denunciations of the "barbarity" of less-Western neighbors are common. In *Balkan Ghosts,* Robert Kaplan shows how on such grounds Croats revile Serbs, Serbs revile Albanians, and so on.[9] The same is true of different regions of the old USSR, where nations rank each other as more—or less—"Western," which is used interchangeably with "advanced," "modernized," or "civilized."

However much one may dislike the idea of cultural deference to the West, it can become a powerful force for democratization when the "other" that is the main target of nationalism—especially the outbound kind—is looked down upon as less Western. Aversion toward a less Westernized neighbor or neighbors can push a country to respect at least basic democratic rules, for today being Western means being democratic. Moreover, having a less Western target for nationalist aversion can strengthen the mobilizational capacity and consensual character of nationalism, for then its reason for being is the impeccably rational desire to free one's country from the benighted domination of a backward land.

Conversely, nationalism that takes aim at a more modernized hegemon (whether or not the nationalists are willing to admit that they are looking up at their target) contains a seed of weakness. The ideology of national autonomy requires the rejection of such a hegemon, but the rejection may not be especially popular or wholehearted if the putative foreign overlord is also the model for and source of development.

In the Baltics, the direction and strength of nationalism lined up in favor of democratization. Baltic-state nationalism was "downward looking," even snobbish: Estonians, Latvians, and Lithuanians all saw themselves as more Western, more advanced, and more civilized than the Russians. This promoted both the mobilizational capacity of their nationalisms and the belief that it was absolutely imperative to follow Western (read: "democratic") ways. The policies of the Baltic states were not beyond criticism in the latter regard—in particular, the Estonian and Latvian reluctance to let Russian-speakers become citizens is dubious on liberal grounds, but dealing with minorities is a longstanding problem in many Western democracies as well, as witness the history of blacks in the United States or Turks in Germany.

Armenia was the only other Soviet land where a "downward-looking" nationalism had mobilizational strength comparable to that seen in the Baltics. In Armenia's case the target was Azerbaijan (seen as an extension of Turkey), and Russia was deemed an ally. Christian Armenians looked down on Islamic Azeris as "less civilized." When it came to democratic standards, Armenia's elites felt at ease with semi-authoritarianism, for even then, was not Armenia still more democratic than Azerbaijan?

In Georgia, the major target of outbound nationalism has been Russia. While Georgia's development has been hampered by ethnic and civic conflicts, Georgians themselves tend to blame these indirectly on Russia. During the fight for independence, Georgian elites insisted that Georgians are personally more Western than Russians (more individualistic, more freedom-loving, and so on), and complained that, "were it not for Russia, we would be more developed now." But the elite's ideology conflicts with the popular perception of Russia as a modernizing power, and Georgian nationalism is weaker because of the clash. Mainstream Georgian policies have so far been nationalist (that is, pro-Western), but there has never been firm consensus about the need to follow Western democratic ways rather than stay in Russia's fold. As a result, while Georgia may have a great deal of Western-style legislation in certain major areas (second only to the Baltic states), its actual record of implementing democratic reforms is much weaker, which is why it fits in with the "Partly Free" trend of the larger "Eastern Christian" realm.

> *It is not by chance that Putin has taken as his model Peter the Great, the paradigmatic Russian Westernizer.*

Russia represents another complicated case. Mainstream Russian nationalism's external other is the West, especially the United States. This split democrats from nationalists in the early post-Soviet years, but nationalism was not central at that time (recent imperial powers usually do not "need" it), and democracy made headway. But the smoldering tension between democracy and nationalism undermined the popular legitimacy of democratic and market reforms.

Russian nationalism also has a semi-external target, which is Russia's "southern tier," especially the Caucasus. Here Russian nationalism becomes "downward-looking," ascribing to Russia a mission to civilize or at least tame the "barbarians." By making a tool of this nationalist sense of superiority toward the "Wild South," Russian president Vladimir Putin may be building a new-model Russian nationalism that is friendlier to Western-style institutions. The idea seems to be to copy the latter insofar as they are needed to make the Russian state stronger and to show Russia's cultural superiority to its unruly neighbors. It is not by chance that Putin has taken as his model Peter the Great, the paradigmatic Russian Westernizer. In this way, Russian democracy may be less liberal, but enjoy greater popular support.

Central Asia is the part of the post-Soviet world that least identifies itself with the West, and it is also notable for the weakness of the nationalism found there. No wonder it is also the least democratic. What support there is for democracy comes from Russified elites, and Russia is viewed as a culturally "Westernizing" power. Therefore, to the extent that there is anti-Russian nationalism in Central Asia, it works at cross-purposes with pressures for democratization. The appeal of Islamist movements is obviously anti-Western, and hence antidemocratic.

In theory, if the countries of Central Asia began to look down on, say, Afghanistan or Pakistan for being too "fundamentalist" and antimodern, that could widen the base of support for democratic reforms in Central Asia. Turkey could serve as a model of an Islamic society whose pro-Western orientation is grounded in opposition to intra-Islamic trends that seem too harshly antimodern. This would require that Central Asia reinvigorate its cultural ties with Turkey, something that seemed to be happening in the early 1990s, but then ran out of steam.

This very short and superficial overview of several cases suggests that the overall success of democratic reforms in the post-Soviet countries correlates strongly with a given republic's perception of its own affinity for the West, as well as the strength of its "outbound" nationalism. Every case is decisively singular, however, for what seems to matter most is the target at which nationalist feeling is aimed, and the type of domestic political project that such nationalism is used to justify.

NOTES

1. In 1999–2000 ratings, Estonia, Latvia, and Lithuania are listed as "Free"; Belarus, Kazakhstan, Tajikistan, Turkmenistan, and Uzbekistan as "Not Free"; and the rest as "Partly Free." See *www.freedomhouse.org/ratings/index.htm.*

2. Rogers Brubaker, *Nationalism Reframed: Nationalism and the National Question in the New Europe* (Cambridge: Cambridge University Press, 1996).

3. Michael Mandelbaum, "Introduction," in Michael Mandelbaum, ed., *Post-Communism: Four Perspectives* (New York: Council on Foreign Relations, 1996), 13.

4. Edward C. Banfield, *The Moral Basis of a Backward Society* (Chicago: Free Press, 1958), 8.

5. Adam Przeworski, Michael Alvarez, José Antonio Cheibub, and Fernando Limongi, "What Makes Democracies Endure?" *Journal of Democracy* 7 (January 1996): 39–55.

6. Ibid., 43.

7. Pierre Manent, *The City of Man* (Princeton, N.J.: Princeton University Press, 1998), 12–14.

8. Samuel P. Huntington, *The Third Wave: Democratization in the Late Twentieth Century* (Norman: University of Oklahoma Press, 1991), 102–3.

9. Robert D. Kaplan, *Balkan Ghosts: A Journey Through History* (New York: Vintage, 1994), 149.

19

FROM DEMOCRATIZATION TO "GUIDED DEMOCRACY"

Archie Brown

Archie Brown, *professor of politics at Oxford University and fellow of St. Antony's College, is the author of* The Gorbachev Factor *(1996), which won the W. J. M. Mackenzie Prize of the Political Studies Association of the United Kingdom for best political science book of the year. More recently, he has edited* The British Study of Politics in the Twentieth Century *(1999, with Brian Barry and Jack Hayward) and* Contemporary Russian Politics: A Reader *(2001). This essay was originally published in the October 2001 issue of the* Journal of Democracy.

While the questions posed by the *Journal of Democracy* are concerned mainly with the post-Soviet period, it is important to note at the outset that the most significant and, in many respects, most successful part of Russia's political transformation—namely, the transition from communism—took place while the Soviet Union was still in existence. Far too often, the breakup of the Soviet Union and the transformation of the communist system are conflated.

The transition from communism had essentially occurred by the spring of 1989. *Glasnost'*, a gift from above, had developed into freedom of speech. The Communist Party's monopoly on power had disappeared de facto with the rise of numerous sociopolitical movements. (It was removed de jure in March 1990, when the Communist Party's "leading role" was excised from the Soviet Constitution.) Within the party, "democratic centralism" had given way to vigorous and open debate among different opinion groupings and factions. Contested elections in 1989 for a legislature with real powers replaced pseudo-elections for a rubber-stamp assembly.

The Soviet economic system was in limbo by that time. A series of laws legalizing individual economic enterprise, devolving power from ministries to factories, and creating cooperatives that became thinly disguised private enterprises produced both intended and unintended consequences. The command economy was ceasing to function but what remained was still far removed from a market economy. Moreover, the legitimizing goal of the building of communism, an ideological feature distinguishing communist parties from socialist parties of a social-democratic type, had been abandoned by Mikhail Gorbachev and by his reformist allies.[1]

While the liberalization and partial democratization of the highly authoritarian and ideologized Soviet system were unambiguously to be welcomed, there is no good reason why the disintegration of the USSR into 15 new states should have been seen as constituting a democratic gain for Russia or all 14 others. For observers on whose scale of values democracy and the rule of law come higher than nation-building and the myth that every nation, however recently constructed, should have a state corresponding to "national" boundaries, the burden of proof that breaking up a larger country will promote democracy lies with the disintegrationists. The existence of historical injustices or of states formed or expanded as a result of territory at some point having been forcibly seized do not in themselves constitute reasons for the dissolution of a modern state. Few states—certainly not the United States—would survive intact if those criteria were sufficient grounds for separatism.

The Baltic States

Even so, it was clear to most outside observers that, if the Soviet Union were democratized, the three Baltic countries would have to become independent. The greater part of their populations would not recognize as legitimate or democratic a political entity, even a confederation, whose center remained Moscow. Their experience following incorporation into the Soviet state in 1940 had powerfully reinforced a preference for independent statehood—a choice that has been largely vindicated. Of all 15 successor states, Estonia, Latvia, and Lithuania, whatever their faults and numerous imperfections, are closest to the democratic end of the political spectrum. While they were better prepared for transition than most other Soviet republics thanks to their connections with their democratic neighbors in Scandinavia, stronger civil society (including major autonomous religious institutions), and higher levels of economic development, they have owed much of their relative success to the greater commitment of their postcommunist elites to the creation of democratic institutions, a tendency strongly reinforced by the prospect of EU membership.

Where the Baltic states were most likely to fall short of democratic standards was in their treatment of the Russians living in their midst. Partly in response to external incentives, however, indigenous Baltic elites have come to realize that, since the Russians are not going to leave, it is necessary to reduce the barriers to their full citizenship and to accept that movement toward bilingualism (or eventual full linguistic assimilation) will be gradual. Although Latvians are far more likely to know Russian than even those ethnic Russians who have obtained Latvian citizenship are to know Latvian, generational change will probably reverse that. The Baltic elites' increasing appreciation of this tendency should help to reduce discord, not only with their Russian minorities, but also with their exceedingly large neighbor, the Russian Federation.

Although the Baltic countries have taken steps toward more inclusive democracy, in most post-Soviet states democracy building has simply not been a top priority for local elites. State building, more often than not as a prelude to asset-stripping of the state's resources, has ranked far higher on their agenda. Presidents, intent on consolidating executive power, have turned most of the successor states into autocracies. Belarus and, more especially, the Central Asian republics were not the most democratic parts of the union in the last years of the USSR, but they were at least more democratic than they are today, having had to respond to liberalization and subsequent democratization in Moscow in the late 1980s.

Russia—Pluralist and Hybrid

Post-Soviet Russia, however, has remained reasonably pluralistic in its politics at the central level, although the most critical voices in the electronic media have been purposefully muted in 2001 and there are few signs of pluralism in most of the republics of the Russian Federation or in many of its regions. Overall, the system is a hybrid—a mixture of arbitrariness, kleptocracy, and democracy.[2]

Boris Yeltsin and his entourage must shoulder a large share of the blame for the weakness of Russia's democratic institutions. Yeltsin's readiness to obliterate one legislature and to bypass its successor, his disdain for political parties, his extensive use of the power of decree, and his blindness to conflicts of interest (between personal enrichment and public service) within his administration all played their part in undermining respect for the post-Soviet political system. A majority of Russians say they have not been living in a democracy, and they are quite right. Western politicians who called Yeltsin's regime democratic did their cause a disservice—unless they were really more interested in stability than accountability and in capitalism (however crooked) than democracy.

Even the manner of Yeltsin's departure was not, as has sometimes been claimed, the ultimate example of his respect for democracy, but rather the reverse. He made it clear that he was not resigning on grounds of poor health but was instead choosing the best moment to secure the election of his favored successor. In a system such as Britain's, which specifically accords the prime minister some discretion in this matter, a government may choose an earlier election date for the sake of party advantage. In contrast, Yeltsin's surprise departure, intended to aid a candidate unknown to the general public half a year earlier, entailed a bending of his own tailor-made 1993 Constitution with its fixed electoral terms.

The Russian political elite has time and again put the pursuit of naked power and personal wealth ahead of respect for democratic institutions, political accountability, and the general welfare. The relationship between unscrupulous businesspeople and Yeltsin and his entourage brought disproportionate political influence to the "oligarchs" and financial gain to both sides at the expense of the people as a whole. The scandalous loans-for-shares scheme—masterminded by the tycoon Vladimir Potanin and his governmental ally Alfred Kokh, supported by Anatoly Chubais, and endorsed by Yeltsin—not only robbed and deceived the population of Russia but also "bound the economic fortunes of the future oligarchs to the political fortunes of the Yeltsin administration."[3] In the run-up to the 1996 presidential election, it enabled the businesspeople who bankrolled Yeltsin's campaign to get their hands on Russia's most valuable national assets, with the two sides united by the fact that formal ownership would come only after victory had been secured. When so much of what has been dignified with the title of "economic reform" has involved dirty deals behind the voters' backs, it is hardly surprising that public opinion turned against the "really existing democracy" of the Second Russian Republic.

Trends in Public Opinion

While the evidence on attitudes toward democracy varies and is not without its ambiguities, the past decade has seen a marked downward trend in support for what passes for democracy in Russia, and even some evidence of declining support for the norms of democracy. In numerous opinion polls, more Russians have picked out the Brezhnev era than any other period as the best time to have lived in Russia during the twentieth century. Moreover, the proportion of Russians who agreed that "it would have been better if the country had remained as it was before 1985" increased from 44 percent in 1994 to 58 percent in 1999. As these data suggest, perceptions of periods of Soviet history have been heavily influenced by the vicissitudes of the post-Soviet experience and changing evaluations of it. Thus, although nothing new came to light about either the Stalin era or the *perestroika* years, between 1994 and 1999 the proportion of the population positively evaluating the Stalin period went up from 18 percent to 26 percent, and favorable evaluations of the *perestroika* years declined from 16 percent to 9 percent.[4]

A similar trend may be detected in attitudes toward the post-Soviet system more specifically. Whereas a modest 34 percent of Russians agreed in 1996 that their political system was a democracy, that figure had declined to 19 percent by 1999. Offered several choices in a survey, more than twice as many Russian respondents in 1999–2000 opted for the pre-*perestroika* system as favored "the political system that exists today." Interestingly, however, Timothy Colton and Michael McFaul found that the largest grouping (41 percent of the population) preferred "the Soviet system, but in a different, more democratic form."[5] When other post-Soviet surveys canvassed opinion on *perestroika* or "the Gorbachev era," they found (as illustrated above) relatively low and declining levels of support. Yet a case could be made for regarding those very years as "the Soviet system, but in a different, more democratic form."

This apparent contradiction can be explained in a number of ways. The Soviet system was no longer communist in any meaningful sense of the term from 1989 onwards; reform had given way to systemic trans-formation. It is possible, then, that Russians wanted a less comprehen-sive dismantling of the Soviet political system. More likely, they re-main nostalgic for the levels of physical and economic security and welfare that the post-Stalin Soviet era offered (however inadequate they were by the standards of West European welfare states). And probably most decisively, the *perestroika* period has come to be associated in the popular mind with the disintegration of the Soviet Union (which most Russians regret), although that was very much an unintended conse-quence of systemic change. In fact, a majority of the component parts of the Soviet Union might have been held together on the basis of a new and voluntary Union Treaty had not Yeltsin played the Russian card against the union and had not the putschists of August 1991 unwittingly aided and abetted him.

In a hybrid political system, the convictions and behavior of elites, especially the principal holders of executive power and the strongest economic interests, are likely to be a better guide to the prospects for democracy than mass opinion. Ordinary Russian citizens cannot be blamed for taking a dim view of what has been presented to them in the name of democracy. That some of the opprobrium rubs off on the prin-ciples of democracy is not altogether surprising. It is fair to say, never-theless, that "the people have assimilated democratic values faster than the elite has negotiated democratic institutions."[6]

When he became president, Vladimir Putin inherited a flawed and skewed pluralistic system, not a democracy. Many of his words about the desiderata of democracy have made better sense than Yeltsin's—especially concerning the need for a serious party system and a rule of law. The Law on Political Parties, passed by the State Duma in summer 2001, provides incentives for party amalgamations and *could* lead not only to fewer but also to stronger parties. Much will depend on the way that law is interpreted. Unfortunately, the attitude of the Putin adminis-tration toward opposition provides grounds for caution. In this and some other areas (above all, Chechnya), there has been a notable gulf be-tween word and deed.

The television station most ready to criticize the state authorities, NTV, and the most independent radio station, Ekho Moskvy, were undermined in the first half of 2001 by a change of ownership backed by Putin's administration. Although Vladimir Gusinsky, their principal owner, had taken from the state more than he ever expected to repay, that scarcely differentiated him from other tycoons. While some Russian economic reformers have rationalized the government's actions on the grounds of defense of property rights, businesspeople whose financial transgressions have been no less than Gusinsky's but whose loyalty to the Kremlin has been above reproach have not been targeted in the same way.

"Manipulated Democracy"

In some respects, the federal authorities, in their attitudes toward political opposition and critical media coverage, are becoming more like their counterparts in the republics and regions. The system by which regional executive authorities control political processes within their domains has been described as "guided" or "manipulated" democracy.[7] Up until now, it has been possible to argue that the federal center has been more democratic and pluralistic than the average constituent unit, of which there are 89. However, at the same time as the central authorities in Moscow are trying to extend their control over the republics and regions, they are learning from the latter and bringing ever more elements of "guided democracy" to the federal level.

What remains encouraging is that within the Russian intellectual elite and, to a lesser extent, the central political elite there are still independent and questioning voices ready to criticize the powers-that-be for their disregard for democratic norms and procedures and for their highly selective application of the law. In the demand for a rule of law, they are joined by actual and potential foreign investors. Since the Russian economy suffers from severe lack of foreign direct investment, as well as from huge domestic capital flight, there are economic incentives for the president and the government to pay more than lip service to a level and predictable legal playing field.

Unfortunately, the kinds of external incentives for the development of *democracy* that have operated in the Baltic states (and in the countries of Central and Eastern Europe) are not present in Russia. Only a minority of Western businesspeople have been sufficiently enlightened to recognize that in the long run democracies provide the greater stability that they crave. There are many who actually prefer authoritarian regimes such as Azerbaijan and Kazakhstan to the more complicated hybrid system of Russia.

Thus, if the Russian political elite is to be given any external incentive to strengthen democratic tendencies, this is likely to depend more on Western politicians than on the business community. It will help if Western presidents, prime ministers, and foreign ministers call things by their proper names and do not designate insider dealing as marketization or creeping authoritarianism as democracy. Given Vladimir Putin's political and economic orientation toward Europe, the European Union, which has provided such effective incentives for the development of democracy in East-Central Europe, could do much more than it has done thus far vis-à-vis the Russian Federation. Within Russia itself and also in the EU there is a minority of officials who are prepared to think the unthinkable and contemplate eventual EU membership for Russia. David Gowan, minister in the British Embassy in Moscow, is among those who have proposed active EU investment "in a structural transformation in Russia, with the aim of achieving a high degree of convergence with EU legislation and norms," while noting that in the long run a closer relationship "depends on Russia meeting many of the democracy and market economy criteria" that are required of all applicant countries.[8]

Given the extent to which the opinion of the mass public, though studied as never before by Western scholars, is marginalized in political practice, nothing will be more important *in the near term* than the choices made by a new and younger Russian political elite. Whether Russia becomes more authoritarian or more democratic is very much in the balance. If the choice is for the former, the losers once again will be the great mass of the Russian people. Having begun, however, to grow accustomed to political freedoms, they are unlikely *in the longer run* to be as manipulable as they were throughout most of the Soviet period—or, indeed, over the past decade.

NOTES

1. These points about the dismantling of the communist system are more fully elaborated in Archie Brown, *The Gorbachev Factor* (Oxford: Oxford University Press, 1996), especially pp. 309–15.

2. For the criteria I deploy in assessing democratization and their application to the Russian case, see Archie Brown, "Evaluating Russia's Democratization," in Archie Brown, ed., *Contemporary Russian Politics: A Reader* (Oxford: Oxford University Press, 2001), 546–68.

3. Chrystia Freeland, *Sale of the Century: The Inside Story of the Second Russian Revolution* (London: Little, Brown, 2000), 173.

4. See Yury Levada, "'Chelovek sovetskiy' desyat' let spustya: 1989–1999" [The Soviet person ten years later: 1989–1999], *Monitoring obshchestvennogo mneniya* [Monitoring public opinion] (VTsIOM, Moscow), 3 (41), May–June 1999, 7, 11.

5. Timothy J. Colton and Michael McFaul, *Are Russians Undemocratic?* (Washington, D.C.: Carnegie Endowment for International Peace, 2001), 4, 7.

6. Timothy J. Colton and Michael McFaul, *Are Russians Undemocratic?* 21.

7. Alla Chirikova and Natalya Lapina, "Political Power and Political Stability in the Russian Regions," in Archie Brown, ed., *Contemporary Russian Politics*, 306, 384–87.

8. David Gowan, *How the EU Can Help Russia* (London: Centre for European Reform, 2000), 45.

20

THE ADVANTAGES OF RADICAL REFORM

Anders Åslund

Anders Åslund is senior associate at the Carnegie Endowment for International Peace. *He has served as a senior economic advisor to the Russian and Ukrainian governments, and as an economic advisor to President Askar Akayev of Kyrgyzstan. This article, which originally appeared in the October 2001 issue of the* Journal of Democracy, *draws on his book* Building Capitalism: The Transformation of the Former Soviet Bloc *(2001).*

The collapse of the Soviet Union initiated a unique political and economic experiment. After half a century or more as part of one state, 15 countries parted company and simultaneously changed their political and economic systems. These states have pursued remarkably different policies since independence, and given that they shared many of the same initial conditions, we can judge the results through quantitative measurements and regression analysis.

Far too often, Russia is discussed on its own or in comparison with Poland or Hungary, countries with far more favorable initial conditions. A comparative analysis of Russia, Ukraine, and Belarus makes more sense, and it renders Russia's performance more impressive. Such a comparative analysis of all the former Soviet republics yields many conclusions.

Strikingly, democracy and market reform have been very closely correlated following communism. The more far-reaching the democratization, the more radical the market reform has been, and both democracy and market reform have been positively correlated with economic growth. Democracy and market reform have also been positively correlated in other regions, but not as strongly as in the postcommunist world.

This observation contradicts the conclusions of a broad social-democratic school of political economy, spearheaded by Adam Przeworski, Jon Elster, and Klaus Offe. They assumed that radical reform would cause higher social costs than gradual reform and that, consequently, voters would prefer the gradual strategy. Neither assumption is borne out by the evidence. They also presumed that continuing material deprivation and the ineffectiveness of representative institutions would undermine popular support for democracy. In truth, however, the real threat to democracy has come from the elite rather than the population, and it has emerged most strongly in countries with little market reform.

Contrary to widespread misperceptions, voters in democratic elections have not rebelled against radical reform. In the countries with the most radical reform programs, Estonia and Latvia, the communist parties were obliterated at an early stage, never to be heard from again; the former Lithuanian Communist Party remains significant, but it has been transformed into a normal social-democratic party. In countries with more gradual economic reform, however, the communists have reformed little and remained retrograde. Even so, they have continued to be quite popular. In Russia and Ukraine, dogmatic communists and their allies usually gather about 35 percent of the vote, and in Moldova they even won a parliamentary majority this year, thanks to chronically gradual— and thus unsuccessful—reforms.

Opponents of democracy, pointing to Deng Xiaoping's China or Augusto Pinochet's Chile, have argued that a benevolent dictatorship is needed to impose arduous market reforms. Yet no such benign despot has emerged in the post-Soviet countries, while quite a few self-serving ones are in evidence. The main threat to market reform has been an egotistical establishment seeking to exploit the omnipotent communist state for its own benefit. The best way of checking this harmful elite has been through democracy.

A small and powerful elite (the *nomenklatura*) is one of the main legacies of communism. As the end of the old regime was approaching, the *nomenklatura* split into two groups: unreformed communists, who remained dogmatic, and pragmatists, who wanted to get rich off the transition. The pragmatists tended to include enterprise managers, young communist officials, and all kinds of operators. Although they facilitated the collapse of communism, they did not desire a normal market economy; they wanted full freedom for themselves but overwhelming regulations for others. They bought commodities at home for a fraction of their world-market prices and sold them abroad, thanks to export privileges. They insisted on massive state credits to themselves at highly negative real interest rates. To make these outrageous practices politically palatable, the pragmatists presented their program as a set of socially conscious gradual reforms. For a variety of reasons, many Westerners played along. Where these parasites won, the outcome was a rent-seeking society.

The communist state was both lawless and kleptocratic, and no successor government has been immune to its lingering corrupting influence. Whoever comes to power finds his collaborators being corrupted over time. Building transparency, as well as checks and balances against corruption, is no easy feat. Strong independent media are vital to expose the malicious elite, and large private enterprises are a precondition of such media. Additionally, one of the most reliable checks on corruption is to oust the rulers every so often (while, incorrectly, many political scientists axiomatically see the stability of government as an important aim). The three Baltic countries have actually exchanged their governments on average once a year, and they are the most reformed in the region; Estonia is also the least corrupt.

Pertinently, all the post-Soviet countries with presidential rule are less democratic than their parliamentary counterparts, and the parliamentary regimes have also produced more market reform. A parliament controls a prime-ministerial government rather closely, while a presidential administration is far less transparent and subject to little legislative supervision. It tends to re-create the central committee of the previously ruling communist party, while at the regional level the gubernatorial apparatus is usually a direct descendant of the regional party committee. In Russia, the presidential administration possesses substantial property that is beyond the control of the treasury, comprising a chronic source of corruption.

The meaning and role of civil society are amorphous. At the outset, the comparatively strong civil society in Russia appeared to be a problem for reform, as any action was subjected to devastating public criticism, complicating the formation of a coherent reform strategy. In the longer run, however, Russia's intense popular debate has contributed to a broad and impressive understanding of market economics, facilitating an extraordinary wave of reform in 2001. By contrast, the main cause behind the spectacular failure of Belarus appears to be the dismal state of the country's civil society, which generated little public understanding of economics. Hence, an inordinately confused population freely voted a populist dictator-to-be into power with an 80 percent majority. In Russia, a far better-informed electorate gave Vladimir Zhirinovsky's similar party only 23 percent of the vote at its peak in the December 1993 elections.

Neither democracy, a market economy, nor privatization was ever a given. Today the former Soviet republics represent three very different political and economic models. The three Baltic countries are categorized by Freedom House as full-fledged democracies with market economies and more than two-thirds of GDP arising from the private sector. Most of the post-Soviet countries are semidemocratic, rent-seeking societies with over half of GDP coming from the private sector. Belarus and Turkmenistan are totally undemocratic and state-controlled, and less than a quarter of their GDP originates in the private sector. Uzbekistan, Azerbaijan, and Tajikistan are also full-fledged dictatorships and not much better economically.

Path dependence has turned out to be important. Countries tend to stick to their initial reform courses, and those that did not jump forward achieved little. Belarus, for example, was one of the most well-developed Soviet republics and is located further to the west than Russia. Today, however, its institutions are as backward as those of Turkmenistan, the most retarded Central Asian country. Belarus never undertook much deregulation, privatization, or democratization. By 1996, populist president Alyaksandr Lukashenka had consolidated a renewed state-dominated dictatorship. Belarus's political and economic retardation is a strong argument for Russia's more radical reforms. It was the real alternative to Boris Yeltsin's program.

With its late, gradual reforms, Ukraine has occupied an intermediate position between Russia and Belarus. In all major regards, it has performed worse than Russia, with greater declines in output and living standards. Late implementation aggravated the quality of privatization, resulting in even more insider ownership than in Russia. On the whole, gradual reforms boosted rent seeking, and rent-seeking societies reinforce themselves in a vicious circle.

Yet Ukraine also shows that you can catch up if you maintain democracy. In 2000, under the reforms of Prime Minister Viktor Yushchenko, Ukraine's vicious circle of rent seeking and rising authoritarianism may have been broken. Yushchenko's trick was to attack on a broad front and play the leading oligarchs against one another, hoping to weaken and eventually destroy them. Clearly, such a semi-reformed oligarchic society is preferable to Belarusan state despotism.

Side Effects and Trade-offs

The slow and gradual reforms that have been dominant in the Commonwealth of Independent States (CIS) have brought socially undesirable results, ranging from the tardy return of economic growth to high corruption and sharply rising income differentials. Indeed, the mythical tradeoff, assumed by gradual reform theoreticians, between high initial social costs of radical reforms and a more promising future never existed. Instead, all radical reform measures and democracy showed strong complementarity, leading to low transition costs and early growth.

The significance of different economic reforms has varied over the course of the transition. From the beginning, it was evident that there was little hope for improvement until inflation had fallen below 40 percent, a level established empirically by Michael Bruno and William Easterly. Yet the hope that financial stabilization on its own would lead to hard budget constraints proved to be in vain. Russian and Ukrainian enterprises were perverted by an abundance of enterprise subsidies and tax exemptions through barter and other nonmonetary transactions, until Russia's financial crash put an end to them in August 1998. Long-term regression analyses show that the reform with the greatest impact

is clearly liberalization, notably price deregulation and external liberalization, including the unification of the exchange rate.

The most controversial reform has been privatization, but cross-
national regressions show that privatization has had a persistently
positive influence. It is true that in countries with little liberalization,
such as Ukraine, no difference was evident between state enterprises
and privatized enterprises for a long time. This is not surprising. With
minimal deregulation, there are few private property rights. In the first
stage of defensive restructuring, enterprises do little but cut costs, and
state enterprises can do that almost as well as private enterprises. The
positive effects of private ownership become apparent, however, when
strategic expansion and innovation are required. Moreover, new owners
usually need some time to take control and to sort an enterprise out.
Who wants to undertake productive investment in already existing
enterprises when the best return on money is to buy enterprises not yet
privatized? Therefore, the beneficial effects of private ownership mount
over time, especially in the most reformed economies.

The prime complaint about privatization has been that it boosts corruption, which is commonly defined as "the misuse of public power for
private gain." Privatization is a one-time process, however, so while it
might be corrupt in itself, it ends the possibility of corruption involving
those enterprises or properties. Moreover, private monopolies rarely
persist, while many public monopolies do, according to surveys by the
European Bank for Reconstruction and Development (EBRD). With more
competition, openness, and transparency, rents and bribes are more difficult to extort. Thus, even though privatization is rarely very clean, it is
bound to reduce corruption in the longer run as politicians and civil
servants have less to sell. Meanwhile, numerous independent proprie-
tors reinforce their independence from the state. The more swiftly early
mass privatization occurs, the more likely it is to mitigate corruption,
because corrupt deals require time for their elaboration. Russia was a
pioneer in mass privatization, and contrary to common prejudices, EBRD
surveys show that Russia is one of the least corrupt post-Soviet countries, besting even Lithuania.

A stark dividing line is apparent in reforms and economic performance between the CIS and Central Europe, but in reality the border is
not so plain. The Baltic countries rival the star performers of Central
Europe, while Romania and Bulgaria have not done much better than
the CIS countries. The explanations vary. One is that hyperinflation, or
at least very high inflation, struck the whole former Soviet Union in
1992–93. Another reason is that the state-trading system persisted among
the CIS countries until 1994, and large implicit subsidies, financed primarily by Russia, dissuaded enterprises in the region from adjusting to
the market.

Russia is the key to the development of all other CIS countries. It remains their dominant export market, and economic recovery is invariably led by exports. When Russia did not liberalize foreign trade within the CIS, nobody else could. If Russia offered underpriced raw materials to the other CIS countries, who would say no? (The Baltic republics actually did.) If Russia could not get the necessary financing for its reforms from the West, everybody else felt that they had no chance. Less tangibly, Russian intellectual debates, TV, and radio continue to dominate the region. Finally, when even the highly qualified Russian radical reformers lost out politically, nobody else was going to forge ahead.

The conclusion is that a "Russia first" policy should have been pursued by the West for the benefit of all CIS countries; unfortunately, it was not. Its essence should have been strong political and financial support for Russia's reformist government in the first half of 1992, but the West provided no financial assistance whatsoever to Prime Minister Yegor Gaidar's reforms. Only later, when the radical reforms had been quashed, did the West provide assistance—to politicians with little or no commitment to real market reform.

Growth and Corruption

Even among the CIS countries, a few achieved early and high growth, notably Georgia, Kyrgyzstan, and Armenia. Although some of the growth might be a matter of statistical vagaries, the effect is too great to be discounted entirely. In comparison with poor performers like Russia, Ukraine, and Moldova, the early-growth states stand out in two ways: lower public expenditures (and revenues) and fewer bureaucrats. Yet Georgia, Armenia, and Kyrgyzstan are clearly more corrupt, as measured by the share of enterprise turnover spent on bribes. Thus even these rather corrupt countries can achieve growth, if only they reduce the size and reach of the state sufficiently.

Many Western analysts assume that the state is good, although the opposite was obviously true under communism. Liberal thinkers who challenged the feudal state in the nineteenth century did not suspect it of being good, and the communist state was clearly far worse. Moreover, an evil state is not easily turned humane. The nineteenth-century liberals sensibly concluded that the role of the state should be minimized to the provision of public goods that offer evident economies of scale, such as defense and law and order. Yet Russia and Ukraine still have public revenues amounting to around one-third of GDP, which is equal to the U.S. level, and their revenues have been quite stable. The much-publicized collapse of their public revenues is nothing but a myth, and efforts should be made to reduce the overextended and incompetent state.

Similarly, the problem of crime has been misperceived. With the collapse of communism, crime rates doubled throughout the region, as is typical with any liberalization after a severe dictatorship. Initially, crime was spontaneous and rather disorganized, but by 1993–95 organized crime had taken over, prompting crime rates to fall. The years 1996–98 saw the rise of oligarchic groups, which edged out real organized crime, and crime rates dropped further. In recent years, the public law-enforcement organs have become the main sources of crime, and law-abiding post-Soviet citizens fear the police more than criminals. Few people hire criminals to take revenge on their enemies any longer, as it is cheaper, less risky, and more effective to call for the tax police. The current challenge for these half-reformed, rent-seeking societies is to bring their lawless law-enforcement organs under democratic control. If they succeed, their market economies are also likely to flourish.

The overall lesson of the post-Soviet transformation is that a maximum of discontinuity is desirable. The most clear-cut example is Estonia, which has been ruled by truly radical reformers. They did not try to assess elusive costs and benefits but instead chose the best long-term solution for their nation: true free markets and full democracy. Rather than reducing import tariffs, the Estonians abolished them, and they introduced a flat income tax early on. All civil servants were sacked, but they were allowed to apply for jobs in a new public administration. Estonia has achieved a high sustainable growth rate and the lowest level of corruption in the whole postcommunist world.

After the Russian attempt at radical reform in 1992, which was only partially implemented, "shock therapy" became a derisory term. Yet true radical reformers, notably in Poland and Estonia, were highly successful. The purpose of shock therapy was to convince enterprise managers to change their behavior by imposing hard budget constraints on all enterprises. Alas, total enterprise subsidies in Russia, including barter and nonpayments, stayed as high as 16 percent of GDP until 1998, according to a World Bank study. The situation was similar in Ukraine. These subsidies and their erosive effects on managerial incentives appear to have been the main cause of the late economic recovery in these two countries. Indeed, Russia had seen too little shock, and thus the other CIS countries suffered from too much Soviet continuity.

In August 1998, however, world financial markets delivered a real shock to Russia, both starker and more credible than the attempted "shock therapy" had ever been. Contrary to universal expectations of doom, this jolt cleaned up both Russian economic thinking and the country's economic system, helping Russia attain a solid GDP growth rate of 5.4 percent in 1999, 8.3 percent in 2000, and at least 5 percent in 2001. The harmful Soviet continuity had at long last been broken, and the financial crash convinced even the Russian communists that a market economy was necessary.

It is difficult to find any systematic evidence supporting the widely held view among Western social scientists that reforms in the former Soviet Union were too radical or disruptive or that valuable institutional and administrative capital was wasted. The obvious truth is that dictatorial communist parties are no good at building democracy, and lawless security police have no comparative advantage in establishing the rule of law. Yet many of their former servants may make significant contributions, once they are compelled to abandon these moral wrecks. Similarly, much of the human and physical capital of state enterprises is valuable, but it has to be broken free from the old state structure to flourish.

21

DISILLUSIONMENT IN THE CAUCASUS AND CENTRAL ASIA

Charles H. Fairbanks, Jr.

Charles H. Fairbanks, Jr., is director of the Central Asia–Caucasus Institute and research professor of international relations at the Paul H. Nitze School of Advanced International Studies of Johns Hopkins University. This essay originally appeared in the October 2001 issue of *the* Journal of Democracy.

When the Soviet Union fell into shards, it was as if Western liberal democracy—at least on the level of words—suddenly vaulted far to the east, into the traditional heartland of "Oriental despotism."

Ten years later, all the countries of the Caucasus and Central Asia now have parliaments, elected presidents, and (Turkmenistan excepted) multiple parties. The Organization for Security and Cooperation in Europe (OSCE) extends across the steppes two-thirds of the way to the Yellow Sea, and the North Atlantic Cooperation Council includes the homeland of Genghis Khan. When Western forms sprang eastwards, so did the hopes of Western democrats and the interest of Western businesses in the Caspian basin. Today, however, in response to the region's authoritarianism, corruption, and limited oil, disillusionment has set in. It is an appropriate moment to take stock.

A serious taxonomy of Caucasian and Central Asian regimes must separate out three political patterns. In the first, which predominates in most of the region, the ruler is a powerful president who typically was the Communist first secretary during Soviet days. There is no effective power sharing, whether with parliaments, local governments, or independent judiciaries. (Tajikistan is a special case. The Russian government forced its local allies into a fragile power-sharing agreement with Islamist guerrilla fighters.)

Yet despite these elements of continuity, there are striking differences from Soviet times. First, the major role that the "center" in Moscow played in the government of the republics has disappeared. Because the center had directed most of the economy, the selection of officials, foreign policy, and the military and KGB, its replacement by the independent republics represents a major achievement of state-building. Second, although these republics typically have government parties, these are personal followings with none of the organizational or ideological capacities of the old Communist Party. Government parties no longer carry out provincial and city administration, and the distrust of all ideology is pervasive. This is the situation in Armenia; Azerbaijan and its secessionist Nagorno-Karabakh region; Georgia and its three "entities" of Abkhazia, Ajara, and South Ossetia; and Kazakhstan, Kyrgyzstan, and Tajikistan.

The countries we are considering are very different from the democratizing societies of Southern Europe, the Southern Cone, and Central America that faced inherited tastes for ideological extremism, authority, and violence. The reaction to communist politicization of life has bred an exhausted tolerance and moderation suspicious of all authority. In the absence of efforts to organize and mobilize society, or to disguise the nature of rule, there is a yawning chasm between the rulers and the ruled.

Third, the basis for free elections provided by civil society, a free press, and a real multiparty system is at best no more than partly present in the southern states of the former USSR. While presidents and parliaments alike are chosen through multiparty elections, chicanery and vote-rigging are common. Parties other than successors to the Communist Party are mostly small and focused on personalities. A February 2001 poll showed Azerbaijanis thinking, by 57 to 26 percent, that voting did not give them "a say in how the government runs things."[1]

Yet in none of these states are elections a mere formality. There are always opposition parties and movements, generally headed by ousted officials, but sometimes by real democrats. One president, Armenia's already unpopular Levon Ter-Petrosian, demonstrated that there can be too much election fraud when he was forced out by the armed forces in early 1998. In my judgment, no president in any of these lands who does not reach office through a multicandidate election will be judged legitimate. Thus, while all of these countries do not qualify as what Larry Diamond calls "electoral democracies," some are more than just "pseudodemocracies." I will argue that the weakness of the state and the presence of democratic culture often allow the diversity of society to intrude into political space.

Fourth, in abrupt contrast with the overly strong Soviet state, all the states in this group are weak or weakening; several have wavered in and out of the "failed state" category. In the winter of 1993–94, for example, the Georgian government could not manage to defend the country, keep order on the streets of the capital, pay state workers, collect taxes, or print the currency in common use.

In such states, people usually have more to fear from local bosses (whether actual government officials or their allies) than from direct abuses by the central government, although it is the latter that tend to draw Western attention. Currently, Tajikistan seems to have the weakest state. There, army units dissatisfied with their share of productive assets have simply fought it out, with the loser being quietly deleted from the order of battle. Armed Chechen war refugees in the Pankisi Gorge expose Georgia to fearsome Russian threats, but Georgia sent no policemen or soldiers there for years. Instead, as I found in August 2000, the police are blocking nearby roads, shaking down motorists for imaginary violations. These states cannot perform essential tasks of self-preservation because they have given their intermittently paid officials the right to live off the population. Some state structures, as in Georgia and Azerbaijan, have grown stronger since independence, but others, such as in Kyrgyzstan, Armenia, and Nagorno-Karabakh, have become weaker. Weakening of the state is a distinctive characteristic of post-communist transitions, equally found in former Yugoslavia, Albania, and Cambodia.

The weakening of the Soviet state meant the breakdown of state-run economic enterprises and social-welfare programs. Next came the end of subsidies from Moscow, the interruption of intra-Soviet trade, civil and ethnic conflicts, weak administration, Western-sponsored "reforms" that often made things worse, and blockades from ethnic conflict or Russian ambitions. Together, these blows have reduced most people to deep poverty.

Because most nonspecialists do not know the depth of the economic crisis, let me cite a few figures. A 1998 survey found that Tajiks are consuming 71 percent less meat and 45 percent less cooking oil than they did in 1991. Farm animals per household average less than half the 1991 figure.[2] In Georgia, average real wages had fallen to one-tenth of the Soviet level by 1995; most countryfolk live by bare-subsistence farming, as their ancestors did hundreds of years ago.[3]

Most of the countries of the Caucasus and Central Asia are trying to make the transition to democracy amid conditions that resemble the Great Depression—or worse. Accordingly, there is much regret about the collapse of the USSR—most in Tajikistan, Kyrgyzstan, Armenia and Nagorno-Karabakh, least in Georgia and Azerbaijan. Polls show far lower support for the new democratizing regimes and far higher approval of the old dictatorial regimes than one sees in comparable bodies of survey data from Southern European, Asian, and Latin American transitional states. Broadly speaking, the post-Soviet public feels that it lost and the ruling elites gained from the transition.

Seizure of state assets disguised as "privatization" has feudalized the state. Since they are not dependent on the budget, officials can afford to ignore public policy and use their offices as private interest dictates. The "weak" state will be hard to overcome because it feeds on itself.

For the elites, the totalitarian past survives less in authoritarian attitudes than in the ever-present question, *Kto kogo?* ("Who shall exploit whom?") Politics is zero-sum, ruthless, and sometimes murderous. It is therefore understandable that people should see their rulers as self-ish, unpatriotic exploiters even when some, such as Levon Ter-Petrosian of Armenia, Eduard Shevardnadze of Georgia, Heydar Aliyev of Azer-baijan, and Askar Akayev of Kyrgyzstan have defied long odds to save their countries from dissolution or reabsorption into a new Russian empire.

In these circumstances, the moderation of ordinary citizens is aston-ishing and surely betokens leftover Soviet-era passivity, as well as the debunking of ideology and violence. But amid so much misery and dis-content, how long can such moderation last? This raises in turn a large question about the future of democracy, which the West has tended to identify with the present political order and with many of its leaders. If, at any point, a democratic leader wished to reintroduce the politics of class conflict and mass mobilization, public discontent could also be a mighty source of energy for democratic change.

The abolition of the Communist Party and the shrinking of govern-mental power have opened a wide space that civil society could poten-tially fill. Currently it is filled by clans, ethnic groups, clientelistic net-works, and criminal gangs; more usefully, it has been filled in a number of republics by quasi-private businesses and by NGOs.

These last form promising features of the political landscape in places where formal democratic institutions are badly compromised. With their Western financing, they create a political sector where the struggle for property is not the primary concern. They tend to draw their members from the elite and can produce an intermingling of the democratic intel-ligentsia and undemocratic governments, as we see in the three Cauca-sian republics and perhaps Kyrgyzstan. In Georgia and Armenia, flowerings of NGO activity followed the dubious elections of 1995 and 1996, suggesting that the NGOs were at least partially replacing more formal channels of political activity. In Georgia, NGOs working with one faction of the government party, the Citizens' Union, were able to block an undemocratic press law.

Strong-State Autocracies

A very different pattern often confused with the foregoing exists in Uzbekistan and Turkmenistan, as it did earlier in Nagorno-Karabakh, South Ossetia, and perhaps Abkhazia. There the old communist system persists. The center in Moscow is gone and with it the parallel Party apparatus, but all else remains, with the state harnessed to the old ideo-logical, organizational, and mobilizational wagons that the Party used to pull. In Uzbekistan, Tamerlane has replaced Lenin, and the govern-ment intrudes into neighborhoods not only through the police but also through the neotraditional *mahalla* or urban-quarter organization. In Turkmenistan, hortatory slogans reminiscent of the Khrushchev era pervade the land, as does the personality cult of President Sapurmarad Niazov. In neither republic is there much privatization.

Yet in Uzbekistan and Turkmenistan—as nowhere else in Central Asia and the Caucasus—the state remains strong and cohesive. Although both governments are shot through with corruption, their presidents maintain tight control over lower officials, and ordinary citizens are not, as elsewhere, completely naked before elites who wield public power for private ends. Instead, the average Uzbek or Turkmen gets about as much predictability, discipline, and public-spiritedness as his father or grandfather got from the Soviet apparat under Khrushchev. While statistics from these republics cannot be wholly trusted, their economies appear not to have collapsed to the degree seen in their neighbors. The chasm between the elite and ordinary people is no wider than it was in Soviet times, and the sense of victimization seems less than elsewhere. Western observers have hardly noted, in their doctrinaire enthusiasm for "reforms," the complex tradeoffs between this model and the foregoing, more prevalent one. To be an Uzbek or Turkmen is to give up all freedom, but to belong to a state capable of furnishing order and protection.

The relative predictability that the Uzbek government can boast of is increasingly threatened by its bitter struggle with a small number of extremist Muslim fighters who have exploited the weakness of the Tajik and Afghan states to find sanctuary. There can be little doubt about the existence of a threat, but the Uzbek government is making its own nightmares come true by identifying Islam with political dissidence, thereby channeling antigovernment feeling into politicized Islam.

Stateless Communities

This third political pattern is the one exemplified by "governments" that lack such essentials as sole control over organized coercion, a regular revenue-collection system, and administrative institutions that function everywhere in the territory. Rebellious Chechnya, internationally recognized as part of Russia but Caucasian in culture, is at the moment the only case. During "independent" Chechnya's interludes of peace with Russia (1991–94, 1996–99), it was teeming with private armed groups, never controlled all of its territory, and paid for public services by ad hoc levies on wealthy Chechen individuals or enterprises. Many parts of the "government," including its "ambassadors" abroad, have been expected to raise their own operating expenses. In these respects, Chechnya resembles classic "failed states" such as Sierra Leone and Liberia. Yet Chechnya is different, for it boasts a powerful sense of communal solidarity that enabled it to win its first war against a vastly more powerful Russia, a victory secured by a centrally coordinated military effort at the August 1996 battle for Grozny.

We could call this pattern the *stateless community*. It resembles the segmentary tribes that still evade government control in a few places such as Yemen and Somalia. Like these tribes, stateless communities present a united front against outsiders even as they seethe with internal strife. They are coordinated by culture, not by formal institutions.

Such formations are obviously limited in size, internal diversity, and life span; Ibrahim Rugova's stateless community in Kosovo (1989–98) collapsed with the rise of the competing Kosovo Liberation Army. It is worth adding stateless communities to a taxonomy of post-Soviet political patterns, however, because they make the prevalent postcommunist weak state look very different. Chechnya is one end point of a continuum along which Georgia, Azerbaijan, and Tajikistan have all oscillated. In such states, the preference for the community over the state emerges in polls showing that not very religious peoples, who have little confidence in political institutions, leaders, or parties, have great confidence (66 percent in Georgia in 2001) in the national church, or in Islam.[4] Perhaps these states are weak, not only because they are poorly crafted out of poor materials, but also because their people have known impersonal modern (read "Soviet") institutions, and at some level crave a stateless community instead—a problem that earlier democratic transitions did not face.[5]

Toward the Future

The ex-Soviet political patterns that I have just sketched cannot endure. Throughout Central Asia and the Caucasus, communist institutions and ways are aging and declining along with leaders formed by the Party apparat and its distinctive ethos. Further change is coming, though it remains to be seen whether it will be sudden or gradual. Leadership successions, already beginning in Azerbaijan and Georgia, open up the easiest path to sudden change. Here democratic change is entirely possible. The decisive moment will be the "free" elections without which no successor president can claim legitimacy. The elites that have ruled will attempt to manipulate these elections, and the question of how much fraud is too much will become decisive. Popular reaction and Western pressure may decide whether elections are in fact free and fair, and whether the winner is accepted. Democracy, pseudodemocracy, or stateless community could be the outcome.

If officials cannot retain communist attitudes indefinitely without communism, neither can the population. The collapse of the economy has already forced young people to unlearn Soviet-style quiescence. If anything, weak states breed criminality rather than passivity. In a few places, ordinary people are organizing spontaneously to deal with weak-state problems such as lack of services or illegal apartment construction.

But will the decay of communist survivals clear a gradual path to full democratization? That depends on factors too numerous to name. However, we should emphasize "the primary role of ideas. Whether or not [leaders] really believe them is secondary in defining the nature of political regimes."[6] The key reality is that after communism's collapse, there is no principled alternative to democracy left. Sunni Islamists can propose a "caliphate" for Central Asia, but a close look at their activities in Kyrgyzstan, Tajikistan, Chechnya, and Daghestan suggests that, like many extremist movements in Islamic history, they have a symbiotic relationship with stateless communities.

Civilizational identities will have an important impact, though we must understand them in a more dialectical way than Samuel P. Huntington has done. For more than two hundred years, Georgians and Armenians have sought a "third force"—some great but distant power that would save them from their alien and dominant neighbors.[7] For Georgians, this force has been for 140 years the West; for Armenians, Russia or the West. The Azeris, shunning a past many of them see as Persian and medieval, have long looked to secular Turkey and behind it, the West. All three peoples regard themselves as emphatically European. Thus they display the historic attraction of small peoples to universal principles. (Consider the Jews.) Together with the ideological monopoly that democracy now has, these civilizational identities will over the long term pull each of these countries toward democratization.

Central Asia is more complicated. Its peoples do not regard themselves as Europeans, although urban Kazakhs and Kyrgyz, like Baku Azeris, mostly speak Russian at home, and seem European in many respects. The Russian government would like to revive the shattered Soviet identity in a different form, but has neither the power nor the tolerance to achieve this over the long run. The larger populace throughout the region has a Muslim identity, but the elites fear and hate Islam. Central Asian elites are also trying slowly to oust or outbreed the remaining Russians and free themselves from Russian hegemony. Central Asian states have toyed with "Asian" as an identifier and "Asian authoritarianism" as a model, but have little in common with East Asia. Tajikistan, the remaining island of Persian language and culture in Central Asia, is likely to be opened to much more intensive influence from Iran in the next few years, as Iran's Islamic regime begins to fade.

While Turkey has tried to emphasize its cultural connections with Azerbaijan and Central Asia through pan-Turkic policies, it does not loom large enough on the cultural map to be very successful outside of Azerbaijan and Turkmenistan. Yet there remains some potential for the future. The civilizational connection with Turkey tends to reinforce Western orientations, including a democratic direction. The Central Asian governments' fear of Islam closes them off (except to a degree in Tajikistan) from the most credible anti-Western and antidemocratic alternative. Thus democracy becomes the object of imitation, however insincere.

What imitation and civilizational choice can do is shown by the history of Italy. After the Risorgimento in the mid-nineteenth century, Italy became formally democratic, but with few of the usual democratic "prerequisites." Intractable problems went unsolved: the poor and unruly *mezzogiorno,* the Mafia, the authority of an antimodern Church hostile to the Italian state, a small middle class, vast corruption, and the apolitical clannishness of the peasantry so well portrayed in the *Godfather* movies. Some of these problems, such as the Mafia, fester still.

These difficulties are similar to the disillusioning conditions now on display before Western eyes in the Caucasus and Central Asia. What seems to have worked most powerfully in Italy's case were civilizational identities and, still more, aversions. In retrospect, it was less the presence of democratic prerequisites than sheer aversion to the political claims of the Church, to Austrian absolutism, and—once the Fascist alternative had failed—to Soviet communism that slowly led Italy toward consolidated democratic rule. Perhaps the civilizational aversions of many peoples of the Caucasus and Central Asia will eventually push them into the same mighty current.

NOTES

1. U.S. Department of State, Office of Research, "Azerbaijanis Allege Election Fraud and Government Corruption," *Opinion Analysis,* M-122-01, 30 May 2001.

2. Payam Foroghi, *1998 Socio-Economic Survey of Households, Farms, and Bazaars,* unpublished paper for Save the Children Federation, January 1999, 34, 32.

3. Ruslan Yemtsov, "Labor Markets, Inequality and Poverty," in the World Bank, *Georgia: Poverty and Income Distribution* (2 vols., Washington, D.C.: World Bank, 1999), 1:35, 2:9.

4. U.S. Department of State, Office of Research, "Georgians' Faith in Their Government Wanes, As Pessimism Mounts," *Opinion Analysis,* M-16-01, 30 January 2001.

5. See G.M. Tamás, "Ethnarchy and Ethno-Anarchism," *Social Research* 63 (Spring 1996): 147–90; Charles H. Fairbanks, Jr., "Party, Ideology, and the Public World in the Former Soviet Space," in Arthur Meltzer, Jerry Weinberger, and Richard Zinman, eds., *Politics at the Turn of the Century* (Lanham, Md.: Rowman and Littlefield, 2001); and "Wars of Hatred and the Hatred of War," *Weekly Standard,* 19 April 1999.

6. Ghia Nodia, "How Different are Post-Communist Transitions?" pp. 3–17 above.

7. Rafael Ishkanian, "The Law of Excluding the Third Force," *Haratch* (Paris), 18, 19, 20, and 21–22 October 1999, trans. in Gerard J. Libaridian, *Armenia at the Crossroads: Democracy and Nationhood in the Post-Soviet Era* (Watertown, Mass.: Blue Crane, 1991), 9–38; and Ghia Nodia, "Konflikt v Abkhazii: Natsional'niye Proyekti I Politicheskiye Obstoyatel'stva," in Bruno Coppieters, Ghia Nodia, and Yuri Anchabadze, eds., *Gruziny I Abkhazy: Put' k Primireniyu* (Moscow: Ves' Mir, 1998), 21–23.

22

SOVEREIGNTY AND UNCERTAINTY IN UKRAINE

Nadia Diuk

Nadia Diuk is senior program officer for Eastern Europe and the former Soviet Union at the National Endowment for Democracy in Washington, D.C. She holds a doctorate in history from St. Antony's College of the University of Oxford and is coauthor of The Hidden Nations: The People Challenge the Soviet Union *(1990) and* New Nations Rising: The Fall of the Soviets and the Challenge of Independence *(1993). This article was originally published in the October 2001 issue of the* Journal of Democracy.

As they emerged from the wreckage of the old Soviet Union, all the non-Russian republics confronted the same triad of mighty tasks: consolidate statehood, reform the economy, and establish democracy. The test was and is formidable. Each republic has had to lay a firm foundation for sovereign statehood and overhaul a Moscow-run command economy while learning to conduct its political life according to internationally recognized principles of freedom and democracy.

As the largest of the non-Russian republics, Ukraine has always been a bellwether of sorts. Its success at handling these three simultaneous "revolutions" and posing a counterweight to Moscow has been crucial in preventing the resurgence of Russia as an imperial power. As it passes its tenth anniversary as an independent state, Ukraine presents a mixed picture of achievements and setbacks.

When Ukraine declared its independence and took its place among the self-governing countries of the world on 24 August 1991, the prognosis for success on all three fronts was not very favorable. At the time, many analysts thought that Ukraine's strongest suit would be economic reform. A much-quoted Deutsche Bank study pointed to the country's well-developed industrial base, its mineral wealth, and its resourceful, highly skilled people as reasons to think that Ukraine would soon become the leading economic performer among all the post-Soviet economies.

By contrast, many commentators rated the likelihood that Ukraine would maintain its independence as rather low. Ukraine's last prolonged experience as an independent state had been in the seventeenth century. Unlike the Estonians, Latvians, and Lithuanians, who had enjoyed a period of independence between the world wars, nearly all of Ukraine's people had no memory of anything but life in a Russian-dominated state. (The only exceptions were the Western Ukrainians who had lived under Polish rule during the interwar period.)

Compared with non-Slavs such as the Armenians, Georgians, and Azeris, and even the Turkic peoples of Central Asia, Ukrainians were also at a disadvantage in terms of defining a coherent national identity. With a language, religious traditions, and culture so similar to what is found in Russia, nationally conscious Ukrainians were hard-pressed to convince many of their own compatriots—let alone a skeptical outside world—that Ukraine could carve out its own independent identity as a state, even though it was the most populous of the "hidden nations" of the Soviet Union.

Contrary to these expectations, the eve of its tenth anniversary finds Ukraine a securely independent state, enjoying a sovereignty that has never come seriously into question. Ukraine traced the same trajectory as most of the other post-Soviet states by rapidly creating the institutions of statehood where previously there had been none. In addition to forming a separate judicial system and government, including a fully functioning foreign ministry, Ukraine moved quickly to establish its own army and navy, national bank, and currency, declared Kyiv its capital, and wasted little time in gathering around itself all the usual trappings of independent statehood.

Meanwhile, the breakup of the Soviet Union was causing alarm in influential Western circles. The boundaries that had marked out the 15 constituent republics of the USSR became the national frontiers of the new states. Worried that the ethnic-Russian minorities now "trapped" in other states and separated from their homeland would rise up against their new non-Russian rulers, or that Russia itself would go to war to defend its nationals in what Russians had begun to call the "near abroad," some feared that the whole vast region might soon be ablaze with armed strife. All eyes were on Ukraine. As the old USSR's second-most populous republic, and one with a 22 percent ethnic-Russian population, hundreds of Soviet-era nuclear missiles, and a long shared frontier with Russia, its situation seemed especially critical. How would the new-old borders hold up? How would the two major ethnic groups get along?

The Crimean peninsula, which Nikita Khrushchev (in what was at the time an empty gesture) had shifted from the Russian Soviet Federated Socialist Republic to the Ukrainian Soviet Socialist Republic in 1954 to commemorate a treaty signed between the Ukrainian Hetmanate and Muscovy three centuries earlier, seemed the leading candidate to become the flash point of a Russo-Ukrainian explosion. The Crimea was peopled mostly by ethnic Russians, plus growing numbers of returning Crimean Tatars whose parents and grandparents Stalin had forcibly removed in 1944. Its largest city, the port of Sevastopol, was a major center for Russian security forces and the home base of the Soviet Black Sea Fleet. The Crimea, in short, seemed to encapsulate all the potential problems of consolidating statehood in Ukraine, as well as the broader problems left in the wake of the Soviet breakup.

For many Russian public figures in the early 1990s, waging a successful campaign to establish control over the Black Sea Fleet went hand-in-hand with regaining the entire peninsula. Politicians from across the political spectrum traveled to Crimea to view the already inflamed situation first-hand, thus encouraging Russian nationalists on the peninsula to dream that reabsorption into the motherland was just around the corner. Ukrainians, for their part, worried that losing the Crimea might presage the dissolution of their whole country. Western analysts brooded over the fate of the Crimea, and Samuel P. Huntington coined the term "cleft country" as a way of describing Ukraine's ills and fitting the Ukrainian case into his own intellectual paradigm.

Even though in retrospect it appears that there never was much chance of another Crimean War, Ukraine's new government deserves credit for ably clearing a major obstacle to the securing of its territorial integrity, and for helping to moderate Russia's ambitions regarding ethnic-Russian minorities in other states. Perhaps the crowning moment of Ukraine's successful state-building effort came in 1997, when it signed an agreement with Russia to divide control over the Black Sea Fleet. To mark this accord—which also included Russian recognition of the Crimea as Ukrainian territory—Boris Yeltsin made a highly symbolic state visit to Kyiv in May of that year. Independent Ukraine had arrived as a full-fledged member of the family of nations. That same year, the confirmation of Ukrainian statehood as a permanent feature of international relations came in the form of a special partnership agreement with NATO, together with a series of bilateral agreements between Ukraine and the United States.

Travails of a Troubled Economy

If the news on Ukraine's sovereignty has been surprisingly good, its economy has been a surprising letdown. At the time of independence, many experts recommended that the post-Soviet states try the same mix of shock therapy and privatization that had worked in Central Europe, hoping to "turn fish soup back into an aquarium." Over the last decade, however, Ukraine has fallen short of its expected economic potential and has not forged ahead of the other republics according to most measures of development.

In retrospect, it is easy to see that Ukraine's swift transition to a free-market economy and the realization of its economic potential would have required a thoroughly reformed political system, firmly based on democratic principles and the rule of law. Yet Ukraine, like the other non-Baltic post-Soviet states, had inherited a political and administrative system shaped by seven decades of communism. Russia opted for price liberalization and voucher privatization in an effort to "kick start" the transition to a market economy, benefiting a broad range of prospective businessmen.

Ukraine chose a slower route. Although perhaps less immediately disruptive, this choice inevitably widened the scope for corruption and undercut the initiatives of many potential small and medium-scale entrepreneurs. Despite its successes in curbing inflation and introducing a new currency, Ukraine's government has stuck to this "go-slow" approach ever since. It pays lip service to reform, but in practice restricts large-scale privatizations and the issuing of licenses to politically connected circles of favored businessmen.

In the fall of 1991, when Vyacheslav Chornovil, the leader of the national-democratic Ukrainian Popular Movement (Rukh), was a leading contender for the presidency, it looked as if Ukraine might follow in the tradition set by Lech Wałeşa in Poland and Václav Havel in Czechoslovakia by choosing a celebrated former dissident and leader of a mass popular movement to be its head of state. In the event, however, the winner of the December 1 balloting was Leonid Kravchuk, who had been the chairman of the Supreme Soviet of the Ukrainian SSR. On December 5, he was sworn in as Ukraine's "second" president. (The first was Mykhailo Hrushevsky, who held office for a brief period in 1918.)

Ten years into independence, Ukraine is like many of the other post-Soviet states in displaying the trappings of democracy: It holds bona fide elections to fill its presidency and its 450-seat Supreme Council (Verkhovna Rada), as the national legislature is called. Political parties form and compete. The government has executive, legislative, and judicial branches (though no real separation of powers). A constitution outlines the rights and duties of the citizens and the functions of different parts of the state.

On the spectrum of post-Soviet states, as on the global scale proposed by Freedom House's annual survey *Freedom in the World,* Ukraine occupies a middling position. It is far freer and more democratic than the Central Asian states, where authoritarianism is worse than it was during communist times, but at the same time does not come close to the standard set by the Baltic states, which are developing institutions that are fully and genuinely democratic. Freedom House rates Ukraine as Partly Free, with scores of four out of seven on both political and civil rights, where "one" denotes freest and "seven" denotes least free.

The withering away of communism left the post-Soviet states with few alternatives in the area of governmental institutions. For all but the Baltic states, parliamentarism was out of the question. The USSR had been administered as a unitary state according to a vertical system of command that came from Moscow via the Communist Party of the Soviet Union (CPSU). In Ukraine, as in most of the republics, the Soviet breakup meant that the center of action shifted from Moscow to the local capital. Other than that, however, there was little change in the way power was distributed and exercised. The CPSU's command and administrative functions simply passed more or less intact into the hands of the newly created presidency and its executive arm, known as the *vertikal*.

Super-presidentialism Rising

In Ukraine, this super-presidentialist system has only grown stronger with the years. While the Ukrainian president does not enjoy the same level of unchallenged rule as his counterparts in Central Asia, his powers have increased over the last decade, especially as a result of the new Constitution that was approved in June 1996 under the guidance of President Leonid Kuchma, who had defeated Kravchuk in a July 1994 runoff. Presidential powers include the authority to appoint unilaterally every cabinet minister (except the premier) and regional leader, without need of legislative advice and consent. The implications of this increase in powers were not obvious at first, as Ukraine at that time could boast the only peaceful transfer of power to date from one president to another in any former Soviet republic.

President Kuchma had been prime minister in 1992–93, and before that had served as director of the Southern Machine Building Plant (the USSR's biggest missile factory) in the large Ukrainian industrial city of Dnipropetrovsk. His 52-to-45-percent victory over Kravchuk signaled a new direction in Ukrainian politics. As a native of the Russian-speaking eastern Ukraine, he symbolized the growing unity of the new state. At the same time, however, as a representative of the former Communist Party structures of Dnipropetrovsk, his election signified the growing influence of regional and criminal interests over the institutions of state power. The operation of clans and mafia groups within the political system was a feature of most post-Soviet states in the 1990s. Indeed, it is clear that the CPSU itself had previously supported regional and family clans through its own system of patronage. But as the twenty-first century approached, the strength of such groups in Ukraine was reaching new heights.

In Ukraine, as nowhere else in the post-Soviet world, corrupt business interests control the major party structures. In April 2001, four of the five major party factions in the Verkhovna Rada could be identified directly with financial-industrial groups, known as "oligarchs." (The major "oligarch" parties are generally considered to be Social Democrats United, Working Ukraine, Democratic Union, the Rebirth of the Regions Party, and the Fatherland Party.) One of the distinguishing features of the oligarchic parties is that some of their leaders hold legislative seats to provide themselves with immunity against arrest.

Another reason for the fusion of political and economic activities that is such a prominent feature of Ukrainian public life is that wealth—whether ill gotten or fairly gained—cannot be safeguarded by the existing legal system, which leaves the wealthy feeling that they must engage in direct political manipulations themselves in order to protect what they have. Even though these parties claim thousands of members, their constituencies are difficult to define. Many voters simply sell their votes to the highest bidder. The close identification of business interests with politics has been one of the major obstacles to democratization in Ukraine. In contrast to most of the other post-Soviet states, Ukraine does not have a strong "party of power" that supports the president, in the way that Unity (Edinstvo) backs Russia's President Vladimir Putin.

The only two political parties that had genuine support and represented the authentic interests of sizable numbers of Ukrainian citizens in the early 1990s were the Communist Party and the Rukh, but only the former has retained its voter base. The Rukh was the direct outgrowth of the national-democratic mass movement that had helped to draw thousands into the streets to support independence in 1991. After the charismatic Chornovil died in a March 1999 car accident, the Rukh's support began to collapse even in its onetime stronghold of western Ukraine, and the party split in two. During the first round of the presidential election in October 2000, the two Rukh candidates combined gained less than 4 percent of the vote. The Rukh's demise is yet another indication of the general malaise of political parties in the region.

If vibrant and integrally democratic parties are notable by their absence in Ukraine, what of civil society? Here, one is relieved to note, there is some cause for optimism. Despite the obstacles to democratization present in the major institutions of government, the country's small civil society organizations have burgeoned over the past ten years. Citizens' organizations of all kinds—devoted to humanitarian assistance and charity, young people's and women's concerns, support for education, or any of a number of other causes—now number in the hundreds in Ukraine.

The influx of U.S. and Western aid and expertise in all areas of civil society development, not to mention the promotion of Ukrainian expertise through targeted programs and exchanges, has helped to foster a rapid increase in the number of people with pro-Western views. Yet even with the growing numbers of nongovernmental organizations, it would be going too far to say that Ukraine has a functioning civil society. As for the media, although they reflect a range of viewpoints, most publications, radio stations, and television channels remain under the control of government or financial interests that still dictate their editorial line.

The Gongadze Affair

At the end of the year 2000 came a crisis that exemplified all of the paradoxical trends within Ukraine's political system and society. The revelation of secret tapes, allegedly recording the complicity of President Kuchma and his top lieutenants in the murder of noted independent journalist Heorhiy Gongadze, threw the country into turmoil. These suspicions brought hundreds of protesters out into the streets and encouraged the creation of several centers of overt opposition to the president. Journalists working for the oligarch-controlled media took on more independent points of view. After ten years, it was clear that civil society had developed to the point where the killing of an anti-regime journalist could no longer be covered up.

At the same time, the crisis showed how poor the political system is at responding to popular sentiments. Parliament formed committees to pursue the criminal investigation and to start impeachment proceedings against the president, but they faltered through inadequate funding and a lack of constitutional mechanisms to carry out their activities. The pro-presidential forces also showed their strength by launching politically motivated criminal proceedings against the one member of the cabinet, then–deputy prime minister Julia Tymoshenko, who had worked to end the system of barter trade and to block financial transactions that had previously been controlled by the major oligarchs.

Another major blow to the democratic forces came on 26 April 2001, when the parliament voted "no confidence" in Prime Minister Viktor Yushchenko by an overwhelming 263-to-69 margin. At the time of the vote, Yushchenko's "favorable" rating among the population stood at around 50 percent. (By contrast, President Kuchma's approval rating at the time of this writing is well below 20 percent.) This vote against a popular premier laid bare both the degree to which oligarchical interests dominate the Verkhovna Rada and the chronic lack of communication that bedevils relations between the people and their elected representatives. The charismatic Yushchenko had tapped into a well of popular support and was generally considered to have been responsible for finally paying state wages and pensions after months of arrears under previous governments. Yushchenko, who was perceived as having no connections with any of the major oligarchical groups, had a reputation for honesty, enhancing his popularity among ordinary citizens.

As Ukraine enters its second decade of independence, large questions loom about its future direction: Will the strength of entrenched interest groups grow and thwart future attempts to democratize the institutions of power? Might Ukraine's struggling, nascent civil society succeed in the long term in achieving an open system of government that will bring Ukraine closer to the West? Or will Ukraine remain somewhere in the middle, with the main institutions of power controlled by a strong presidency, but with ordinary citizens allowed to exercise considerable personal freedom as long as they do not challenge the powers that be?

23

RUSSIA'S HYBRID REGIME

Lilia Shevtsova

Lilia Shevtsova, senior associate at the Carnegie Endowment for International Peace, is the author of Yeltsin's Russia: Myths and Reality *(1999) and coeditor of* Gorbachev, Yeltsin, Putin: Political Leadership in Russia's Transition *(2001). This essay, which was translated from the Russian by Mark H. Eckert, originally appeared in the October 2001 issue of the* Journal of Democracy.

Ten years after the Soviet Union broke up into 15 independent states, it is possible to form some preliminary conclusions regarding the challenges and problems faced by these transitional societies. First of all, despite their common Soviet roots, their paths of post-Soviet development are becoming ever more divergent—evidence that there are more influences at work than just the legacy of the USSR.

One can provisionally identify three groups of states, based on the degree to which they have moved toward "polyarchy." The first group, the Baltic states, have come closest to liberal democracy, although even here it is premature to speak of democratic consolidation. The second group includes those states that have been able to form weak institutions but still suffer under personalistic government, or those in which the Soviet bureaucracy, which has disintegrated into clans, still holds sway. There are as yet no guarantees that democratic changes are irrevocable in these states—Russia, Ukraine, Armenia, Georgia, and Moldova. The third group includes neopatrimonial and even openly sultanistic regimes of varying degrees of authoritarianism. It comprises Kazakhstan, Azerbaijan, Uzbekistan, Kyrgyzstan, Belarus, Tajikistan, and Turkmenistan.

In the overwhelming majority of post-Soviet states, the fundamental problems of democratic development—building the foundations of the rule of law, dismembering the traditional monolithic government, training society and the elite to live under independent political institutions, ensuring political accountability and alternation in power, and forming a consensus in society that democracy is "the only game in town"—have still not been resolved. True, in almost all the newly independent states people have realized that the old mechanisms of legitimation—party, ideology, heredity, and force—are exhausted, and the elites have thus been forced to legitimate their rule through elections. But in a situation where power remains undivided, authoritarian elements linger, and civil society is weak, democratic institutions (above all, elections) increasingly take on an imitative, surrogate character and begin to ring hollow.[1]

Several factors have influenced the evolution of political regimes in the post-Soviet era. Some of these loomed larger during the transition, while others matter more now. The decisive influence on the character of the postcommunist transition was the inability of the political class (including its liberal-democratic wing) to transcend the previous civilizational model, which had been founded on a faith in a "special path" of development. Important elements of this model included a reliance on personalized networks rather than on institutions, a stress on the subordination of society rather than dialogue with it, and an attempt to impose modernization "from above" without the active participation of the masses.

The old paradigm endures partly because Gorbachev's *perestroika* era was so brief, because there was no alternative elite ready to step in, and because the old habits of state paternalism and societal passivity lingered.[2] The pragmatic part of the Soviet *nomenklatura*—which rose to power on the ashes of communism and faced no pressure from below or from an alternative elite—was unable or unwilling to embrace new democratic "rules of the game," although it did learn to give the appearance of doing so.

The three simultaneous transformations of state-building (especially where the traditions of the state were either weak or nonexistent), democratization, and economic reform—which at times required incompatible methods of implementation—have also had an influence on the character of the post-Soviet period.[3] Moreover, one must note the dramatic paradox faced by all post-Soviet states. On the one hand, the challenges of globalization and postindustrial development demand that these states seek inclusion in the world economic and political community, which means downplaying the old themes of territory, sovereignty, and force. On the other hand, they face these challenges at a time when they have only just begun to build their own national states, a process whose logic conflicts with that of globalization. It is not yet clear how these two tasks can be reconciled.

As transitions in Latin America and Asia have shown, Western influence and assistance, as well as the presence of leaders who accept the liberal value system and are ready to limit the government's paternalism and authoritarianism, can compensate for an undeveloped civil society, weak pluralist traditions, continuing degradation of economic potential, and the absence of influential groups of liberal democrats.[4] The presence of such leaders in the Baltic states made it easier for them to overcome the remaining obstacles to transformation. Most of the other post-Soviet states, however, cannot draw on these compensating factors.

Of course, historical, cultural, and civilizational differences among the post-Soviet states also figure in the story. In the European post-Soviet states, which have ties to Christian culture and consider themselves part of European civilization, there has been more of a move toward liberal values. In the Asian part of the former Soviet Union, by contrast, one may observe a return to pre-Soviet traditions of sultanism.

Russia, of course, is the country to watch. The course of its transformation will have a major impact on the other independent states and will go far toward shaping the entire post-Soviet world. Russia's claim to continued superpower status and its possession of certain world-power attributes—in particular, lots of long-range nuclear weapons—have played a substantial part in the country's evolution. Its persistent longing for recognition as a superpower has undoubtedly preserved elements of the previous political system, including the domination of the executive branch, "top-down government," and personalistic leadership, with the president playing the role of "elected monarch."

Democrats versus Liberals

The persistent split between democrats, oriented toward building political institutions and strengthening civil society, and liberals, who have been ready to support authoritarianism for the sake of economic reform, has also influenced the formation of Russia's postcommunist regime. The co-optation of liberals into Russian power structures has, to a certain extent, made it easier to carry out privatization and other marked-based reforms. From a broader perspective, however, their participation in the "elective monarchy" has discredited the principles of liberal democracy in the eyes of many. Moreover, Russian bureaucrats exploited the liberals' role in carrying out such reforms in order to fuse business and government and create a shady, oligarchic type of capitalism.

In sum, Russia has a hybrid regime, founded on the principle of weakly structured government and relying on both personalistic leadership and democratic legitimation. This combination of incompatible principles enables the regime to develop simultaneously in various directions: toward oligarchy, toward authoritarianism, and toward democracy as well. Yet such a regime can hardly be consolidated; its contradictory tendencies are a sure recipe for instability.

The Russian regime rests mainly on the bureaucracy, which has been the gravedigger of all attempts at modernization in Russia, and on the military and security services, which even in their currently somewhat parlous condition add a note of intimidation, if not brute force, to political life. The regime survives by co-opting representatives of the main political and social groups into the framework of the government, replacing ideology with constantly changing eclectic rhetoric, deliberately postponing strategic choices, and orienting itself toward stability rather than breakthroughs. All this allows the regime to preserve its diverse base of support and its leader's high poll ratings, and makes it hard for an alternative or an opposition to form. At the same time, however, the refusal to answer the country's existential questions (such as "Where does Russia belong?") is a reflection of the weakness, powerlessness, and disorientation of both the leader and the ruling elite.[5]

Can a regime founded on a less-than-heartfelt imitation of foreign ways, a reluctance to make strategic choices, and a desire to please all groups at once be sustainable or economically effective?

The postcommunist Russian regime remains in flux. After coming to power, Vladimir Putin attempted to rationalize Boris Yeltsin's "elective monarchy" and to regulate relations among the various segments of the political class. He succeeded in weakening the patrimonial character of the regime and, in place of Yeltsin's "atmosphere of mutual tolerance," introduced elements of subordination and subjection. Yet the preservation of the mechanism of personal rule and the weak separation of powers are obvious reasons why even this rationalized system remains vulnerable. At any moment, the atrophy or weakness of one block within the vertically organized "presidential pyramid" could lead to the collapse of the whole structure, as happened with the Soviet state.

We might call the system that has tentatively developed in Russia "bureaucratic quasi-authoritarianism."[6] Certain democratic elements persist, but the government does its best to manipulate them. At the same time, the administration, without an obedient and monolithic bureaucracy or a truly prestigious and well-paid army, is not purely authoritarian. This does not, however, rule out the possibility that it might drift or lurch in an authoritarian or even a totalitarian direction, even if more out of weakness than strength.

Can a regime founded on a less-than-heartfelt imitation of foreign ways, a reluctance to make strategic choices, and a desire to please all groups at once be sustainable or economically effective? One may assume that, if there are no serious social tensions, if the opposition is weak, if the ruling class strives to solve all its problems on the basis of loyalty to the leader, and if the economic situation remains relatively satisfactory, such a regime could exist for a rather long time in a condition of "stagnant stability."

Yet surely the structural flaws inherent in such an arrangement will sooner or later be laid bare and tested. I refer, above all, to legitimacy. A leader who tries to take credit for every success will, in the end, also have to shoulder the blame for every failure, even those at the local level, and this will wear down his legitimacy. To avoid this, he will have to resort to Yeltsin's practice of constantly reshuffling personnel, returning the country to the revolutionary cycle.

There is yet another trap connected with the imitative nature of the regime: If it continues to mimic an independent parliament, a multi-party system, and self-government, in the end the leader may end up having to face the fact that his own strong leadership is also just a counterfeit. A leader who has to confront too many challenges will inevitably be forced to share power, and without independent institutions, he may end up hostage to influential groups at his court.

Can Russia's "bureaucratic quasi-authoritarian" regime become the engine of economic modernization? Judging from recent years, this regime is quite capable of making moderate market reforms, but only insofar as they strengthen executive power rather than society. Can such a regime undertake the long-postponed restructuring of the economy, which would introduce new, transparent rules of the game, liquidate the shady interdependence of government and business, change the role of the bureaucracy, and build the rule of law? It is doubtful; such reforms would inevitably lead to the formation of powerful strata that would have an interest not only in economic freedom but also in political freedom and self-expression, which would require a fundamental restructuring of the government. One can hardly expect the regime to annihilate itself.

In Russia, where about 45 percent of the population says that it supports liberal democracy, there is reason to attempt to strengthen the democratic vector of development. This choice will not take place, however, until the political class realizes that "stagnant stability" and the attempt to crossbreed the old civilizational model of "paternalism and passivity" with democracy will only lead to a dead end. But it is likely, however, that Russia—and many another post-Soviet state as well—will have to travel a long road before the hopes it has invested in its patrimonial vision of leadership are finally dashed.

NOTES

1. In this case, it is not even a matter of the gap "between formal rules and what most people most of the time actually do," that Guillermo O'Donnell describes. See Guillermo O'Donnell, "Horizontal Accountability in New Democracies," *Journal of Democracy* 9 (July 1998): 116. Here, democratic reforms are just the framework that conceals the dominant authoritarian or oligarchic style of rule.

2. Francis Fukuyama was right when he wrote that liberal democracy meets its greatest challenges on the level of civil society and the development of culture. See Francis Fukuyama, "Democracy's Future: The Primacy of Culture," *Journal of Democracy* 6 (January 1995): 7–9.

3. Juan Linz and Alfred Stepan have written that the problem of combining *demos* and *polis*, especially in multinational societies, is one of the most serious challenges of transformation and that "some methods of dealing with the problem of 'stateness' are inherently incompatible with democracy." Juan J. Linz and Alfred Stepan, "Toward Consolidated Democracies," *Journal of Democracy* 7 (April 1996): 24.

4. On the decisive influence of the international context on the postcommunist transformation of Eastern and Central Europe, see Jacques Rupnik, "Eastern Europe: The International Context," *Journal of Democracy* 11 (April 2000): 115–30.

5. The presence throughout the post-Soviet states of presidents who are ostensibly all-powerful, who concentrate all power in their hands, is frequently a sign not of strong power but of the "impotent omnipotence" of which Guillermo O'Donnell has written. Here the problem arises, not just of limiting the powers of the executive branch, but of reformulating these powers to create conditions for real, strong leadership, which would be responsible only for the general issues of the consolidation of society and would not interfere in day-to-day control over events.

6. This regime resembles the bureaucratic-authoritarian regimes described by Guillermo O'Donnell and Fernando Henrique Cardoso and is also an attempt to regulate power on the basis of the primacy of the executive branch. See David Collier, ed., *The New Authoritarianism in Latin America* (Princeton, N.J.: Princeton University Press, 1979). The difference between bureaucratic authoritarianism in Latin America and the bureaucratic quasi-authoritarian regime in Russia is that the Russian government is still weak and incapable of accomplishing its main goals; for the time being, it strives only for illusory stability, which, for the most part, rests on hopes and expectations.

24

PUTIN'S PATH

M. Steven Fish

M. Steven Fish is associate professor of political science at the University of California–Berkeley. He is author of Democracy from Scratch: Opposition and Regime in the New Russian Revolution (1995) and coauthor of Postcommunism and the Theory of Democracy (2002). In 2000–2001, he was a Fulbright Fellow and visiting professor of political science at the European University at St. Petersburg. This essay originally appeared in the October 2001 issue of the Journal of Democracy.

Over the past decade, the lands of the former USSR have followed diverse trajectories with respect to democratization. The Baltic states established robust democratic regimes. Georgia and Moldova entered the postcommunist period under conditions of chaos and authoritarianism, but thereafter moved toward more democratic and stable politics. Belarus, Azerbaijan, and Kyrgyzstan experienced substantial openings but subsequently reverted to despotism. Uzbekistan and Turkmenistan slid directly from Soviet rule to sultanism, with personalist dictatorships quickly replacing the rule of the communist party. Russia, Ukraine, and Armenia, following antiauthoritarian breakthroughs in the late 1980s and early 1990s, gradually drifted back toward political closure, albeit without the unequivocal consolidation of authoritarian rule witnessed in Belarus and Central Asia.

In Russia, by far the region's dominant country, a political transformation has been under way since Vladimir Putin's ascension to power at the beginning of 2000. After the paralysis of Boris Yeltsin's second presidential term, Russian politics has again become dynamic and extraordinarily interesting. Although Putin's path is usually portrayed in the West either as a continuation of the Yeltsin era's erosion of democratic advances or as a rush back to hard authoritarianism, its effects may prove to be mixed and complex. Some changes are indubitably reversing previous democratic gains, but others may advance democratization.

Putin's political project stands on four pillars: centralizing state power, formulating a practical ideology, restoring state control of communication, and structuring political competition.

Recentralizing state power is the centerpiece of the Putin agenda. Decentralization, in a form that granted various territorial entities of the Russian Federation dissimilar rights and obligations, was a hallmark of the Yeltsin era. From the beginning of his political ascent, Putin made clear his intention to reestablish Moscow's supremacy and to humble the regional barons who had profited most from the policies of the previous administration.

Many Western observers hold that Putin's effort has already failed. After a decade of watching power flow from the center to the regions, many leading experts on Russian subnational politics doubt that measures such as the creation of "supergovernors" to supervise the new "super-regions" have any chance of reestablishing Moscow's primacy.

Yet this conventional wisdom lags behind events. St. Petersburg is now under virtually direct rule by the presidential administration. City governor Vladimir Yakovlev, whom Putin despises (or used to despise), has wisely decided that serving Putin with exquisite solicitousness is vastly preferable to resisting him. Even Yuri Luzhkov, the once-invincible mayor of Moscow, has begun to show great deference. Putin's successful effort to rid Primorskiy kray (the Maritime Province) of its gangster of a governor, Yevgeni Nazdratenko, represented a spectacular reassertion of central authority. Observers who are not impressed emphasize that the price of Nazdratenko's peaceful resignation was his receiving a top post in the fisheries ministry. But bringing Nazdratenko to Moscow, where he can be monitored and hemmed in, actually represents a remarkable step toward recentralization.

Nazdratenko's fate has not eluded the notice of other regional leaders, most of whom prefer their baronies to the fisheries ministry. Governors and republican presidents have striven to cultivate good relations with the "supergovernors" whom Putin has placed above them and with the provincial-level "inspectors" whom he has installed beside them. Putin's intimate personal control over the agencies of state security—an asset Yeltsin lacked—has enabled him to launch his bid for recentralization forcefully but quietly.

If some recentralizing is actually taking place, as I argue it is, how might it influence democratization? *Prima facie,* its effect would seem wholly negative. Democratic theory usually places local and provincial self-government at the heart of democratic practice. In the early post-Soviet years, knowledgeable and well-intentioned Western experts emphasized the need for a massive devolution of power. Given the dysfunctional hypercentralization of the Soviet regime, moving government closer to the governed seemed to make good sense.

What is more, the Russian government's most brutal and potentially

self-destructive policy—the grim prosecution of the war in Chechnya—
is an integral part of Putin's scheme for reasserting Moscow's control.
The insurgents' challenge to Russia's territorial integrity and to
Moscow's primacy undoubtedly provides an even more urgent motive
for Putin's unyielding policy on Chechnya than does the threat of ter-
rorism and Islamic fundamentalism. Nowhere does the recentralizing
urge appear more inimical to democratization than in policy on the north
Caucasus.

The effects of recentralizing power, however, may be equivocal.
Yeltsin's policies of devolving great power to regional governments
and granting enormous privileges to the autonomous republics may have
mitigated the hazards of ethnic conflict during the early post-Soviet years.
By the end of the 1990s, however, these policies had incited widespread
resentment among the majority who lived in provinces other than the
autonomous republics and had conferred upon the presidents of the autonomous republics the powers of unchecked overlords.

Indeed, most abuses of power in Russia occur on the provincial and
local levels. Reigning in the Nazdratenkos, Luzhkovs, and Yakovlevs—
not to speak of the highhanded presidents of the republics of Tatarstan,
Bashkortostan, and Kalmykiya—is not necessarily the worst thing that
could happen in terms of the prospects for a more open polity. A feeble
central state can impede democratization as surely as an overly strong
one. Might the erosion of central authority have actually exacerbated
the de-democratizing trends of the 1990s? Might some recentralization
eventually prove consonant with a resumption of democratization?

Formulating a Practical Ideology

Putin's push to recentralize is first and foremost about power, administration, and state capacity. But recentralization also serves another
part of Putin's agenda: separating ethnicity from identity. Putin is deeply
dedicated to formulating and propagating what Ken Jowitt calls a "practical ideology," an effort that involves reducing the salience of ethnicity
in public consciousness as well as in territorial administration. The questions "What is a Russian?" and "Who are we?" dominated discourse
during the 1990s. The debate took mind-numbing forms: interminable
essay contests on "the Russian idea," competitions to find new lyrics
for the wordless (and virtually tuneless) interim national anthem, and
government commissions charging armies of social scientists with de-
vising "new national conceptions" of such matters as social welfare and
Russia's place in the world.

Mercifully, the Putin government has put such antics to rest. In its
attempt to develop and instill a practical ideology, it has aggressively
promoted its own brand of supraethnic, statist nationalism. To this end,
Putin not only has attacked the ethnic republics' special privileges but

has also promoted many non-ethnic-Russians in government and in the political party he controls, Edinstvo (Unity). The chairman of Edinstvo is a minister in Putin's government, Sergei Shoigu, a Tuvanese whose handsome and distinctly Asian countenance adorns Edinstvo party offices and appears frequently on television.

Yet Putin's effort to build an inclusive sense of national belonging does not mean that he advocates a rights-based, civic conception. Rather, his understanding of citizenship is distinctly statist. Membership in the national community, social solidarity, and unwavering loyalty to the state and regime should, in Putin's view, form the core of citizens' public consciousness and identity. The social cement Putin is intent upon manufacturing is largely a neo-Soviet elixir. In place of the communist party and allegiance to it, however, Putin seeks to substitute the state, the constitution, and devotion to them.

Since the state and the constitution are rather abstract entities, however, they require concrete embodiment if they are to dominate public consciousness. In its effort to propagate a practical ideology, therefore, Putin's team has elected to promote three readily visible institutions as objects of affection and respect. The first is the presidency and the president himself. Since Russia's constitution invests enormous power in the executive office, loyalty to the constitution and loyalty to the president are easily conflated. Putin's own personal vigor and political ingenuity, which stand in stark contrast with his predecessor's debility and detachment, facilitate the promotion of the president as the embodiment of the state.

The second source of allegiance that Russian rulers extol is the military. In imperial and Soviet times, the military sometimes served as an agency of national integration and a source of pride, and Putin explicitly seeks to resurrect its social and symbolic functions. He has revived "military-patriotic" education in schools, which lapsed at the end of the Soviet period, and has portrayed the armed forces as an embodiment of national virtue.

The third institutional vehicle for the propagation of a practical ideology is the law. Putin speaks frequently of establishing a "dictatorship of the law," but he knows that such talk is cheap and that his countrymen, for good reason, do not regard the law as a source of protection or an object of veneration. To change that attitude, Putin has pushed through major reforms, most notably in criminal law. The new criminal code divests prosecutors of the power to issue arrest and search warrants and invests such power in judges. Additionally, it guarantees trial by jury. Juries heard only about 2 percent of criminal trials during the 1990s; under the new code they are to hear all criminal cases. During the 1990s, acquittal rates were about 20 percent in the small portion of cases heard by juries. In contrast, so few of the accused—about 1 percent—were freed in the usual old-style trials that prosecutors often did not bother to show up in court. The new code also allows defendants to retract confessions and disallows the use of retracted confessions as evidence. Given the frequency with which the police extract confessions by beatings and torture, this reform may very well transform criminal procedure.

The effects of Putin's effort to forge a new practical ideology are likely to be mixed and contradictory. There is nothing antidemocratic about reducing the salience of ethnicity and promoting an inclusive nationalism. Yet the statist character of that nationalism and the types of institutions selected as embodiments of the nation leave room for skepticism. Furthermore, although the presence of a widely respected president represents a healthy change, exalting the president as the personification of the state requires the creation from above of a miniature personality cult—a process that is well underway and that manifestly contradicts democratization.

Raising the status of the army is laudable, particularly after two decades of deteriorating morale and public standing following the war in Afghanistan. In the Russian context, bolstering the image of the armed forces is not at odds with democratization. But the soundness of the effort remains uncertain at best. Extolling the military as the embodiment of national greatness may well fall flat at a time when the army is committing more atrocities against civilians than it is winning battles against insurgents in Chechnya.

More encouraging and promising is the effort to establish a "dictatorship of the law." Even if Putin is motivated entirely by a desire to get Russians to take the law seriously and not by any affection for rights, the change in criminal procedure might serve democratization. But the ink is not yet dry on Putin's legal reforms. Whether the law in Russia outgrows its longstanding, inglorious role as the redundant codification of the state's subordination of society and becomes a viable institution that citizens embrace depends on whether it is really overhauled and really enforced. What is more, discrepancies between the letter of the law and the rulers' behavior have actually widened since the end of the Yeltsin period.

Restoring State Control of Communication

The growth of illegal action by officialdom has been most dramatic in the realm of political communication. During the 1990s, local and provincial officials often intimidated critics, and violence against journalists was a serious problem. Still, Article 29 of the Constitution, which guarantees freedom of speech and information, was no dead letter. The media in Russia were hardly unbiased or totally open, but a high degree of pluralism obtained at the national level and in many regions. Critical scrutiny of officials, including the president, was incessant and clamorous. Furthermore, Article 23, which prohibits official monitoring of telephone conversations or written correspondence without a court order, was widely respected. Much mischief took place at the highest levels, but the surveillance of private citizens' personal communications and lives—a hallmark of totalitarianism—for the most part ceased.

> *Putin has effectively brought all television stations with national reach under government control. If current trends hold, criticism of the president in the electronic media may become as scarce in Russia as it is in full-blown autocracies like Belarus and Kazakhstan.*

Since early 2000 the situation has changed. Putin has effectively brought all television stations with national reach under government control. The tone of reporting has altered markedly. If current trends hold, criticism of the president in the electronic media may become as scarce in Russia as it is in full-blown autocracies like Belarus and Kazakhstan. Anything resembling balanced and comprehensive coverage of the war in Chechnya has simply disappeared from the airwaves. Many regional officials, taking their cue from the center, have tightened control over the media in their bailiwicks. Censorship—which Article 29 forbids—is back.

Article 23, which guards the secrecy of private communication, is also taking a beating. The secret police have returned to their monitoring and meddling. In a reversion to the policy of squandering colossal resources on useless and socially degrading operations, agents of the FSB (the successor to the KGB) once again prowl the halls of universities and squeeze administrators for information on foreign students and Russians who associate with them. The telephones of political, social, and religious organizations are again being tapped. Monitoring of e-mail has become commonplace.

Even as he has used surrogates and coyly denied involvement in the assault on the independent media, Putin has not concealed why he would like to see the media back under government control. He has suggested that Russia's defeat in the first round of the war in Chechnya in 1994–96 was due to the lack of a proper moral climate in society. The mass media, of course, shape society's moral climate, and Putin does not intend to leave such an important matter to the whims of chance or to critically minded journalists. Control of the media is also crucial to his effort to instill his ideology.

The assault on private communication is harder to justify. Putin has made fighting organized crime and corruption a high priority, and the revival of the secret police might seem necessary for such purposes. But the myth of KGB probity is entirely apocryphal, as all Russian businessmen (and many ordinary citizens) know. It is not at all clear, more-

over, how tapping the telephones and meddling in the affairs of the
Committees of Soldiers' Mothers—an organization that resists official
mendacity in reporting on casualty counts in Chechnya—serves to fight
crime and restore public order. Whatever Putin's motives, his policies
on the mass media and private communication flagrantly violate Articles 29 and 23 of the Constitution.

Structuring Political Competition

Putin's plan for altering the basis of political competition is not necessarily as poisonous in its implications for democracy as is his policy
on communications. Putin's main aim is to give structure and regularity
to political competition. The new law on political parties sets minimum
requirements on membership for organizations to register as parties and
enjoy the right to compete in elections. The law also provides for state
financing of parties.

The law has been widely portrayed as a naked bid to eliminate most
parties and assert full state control over the few that survive. But the
actual effects of the law are unpredictable. Most of the parties that the
new rules will eliminate are insignificant groups that create more noise
than choice during elections. The law compels the major parties, if they
wish to survive, to recruit members aggressively—a task that many leaders, especially in the liberal parties, have heretofore regarded as be-
neath their dignity. The law's promulgation is being accompanied by a
government-backed campaign to de-stigmatize the idea of "party," with
commentators frequently asserting that politics will remain amateurish
and politicians unaccountable until parties rather than personalities dominate political competition. Putin has shown that he takes party-building
seriously. While leaving Edinstvo's daily operations in the hands of others, he has invested a great deal of energy—and government money—
in building up the party. Unlike Yeltsin, Putin is seeking to create an
organizational weapon in parliament and in society more broadly.

The effect of the new rules may cut either way. On the one hand,
they threaten to abolish all but a handful of parties and even to exclude
entire portions of the political spectrum from representation. On the
other, the new regulations may spur the overdue emergence of several
substantial parties that cover the breadth of the political spectrum and
that are more disciplined, internally coherent, and deeply rooted in society than the parties that Russia has known since the demise of the
Soviet Union. In addition, although mandatory state financing raises
the specter of official tutelage, it could liberate parties from the undue
influence that private and semiprivate businesses, including criminal
interests, currently exert. Americans who realize that their campaign
finance system—which is largely party finance—has reduced their country to a plutocracy might think twice before condemning the Russian

scheme. In a word, the new law could "party-ize" political competition and thereby impel democratization, or it could decimate the party system and turn parties into wards of the state.

Getting What They Asked For

Putin's path may lead directly to hard authoritarianism. Yet it is also possible that some aspects of it will—even if inadvertently—spur a resumption of democratization. In whichever direction it leads, Russians are to a large extent getting what they want. Even after nearly two years in office, Putin remains widely popular and respected among one of the world's most skeptical and cantankerous electorates. Western analysis has brimmed with condescending claims that Putin was shoved down the electors' throats or that the electors chose Putin without the slightest idea of who they were voting for. Few voters, however, failed to recognize in Putin a stern, cunning statist who placed competent administration and public order above rights but who also did not reflexively detest liberalism and modernity. Voters enjoyed a long and intimate acquaintance with the alternatives: the liberal idealist, Grigory Yavlinsky; the nationalist demagogue, Vladimir Zhirinovsky; the anachronistic communist, Gennady Zyuganov; the wily pragmatist, Yevgeni Primakov; and the imperious taskmaster, Yuri Luzhkov.

Electoral choices reveal preferences. Most Russians want the right to elect their president but are not passionate about their right to criticize him or to watch truthful, disturbing reports on what their government is doing to counter threats to the country's territorial integrity. They favor some local and regional autonomy but are horrified at the threat of national disintegration and are prepared to sacrifice blood, treasure, and freedom to avert it. They want the right to choose their governors and mayors but do not mind Moscow keeping an eye on their choices. They want genuine political choice but see little reason why 40-odd parties should muddy the waters at election time. They are nationalists but prefer an inclusive conception of their nation to an ethnic one.

Genuine democracy, with its panoply of rights, protections, and mechanisms for enforcing official accountability, has not taken hold in Russia, and some current trends are starkly inauspicious. But if democracy is at least partly about people getting to vote for whom they want and then getting what they voted for, and if one recalls the nature of the regime that the population lived under for most of the twentieth century, Russians could be faring worse.

25

GOING BACKWARDS

Grigory Yavlinsky

Grigory Yavlinsky is a member of the Russian State Duma (parliament) and co-founder and chairman of the Yabloko party and its Duma faction. An economist by training, he held a series of high positions during 1990–91 in the governments of the Russian Republic and the USSR. In June 1996, Dr. Yavlinsky came in fourth in his bid for the presidency of Russia. Running again in 2001, he came in third, after Vladimir Putin and Gennady Zyuganov. This essay, which was translated from the Russian by Mark H. Eckert, originally appeared in the October 2001 issue of the Journal of Democracy.

Russia has lived for almost two years without President Boris Yeltsin; a new age, a new millennium even, has begun. Yet it is becoming increasingly clear that political time in Russia is flowing backward. Increasingly, the old, updated, is returning in the guise of the new.

I am not referring simply to the return of the Soviet national anthem or the triumphal concert in the Kremlin on the anniversary of the creation of the Cheka (the predecessor of the KGB). There is much in our politics today that is reminiscent not of yesterday but of the day before yesterday. We are returning to the "familiar things" of days gone by: the renunciation of freedom of speech, the renunciation of freedoms in general, the renunciation of the principle that the army should not be used in internal conflicts, the renunciation of private initiative, the renunciation of enterprise, the renunciation of truth-telling, and the expectation that benefits will be distributed from above. This is connected with the nostalgia that a very large number of people in Russia, a majority in fact, feel for the most stagnant Soviet times and traditions. Indeed, the main thrust of official policy is to encourage this mentality.

What we have in our country today is artificial, formal, sham democracy.

Our freedom of speech is a sham because, with rare exceptions, the only thing that one can do freely in the mass media is praise the government. It is easy to trump up criminal charges against anyone who understands freedom of speech as the right to say what he really thinks.

Our elections are a sham because citizens are virtually deprived of the possibility of changing the government as they wish. The best they can hope for is to replace the local elite with someone whom the Kremlin supports.

Our multipartism is a sham because the "party of power," whose place is occupied by Edinstvo (Unity) today, is in a uniquely privileged position. All the other parties have to make a choice: Either become loyal or lose any chance to influence what is going on in the country.

Our legal system is a sham because the courts are not independent. Often they do not so much hand down sentences as offer their services to the authorities.

Our separation of powers is a sham because the executive branch is not checked by the legislature and does not execute its laws. In a normal democratic country, parties fight for places in parliament in order to win the right to form the government; in Russia, the government creates a party so that it can form the parliament it needs.

The political scientists at Putin's court call this sham democracy a "guided" democracy. The bosses can remain in power regardless of the will of the voters, or they can form this "will," if they have to, by deceiving the people on a grand scale, as happened in the 1999 and 2000 elections. The people were shamelessly duped, and the results of the elections were just as shamelessly manipulated to favor the "party of power."

This is a renovated version of the system in place 15 years ago, when we also had a virtually unchangeable government, courts that churned out made-to-order decisions, *pro forma* elections that convinced no one, and the guiding and directing role of one party. And, as with our current system, that party's ideologists and commentators "freely" praised it in the mass media.

Politics as a Covert Operation

Official politics today is like a covert operation in which those in power say one thing, think another, do something else, and want something entirely different. As a result, they get something they never intended. Normal, public, open politics has been replaced by intrigue, lies, the "black PR" of political provocateurs who call themselves "political technicians," and behind-the-scenes struggles.

Those in power do not debate the opposition, refute its arguments, or counter its political programs with their own. Instead, they spread nasty rumors about their opponents, release made-to-order articles and television programs against them, get the tax inspectorate to raid them, bring criminal charges against them, or take their names off the ballot three hours before the election. They have no qualms; the end justifies the means. This Bolshevik thesis has become dominant again. Recruitment and "active measures"—that is, tactics characteristic of the security services—are the two main forms of state policy today.

The Kremlin is striving to limit the governors constitutionally, but in a way that destroys local self-government. It is fighting the "oligarchs" with criminal charges and raids from the tax police, but faith in private property and personal initiative is being destroyed in the process. When federal districts are introduced, generals are appointed as their governors; the result will be either nothing or the opposite of what was intended. And I am sure that if the Kremlin wants to form a Constitutional Assembly to amend the Constitution, it will end up being the kind of assembly that will turn the document in a completely different direction. Anything, even something positive in principle, can be turned in the opposite direction. It is the "law of the fork": You can use a fork to eat sausages, or you can stab your neighbor with it.

We do not have laws; personality and official position are completely decisive. In other words, the government's activity depends only 5 percent on the laws and 95 percent on the personalities (or groups) who occupy top government positions. Their interests and their whims rule.

No matter what problem one tries to solve, one ends up having to face the fact that the democratic form simply cannot hold the criminal content. The entire personnel structure of the Yeltsin administration has been preserved, both in spirit and in form, thereby maintaining the whole carcass of the system of government created in the 1930s. Yeltsin kept the system of *nomenklatura* government, as well as the Stalinist worldview that divided everyone into "our people" and "outsiders."

The attitude of politicians, both in and out of power, toward the people has changed only minimally, if at all. A striking example of this was the Duma's consideration of a bill on importing nuclear waste into Russia, usually interpreted as yet another sign that the legislature is dominated by the executive branch. But the problem is more serious than that: Our politicians' thinking and style have remained fundamentally unchanged since Soviet times. Instead of heeding the nine out of ten Russians who oppose the importation of nuclear waste, the bill's supporters tried to persuade them that the decision made was the correct one. In essence, the deputies of Edinstvo, Otechestvo (Fatherland), and other parties acted as if they had not been *elected* to the Duma by the people but rather *appointed* to it by the president's administration or some governor or mayor.

For these reasons, and also because of Yeltsin's incompetent economic policy, Russian citizens have been hit with two wars, two defaults (in 1994 and 1998), a hyperinflation of 2,500 percent in 1992, and the shelling of the Supreme Soviet in 1993.

One cannot but feel sorry for what has happened to the Russian people over the past ten years and understand why they have been overcome with disillusionment and passivity. Yet one must also remember that they went into the 1996 presidential elections with their eyes open. (And at the time, their predicament was not as serious as it is now.)

Why did many choose according to the principle of "This one's better, but we'll vote for the boss anyway"? Most likely, it was spiritual laziness or even deep-rooted amorality. Well, they got what they asked for. No one, as they say, forced them. "Black PR" was not as prevalent as it is today, nor were votes stolen so brazenly or so massively. But this choice—ostensibly the "lesser of two evils"—has determined our present and our future.

It is worth remembering now that all of the violations, manipulations, and falsifications of the 1996 elections were justified by the need to "keep the communists from returning to power." It is worth remembering because a strategic alliance with the communists and their control over the State Duma is openly defining policy today. As a result of their alliance, a mechanical, obedient, rubber-stamp Duma has been created. In this sense, it is a very good reflection of the country we have today.

Sham Civil Society

Now sham democracy has been taken to a new level, encompassing not only the branches of government but civil society as well. On June 12, President Putin met with representatives of social organizations handpicked by the Kremlin: athletes, stamp collectors, political scientists, women, divers, and the like. In the course of the meeting, there was talk of creating a "Union of Social Unions."

This is a step toward transforming civic organizations into a component of the corporate state, replacing civil society with a Soviet-style society that exists only to approve the decisions of "the party and the government." The "Union of Unions" will lay claim to a monopoly on the third sector (civil society) and will resemble the creative unions of Soviet times. If you were not a member of the Writers' Union, you were not a writer but just a "parasite" like Joseph Brodsky; if you do not join the Union of Unions, you will not be part of civil society. The criterion for selection will undoubtedly be loyalty, which, even now, has become the price for receiving privileges and financial support.

There is a real danger that classical democratic procedures will be replaced by such "direct" forms of democracy as "assemblies of society" or "nationwide discussions." It is no accident that the idea of replacing the institutions of representative government with an annual assembly of "the most respected members of society" has been floated in public discussions.

In neighboring Belarus, this idea has already been implemented. The All-Belarusan Popular Assemblies, organized by the government, have become a tradition. The "progressive society" that participates in these assemblies is directly contrasted with "unconstructive forces"—that is, those who do not agree with the president.

The Russian government and the structures that support it engage in the same sort of "dialogue" with their opponents. The recent history of the television station NTV and the radio station Ekho Moskvy demonstrates how such dialogue works. NTV journalists who spoke out openly against the seizure of the station by the state-controlled concern Gazprom were accused of being "unconstructive" extremists who were "unwilling to negotiate." In the same situation, the leadership of Ekho Moskvy negotiated in every possible way, trying by any means to obtain a controlling interest for the employees. After long negotiations, however, it became clear that Gazprom had no intention of selling shares to the journalists. When the station's representatives tried to complain, they were immediately hit with the familiar accusations of being "unwilling to negotiate."

It has become clear that, for the government and its satellites, "dialogue" is only a fig leaf to cover the establishment of direct or indirect state control over the institutions of civil society and the nongovernmental mass media. The only real subject of these negotiations is the terms of surrender and the payment for loyalty. What is especially dangerous is that this course has begun to seem, if not justified, then at least reasonable, even in the eyes of those who in principle hold very democratic views.

Some think that what is going on may be best for Russia. They see in the elements of authoritarianism a certain originality, even a mystique. Others see the return of authoritarian elements as something like the "growing pains" of Russian democracy, short-lived relics of a past to which it is impossible to return completely because the president has "positioned himself as a liberal" on economic issues. Still others have come to the conclusion that, since nothing can be done about it, we have to adapt. Publications and journalists who are not at all communist are analyzing the possibility of life under "guided democracy" and examining the laws that govern the functioning of the "one-and-a-half-party system."

We are returning rather quickly to the time of doublethink, when a person's real views had nothing to do with what he said publicly, when secretaries of Komsomol (the communist youth organization) made "correct" speeches during the day and cursed the Soviet regime at night. At that time, living according to one's views meant getting involved in the fight, and not everyone was capable of that.

The advantage of democracy—one of its most important virtues, in fact—is that living in accordance with one's views and conscience does not demand everyday feats of heroism and sacrifice; it is simply the norm. Today, we are far from that norm.

The pseudo-intellectual attempt to excuse the government's actions by invoking the myth that Russia is unlike any other country or by appealing to the hopelessness of the situation could cost our country dearly. It is also important to understand that, in spite of obvious associations with the not-so-distant past, it would be a mistake to see today's authoritarian elements as connected exclusively with orthodox communism. The most serious danger today is the formation of a new authoritarian or totalitarian system that is completely compatible with a banal market economy. Whether such an economy will be effective in meeting the challenges of the twenty-first century is a separate question.

A "Loyal" Economy

If Russia remains as it is for the next five to seven years, we can say goodbye to all our dreams of a new, modern economy for the new century, since we will remain within the framework of the current economic system. It is a "pipeline economy," based on selling natural resources; it is an economy that is technically backward, that remains uncompetitive, and that has nothing to do with computers, the Internet, or new technologies; it is an economy in which whole sectors are transformed into corporations whose resources and expenses belong to the state, but whose profits are private.

Today people speak of imposing "order," a notion that has nothing to do with reality. What is taking place in the name of "order" today is not a "dictatorship of the law" but rather a redistribution of property in favor of certain groups that are close to the new authorities.

A market economy without democracy is tantamount to oligarchy. That is why President Putin's struggle with the oligarchs is not a battle against oligarchy in principle. No one man, even if he is president, can conquer oligarchy; like corruption, oligarchy can be conquered only by civil society. Fighting oligarchy by fighting an individual magnate like Boris Berezovsky is nonsense, because oligarchy is more than just one man: It is a system of social ties. Oligarchy—that is, the system based on the "pipeline economy"—is something that the Russian government does not intend to renounce. On the contrary, government programs, in essence, have become its fig leaf.

Some people, pleased by the appointment of supposed liberals to important government posts, think that this will make the Russian system liberal. But our economy is not liberal; it is loyal. A new type of economic system has been created in which the determining factor for succeeding in business is absolute loyalty to the authorities.

As for the people who ostensibly make up the "liberal wing" of the government, let us not forget that quite recently, this very same "team" implemented its own version of "liberalism" in Russia, which can be described only in legal terms: Just as the Criminal Code speaks of "embezzlement on an especially large scale," this team implemented "liberalism on an especially large scale." It is these very people, who admire General Pinochet and dream of a strong hand, who have become "great-power nationalists" and call for the creation of a "strong state," although, for some reason, the state has become not strong but merely brazen. And it is these people who are the leaders or founders of parties that, in spite of their supposed liberalism, do not consider human rights and freedoms to be worth defending.

Therefore right-wing parties have appeared that defend big private property, ignore human rights, and, when it benefits them, call for war and violence in an outburst of loyalty and pseudopatriotism. I must remind you—and world history testifies—that such parties, sooner or later, risk sliding into fascism. After all, the creation of dictatorships has always been accompanied by cries for order and a strong government.

For us, playing at dictatorship is especially dangerous. Our political system has not yet renounced the crimes of the Stalin era. In recent times, in fact, Stalin has returned to the political pantheon of "positive heroes of history." It seems that there are many who not only wish to respect "the Leader" but are seriously following his teachings. If this is so, then Russia is doomed to self-destruction.

Russia and the West

Perhaps, I am told, the West will not tolerate such a turn of events. Perhaps they will not allow the creation of "guided democracy" in Russia, a regime that precludes alternation in power and virtually deprives people of the right to decide their own fate.

I think that we must not have any illusions or hopes on this point. The Western establishment will go along with everything and will object to nothing. First of all, it is not the West's duty to fight for the cause of free self-government in Russia. It is *our* duty. We will create—or not create—an open society in Russia, not because we owe it to the West to do so, but because we owe it to our children and our country. Moreover, Europe and the United States are not charitable organizations but states with their own interests.

Of course, when we speak of the West, we must distinguish between the people and the establishment. People in the West wish Russia well and are ready even to give some of their money so that Russia may become a prosperous, democratic country. As for the present establishment, they often have a view of Russia that is both cynical and simple: They tried to help us as best they could for ten years, but nothing worked. They had no idea what to do or how to do it. Now, having lost their faith, they are trying to conceal their failure. Among themselves, they say that the Russians do not understand democracy, freedom, or the market economy. Therefore, they argue, you simply have to have a strong leader in the Kremlin, a man who can hold his subjects in his fist and promise the West that Russian missiles will not be launched in its direction. And the Western leaders, in turn, must make friends with this Russian leader—drink beer with him, go to the sauna, meet without jackets and ties, and sometimes even give him a little money so that he can become stronger.

In general, we need to understand that the development of Russia as a full-fledged European country is *our* difficult job, that it is in *our* vital national interest, and that no one is obliged to help us.

What Next?

Unfortunately, the "cumulative effect" of everything that has happened in Russia in recent times is that the country has stopped counting its dead. People no longer pay attention to the fact that hundreds are dying, day after day, month after month, in Chechnya, that servicemen are dying in many other parts of the country—even among those not taking part in military operations. At the same time, strong internal forces of a very specific and negative character are building up in the country. The characteristics of the new political system, which I would call "national bolshevism," are becoming increasingly clear. In this sense, the combination of the Stalin-era national anthem and the imperial double-headed eagle is quite natural. Indeed, it is quite understandable—after all, nationalism naturally grows out of bolshevism, especially in Russia.

Is there a way out? The only way is to respect fundamental civil rights; everything that goes against this principle will lead in the wrong direction. We need an independent judicial system, governmental account-ability and "transparency," strong and financially independent local self-government, absolute guarantees of private property, sources of infor-mation independent of the state, and so on.

Unfortunately, virtually all politics in the country is headed in absol-utely the opposite direction. The authorities have no use for independent courts that cannot be ordered to disqualify an inconvenient candidate or jail an inconvenient businessman. Nor have they any use for accountable government, strong local self-rule, or independent mass media; mass propaganda is so much more convenient.

Nothing good will come of this. It will not give us an effective econo-my, or the rule of law, or justice, or security, or the status as a world power that the president wants so much. My colleagues in Yabloko and I speak from experience, having formed the democratic opposition to the Yeltsin regime for many years. We were not wrong in our assess-ment then, and I am sure that we are not wrong now.

People talk a lot about "stability" today. But "stability"—the preser-vation of an oligarchic-criminal regime, a "pipeline economy," and a "guided democracy"—is unacceptable for Russia. For us, as in Lewis Carroll's *Through the Looking Glass,* "It takes all the running you can do to keep in the same place." If we stand still, we will be carried back into the past. And we know that past very well.

26

A MIXED RECORD,
AN UNCERTAIN FUTURE

Michael McFaul

Michael McFaul *is associate professor of political science and a Hoover Fellow at Stanford University. He is also a senior associate at the Carnegie Endowment for International Peace, and author, most recently, of* Russia's Unfinished Revolution: Political Change from Gorbachev to Putin *(2001). This essay was originally published in the October 2001 issue of the* Journal of Democracy.

The defeat of the Communist hard-liners' August 1991 coup attempt marked one of the most euphoric moments in Russian history. For centuries, autocrats had ruled Russia, using force when necessary to suppress society. This time, emboldened by liberalization under Soviet leader Mikhail Gorbachev, Russian society organized to resist the use of force by Kremlin dictators. To be sure, all of Russia did not rise up against the coup plotters; only citizens in major cities mobilized. Yet the ripple effects of this brave stance against tyranny in Moscow and St. Petersburg proved pivotal in destroying communism, dismantling the Soviet empire, and ending the Cold War.

The end of the Soviet dictatorship, however, did not lead immediately or smoothly to the creation of Russian democracy. Sadly, the tenth anniversary of this momentous event did not prompt national public celebration. On the contrary, in response to a December 1999 survey, more than seven-tenths of Russian voters said they believed that the Soviet Union should not have been dissolved, while a paltry 12 percent expressed satisfaction with the way Russian democracy was developing.[1] As reflected in the preceding essays, analysts share the Russian public's perception of Russian democracy. Even those most optimistic today about the prospects for Russian democracy offer only the faintest echo of the August 1991 euphoria. Nor has democracy fared better in most of the other post-Soviet states. What happened?

Part of the problem is with us analysts. A distorting interpretive framework has exacerbated our disappointment with the lack of democratic progress in the post-Soviet lands. We assumed that Russia and the rest of the region belonged to the "third wave" of transitions to democracy that began with the fall of the Portuguese dictatorship in 1974. The democratic rhetoric of anticommunist leaders in the region encouraged the comparison.

But "transition" is an imperfect metaphor. As several of our authors emphasize, political change has been only one component of the grand post-Soviet transformation, which also involves economic transformation, state building (after state destruction), and decolonization. Analogies drawn from Latin America or Southern Europe do not capture the scale of what is taking place in the post-Soviet world. On the contrary, one of the conditions for successful democratization in these other regions was that economic transformation was not allowed to occur simultaneously.[2] Such postponement or sequencing of change could not take place in communist regimes, where the economy and polity were so intertwined. The transitions paradigm captured only one component of change in the postcommunist world. Other historical analogies—such as economic reform, decolonization, or revolution—may provide a better guide.

Successful transitions from authoritarian rule often have included a pact between soft-liners in the outgoing regime and moderates among the opposition. Pacts are agreements on a path from autocracy to democracy. In the post-Soviet world, however, pacts have not guided regime transformation. Instead, the victors—be they democrats or autocrats—have simply dictated new rules. As highlighted by Charles Fairbanks, politics in the region is a win-or-lose affair. Where there is no predominant power, the result has been (sometimes violent) confrontation, and events that look more like revolution than democratization.

Initial conditions in the Soviet Union also did not conform to the transitions model. In Latin America and Southern Europe, the successful cases were typically *re*democratizations. Democratic constitutions, political parties, and civil society were resurrected. The states that emerged from the Soviet Union, however, had no civil society to resurrect. Nor could Russian or Georgian democrats dust off democratic constitutions of previous eras or breathe new life into old political parties of a democratic orientation. Instead, these new states inherited social and institutional legacies from the Soviet era (and before) that impeded democratic consolidation. The post-Soviet states were not even starting with a *tabula rasa,* but with a cluttered political landscape that had to be cleared before democracy building could begin.

In fact, consolidating a democratic polity has not been the central aim of *any* rulers in the region. Reorganizing property rights, defining new borders, dismantling state institutions, building state institutions, and (in some countries) creating opportunities for theft and graft have all ranked as much higher priorities. If, as Fairbanks recounts, the Georgian state in the early 1990s could not collect revenues, print currency, or defend its borders or streets, then building democratic institutions could not have been a high priority for government leaders. If, as Fairbanks reminds us, meat consumption in Tajikistan has dropped 71 percent in the last decade, then we should not be surprised that democratization has not made the list of priorities for the Tajik people. If, as Nadia Diuk shows, postcommunist leaders and parties in Ukraine have been beholden to mafias and oligarchs, then why would we expect them to build democratic institutions? Even in the Baltic states, where democracy has progressed farthest, achieving and maintaining independence from Russia were always more important than democracy; it so happened that building democracy complemented and promoted independence.

If democratization was only one of many aims, and a lesser priority to boot, then we should not be surprised if it has proceeded slowly. Other metaphors, especially revolution, would have altered expectations regarding the speed of change. Compared to other transitions to democracy, Russia's ranks as one of the longest. Compared to other revolutions, however, the speed of change in Russia looks rather average.

Explaining Variation

The scale and complexity of revolutionary change in the post-communist world cannot provide a universal explanation for failed democracy. Some countries already have consolidated democratic regimes while also managing economic transformation and decolonization. Anders Åslund, Zbigniew Brzezinski, Ghia Nodia, and Lilia Shevtsova do not agree precisely as to which countries fall where, but they all identify three regime types that emerged from the Soviet Union. At one extreme are the dictatorships—the regimes of Central Asia, Belarus, Azerbaijan, and maybe Armenia. None of these countries are any closer to democracy now than they were ten years ago. Estonia, Latvia, and Lithuania constitute the other extreme—consolidated democracies with some lingering transitional problems (for example, minority rights in Latvia). In the middle are regimes in Russia, Ukraine, Georgia, and perhaps Moldova that some (myself included) might label electoral democracies. Others, like Shevtsova, might call them bureaucratic quasi-authoritarian regimes.

Different authors emphasize competing explanations of this variation. Brzezinski points to history and culture, while Archie Brown and Nodia think that elite commitment to democracy is the key. Both perspectives illuminate aspects of postcommunist change, and yet both must also add additional variables to provide a complete explanation. In the region, as recognized by Nodia, regime type correlates strongly with culture, history, and geography. Put starkly, the more Western a country is in its culture (including religion) and geography, the more likely that a democratic regime emerged after communism. The converse is

also true. Those farthest from the West both geographically and culturally are also least likely to have democratic regimes today.

At the same time, many anomalies undermine this simple theory. First,
as Nodia also emphasizes, the variation among postcommunist experiences in the region demonstrates that the shared history of communism
was not as consequential as we originally assumed.

Second, some countries with shared histories, cultures, and even
geographies have followed very diverse regime trajectories. No two
countries share more history and culture than Belarus and Russia, yet
they have very different regimes today. The same could be said of
Moldova and Romania. Likewise, countries like Belarus and Uzbekistan
have very different histories, cultures, and locations yet have emerged
from Soviet communism with relatively similar regimes.

Third, regime types *within* countries—one thinks of Russia, Belarus,
Armenia, Kyrgyzstan, and Tajikistan—have sometimes changed considerably just in the last decade. Long-term structural forces cannot explain this variation. Even the region's biggest success stories, the Baltic
states, did not always appear to be on a democratic trajectory when
viewed against a longer-term historical background. For most of the
twentieth century, fascism and communism were much more prominent
features of these regimes than liberalism. In the long, long run, culture
and history can usefully be deployed to explain broad sweeping trends.
In a term as short as a decade, however, broad generalizations can hide
as much history as they uncover.

On the other hand, the orientation of elites may be too ephemeral,
unstable, and unquantifiable to explain such a complex phenomenon as
regime change in the postcommunist world. Moreover, when
decolonization is allowed to compete with the transitions metaphor,
"prodemocracy" orientations become "anti-Russian" preferences. Yet
even unstable, ill-defined preferences can have path-dependent consequences during periods of revolutionary change. It is not important what
attitudes Lithuanian or Russian elites have had about democracy over
the course of centuries, but the orientations they held in 1991 were crucial. Bringing actors, their interests, and their power into the equation is
central to developing explanations of regime change in the former Soviet Union.

An orientation in favor of democracy only affects regime change if
the democratically oriented hold power, or at least have powerful allies.
Many people in Uzbekistan are democrats, but their relative power in
that country is weak compared to those with antidemocratic instincts.
The balance of power between democrats and nondemocrats, therefore,
must figure prominently in any explanation of democracy and dictatorship in the postcommunist era. Three different balances of power caused
the three different kinds of regimes that have emerged in the region. In
the Baltic states, democrats clearly enjoyed a preponderance of power

at the moment of Soviet collapse. In elections held in 1990, democrats won sweeping majorities. In Central Asia, dictators enjoyed a preponderance of power over local democrats, controlling elections and limiting liberalization to maintain their autocratic hold on the state. In Russia and Ukraine, the distribution of power between democrats and dictators was *relatively* balanced in the late Soviet and early independence period. Earlier analyses of noncommunist democratic transitions had concluded that such equal distributions of power—stalemates—between challengers and the challenged produced pacts or transitional agreements, which paved the way for the emergence of stable democratic regimes.[3] Russia and Ukraine have not followed this path. A decade later, the potential for democratic consolidation remains, but so too does the potential for democratic collapse.

The Centrality of Russia

The kind of regime that eventually consolidates in Russia will have major implications for the rest of the region, a theme that is echoed in several of these essays. Before Gorbachev, the pro-Western orientation of elites in the Baltic states had little impact on democratization in these Soviet colonies. Political liberalization in the metropole, however, created permissive conditions for democratization in the periphery. The triggering event for Baltic independence and democracy occurred in Moscow, not Vilnius, when Russia's democrats succeeded in defeating the August 1991 putsch. In contrast, as Brown notes, Moscow's push for liberalization in Central Asia ended after the Soviet collapse.

Consequently, the future of Russian democracy will affect the future of democracy in the region as a whole. (Åslund makes a similar argument about the centrality of Russia's economy for the rest of the region.) A consolidated democracy in Russia would destabilize the dictatorship in Belarus, undermine autocratic forces in Ukraine, and help to ensure the consolidation of Baltic democracy. A democratic Russia might also promote democracy in the Caucasus, and eventually even in Central Asia. Remember, as Nodia asks us to do, the impact of Iberia's democratization on the former colonies of Spain and Portugal. Conversely, a newly authoritarian Russia would have imperial designs on the Caucasus, could destabilize the Baltics, and would station forces in (if not simply incorporate) autocratic Belarus. As Russia goes, so goes the region.

The most striking conclusion shared by many of the authors in this symposium is how uncertain Russia's democratic future remains. The liberal democracies in the Baltic states—like liberal democracies around the world—are stable regimes. The authoritarian regimes in Central Asia also have demonstrated real resilience. Fairbanks rightly emphasizes that some autocracies are stronger than others are, with Uzbekistan and Turkmenistan topping the list. And opportunities for regime liberalization might appear when the strongmen who have ruled Central Asia since independence finally cede power. Yet none of these regimes seems as ill-defined today as Russia. After ten years of transition, Russia is neither a full-blown democracy nor a full-blown dictatorship. Both outcomes are still possible. Two different sets of questions confound our capabilities for predicting Russian regime change. First, how democratic is Russia's current regime? Second, how stable is this current regime?

Democracy and Stability

Tellingly, none of our authors is willing to call Russia a liberal democracy. Many key liberal institutions, including an independent judiciary, a structured party system, a vibrant civil society, and checks on the executive, simply do not exist in Russia today. The brutal conduct of the war in Chechnya also calls into question whether the current regime even respects basic civil liberties. At best, the current regime is an electoral democracy, a system in which elections with certain procedures but uncertain outcomes determine who governs. Many, including Shevtsova and Grigory Yavlinsky in this symposium, have concluded that Russia already has fallen below this minimalist standard. Yavlinsky makes a strong case that dictatorship already has arrived. Shevtsova favors qualifying adjectives—"elective" monarchy, "quasi-" authoritarianism—but the nouns are the same as those used by Yavlinsky.

Without delving too deeply into definitional debates, our authors would be unlikely to take issue with the modest claim that Russia has *some* democratic attributes. The Russian state has not limited all individual liberties. A real dictatorship would not allow a parliamentarian to write the essay that Yavlinsky has contributed to this journal. Elections still occur and they still have consequences; ask the hundreds of former Duma deputies and dozens of governors who lost their positions in the last electoral cycle. And as Slobodan Milošević discovered in Yugoslavia, even imitative democratic institutions can unexpectedly become weapons for democratic challengers. Whatever is left of Russia's flawed and fragile democratic institutions is worth preserving.

Since his election in March 2000, President Vladimir Putin has shown scant interest in consolidating democracy. M. Steven Fish rightly highlights reforms initiated by Putin that could foster democratization, and Brzezinski correctly emphasizes that the end of anarchy in certain spheres should not be equated with the end of democracy. Yet, as Yavlinsky eloquently states, the short-term consequences of Putin's rise have been bad for Russian democracy.

How far will he or can he go? Regarding his own preferences, it is too early to know. Putin did not spend the first decades of his career fighting for human rights, and his initial policies as president have eroded already weak democratic institutions. Yet Putin also seems too pragmatic, too modern, and too Western to want to resurrect Soviet-style dictatorship. He also may understand or come to realize, as Åslund forcefully argues, that in the postcommunist world democracy complements and promotes market reform, an objective that Putin clearly embraces. Nonetheless, his advisors speak openly of building a "managed democratic" system that is far more "managed" than democratic, and he has yet to discourage them.

And yet, even if Putin wants "managed democracy," it remains far from certain that he can get it. To emasculate all independent centers of power and silence all critical voices, Putin and his surrogates would have to close down hundreds of media outlets, arrest thousands of human rights activists, environmental leaders, and trade union organizers, and sack dozens of elected governors and parliamentarians. In doing so, Putin would be acting against the will of the Russian majority. Despite a rocky first decade, two-thirds of Russian voters still voice support for the idea of democracy (only 18 percent do not); more than 80 percent think that it is important to elect the country's leaders and to have freedom of expression and of the press; and majorities are not willing to introduce censorship or declare a state of emergency in order to bring about more order in the country.[4] Such societal support for democratic norms may be the best guarantee of Russian democracy in the long run, even if Russian leaders diverge from democratic practices in the short run. In addition, as emphasized by several authors in this symposium, time is on democracy's side, since the youngest people in the region are also the most democratic.

Since coming to power, Putin has emphasized repeatedly his desire to "end the revolution" and restore stability. He consciously deploys the imagery of revolution to emphasize his historic role as the leader of the Thermidor. As highlighted in Yavlinsky's essay, Putin has accompanied promises of stability with the resurrection of symbols from the *ancien régime*. Fish points out that Putin also has sought to replace the anticommunist and liberal ideologies of the 1990s with more usable symbols and slogans. But Putin does not seek to restore the Soviet communist system, command economy and all. Rather, he seeks to bond old practices onto the new postrevolutionary system, and nationalism is the glue of this bond. There are uncanny parallels between Putin's actions and the policies of the Thermidorean leaders in France, as described so well by Crane Brinton in his 60-year-old classic *The Anatomy of Revolution.*

Stretching the metaphor of revolution further, however, reveals that a lot of history is still to come. The disturbing question raised by this analogy is whether Putin also emerges as the Napoleon or the Stalin of Russia's current revolution. Our authors are split. Strikingly, the two Russians—Yavlinsky and Shevtsova—are much more worried than their Western colleagues that authoritarianism could yet make a comeback.

That we cannot accurately assess the impact of Putin's reign on Russian democracy indirectly answers our second question about the stability of the Russian regime. Writing a decade after the Soviet collapse, all our authors express uncertainty about the future of the Russian regime. Those guardedly optimistic about democracy's prospects still add cautions about the potential for erosion. Those already convinced of autocracy's reappearance still qualify their pessimism with hopeful hints of future crises and instabilities that might rattle the new dictatorship.

There may be a third trajectory—no trajectory at all. Ten years from now, the Russian polity might be neither a democracy nor a dictatorship, but something in between—something very similar to the regime in place today. A "transition" implies movement. But Russia's regime may have stopped. Along with several other countries in the region, it may be stuck in a twilight zone between dictatorship and democracy—some new form of hybrid regime that does not readily fit existing categories.

Stability is not the worst outcome, but neither is it the best. When businesspeople and foreign policy makers discuss Russia, they often assume that stability is so valuable that it must be fostered. Paradoxically, though their analyses of the Russian economy have diverged for over a decade, Yavlinsky and Åslund echo an opposite, provocative hypothesis—stability can have negative consequences for reform. Crises, on the other hand, can create opportunities for positive change. As summarized by Diuk, the recent explosion of democratic fervor in Ukraine in the wake of the Gongadze affair demonstrates how authoritarian drift can still be challenged, and perhaps even checked, in these postcommunist regimes.

Attempting to predict crisis in Russia seems unwise. Hoping for crisis in Russia seems inhumane. Writing in these pages almost a decade ago, I concluded, "The democratic triumph over the August putsch was not a consummation, then, but only one critical step in a long journey toward democratic rule in Russia."[5] A decade later, it is clear that many more steps are yet to come.

NOTES

1. Timothy J. Colton and Michael McFaul, *Are Russians Undemocratic?* (Washington, D.C.: Carnegie Endowment for International Peace, 2001), 5–6.

2. Guillermo O'Donnell and Philippe Schmitter, *Transitions from Authoritarian Rule: Tentative Conclusions* (4 vols., Baltimore: Johns Hopkins University Press, 1986), 4: 69.

3. Dankwart Rustow, "Transitions to Democracy: Toward a Dynamic Model," *Comparative Politics* 2 (April 1970): 337–64; Terry Lynn Karl, "Dilemmas of Democratization in Latin America," *Comparative Politics* 23 (October 1990): 1–22; Adam Przeworski, *Democracy and the Market: Political and Economic Reforms in Eastern Europe and Latin America* (Cambridge: Cambridge University Press, 1991).

4. Timothy J. Colton and Michael McFaul, *Are Russians Undemocratic?*

5. Michael McFaul, "Russia's Emerging Political Parties," *Journal of Democracy* 3 (January 1992): 39.

INDEX